Y0-CUQ-262

Sepharad as Imagined Community

STUDIES IN JUDAISM

Yudit Kornberg Greenberg
General Editor

Vol. 8

This book is a volume in a Peter Lang monograph series.
Every volume is peer reviewed and meets
the highest quality standards for content and production.

PETER LANG
New York • Bern • Frankfurt • Berlin
Brussels • Vienna • Oxford • Warsaw

Sepharad as Imagined Community

Language, History and Religion from the Early Modern Period to the 21st Century

EDITED BY Mahir Şaul
AND José Ignacio Hualde

PETER LANG
New York • Bern • Frankfurt • Berlin
Brussels • Vienna • Oxford • Warsaw

Library of Congress Cataloging-in-Publication Data

Names: Şaul, Mahir, editor. | Hualde, José Ignacio, editor.
Title: Sepharad as Imagined Community: language, history and religion from
the early modern period to the 21st century / edited by Mahir Şaul,
José Ignacio Hualde.
Description: New York: Peter Lang
Series: Studies in Judaism; Vol. 8 | ISSN 1086-5403
Includes bibliographical references and index.
Identifiers: LCCN 2016007129 | ISBN 978-1-4331-3137-0 (hardcover: alk. paper)
ISBN 978-1-4539-1635-3 (ebook pdf) | ISBN 978-1-4331-3924-6 (epub)
ISBN 978-1-4331-3925-3 (mobi) | DOI 10.3726/b10502
Subjects: LCSH: Sephardim—History. | Ladino language–Spain.
Sephardim—Languages. | Sephardim—Religious aspects. | Spanish
literature—History and criticism. | Judaism—Sephardic rite—Customs and
practices. | Sephardim—Spain. | Spain–Languages.
Classification: LCC PC4813 .S44 | DDC 467/.9496—dc23
LC record available at https://lccn.loc.gov/2016007129

Bibliographic information published by **Die Deutsche Nationalbibliothek**.
Die Deutsche Nationalbibliothek lists this publication in the "Deutsche
Nationalbibliografie"; detailed bibliographic data are available
on the Internet at http://dnb.d-nb.de/.

The cover image, a watercolor by Charles Gleyre of a young Jewish woman, was painted
in 1840, based on an original the artist made in 1834 from live model in Izmir.
Charles Gleyre (Chevilly, 1806–Paris, 1874) Femme turque, Angelica, Smyrne, 1840
Aquarelle sur papier, 36.8 × 27 cm Musée cantonal des Beaux-Arts de Lausanne.
Acquisition, 1908. Inv. 1233 Photo: J.-C. Ducret, Musée cantonal des Beaux-Arts,
Lausanne. Reproduced by permission

The paper in this book meets the guidelines for permanence and durability
of the Committee on Production Guidelines for Book Longevity
of the Council of Library Resources.

© 2017 Peter Lang Publishing, Inc., New York
29 Broadway, 18th floor, New York, NY 10006
www.peterlang.com

All rights reserved.
Reprint or reproduction, even partially, in all forms such as microfilm,
xerography, microfiche, microcard, and offset strictly prohibited.

Printed in Germany

Contents

Chapter One: Sepharad as Imagined Translocal
   Mediterranean Community: Introduction..1
   Mahir Şaul and José Ignacio Hualde

Part One: The Origins: From the Fifteenth to the Nineteenth Century
Chapter Two: An Overlooked 15th Century *demand d'amor* in Hebrew
   alxamía: Parma Biblioteca Palatina 2666, folio 207 *verso*.................... 29
   John Zemke
Chapter Three: How Old Is Ladino Literature?.................................... 43
   Olga Borovaya
Chapter Four: Historical Overview and Outcome of Three Portuguese
   Patterns in Judeo-Spanish: *quer(em)-se* + PART. in Active Constructions,
   the wh-operator *o que*, and the Inflected Infinitive........................ 53
   Aldina Quintana
Chapter Five: The Syntactic Structure of Liturgical Ladino: Construct State
   Nominals, Multiple Determiners, and Verbless Sentences 87
   Matthew Maddox
Chapter Six: *Ke Haber/Ne Haber*: Linguistic Interference, Cross-Meaning, and
   Lexical Borrowing between Ottoman Turkish and Judeo-Spanish 107
   Pamela Dorn Sezgin

Part Two: Fin de siècle Judeo-Spanish Language, Literature and Culture

Chapter Seven: Networks of Patronage and the Making of Two Ladino Newspapers.. 133
    Matthias B. Lehmann

Chapter Eight: Itzhak Benveniste and Reina Hakohén: Narrative and Essay for Sephardic Youth 147
    Elisa Martín Ortega

Chapter Nine: The Invention of Eastern Judeo-Spanish: The Betrayals of Spanish in the Re-romanization Process (End of 19th Century) and Its Consequences.. 163
    Marie-Christine Bornes Varol

Chapter Ten: Salomon Israel Cherezli's *Nuevo chico diccionario judeo-español–francés* (Jerusalem 1898–1899) as a Judeo-Spanish Monolingual Dictionary 191
    Aitor García Moreno

Chapter Eleven: The Creation of the State of Israel and Its Impact on the Self-Image of the Sephardim, as Reflected in Judeo-Spanish Parodic War Haggadahs 213
    Eliezer Papo

Chapter Twelve: The Hispanic Legacy and Sephardic Culture: Sephardim and Hispanists in the First Half of the 20th Century 231
    Paloma Díaz-Mas

Part Three: Judeo-Spanish Language and Culture Today

Chapter Thirteen: Contemporary Judeo-Spanish Poetry in Its Rediscovery of the Past... 257
    Agnieszka August-Zarębska

Chapter Fourteen: *En tierras virtualas*: Sociolinguistic Implications for Judeo-Spanish as a Cyber-vernacular 275
    Rey Romero

Chapter Fifteen: Judeo-Spanish on the Web.................................. 291
    Ana Stulic and Soufiane Rouissi

    Index of Personal Names 315
    Index of Subjects....................................... 319

CHAPTER ONE

Sepharad AS Imagined Translocal Mediterranean Community

Introduction

MAHIR ŞAUL AND JOSÉ IGNACIO HUALDE
University of Illinois at Urbana-Champaign

1. SEPHARAD IMAGINED AS COMMUNITY

In mid-1970s, when she was almost forty, award-winning French novelist Clarisse Nicoïdski, née Abinun, started writing poetry. It was not composed in French, which was the language of her novels, but in the language of her parents, who hailed from Yugoslavia and called this language "spagnol muestru." She gave a copy of her compositions to the linguist Haïm Vidal Sephiha, who in a brief article was the first person to publish a sampling, which included seven numbered sections making up what we now know as her first poem, "Lus Ojus." This poem was followed by a prose text, "La Vyeja," a heartbreaking short story set in World War II Yugoslavia, with Jewish protagonists under the reign of terror of Free Croatia's Ustashi before liberation by the Partisan army. Sephiha applauded her as "la dernière poétesse judéo-espagnole" (Sephiha 1977).[1] The following year, Nicoïdski produced a small book of her Judeo-Spanish poetry in a run of 300 copies, including an English translation of each poem by Kevin Power (Nicoïdski 1978). Three years later a new garland of nineteen short poems appeared: "Caminus di palavras".[2] In her short but prolific life Nicoïdski published over twenty titles—novels, plays, historical pieces—all in French, which brought her added accolades. However, she did not publish any more Judeo-Spanish poetry.

This already peculiar story assumes uncanny proportion after the exceptional responses that the little poetic sideline stirred. Perhaps Nicoïdski did not need to bother with an English translation of her poems, because the refinement of her verse and the images limned in her sparse style produce an extraordinary effect on modern Spanish readers, and her poetry has received a great share of critical attention. At the turn of the new century, four leading poets of Spain and Latin America were asked to prepare a landmark anthology of the second half of the twentieth century (Milán, Robayna, Valente, Varela 2002). In their selection of 100 laurels of Spanish language poetry, they included Nicoïdski.[3] Forced to make hard choices, and setting aesthetic merit above balance, as the publisher explains, the anthology's selectors had resigned themselves to not representing certain Spanish-speaking countries of Latin America, a decision that reviews following publication contested. No one objected, though, that Nicoïdski, the only one among those sharing the honor who was not from a Spanish-speaking country (her country listed as *Francia*) had been allotted five pages for nine poems, an amazing ratio considering her concise poetic output. Acknowledgment by a poet like José Ángel Valente, arguably Spain's greatest poet in the postwar period, was not all. The Argentine poet Juan Gelman, one of South America's most significant writers and also Nicoïdski's senior, went one step further. He created his own corpus of twenty-nine poems in Nicoïdski's Bosnian Judeo-Spanish, emulated by studying her compositions, an unprecedented tribute paid by one poet to another (Balbuena 2009).

Nicoïdski was not to be "the last" Judeo-Spanish poet, female or male, nor the last one to write in this language with a literary talent and contemporary sensibility that brought transnational recognition. Two more recent poets writing in Judeo-Spanish, Margalit Matitiahu and Avner Perez, both of Salonikan ancestry and bilingual Israeli authors, along with other celebrated Judeo-Spanish poets of their cohort, are the subject of August-Zarębska's contribution to our volume. Their first verse collections, published in the 1980s, generated enthusiasm and their success was confirmed in subsequent publications.[4] A good deal of prose work is also being created in Judeo-Spanish (ranging from the writings of the versatile veteran Matilda Koen-Sarano to the recent contributions of memoirist Roz Kohen). Along with these, we may mention the less noticeable but critical supportive, editorial, and lexicographic work of people such as Gad Nassi, Moshe Shaul and others serving on the editorial boards of *Aki Yerushalayim* or *El Amaneser*, as well as the website LadinoKomunita, which is discussed here by Rey Romero.[5] At the same time we observe a modest recovery of the use of Judeo-Spanish in academic articles and essays, hosted mostly in Spanish university publications, by both senior authors and those belonging to the younger generation.

Why would recognized authors who can reach wide audiences in national languages with a great number of speakers choose to create and publish works in a language that has long been declared severely endangered, due to its low number of adult speakers and its absence in the home environment where children can learn it? We leave the assessment of their personal motivations to literary critics specialized in these authors. Instead, we are interested in addressing the social and historical factors that illuminate such choices. If writing in Judeo-Spanish—against unreasonable odds from the perspective of an author's natural desire to gain readership—can be conceived as a "journey home" (Piser 2012), the writers who undertake this journey come from two generations of geographical and metaphorical displacement, while being dispersed in different countries and continents, and absorbed in different tongues of national and international currency. It may be a rewarding exercise to explore the nature of this "home."

This home seems to be located first of all in the language. We find evidence for this also in works of a very different nature. The memoirs and autobiographic novels of Sephardic authors from Western Europe or South America, who hail from families that had immigrated to those places in recent times, often include Judeo-Spanish words and expressions inserted as quotations. Romeu Ferré and Díaz-Mas, who make this observation, remark that such examples suggest a strong identification with the Sephardic Jewish world of remote Iberian origin as well as a shared collective past in the Eastern Mediterranean (2011: 129). This identification with the language is present, even if in somewhat contradictory fashion, in the life and work of Bulgarian-born Elias Canetti, who came to terms with his heritage in his memoirs and once defined himself as "a Spanish poet in the German language" (Ascher 1990, Esformes 2000).

Romeu Ferré and Díaz-Mas refer to the late nineteenth or early twentieth century dispersal of the Hispanic Sephardim out of the Ottoman world as a "second diaspora." Yet considering the historical Septuagint roots of the term, in the longer stretch of Jewish history it can be called at least a "third diaspora," since the fanning out of the Sephardim into the Mediterranean and Atlantic worlds after their expulsion from Spain was already a second diaspora, following the first, original diaspora out of the Holy Land. This realization prompts further reflection. Western European and American authors of Sephardic origin are not the only ones to reveal attachment to Judeo-Spanish in their work. As we have seen, a number of second-generation Israeli authors also do so and with even greater commitment. The closing of the first diaspora does not seem to bring an end to the second or third Diasporas. The vaunted ingathering from one sort of exile still leaves Sephardim attached to and longing for the image of a "home" remembered as language.

The title of our volume invokes Benedict Anderson's influential analysis, which has a great deal to say on language (Anderson 1983). Anderson's book-length essay presents a reflection on the emergence of the nation as political vessel for the formation of the modern state, and following the gradual collapse or transformation of amalgamated empires, of the international system of states. The Sephardic diaspora, as the use of the term already intimates, is not a nation in that modern sense (although it was in an earlier sense, not irrelevant for the process Anderson delineates—as the rubric *nación* or *nação* applied to New Christian communities of Spanish and Portuguese origin in western Europe and *millet* later in the Ottoman administrative system attest). The analogy of Anderson's story for our case is, therefore, only partial, and the contrast itself is worth pursuing.

Anderson notes at the start that all communities are imagined, except for very small ones allowing members to have face-to-face contact. What needs to be distinguished is the different ways in which they are imagined, which may suggest where their boundaries are likely to be laid. This idea of imagined community is useful for understanding sub-political cultural ensembles that exhibit centripetal force and cultural continuity across changing times, even if they do not ripen into modern nations. Anderson identifies two developments that paved the way for the modern nation: The loss of identification with dynastic realms associated with the decline of sacral monarchies, and a radically new way of apprehending time, including the replacement of religious parable as prefiguration of present and future with time as a flow that transforms and remains irreversible.

Only the first of these two has a correlate in the formation of a Sephardic diasporic identity. For the Iberian Jews, the Edict of Expulsion of 1492 was a fatal blow to any identification with the dynastic realm. This identification was already weak to begin with, because of suspect religious minority status and the test of periodic mass violence. Thus, for instance, whereas Sem Tob de Carrión (Sem Tob ben Ishaq ibn Ardutiel, b. Carrión de los Condes, 1290–c. 1369), one of the most prominent poets in the Castilian language of his time, addresses his *Moral Proverbs* to the King of Castile, Don Pedro I, at the same time he stresses his Jewish identity: *Señor rey, noble, alto, oí este sermón/que viene dezir Santo, judío de Carrion* ["Lord King, noble and high, hear this discourse which Santob, the Jew from Carrión, comes forward to speak"];[6] and, in what are perhaps the best-known lines from the book, he feels the need to remind the imagined reader (the King) not to disregard the wisdom contained in the book because of the author's religious identity: *Non val el açor menos por nascer de mal nido,/nin los exemplos buenos por los dezir judío* ["Nor is the hawk worth less, if born in a poor nest; nor are good proverbs [of less value] if spoken by a Jew"]. Allegiance to the monarch is accompanied by a clear sense of distinctiveness.

The post-expulsion period was not more favorable for the settlers' reinsertion in other dynastic worlds, as during those two hundred years significant proportions of the Sephardic community moved in and out of apostasy in peripatetic existence in search of new homelands between the North African coast, Italian cities, the Ottoman Balkans and Near East, the Atlantic harbors, and Protestant enclaves in northern Europe. There were powerful motivations for a sense of distinction and singular destiny even when the immigrants demonstrated loyalty to the monarchs or to the cities that welcomed them. Since medieval times, for example, the Sabbath services included an official prayer for the king.[7] Beyond this custom, after the expulsion the refugees and their descendants expressed abundant gratitude without practical motivation toward rulers who gave them safe haven. A sense of autonomy persisted regardless. In almost every Hebrew book printed in Constantinople after the Jews established a press there in 1493, the title pages or the colophon included lengthy formulas of blessings and praises for the sultan, even though these books were not dedicated to the monarchs. The Ottoman authorities were completely indifferent to these publications, and no one other than a few Jewish students of law could have been expected to see and understand these inscriptions (Rozen 2010: 43; Lehmann 2005: 17). In contrast, during the same period books printed in the republic of Venice do not contain similar statements of praise to the city or to the doge. One can conclude, therefore, that these inscriptions expressed genuine gratitude. They are also consonant with the open appreciation of Ottoman rulers in the writings of sixteenth century scholars of Iberian origin, such as the Rabbis Samuel de Medina and Moshe Almosnino. Nonetheless, the "we" and "they" distinction, a sense of collective risk and vulnerability in an alien environment, and commitment to Jewish and often more narrowly Sephardic wellbeing first, are also present in these writings (Rozen 2010: 40–41, 305). This may be one of the ways in which the Sephardic subject of early modern times anticipates aspects of fully modern political awareness.

When it came to the approach to religious myth and time, however, the Mediterranean Sephardic world remained attached to the earlier conception. Even when during early eighteenth century the colloquial register of Spanish of the Sephardim of the eastern Mediterranean blossomed as the medium of written literature, the new Judeo-Spanish style was born as a religious product of rabbinic pedagogy, linked to the weekly readings of the Torah and to Talmudic images as guidance for righteous life. In the nineteenth century this written language was relatively secularized by shedding, in the hands of a new intelligentsia, the rabbinic habit of code switching to scriptural Hebrew. A greater proportion of spoken vernacular in writing resulted in increased Romance content. The trend towards secularization of the language was strengthened in the abundant journalistic publications of the twentieth century, even if at times it meant clumsily following French and Italian models. These developments, however, never shook the ties to a religious worldview and an ecumenical understanding of worldwide Judaic community as a dispersed (and fractious) tribe.

Sephardic awareness sprang, therefore, from a hybrid nature: a sense of distinctive identity, but one attached to a religion that imparts a sense of kinship group, whose boundaries lay beyond the Sephardic world; and a proper ideographic sacred language, the elements of which suffuse the vernacular that became literary Judeo-Spanish. The sense of being Hispanic Sephardic did not produce a political vessel, which is Anderson's concern to explain, but an enduring feeling of distinctiveness within a larger religious entity, itself explicitly likened to a descent construct. The language, the vernacular that provided the medium of writing and printing, did not become the basis for a political grouping, but was consolidated as the very backbone of Hispanic Sephardic distinctiveness, taking on the roles that geography and shared history play in other contexts.

The Iberian Sephardic "imagined community" was forged during the first two centuries after the expulsion of 1492, under trying circumstances: The protracted period of migrations and relocations put a stamp on several generations after 1492 as it caused traumatizing losses to life and property; many migrants and their descendants went from one distant location to another because they could not find the safety of a country of permanent settlement; migrants belonging to successive waves intermingled, starting with the first refugees who left Castile and Aragon following the first expulsion to maintain their religion, all the way to the seventeenth century New Christians who, often after several peregrinations and a few generations of religious secrecy, openly embraced Judaism in the Ottoman Empire or in the cities of the Low Countries. The migrants originating in Spain and Portugal were already plural in their make up, as they had been formed in the diverse cultural worlds of the different kingdoms and cities of Iberia, and were also stratified by status and class. The drawn out period of exodus added new elements of heterogeneity among them. Yet the experience produced a convoluted process of self-fashioning and the formation of a singular Hispanic Sephardic identity, along with a concomitant process of linguistic shift and re-identification.

The first Iberian exiles to arrive in the large Ottoman cities founded congregations based in their city of origin and their narrow cultural affinities. In Constantinople, for example, the first Gerush Sepharad (Expulsion from Spain) congregation split quickly into several, and then witnessed the founding of yet other congregations by newer arrivals: Cordova, Aragon, Messina, Sicilia, and Portugal. By mid-sixteenth century there were ten congregations of Iberian origin in the city (Rozen 2010: 78–81). In Salonika the Jews who arrived from Spain established Gerush Sepharad, Castilia, Aragon, Catalan, Majorca; and those who arrived from Portugal: Portugal, Lisbon, and Evora (Goodblatt 1952: 12). As Ibn Abi Zimra, a leading rabbinic scholar among the first generation of exiles from Spain, wrote: "And it is the custom throughout the Jewish Diaspora that Jews who are of the same city of origin or language make a community for themselves, and do not mix with men of different city or language" (quoted by Ray 2013: 80; see Goldman 1970: 86). In the second and third generations, the sharp boundaries between these congregations softened. Their original names survived, but their membership started mixing, with intermarriages and transfers among them for pragmatic reasons. Eventually, newer Jewish arrivals of Iberian origin to Istanbul and Salonika were allotted to the existing congregations with an eye to maintaining balance between the groups and no longer on the basis of the newcomers' languages or originating cities, evidence of the blurring of cultural boundaries between them (Ray 2013: 86). Divisions among Jews of Castilian, Aragonese, Valencian, Catalan, Leonese, and eventually Portuguese heritage faded, giving way to new communities, which were seen by others and also self-understood as "Espanyol."

A number of factors, concerning both trans-Mediterranean connections and the circumstances of the places of settlement, can be invoked to perceive how this happened. The itinerant nature of the early Sephardic Diaspora and the need for the exiled Jews and *conversos* to rely on one another helped foster mercantile networks (Ray 2013: 112). These networks encompassed artisans such as dyers, weavers, and embroiderers, as well as bankers.[8] While the poor, who formed the majority everywhere, remained outside of these expanded translocal communities, the wealthy assumed local leadership. The economic élites were the founders of new congregations or their administrators and set the tone for the rest. They became emulated models for a pan-Mediterranean Hispanic identity in the sixteenth century. Their social role was thus similar to their counterparts in the late nineteenth century in Westernization and modernization (and later on even in Turkification, Hellenization, etc.).

The rabbis provided a different kind of leadership, forming another network stretching throughout the Mediterranean. They led Jewish courts with jurisdiction over pecuniary matters, religious questions, marriage and divorce, and cases involving Jewish ordinances. The *responsa* literature made available in contemporary scholarship provides abundant testimony showing that in these matters their reach as well as the resources they mobilized extended to far-flung localities. Whereas the *Halakha*, the formulated statutes of Jewish law and norms relating to religious sanctity, has no boundaries and does not recognize a delimited Sephardic sphere within it, next to it is *Minhag*, the notion of prevailing custom. The large influx of exiled migrants, each group bringing with it its own *Minhagim*, together with those of native Jews of Egypt, Palestine, Ottoman Anatolia and the Balkans necessitated creative yet, legal responses to meet the demands of everyday life (Goldman 1970: 45). The leaders of the Sephardi congregations surmounted their own perspectives through compromise. They formed supra-congregational institutions soon after settlement. In Constantinople this behavior prevented the founding of joint voluntary societies with the native Jewish community of the Romaniyot (Rozen 2013: 85). Extra-locally too, rabbis of the Iberian communities often conferred with each other regarding mutual concerns (Benaim 2012: 24). Affective bonds to relatives, teachers, and disciples in distant lands transformed the Sephardic rabbis' conception of the pale of Judaism in unexpected ways toward pan-Hispanism.

This is illustrated by rabbinical decisions regarding the status of widows, which was one of the recurrent difficulties of the era of exile and dangerous travel. One decision taken by first generation immigrant rabbinic scholar Yaakov Ibn

Haviv of Salonika, who was born in the Leonese city of Zamora, involved a difficult case in which the brother of the deceased householder was a *converso* who had stayed in Spain. According to the *Halakha*, when a married man dies without the issue of a son, his brother has the obligation to marry the widow in leviratic union to produce a descendant for the deceased. If he was not so inclined, the brother had to liberate the widow with the equivalent of a divorce. The question in this case was whether the widow was bound by this rule. The case hung on whether the surviving brother was considered Jewish, and therefore in possession of his leviratic rights. Rabbi Ibn Haviv ruled that the missing *converso* brother was a Jew and the leviratic principle was in effect. Thus he asserted that the Jewish people encompassed those who had been compelled to stay in the Iberian Peninsula after the expulsion, because "tomorrow they will come here, and how can we oust them now by judging them to be utter apostates" (Rozen 2010: 93–95). For Ibn Haviv and all other Iberian Jews, the nation meant the Jewish-Iberian Nation, including both the immigrants and the New Christians who did not emigrate. Other eminent rabbinic authorities that were not of Iberian origin, such as Constantinople's Moshe Capsali and Eliyahu Mizrahi, differed and took contrasting decisions in their rulings, but Ibn Haviv's principle was upheld and ratified five decades later by the second-generation Iberian immigrant rabbis of mid-sixteenth century; this view persisted for generations.

Local circumstances reinforced the trend toward pan-Mediterranean Iberian Jewish reconfiguration. The Iberian exiles settled among Italian, Ashkenazi, and, in the Ottoman Empire, Greek-speaking Byzantine Romaniyot Jewish communities. Their affinities in religious and social custom brought the Iberian congregations closer together, despite all their differences and rivalries, against these native communities. In the case of Constantinople there was a further political distinction that contrasted the Iberian settlers with the local Romaniyot community, and undermined the latter. Joseph Hacker's writings brought to scholarly attention the fact that the Romaniyot Jewish communities of Constantinople had formed after the conquest of the city, when Ottoman authorities relocated the existing Jewish communities of the provinces and force-settled them in the new capital, alongside others, according to a well-known demographic policy known as *sürgün*, in order to repopulate the destroyed city. This origin gave the Romaniyot Jewish community a sort of serf status curtailing their right to travel, a restriction that paralyzed their economic and social activities until the seventeenth century (Hacker 1992a). The newly arriving Iberian refugees reached an altogether different position. They constituted a new category of Jews, free of such restrictions, because the Ottoman rulers considered them as having the legal status of willingly submitted rather than vanquished in war (*kendi gelen*). Accordingly, the local Greek-speaking Romaniyot Jews and the Iberian immigrants differed in their sentiments toward the authority. The Romaniyot bitterness about their coerced displacement lasted, and they saw no difference between their erstwhile Byzantine overlords and the current Ottoman ones, whereas the Iberians felt grateful and blessed, their chroniclers eventually producing the myth that the Ottomans had invited the Spanish expellees (Rozen 2010: 44).

There were practical consequences to this history. In many towns and cities of Anatolia, Thrace, and Macedonia the previous Jewish inhabitants had been removed and the Iberian expellees who settled in those places found no obstacle to establishing Sephardic custom as supreme. In Constantinople, where the Iberian Jews did encounter Romaniyot, they avoided intermarriage with them, which could jeopardize the civil status of children of such marriages, and group endogamy hardened the boundaries between these two social categories. As the Iberians overcame their differences and consolidated and centralized into Spanish Sephardim, the status difference facilitated their prevailing over the Greek-speaking group. The pluralism of customs in Ottoman Jewish Mediterranean evolved into Sephardi-Castilian tradition (Hacker 1992b: 115).

For the second and third generation of exiles of 1492 the pain of expulsion began to fade. New collective memories were developed. Memory of exact origins and the importance of an identity attached to a particular place in Iberia were overshadowed by an invented shared and homogeneous Sephardic group identity (Ben Naeh 2008: 418). The rabbinic Sephardic chroniclers helped replace painful personal memories with accounts of the glory of the pre-exilic past. The Sepharad that was invoked was a land and a community born of nostalgia, a longing for a better time (Ray 2013: 126, 161). New Christian arrivals later in the sixteenth and during the seventeenth century reinforced connections with Iberia and the hold of the Castilian language, which had in the meantime developed into an inter-community medium (although a fraction of them chose not to associate with the first wave of immigrants and developed an alternative identity as "Portuguese"). The Balkan and Middle Eastern Sephardim of Ottoman lands emphasized their heritage in Christian Spain and Portugal over their distant roots in Muslim Al-Andalus. Cultural traits such as knowledge of new weaving techniques, firearms, printing, and Romance languages helped them bring vitality to the economies of the places where they settled, and to foster mercantile ties to Europe through the ports of Venice, Ancona, Ragusa, and Livorno, making them also valuable subjects for the Ottoman rulers.

The social development outlined here has a linguistic concomitant and counterpart, to which we now turn. Expressions such as "langue Espagnolle," "en Español," "lingua spagnuola," or "spagnoli ebrei" emerge in historical documents concerning Iberian Jews in various languages from all over the Mediterranean; they are mirrored in *Taife-i Espanya* 'community of Spain,' which is the way Salonika's earliest sixteenth century Ottoman register labeled the city's growing Iberian migrant Jewish population (Lowry 1994: 207).

1.2 The Language

The late fifteenth century Jewish exiles from Iberia were linguistically heterogeneous and spoke *different* Ibero-Romance languages (see Lleal 1992, Penny 2000), a crucial point that until recently has rarely been fully taken into account in socio-historic accounts, even though it is at the heart of the issue of how the Sephardic community came to be imagined.

For three of the Romance languages that the Jews spoke in Iberia, a relatively large number of examples written in Hebrew script have come down to us (Castilian, Aragonese, and Navarrese). For the other languages, such as Leonese, Galician, Catalan, or Portuguese, we resort to other sorts of evidence. When Jews wrote Romance languages in Hebrew script, and perhaps when they spoke them as well, they incorporated a good quantity of Hebrew vocabulary in them—mostly but not exclusively pertaining to the religious domain. An example is the word *alhad*, a borrowing from Arabic used by Jews and Muslims to replace *domingo* 'Sunday' (Quintana 2014b: 40), from Latin *dominicus dies*, whose original Christian meaning of 'day of the Lord' must have been evident. When it came to phonology, morphology, and syntax, however, these languages were no different than the varieties that their non-Jewish fellow countrymen spoke and wrote at the time (Lleal 1992, Minervini 2006a: 18, Benaim 2012). Familiarity with Hebrew may nevertheless have resulted in the incorporation in the speech of Iberian Jews of a back fricative, perhaps a uvular /χ/ (a phoneme that did not exist in any Ibero-Romance language at the time) not only in Hebrew words, but also in borrowings from Arabic such as *alhad*, *hazino* 'sick' and *haragan* 'lazy'. It appears that a trait of Jewish Castilian pronunciation must have been a contrast between /h/ (which was later lost or replaced by non-Castilian /f/ in Judeo-Spanish) in *harina* /harína/ 'flour' (< Lat *farīna*), *horno* /hórno/ 'oven' (< Lat *furnu-*), etc., and /χ/ (which was preserved) in /alχád/, /χazíno/, etc. A second minor point of pronunciation is that although word-final /-m/ was not possible in Castilian Spanish or in most other Ibero-Romance varieties, Jewish speakers of these languages may have learned to pronounce it in Hebrew words, including plurals in /-im/. Although these are minor details of pronunciation, they may have served as sociolinguistic markers.

We need to bear in mind also a point to which contemporary sociolinguistic research alerts us: various registers, idiolects, and sociolects existed in each one of these languages and the Jews presumably participated in them.

The expellees who left Castile and Aragon, and later Navarre and Portugal throughout the sixteenth century, brought this plurality of Romance languages to the places where they settled. Different Romance languages and dialects (Castilian, Aragonese, Catalan, Portuguese, etc.) *co-existed* for some generations and the immigrant Iberian Jews used them in private communication (Penny 1992;

Minervini 2006b: 148). As the process of Sephardization we have just delineated set off, these languages competed with each other (Quintana 2002, 2014a). Although the genetic closeness of these languages made them mutually intelligible and a degree of hybridization took place, the outcome was the disappearance of Romance multilingualism and the triumph of one language for the Jews of Iberian heritage in the Mediterranean. Révah, for example, noted that among the sixteenth century Jews who arrived in Salonika, the ones originating in Castile were only a small minority compared to those of Aragonese, Catalan, or Portuguese background; yet, "all the Judeo-Spanish speech forms of the Balkans, without exception, derive essentially from the speech forms that New Castile and Andalusia had in 1492" (Révah 1965: 1354). Due to the absence of politically enforced normative pressure, a colloquial form of this language became dominant, which, following its own course of evolution, came down to the twentieth century as Judeo-Spanish.

It should be noted that at the time of the expulsion, Castilian Spanish was already perceived as more prestigious than other Ibero-Romance varieties. Castilian was progressively replacing other Romance varieties in urban areas in much of the Iberian Peninsula. In the case of the most closely related languages with a very high degree of mutual intelligibility with Castilian, such as Leonese, Navarrese and Aragonese, this replacement took place by a gradual process of adoption of Castilian forms instead of local forms. Let's consider an example from the phonological domain. Among the Ibero-Romance languages, only Castilian transformed Latin /kt/ into /tʃ/ as in *noche* 'night' (< Lat NOCTE), *leche* (< LACTE), *ocho* 'eight' (< OCTO) and *hecho* 'fact, made' (< FACTU), among many other examples. All other Ibero-Romance languages preserved a pronunciation /(i)t/ (cf. Port *noite, leite, oito, feito*; Cat *nit, llet, vuit, fet*). At a certain point, however, Castilian forms with *ch* started intruding in Aragonese and Navarrese texts. A good example is found in the fourteenth century Navarro-Aragonese *siddur* transcribed and studied in Quintana and Révah (2004), where together with *nueyti (de alhad)* 'night (of Sunday)' we also find *lechuga* 'lettuce', instead of the expected Navarro-Aragonese form *leituga*, as the authors point out (see also Lleal 1992: 9). With time, non-Castilian forms become residual and eventually completely disappear from documents written in Navarre and Aragon, reflecting trends in the speech of the urban classes of these kingdoms.

The first generation of Jewish immigrants undoubtedly brought with them to the new communities the sociolinguistic dynamics that existed in the Iberian Peninsula at the time. This would have as a consequence a tendency to give preference to Castilian variants, not only on the part of speakers of Castilian, but also by speakers of other varieties. Thus, to return to the example just considered in the previous paragraph, Castilian forms like *noche, ocho*, etc., are universally found in Judeo-Spanish. To give another telling example, Judeo-Spanish forms like *ojo*

(< Lat OCULU) 'eye', *mujer* (< MULIERE) 'woman', *oreja* (< AURICULA) 'ear' etc., with /ʒ/ from Latin K'L, LY, are exclusively Castilian, cf. Port. *olho, mulher, orelha*, Leon. *güeyu, muyer, oreya*, Arag. *güello, muller, orella*; Cat. *ull, muller, orella*. An exception, however, is found in the choice among /f-/ ~ /h-/ ~ 0. Among the Ibero-Romance languages, Castilian is also unique in having undergone a sound change whereby Latin /f-/ was aspirated to /h/ before a vowel. This aspiration was subsequently lost, starting from the area around Burgos, in Old Castile. Interestingly, Judeo-Spanish has preserved non-Castilian forms with /f-/ in a greater or smaller number of lexemes depending on the geographical area (see Quintana 2006: 93–100).

Recent advances in historical Judeo-Spanish linguistics provide now a better picture of how this process happened. Brief references in the earlier scholarly literature made it sound as if these various Romance languages simply amalgamated or merged together to result in Judeo-Spanish, overlooking the details of the historical evidence on the matter, or the analogies available in our own time. Languages have inherent structures and do not mix in this way. Consequently, the outcome of the historical process, Judeo-Spanish, is not simply a merger that is equidistant to all Romance language antecedents.

After the expulsion, the exiles went through a period of Romance multilingualism involving different Romance linguistic codes. In their new lands of settlement, some of the immigrants acquired—in addition to their pre-Expulsion language—new Romance varieties from fellow immigrants from Iberia, and local forms in the Italian peninsula and in Portugal. As the sixteenth century wore on, the use of the Castilian language spread in the diaspora and started displacing the other Romance varieties. Castilian Spanish, however, was not homogeneous. Like all languages at all times, fifteenth century Castilian had some internal variation. It consisted of various norms connected with social and cultural stratification as well as geographical location (Minervini 2006b: 148). Even restricting our scope to consonant phonology, this variation included, among other phenomena, (a) the conservation or deletion of /h/ (e.g. [hórno] ~ [órno] 'oven'), (b) the devoicing of fricatives (e.g. [káza] ~ [kása] 'house', [óʒo] ~ [óʃo] 'eye'), (c) the fronting of (post-)alveolar fricatives (e.g. [páso] ~ [pás̠o] 'step') leading to their neutralization with the dental fricatives that had resulted from older affricates (e.g. [brás̠o] < [brátso] 'arm'), (d) the weakening of /b/ in certain positions (e.g. [lóbo] ~ [lóβo] 'wolf'), causing its neutralization with /β/ (e.g. [láβa] 's/he washes') and the delateralization of the palatal lateral /ʎ/ (e.g. [éʎa] ~ [éja] 'she'), known as *yeísmo* (see, e.g. Lloyd 1987: 322–348). The analysis of early Judeo-Spanish texts has shown that this variation was also found in the new communities of the Eastern Mediterranean at an initial stage (Minervini 1999, Quintana 2014). The fact that the ultimate outcome of this variation did not always favor the same solutions as in Spain or Latin America is not particularly surprising, but the particular circumstances of language and dialect contact no doubt played a role (for lenition phenomena see Hualde 2014).

We may envision a number of situations among the Iberian-born immigrants. For native speakers of Galician-Portuguese and Catalan, Castilian must have been perceived as a different language, albeit intelligible to a certain degree, with which they may or may not have had familiarity before leaving the Iberian Peninsula, depending on personal circumstances. Speakers of Leonese and Navarro-Aragonese varieties, on the other hand, may have considered Castilian a prestigious version of their own native language, within a linguistic repertoire that allowed different choices depending on style and interlocutor.

Already by mid-sixteenth century spoken and written Castilian, which was a language of prestige, culture, and imperial power and dominant in the sea lines of the Mediterranean, had become the vehicular language of the Mediterranean Jewish world, used in business and everyday communication, marginalizing the other Ibero-Romance languages and dialects, which became family languages (Quintana 2002: 133–134, Minervini 2006a: 22).

This development is revealed, for example in the statement made in 1600 by Meir Lombroso, a person accused at the Inquisition tribunal of Pisa, to explain why he spoke Castilian even though he had not been born or brought up in Spain:

> in Salonica tutti gl'Hebrei e la maggior parte de Turchi parlano spagnuolo et qui in Venetia et in tutto il Levante li nostri rabini non fanno le prediche in altra lingua que in lingua spagnuola e per questo l'intendo et anche la parlo.[9]

What makes this testimony even more pertinent in the present context is that Lombroso, trying to save his skin, was not being truthful, as he actually belonged to a family of New Christians from Lisbon.

In such instances, the linguistic transfer involved not only influence or modification, but in some cases actually language shift through the acquisition of Castilian outside of Castile and Aragon. The existence of a phase of Romance multilingualism in the diaspora is somewhat obscured, because the speakers did not always gave a precise name to the Romance language that they spoke. Speakers of a language do not always need to designate it with a proper noun. Proper names for languages emerge and gain currency only in particular historical circumstances, and frequently it is outsiders who assign them, not the native speakers. In rabbinic writings the Romance varieties that the Iberian Jews spoke are referred to as *la'az*, which means "foreign" and could designate any language in contrast to the holy tongue. It could be Castilian, but it just as well could be Aragonese, Leonese, Catalan, or Portuguese. Expressions such as *ladino* or *franko* seem to have been used as Romance equivalents for *la'az*, in the sense of "vernacular", "not-the-Sacred Language," rather than as proper names. We can call these expressions *descriptors* (adopting a term from computer science) and contrast them with proper names.

For the Jews "sacred language" in itself was a descriptor, not a proper name, as it designated indiscriminately Hebrew or Aramaic. Nevertheless, the logic of language boundary operates because of the systemic properties of phonology, morphology, and syntax.

The description of a scene from the mid-sixteenth century may provide an illustration of the daily incidence of Sephardic Romance multilingualism, as it suggests at the same time the presence of language boundaries, ready to take over and regulate communication when possible. The event is reported in Ray (2013: 139). In 1565 the Portuguese friar Pantaleão de Aveiro and fellow monks who were in pilgrimage in the Holy Land encountered at the Shiloah pool outside of Jerusalem a group of Jewish women who were bathing in the public bath. One of the women, identifying the men as Europeans, addressed them, first using a language that De Aveiro describes as "a mix of Spanish and Italian." But then she was delighted when she heard that the monk replied to her in Castilian and they quickly fell into friendly conversation. We see here that the initial "mix" was a fleeting and spontaneous product of lack of clarity at the moment of encounter, but the proper code was established once competence in it could be ascertained, although it was not the native language of at least one of the parties, and maybe of neither.

Castilian eventually replaced the other varieties of Romance not only in the Ottoman cities such as Salonika, Constantinople, Alexandria, and Cairo, but also in Venice, Ancona, Ferrara, and Pisa. Inquisition records indicate that in Pisa it was common practice for Jews of Iberian origin to hire tutors to teach their children to read and write Castilian in Hebrew characters (Ray 2013: 138). The large Jewish Portuguese community of Ancona spoke Castilian (Benaim 2012: 183). In Bucharest, too, Portuguese and Catalan Jews abandoned their language and adopted Castilian, although this history left linguistic traces in their speech as usages from these former languages (Sala 1971: 12–13).

Romance multilingualism is reflected in their sixteenth century publications of the Jews of Iberian origin. For example, it is well known that Abraham Usque of Ferrara (born in Portugal) and his son Abraham printed in their press back-to-back books in literary Portuguese or Castilian, some of which were dedicated to the same patron, Doña Gracia Nasi, who lived in Constantinople. They themselves authored works in various genres in Castilian, Portuguese, and Italian.

Literary creations in Castilian that were produced in the Ottoman cities, in turn, reveal a variety of linguistic norms. At the high end were the writings of Rabbi Moshe Almosnino of Salonika, who was born of Iberian immigrants in the Ottoman diaspora, but who published works that are close in language and style to the literary norms of Castilian prevailing in Spain at the time.[10] These writings were addressed to a limited circle of Jews who carried or reproduced the standards of the educated in peninsular Spanish (In the case of *Crónica*, they have been described as the author's acquaintances in Salonika and Constantinople, close to the highest echelons of Ottoman administration, who wished to understand how the Ottoman state operated in order to better plan their next political steps [Rozen 2004: 41–42]). In the same category of language belongs a medical treatise, *Diálogo del Colorado*, published in 1601 in Salonika by the physician Daniel de Ávila Gallego, who was from a family of *conversos* and a student at the university of Salamanca, before moving to Amsterdam and eventually to Salonika (Romeu Ferré 2014). It is notable that Almosnino, and perhaps De Ávila Gallego as well, had family backgrounds of non-Castilian Romance heritage, but created works in Ottoman cities in the high register of educated Castilian.

At the other end of the scale of registers were a number of genres, which remained mostly unpublished, but occasionally made their way into manuscript collections or print as "texts lacking literary ambition" (Minervini 2006b: 149). Oral sermons and homiletics proliferated in the sixteenth century and, as they were usually delivered in the vernacular, may have influenced the speech habits of the population. When rabbis moved from one place or one congregation to another, they gave wider currency to local linguistic innovations and parochial traits, or to elements of rabbinic discourse, such as code switching to scriptural language or lexicalization of its elements for daily conversation. But such texts were generally later published in Hebrew. Another kind of text that has recently become more accessible for scholarly purposes are the occasional long Judeo-Spanish extracts lodged in the Hebrew documents of rabbinic *responsa*, which were given and reproduced as testimonies, or the contracts, letters, and other documentary evidence supplied for the case. Benaim provides 84 such extracts from the sixteenth century (Benaim 2012). Although redacted by a scribe or the scholar presenting the case, the passages provide evidence for a range of colloquial speech forms of the Castilian spoken by the eastern Mediterranean Iberian Jewish immigrants or their descendants, occasionally showing traces of other spoken varieties of Romance, such as Leonese, Aragonese, or Portuguese and Italian.

The people who produced these specimens or those who committed them to writing had little contact with the higher modalities of peninsular Spanish. Their discourse represented the popular Castilian norm that spread among the Jewish exiles, and then formed the basis of the new Judeo-Spanish common language of the Mediterranean diaspora (Minervini 2006b: 148). A prayer book printed in Salonika around 1565 affords a better window on this process. It was written in Spanish for women, who were normally not educated in Hebrew, and its author has only recently been identified as Rabbi Meir Benveniste (Quintana 2014). The main text of prayers and blessings shows the characteristics of the scriptural translations that Sephiha dubbed "calque language," but in his instructions and explanations Benveniste's language reveals northern colloquial Castilian with some Aragonese pronunciation influences. Its written models were not those of the peninsular literary language, but Hebrew, resulting at times in narrative incoherence or flaws in expository logic or argumentation (Quintana 2014: 57). These very same features became characteristic of the prose that blossomed two hundred years later in the *Me'am Lo'ez* series initiated by Yaakov Huli. The difference is that the eighteenth century language of *Me'am Lo'ez* is more fluent and readily understandable (Benaim 2012: 187)—when compared both to the Judeo-Spanish of *responsa* texts and to the explanations and expositions of Benveniste's prayer book—thanks to Huli's own gift and as befits a text published for a popular readership.

The classic rabbinical *Ladino* prose of the eighteenth century reveals no more contact with peninsular literary norms and emanates from colloquial speech forms, which may have survived in regional popular speech in Spain, but would not be encountered in writing. Throughout the sixteenth century, however, when the Mediterranean community of Sepharad was gaining shape in the imagination, contact with the Castilian language and the culture of Iberia had not ceased. It was maintained not only through orality, due to the flow of New Christian exiles which continued all the way into the seventeenth century, but also through print. Some of the Hispanic Sephardim of the eastern Mediterranean had access to publications from Spain and read the Latin script. Evidence for this exists in the Hebrew translation of Garci Rodríguez de Montalvo's immensely popular 1508 chivalric novel *Amadís de Gaula*. This novel had led to a very profitable franchise in a series of sequels, which eventually inspired Cervantes's clever lampooning in Don Quixote. According to Wacks, Ottoman Sephardim also were avid readers of the adventures of Amadís and the similar novels of Palmerín de Olivia [Oliva]. In the early sixteenth century Rabbi Menahem di Lunzano chastised in verse his community in Jerusalem for reading such books on Shabbat instead of coming to the synagogue (Wacks 2011, 2012). The translation of Amadís was undertaken by Jacob Algaba in 1541, and seems to have been a commercial initiative meant for a wider readership among the non-Hispanophone Jews. Thus Iberian Jews' competence in Castilian Spanish, which was partly inherited and partly achieved through language shift after the Expulsion, served them not only in their historical self-fashioning as translocal community, in finding economic recovery, and in contributing to the vitality of the Ottoman realm, but also in interposing themselves as mediators of this culture for the Jews of other lands.

Benedict Anderson includes in his book a discussion of how newspapers shaped anonymous crowds of vernacular readers into an imagined community of fellow citizens. The nearly nine decades of Judeo-Spanish journalism developed in contrasting circumstances. Sephardic periodicals thrived from the last quarter of the nineteenth century and resulted in a bibliography of nearly four hundred periodical titles from two dozen cities in the Middle East, the Balkans, Central Europe, and also North America. This previously neglected topic is now a burgeoning field of study, as attested to by the contributions to Sánchez and Bornes Varol (2013). Mostly the work of small-scale printers or isolated visionaries in precarious living conditions, the Judeo-Spanish press and the new genres it incubated—such as the novel, theatrical play, or modern poetry—produced the largest volume of published material in this language. It refashioned the language, reconnecting it with its Romance heritage, and provided a forum for expressing the joys and pains of the encounter with modernity. The difference from the situation described by Anderson, however, is once again evident. The early gazettes that shaped imperial provinces into nation-states reinforced a sense of common destiny in a bounded space: "*this* marriage with *that* ship, *this* price with *that* bishop" (Anderson 1983: 62). The Judeo-Spanish newspapers, in contrast, served a dispersed community spanning the length and breadth of a crumbling empire, from Cairo and Jerusalem to Vienna, surviving in successor states hostile to one another and suspicious of minorities, and encompassing new migrant communities in the far-off New World. They took on the mission of keeping this community connected by overcoming geographic distance; in fact, turning distance and travel into one of its distinguishing traits. To some extent the spirit of that press, its language, and perhaps even its cosmopolitan parochialism breathe today anew on the Internet of the Judeo-Spanish community.

2. ORGANIZATION OF THE BOOK

The contributions to this book cover the whole range of the history sketched in the foregoing paragraphs, from the fifteenth century to contemporary times. They derive from a selection of papers that were originally presented at the symposium "Sepharad as Imagined Community," which took place in September 2014 on the campus of the University of Illinois, Urbana. The three exceptions are the chapter by Eliezer Papo on Ladino parodies of the Passover Haggadah, and the two chapters by Rey Romero and by Stulic and Rouissi respectively, which examine different aspects of the presence of Judeo-Spanish on the Internet. The book's chapters are written from a variety of disciplinary perspectives, but we have organized them in an approximate chronological order.

2.1. The Early Period: From the Fifteenth to the Nineteenth Century

The first chapter in our collection, John Zemke's "An overlooked fifteenth century *demand d'amor* in Hebrew *alxamía*," concerns a poem in Castilian found in a manuscript written in Hebrew characters in the second half of the fifteenth century in Spain. The work predates the expulsion and belongs to our imagined Sepharad in terms of the presumed identity of its copyist and intended readership. What else can be said about its language and style, and the connections it reveals between the Jews and non-Jews at that time? Zemke, in his discussion of this rare find addresses its language and compositional features, locates the poem within what is known of Castilian Spanish folk literature at that time, and comments on the relevance of its features for interpreting the participation of Jews in the non-Jewish culture of their surroundings.

Olga Borovaya's contribution "How old is Ladino literature?" focuses on continuity in the literature that the Sephardim created after they left Iberia and questions whether only formal characteristics of the language are sufficient to exclude the early centuries of this period as not yet belonging to Judeo-Spanish writing. She objects to considering literary works written outside of Spain in the centuries immediately after the expulsion and clearly intended for a Jewish readership simply as an extension of Spanish literature, instead of seeing them also as part of a distinct literary tradition. We understand this in the following manner: If the register of Castilian in which Rabbi Moshe Almosnino of Salonika wrote in the mid-sixteenth century, which was close to the standards valid at the time in Spain, became inaccessible to most Sephardic Jewish readers of the Ottoman Empire in the eighteenth century, this observation itself is highly pertinent to the history of Judeo-Spanish literature.

The two chapters that follow are more specifically on linguistic matters. Intense contact with other languages has no doubt had an important role in the formation of Judeo-Spanish as a linguistic code standing apart from the Spanish of Spain and Latin-America (emerging, as it were, of diverging evolutions that would be an expected outcome of languages of the same source spoken in different places with no communication between them). In the case of Judeo-Spanish, we find three rather different types of linguistic contact. The first is the influences of the other Romance languages on Castilian, which has been discussed in the preceding section. It may have started already in Iberia, during the bilingual phase which is referred to as "Castilianization," and accelerated during the multilingualism that developed in the new lands of settlement of the Jewish immigrants. Secondly, in the multilingual context of the Ottoman Empire, communication outside of the Jewish community required some mastery of Turkish and other languages. Finally, there was the continued use of Hebrew (and Aramaic) as the language of religion, liturgy, biblical study, and scholarly composition. This volume includes a chapter devoted to each of these three contexts of linguistic contact.

Aldina Quintana in "Historical overview and outcome of three Portuguese patterns in Judeo-Spanish: *quer(em)-se* + part. in active constructions, the wh- operator *o que*, and the inflected infinitive," offers a lucid analysis of three Judeo-Spanish structures, for which she proposes a Portuguese source. This chapter is an example of how detailed linguistic research can elucidate the origins and evolution of the Judeo-Spanish language.

A special register of Judeo-Spanish is the calque language used in liturgical translations, which closely follow the Hebrew original. This liturgical language, for which the term *Ladino* was originally proposed by Sephiha and largely adopted, is the topic of Matthew Maddox's contribution "The syntactic structure of liturgical Ladino: Construct state nominals, multiple determiners and verbless sentences."

Pamela Dorn Sezgin's chapter "*Ke Haber/Ne Haber*: Linguistic interference, cross-meaning and lexical borrowing between Ottoman Turkish and Judeo-Spanish" examines the impact of Ottoman Turkish on Judeo-Spanish, by focusing on some specific cases of borrowing.

2.2. Fin de Siècle Judeo-Spanish Language, Literature and Culture

A very important development in the evolution of Judeo-Spanish writing outside of religious context was the printing of a relatively large number of newspapers in this language in the nineteenth century and the early twentieth century. Matthias Lehmann's "Networks of patronage and the making of two Ladino newspapers" focuses on the biography of two important publishers of such newspapers and the reasons that led them to engage in these activities.

During the transition from the nineteenth to the twentieth centuries, the flourishing secular writings in Judeo-Spanish also provide a record of debates between contrasting worldviews and the questioning of traditional mores. In "Itzhak Benveniste and Reina Hakohén: Narrative and essay for Sephardic youth," Elisa Martín Ortega analyzes a polemical exchange between two authors, carried out in different genres, but vying for the same audience and reflecting the tensions present in Ottoman Sephardic society at the time. The polemic addresses the role of religion and tradition in young women's life. Reina Hakohen, of Salonika, one of the first women to write in Judeo-Spanish, wrote in 1898 an essay she entitled "Las muchachas modernas" [Modern young women] in which she defended traditional values. A year later, Itzhak Benveniste, also of Salonika, responded with a novel, *Konfidensias de un amigo* [Confidences of a friend], which is directly framed as a response to Reina Hakohen's essay. Elisa Martín Ortega's chapter, which is based on her own transliteration and edition of the works she discusses, offers us an analysis of two works that, together, give us a glimpse of the profound transformations that Judeo-Spanish culture underwent in this period.

The use of Judeo-Spanish in journalistic and literary works required an adaptation of a language which, aside from its oral use, had been cultivated only in religious writing. This was often accomplished by seeking models in other prestigious Romance languages. In her chapter "The invention of Eastern Judeo-Spanish: The betrayals of Spanish in the re-Romanization process," Marie-Christine Bornes-Varol studies the effect of contact with other Romance languages such as French, Italian and, especially, Iberian Spanish, on the evolution of written Judeo-Spanish at the end of the 19th century. She points out that this contact had a major impact on the development of the written language. Whereas Judeo-Spanish writers' concern was with creating a written language valid for their purposes, the adoption of foreign models often gave rise to interference and linguistic insecurity. Bornes-Varol focuses on verbal morphology. She shows how the impact of other Romance languages on a language that lacked a written norm resulted in a multiplicity of variants for many verbal forms.

The new usages to which the language was being put also required the production of dictionaries. Aitor García Moreno's chapter "Salomon Israel Cherezli's *Chico diccionario judeo-español–francés* (Jerusalem 1898–1899) as a Judeo-Spanish monolingual dictionary" studies the sources, genesis, features and significance of one such dictionary. He explores the intended readership and purpose of this work on the basis of its internal characteristics, as it was obviously intended for Judeo-Spanish speakers who could read French as a second language, and not the other way around, as the title might suggest.

In "The creation of the State of Israel and its impact on the self-image of the Sephardim, as reflected in Judeo-Spanish parodic war Haggadahs" Eliezer Papo provides an overview of the humorous parodic Haggadah genre, which flourished within the medium of newspapers in the final decades of the nineteenth century, as these works mostly appeared in the special holiday editions of the Judeo-Spanish weeklies. One set of humorous Haggadahs expresses debates in the larger Balkan Sephardic communities. Papo concludes with a discussion of the impact of the establishment of the State of Israel on Sephardic self-understanding as revealed in the last known example of such Haggadahs, which no longer shows the irony that had characterized the genre.

At the waning of the nineteenth century, at the time when the Ottoman Sephardic society came into contact with western modernity, there was a simultaneous rediscovery of the Judeo-Spanish language and tradition on the part of Spanish philologists and European Romanists. In turn, the encounter led some Sephardic intellectuals to develop an interest in their own Judeo-Spanish culture and in Spanish philology. Paloma Díaz-Mas in her chapter, "The Hispanic legacy and Sephardic culture: Sephardim and Hispanists in the first half of the twentieth century" discusses the contribution that several Sephardic intellectuals made to the development of Spanish philology, through their investigation of their own language and oral culture, and their interaction with Spanish scholars in labors such as the compilation of old Spanish ballads.

2.3. Judeo-Spanish Language and Culture Today

Although Judeo-Spanish is no longer a language that is used as a main means of communication in any physical location, as there are no Judeo-Spanish speaking towns or neighborhoods anywhere, the language continues to play a role for its speakers. We began this introduction by stressing the contemporary phenomenon of Judeo-Spanish becoming the language for the creation of significant bodies of lyrical poetry. One chapter in the volume, Agnieszka August-Zarębska's "Contemporary Judeo-Spanish poetry in its rediscovery of the past" considers present-day Judeo-Spanish poetry, a topic that is still a rarity in the philologically and historically oriented Sephardic studies. The poets on whom she focuses created their work after 1980 and are second-generation descendants of the Turkish-Balkan diaspora. They live in cities such as Paris, Tel Aviv, or San Miguel de Tucumán (Argentina). The critical attention she devotes to these creations emphasizes the assertion that Judeo-Spanish continues to hold central symbolic space and to serve as emotional anchor for the people who identify with its heritage; her scholarship indeed demonstrates the aesthetic afterlife of Judeo-Spanish.

The last two chapters in the book address the important and current topic of Internet portals in and on Judeo-Spanish. The study of the presence of Judeo-Spanish on the Internet is a field that is still in its infancy and has only begun to receive the scholarly attention that it no doubt deserves. Today the Internet includes virtual communities where the Judeo-Spanish language lives and continues to evolve, giving vitality to the language. Studies on the make-up of the participants in these communities, and the philosophies, procedures, editorial policies, and content of the sites hosting them are thus essential for our understanding of Judeo-Spanish in the 21st century.

In "En tierras virtualas," Rey Romero provides a survey of current online communities, their language policies, their participants, and topics. He also discusses several ethical and methodological issues regarding research on online communities. Finally, he also presents his results regarding morphological (subjunctive) variation and dialect accommodation in these web sites.

In "Judeo-Spanish on the Web," Ana Stulic and Soufiane Rouissi present a different kind of perspective on the presence of Judeo-Spanish on the Internet, by including sites that do not address specifically heritage users. They discuss the stakes in the presentation of the language to neutral third parties, in revitalization efforts on the Internet, providing insights into the constituencies and at times extreme perspectives of the content for these sites. Their examination also has a technological perspective, concerning the codification and recognition of Judeo-Spanish in the digital media, and a sociolinguistic dimension, including the measurement or evaluation of textual, oral and audiovisual content in Judeo-Spanish, as well as the observation of Judeo-Spanish spaces on the Web.

We hope this volume bears witness to the vibrancy of the field of Judeo-Spanish studies from so many novel and multidisciplinary perspectives.

We want to thank Joyce Tolliver and Matthew Maddox, who read several of the chapters and offered us stylistic suggestions. For providing funds for the conference and for the production of this book, we are also grateful to a number of units at the University of Illinois at Urbana-Champaign, including the Illinois Program for Research in the Humanities, the Center for Advanced Study, the

Program in Jewish Culture and Society, the College of Letters, Arts and Sciences, the School of Literatures, Cultures and Linguistics, and several academic departments and area study centers. Finally, we also want to thank the Editor of Peter Lang's Studies in Judaism series, Dr Yudit Greenberg.

NOTES

1. Sephiha published these extracts once again after the poet's untimely death, with linguistic explanations and French translation (Sephiha 1999). Nicoïdski did not publish any other prose written in Judeo-Spanish. If she wrote more short stories, and from the quality of this single example one hopes she did, they await publication.
2. Nicoïdski's complete verse was later gathered in a slim volume under the title *La culor dil tiempu* (Nicoïdski 2014).
3. In this anthology Nicoïdski's poems are produced in her original spelling, not with facing normalized Castilian Spanish versions, as her work is frequently printed in Spanish editions.
4. Margalit Matitiahu and Avner Perez, along many others, are anthologized and commented upon in Refael 2008.
5. For a rare statement of policy adopted when facing the practical tasks of editing, see Shaul (1999).
6. We follow the edition by Díaz-Mas and Mota (Sem Tob de Carrión 1998) and Perry's (2014) English translation.
7. The earliest mention of this religious custom is found in a commentary on the liturgy composed in fourteenth century Spain (Rabbi David Abudraham's).
8. Benbassa and Rodrigue (1995) give a historical account of the commercial life of the sixteenth century Ottoman Jews.
9. "In Salonika all the Jews and the majority of the Muslims speak Spanish and in Venice and all over the East our rabbis do not preach in any language other than in the Spanish language and for this reason I understand it and also speak it." (Reproduced from Ioly Zorattini 1991 by Minervini 2006b: 153).
10. Almosnino's homiletic text *Regimiento de la Vida* and his treatise on dreams *Tratado de los sueños* were published together in Hebrew characters in Salonika in 1564 and had Latin character editions in Jewish presses in Amsterdam during the eighteenth century (Zemke 2004). His *La crónica de los reyes otomanos* circulated in manuscript form among Ottoman Jews of Iberian origin; a selection of chapters from it was published under the title *Extremos y grandezas de Constantinopla* in Madrid in 1638 at the expense of Jacob Cansino, a Jewish notable from Oran, who served as interpreter to the Spanish crown (Romeu Ferré 1998). Rabbi Almosnino wrote other books in Hebrew.

REFERENCES

Anderson, Benedict. *Imagined Communities: Reflections on the Origin and Spread of Nationalism*. London: Verso, 1983.
Ascher, Gloria. "Elias Canetti and his Sephardic heritage". *Shofar* 8.3 (1990), 16–29.

Balbuena, Monique R. "A Comparative Analysis of Clarisse Nicoïdski's and Juan Gelman's Bilingual Poetry." *Romance Studies* 27.4 (2009): 283–297.
Ben Naeh, Yaron. *Jews in the Realm of the Sultans: Ottoman Jewish Society in the Seventeenth Century.* Tübingen: Mohr Siebeck, 2008.
Benaim, Annette. *Sixteenth Century Judeo-Spanish Testimonies: An Edition of Eighty-four Testimonies from the Sephardic Response in the Ottoman Empire.* Leiden: Brill, 2012.
Benbassa, Esther and Aron Rodrigue. *The Jews of the Balkans: The Judeo-Spanish Community, 15th to 20th Centuries.* Oxford: Blackwell, 1995.
Díaz-Mas, Paloma and Pilar Romeu Ferré. "El léxico de la memoria: expresiones judeoespañolas en autobiografías sefardíes" In *Lexicologia y lexicografia judeoespañolas.* Edited by Winfried Busse and Michael Studemund-Halévy, 123–141. Bern: Peter Lang, 2011.
Esformes, Maria. "The Sephardic voice of Elias Canetti". *European Judaism* 33.1 (2000), 109–117.
Goldman, Israel M. *The Life and Times of Rabbi David Ibn Abi Zimra: A Social, Economic and Cultural Study of Jewish Life in the Ottoman Empire in the 15th and 16th Centuries as Reflected in the Responsa of RDBZ.* New York: The Jewish Theological Seminary of America, 1970.
Goodblatt, Morris S. *Jewish Life in Turkey in the 16th Century as Reflected in the Writings of Semuel de Medina.* New York: The Jewish Theological Seminary, 1952.
Hacker, Joseph. "The *Sürgün* System and Jewish Society in the Ottoman Empire during the Fifteenth and Sixteenth Centuries." In *Ottoman and Turkish Jewry: Community and Leadership.* Edited by A. Rodrigue, 1–65. Bloomington: Indiana University Turkish Series, 1992a.
Hacker, Joseph. "The Sephardim of the Ottoman Empire in the Sixteenth Century." In *Moreshet Sepharad: The Sephardi Legacy,*" vol. 2. Edited by Haim Beinart, 109–133. Jerusalem: The Magnes Press, 1992b.
Hualde, José Ignacio. "Intervocalic lenition and word-boundary effects: Evidence from Judeo-Spanish". *Diachronica* 30.2 (2013), 232–26.
Lehmann, Matthias. *Ladino Rabbinic Literature and Ottoman Sephardic Culture.* Bloomington: Indiana University Press, 2005.
Lleal, Coloma. *El judezmo: El dialecto sefardí y su historia.* Barcelona: Universitat de Barcelona, 1992.
Lloyd, Paul. *From Latin to Spanish.* Philadelphia: American Philosophical Society, 1987.
Lowry, Heath W. "When Did the Sephardim Arrive in Salonika? The Testimony of the Ottoman Tax-Registers, 1478–1613." In *The Jews of the Ottoman Empire.* Edited by A. Levy, 203–214. Princeton: The Darwin Press, 1994.
Milán, Eduardo; Andrés Sanchez Robayna; José Ángel Valente; Blanca Varela. *Las ínsulas extrañas: Antología de poesía en lengua española (1950–2000).* Barcelona: Galaxia Gutenberg, 2002.
Minervini, Laura. "The Formation of the Judeo-Spanish koiné: Dialect Convergence in the Sixteenth Century". In *Proceedings of the Tenth British Conference on Judeo-Spanish Studies.* Edited by Annete Benaim, 41–52. London: Queen Mary and Westfield College, 1999.
Minervini, Laura. "El desarollo histórico del judeoespañol," *Revista Internacional de Lingüística Iberoamericana* 4.2 (2006a): 13–34.
Minervini, Laura. "The Development of Judeo-Spanish in 16th Century Saloniki." *Judenspanisch X*, edited by Winfried Busse. *Neue Romania* 35 (2006b): 145–155.
Nicoïdski, Clarisse. *Lus Ojus Las Manus La Boca.* Loubressac-Bretenoux, Lot, France: Braad Editions, 1978.
Nicoïdski, Clarisse. *El color del tiempo/La culor dil tiempu: Poezia kompleta.* Edición bilingüe. Transated into Spanish by Ernesto Kavi. Madrid: Sexto Piso, 2014.

Penny, Ralph. "Dialect Contact and Social Networks in Judeo-Spanish." *Romance Philology* 46.2 (1992): 125–140.
Penny, Ralph. *Variation and Change in Spanish*. Cambridge: Cambridge University Press, 2000.
Perry, Theodore Anthony. *The Moral Proverbs of Santob de Carrion: Jewish wisdom in Christian Spain*. Princeton: Princeton University Press, 2014.
Piser, Celine. "The Journey Home: Language, Exile and Identity in Clarisse Nicoïdski's *Lus Ojus Las Manus La Boca*." In *Selected Papers from the Fifteenth British Conference on Judeo-Spanish Studies*. Edited by Hilary Pomeroy, Christopher J. Pountain and Elena Romero, 157–165. London: Department of Iberian and Latin American Studies, Queen Mary, University of London, 2012.
Quintana, Aldina. "Geografía lingüística del judeoespañol de acuerdo con el léxico." *Revista de Filología Española* 82 (2002): 105–138.
Quintana, Aldina. *Geografía lingüística del judeoespañol: Estudio sincrónico y diacrónico*. Bern: Peter Lang, 2006.
Quintana, Aldina. "Judeo-Spanish in Contact with Portuguese: A Historical Overview." In *Portuguese-Spanish Interfaces: Diachrony, Synchrony, and Contact*. Edited by Patrícia Amaral and Ana M. Carvalho 65–94. Amsterdam: John Benjamins, 2014a.
Quintana, Aldina. "*Séder Našim* (c. 1565) del rabino Meir Benveniste: Variación en la lengua de un miembro de la primera generación de hablantes nativos de Salónica." In *La lengua de los sefardíes. Tres contribuciones a su historia*. Edited by Winfried Busse 9–64. Tübingen: Stauffenburg Verlag, 2014b.
Quintana, Aldina and I.-S. Révah (posthumous). "A Sephardic Siddur with ritual instructions in Aragonese Romance, M.S. Oxford Bodleian Library 1133 (Opp. Add. 8º 18)." *Hispania Judaica Bulletin* 4 (2004): 141–151.
Ray, Jonathan. *After Expulsion: 1492 and the making of Sephardic Jewry*. New York: New York University Press, 2013.
Révah, Israel S. "Formation et évolution des parlers judéo-espagnols des Balkans." In *Actes du Xe Congrès International de Linguistique et Philologie romanes*. Edited by G. Straka, vol. 3, 1351–1371. Paris: Librairie C. Klincksieck, 1965.
Romeu Ferré, Pilar, ed. *Crónica de los Reyes Otomanos/Moisés Almosnino*. Barcelona: Tirocinio, 1998.
Romeu Ferré, Pilar, ed. *Daniel De Ávila Gallego, Diálogo del colorado. Interpretación académica de la escarlatina*. Barcelona: Tirocinio, 2014.
Refael, Shmuel. *Un grito en el silencio. La poesía sobre el Holocausto en la lengua sefardí: Estudio y Antología*. Barcelona: Tirocinio, 2008.
Rozen, Minna. *A History of the Jewish Community in Istanbul: The Formative Years, 1453–1566*. Leiden and Boston: Brill, 2010.
Sala, Marius. *Phonétique et phonologie du judéo-espagnol de Bucarest*. The Hague: Mouton, 1971.
Sánchez, Rosa and Marie-Christine Bornes Varol, eds. *La presses judéo-espagnole, support et vecteur de la modernité*. Istanbul: Libra, 2013.
Sem Tob de Carrión. *Proverbios morales*. Edited by Paloma Díaz-Mas and Carlos Mota. Madrid: Cátedra, 1998.
Sephiha, Haïm Vidal. "Clarisse Nicoïdski, la dernière poétesse judéo-espagnole." *Homenaje a Mathilde Pomes: estudios sobre la literatura del siglo XX* 108 (1977): 293–301.
Sephiha, Haïm Vidal. "Le Judéo-espagnol de Sarajevo: Clarisse Nidoïdski, née Abinun, conteuse et poétesse judéo-espagnol." In *Proceedings of the Tenth British Conference on Judeo-Spanish*

Studies, 29 June–1 July 1997. Edited by Annette Benaim, 53–64. London: Department of Hispanic Studies, Queen Mary and Westfield College, 1999.

Shaul, Moshe. "Kreasion leksikala en la Emision Djudeo-espanyola de Kol Israel." In *Proceedings of the Tenth British Conference on Judeo-Spanish Studies, 29 June–1 July 1997*. Edited by Annette Benaim, 65–71. London: Department of Hispanic Studies, Queen Mary and Westfield College, 1999.

Wacks, David A. "Reading Amadís in Istanbul" and "Translation in Diaspora: The Hebrew Amadís de Gaula." Blog Posts of October 29, 2011 and January 2, 2012. http://davidwacks.uoregon.edu

Zemke, John M., ed. *Moše ben Baruk Almosnino*. Regimiento de la vida: Tratado de los suenyos *(Salonika, 1564)*. Tempe, AZ: Medieval and Renaissance Texts and Studies, 2004.

PART ONE

The Origins

From the Fifteenth to the Nineteenth Century

CHAPTER TWO

An Overlooked 15th Century *demand d'amor* IN Hebrew *alxamía*

Parma Biblioteca Palatina 2666, folio 207 *verso*

JOHN ZEMKE
University of Missouri-Columbia

"Wie alle mittelalterlichen jüdischen Literaturen—arabisch, persisch, griechisch, deutsch etc.—*sind auch die romanischen Text der Juden meist in hebräischen Lettern greschrieben.*"
— Navè (225)

ABSTRACT

This chapter studies a 15th century Spanish debate poem copied in Hebrew letters found on folio 207 *verso* of Parma Biblioteca Palatina 2666 (see Hamilton 2010). The debate develops a disjunctive challenge regarding preferred modes of amatory relations. The poem merits attention as one of the few extant poetic expressions of contemporary Sephardic attitudes, in this case, an agonistic and ludic masculine viewpoint that deprives the female partner of agency in sexual relations. The essay also offers the Spanish text and English translation together with a glossary, notes on versification, and interpretation; appendices include a Hebrew transcription and a congener poem.

1. INTRODUCTION

Why is this short Spanish debate poem worthy of attention?[1] Its subject matter is, in one respect, disturbing, but there is nothing very serious in general or in particular about the poem, which is not to say that poetry is not a serious matter. Copied in Hebrew characters in Parma Palatina 2666 on the *verso* of folio 207,[2] this unique composition articulates a dialogue, a fictitious debate over a love dilemma, a test question for which there is no right answer (See appendix A for a Hebrew transliteration of folio 207 *verso*). The voices of its male protagonists take evident delight in their contemplation of platonic and corporal venereal pleasures while the reified feminine persona who is the object of their speculative desires remains ever mute. Couched in the idiom of courtly love, the contentious question fundamentally serves as the pretext for a concluding boast. Abandoning the ambiguity and euphemism that is characteristic of the first two strophes, the boast narrates an unambiguous sexual aggression, the rape of the beloved. It is, to be sure, a fictional perpetration of masculine violence on the feminine body, the wish fulfillment of an erotic fantasy, but is it inconsequential? Its seeming trivialness again prompts the question: Why is this poem worthy of attention? I set the question aside now to return to it later.

A congener of this debate is recorded in poems number 369 through 377 of the *Cancionero de Baena* (see appendix B).[3] These verses report a dispute between Juan Alfonso and Ferrant Manuel de Lando about the same dilemmatic question couched in a slightly different formulation: which amatory mode do you prefer, visual or verbal? The *alxamía* verses are sufficiently proximate in theme, rhetorical style, form, and probable copy-date to invite legitimate comparison with the *Cancionero* debate and to be reminded that the role of Jews and *conversos* in the social milieu depicted by the *Cancionero* poems is itself a question among literary critics, historians, and others.[4] The central issue our poem raises lies at a remove from what Yirmiyahu Yovel has enumerated in "Residual Words as Mental Signifiers," the *topoi* of *converso* identity (14).[5] It makes no mention of the metaphysical, political or sociological questions—crucifixion, *kashrut*, pork, invective, Judaizing, circumcision, castration, guilt (though the latter may by implication be in play), heresy, *meshumad*, Will or Intellect—that loom large in the study of *Cancionero* society *conversos*. I mention the point not to construct a straw man to be struck down, but rather, to insist that the poem's location along the continuum of poetic discourse falls within the ludic register.

Similarly, nothing in its literary form or content would make the poem unmistakably Jewish in character, in the way that a *qettubah* or a Torah scroll inescapably is. Being a verbal creation, it is a prime product of the human imagination. Only an incidental empirical detail links it to a Jewish milieu: an individual amanuensis preferred to copy the poem in Hebrew characters. It is this secondary aspect of the poem, the Hebrew letters inked on the manuscript, the physical artifact, and *not* its primary verbal form, that circumscribes a readership, and situates the poem in a manuscript recording philosophical texts that also do not entertain exclusively "Jewish" questions. To review, my claim is the following: (1) The Hebrew alphabet of this copy excludes readers unlettered in *alefbet* and correlates the poem with an intended readership; and (2) it is the quality of being a verbal product of the imagination that licenses the poem in an imagined Sepharad. To the extent that this slight entertainment sheds a ray of light onto recesses of one social circle's literary appetites, it hints at one reason why the poem should merit attention.

2. THE MANUSCRIPT

Benjamin Richler describes Parma Biblioteca Palatina 2666 thus: "a collection of philosophical works in Spanish in Hebrew characters" (*Catalogue* 307), but our poem is not a philosophical one. Copied in the second half of the fifteenth century, most probably in 1468, its contents include the following titles: *Visión deleytable* by Alfonso de la Torre (1r–96v), *Proverbios* culled from Seneca (121r–137); *Arte alla memoria*, a treatise on memory (139r–140v); a vocabulary or glossary of philosophical terms, Spanish–Hebrew (143r–v), Hebrew–Spanish (144r–145), Hebrew–Spanish list of terms from Moses ben Maimon's *Millot ha-Higgayon* (196r–197r); a Spanish poem that interprets the *akedah* (198r);[6] the *Danza general de la muerte* (199r–206v), and the present Spanish *demand d'amour* (207v). Several different Sephardic semi-cursive scripts are used. A first owner is identified as Solomon ibn Crispin (fol. 1r). A table of contents mentions no longer extant titles including: *Regimientos* (fol. 146), *Casos del Rey* (fol. 151), *Práctica de Gelí* (fol. 157), and *Tesoro de pobres*. Nelson Novoa considers Parma Palatina 2666 to be "a precious sample of the kind of texts Sephardi Jews read and wrote in the fifteenth century in the language they shared with their Christian peers" ("MS. Parma Pal. 2666 as a document of Sephardi Literary and Philosophical Expression," 21).[7]

As far as I have been able to determine, the number of extant medieval Spanish and Catalan texts in Hebrew *alxamía* that treat Jewish subjects is slight: glossaries, prayerbooks, *Haggadot*, paraliturgical poems, wedding songs, and polemic writings. Other items pertaining to subjects of general interest include treatises on illumination, mathematics, medicine, logic, ethics, legal documents, and notebooks. It is a small universe of texts. Preserving as it does even this exiguous number of compositions, Parma Palatina 2666 represents for students of medieval Spanish in Hebrew *alxamía* the equivalent of the *Oxyrhyncus* papyri.

3. TRANSCRIPTION AND ENGLISH TRANSLATION

A. Demanda | Question

1. Vos ke tanto sabés | You, so learned
2. y tanto valés | and meritorious
3. en la arte del amar, | in the art of love,
4. akordé de preguntar | I resolved to ask
5. por me abisar. | for my instruction.
6. ala ke más keréis | Regarding your beloved
7. ¿kual desto eskogerés?: | which will you choose?:
8. a vuestra guisa tratalya | To have your way with her
9. y non fablalya | and not speak to her
10. nin sola mente miralya | nor even gaze at her
11. o bien beer y fablar | or, rather, see and speak
12. y nunka aelya lyegar. | and never draw near her.

B. Respuesta | Response

1. El saber vos le tenés | Knowledge you possess,
2. y entendéis | and understanding,
3. keréisme preguntar | you want to ask me
4. por probar | to test
5. el mi sentido, ¿kuál es? | my opinion, which it is?
6. si yero enmendaréis. | If I err, you will emend.
7. ke digo ke kiero sin falya | I say that I want without fail
8. desealya | to desire her
9. y fablalya | and speak with her
10. y non tokalya | and not touch her
11. y kiero la ber y mirar | and I want to see and regard her
12. y nunka aelya lyegar. | and never draw near her.

C. Otra | Another

1. Tan perfundo traçendéis | So profoundly do you transcend
2. ke me traés | that you bring me
3. en punto de filas tomar | to the brink of animosity
4. y por otra parte katar | and on the other hand to regard
5. y konsolar. | and console.
6. de akí non me traerés | That is why you will not dissuade me
7. nin me kansarés | nor weary me

8. de korelya   from pursuing her
9. y alkançalya   and catch her
10. y luego presto enklabalya   and then quickly nail her
11. y sobre elya reçemlar   and upon her sow and sow seed
12. fasta la bida apokar.[8]   until life is lessened (ejaculation achieved).

4. VOCABULARY

Several words deserve brief elucidation: *apokar,* seems to be a double *entendre,* "to diminish" as well as *"mollis"* (*Floresta de poesía erótica del Siglo de Oro* = PESO, 13); *bida,* "algo que causa mucho placer" (*Diccionario de uso del Español* = *María Moliner,* no. 9), here the meaning is "semen"; *enklabar,* "clavo. clavus – pro pene"* (*Glossarium eroticum linguae latinae*, 124), and "1. Es metáfora formal (el pene semeja un clavo)" (*Enciclopedia del erotismo,* 2: 19), cf. "que la novia saltó y enclavóse el clavo" (*PESO*, 97, n. 27); *filas tomar,* "sorprender a alguien en culpa o delito" (*María Moliner,* no. 21) or "cubrir el macho a la hembra" (*ibid*, no. 26); *katar,* "Es eufemismo de intención festiva por sexualización de sentido. Desvirgar" (*Enciclopedia del erotismo*, 1: 792); *konsolar,* "Es eufemismo de intención irónica. Copular" (*ibid.,* 2: 193); *korer,* "1. Copular […] 2. Experimentar el orgasmo" (*ibid.,* 2: 254); *punto,* "Es antonomasia en ambas acepciones. 1. pene […] 2. vulva" (*ibid.,* 4: 239), and "el *punto* es efectivamente término de astrología para indicar la posición de un astro, aunque aquí se trata de otra conjunción" (PESO, 97, n. 27); the otherwise unattested *reçemlar* is probably a focalizing form of *sembrar*, "Es eufemismo. Copular el varón, eyacular el semen" (*Enciclopedia del erotismo,* 4: 406) or "sembrar nuevamente un terreno o parte de él por haberse malogrado la primera siembra" (*María Moliner*); *traçender,* "dicho de algo que estaba oculto: empezar a ser conocido o sabido" (*Diccionario de la Real Academia Española,* no. 5); *tokar,* "Es antomasia. 1. Magrear, sobar" (*Enciclopedia del erotismo*, 4: 593).

5. VERSE

Overlapping structures of meter, rhyme, and rhetoric organize the content and discourse. A duple-triple-duple-triple-duple rhyme pattern organizes the twelve-verses of strophes A and C; a slight exception to the pattern occurs in the duple-duple-duple-quadruple-duple sequence of strophe B:

A aa bbb aa ccc bb
B aa bb aa cccc bb
C aa bbb aa ccc bb

This nearly conforms to the expectation of strict repetition of the rhyme established by the *demanda*[9] to answer in the *respuesta "por los consonantes."*

Scansion suggests a nucleus of octosyllabic and tetrasyllabic verses, several are hypometric (A1, A6, C7), and others are hypermetric (A5, A9, B7, B10, C3, C4, C5). The poetic licenses of diaeresis (B8) or synalepha (B12, C3, C6, C9, C10, C11, C12) may be invoked.

```
A   748857885 8 8 8
B   848848894 5 8 8
C   849958644 8 8 8
```

6. DRAMATIS PERSONAE AND PERIPETEIA

The initial strophe introduces three *dramatis personae* that advance the poem's *peripeteia*. The protagonists Vos_1 and Vos_2 have speaking roles while the dative of interest *la ke más keréis* is denied any voice in the matter under discussion. These verses initiate the dialogue and state its theme, an amorous dilemma. The disjunctive question is derived from the courtly love code governing the lovers' relations in ascending steps of intimacy: *visus, colloquium, contactus,* and *factum*. The question pairs the senses of sight and speech, *visus* and *colloquium*, together in one set or *lemma*, with *contactus* and *factus* forming a second *lemma*. The tandem *lemmata* stand as mutually exclusive terms in the central optative proposition, the apparent main business of the poem.

Vos_1, citing as *causa scribendi* a previous decision to seek instruction from Vos_2, initiates the exordium by enunciating a *captatio benevolentiae laude* that exalts his interlocutor's erudition and esteem in the *ars amandi*. The mute *la ke más keréis*, upon whom the entire question turns, is alluded to when the petitioner challenges the addressee to choose between the *lemmata*, declare his preference for one mode of amatory relations and thus refrain, by implication, from engaging in the excluded pair. The respondent's forthcoming instruction will satisfy his interrogator's quest for knowledge. Thus far is the action advanced by strophe A: statement of a disjunctive optative proposition that presses hard on the respondent's acumen and expertise.

Recognizing his petitioner's conundrum for the thinly veiled test that it is, Vos_2 begins his exordium with a reciprocating *captatio benevolentiae humilioris* that invokes his counterpart's superior understanding and knowledge in the matter at hand and, with a neat play-on-words, reiterates that it is his sense and his opinion that the petitioner is seeking. Faced with a fraught decision, Vos_2 formulates a gambit against the potential humiliation of choosing unwisely, voicing the assurance that, should he err, his erudite interlocutor's correction will swiftly be forthcoming. Hesitation dispatched, Vos_2 emphatically claims his preference for the visual and verbal modalities of courtship over their tactile complements.

Strophe B, then, advances the action to a second stage: the respondent makes his choice of one of the *lemmata* presented in the initial provocation.

With the conclusion of strophe C it becomes abundantly clear that the ostensible genteel courtly nature of the question is nothing but a ruse, a hoax and a sham, the mere pretext for a grand and virile rooster-crowing boast, an occasion for euphemism and titillation, talking dirty, if you will. This exordium expresses praise as well as an affective reaction, a double incitement to aggression on the one hand but consolation on the other. The poetic voice simultaneously and emphatically contends his rival's impotence to ever dissuade him from pursuing tactile relations with the beloved. A reader may puzzle over which poetic voice enunciates these verses, the rubric "*otra*" (< Lat. ALITER 'other') signals an alternative not an identification. Yet the dictates of the *partimen* require the challenger to argue the position his adversary declined to defend.[10] Thus by generic stipulation it is the debate's provocateur who acknowledges that his opponent's transcendent response has incited him to the point of physical aggression while paradoxically eliciting the desire to console. His response appears to cheat the rules of the game by formulating a decided preference for having it both ways, regard and console, and also physically possess her (glossing *katar* as "to regard," in accord with the terms of the question, but see vocabulary *supra*). Depiction of coitus with the beloved brings the poetic action of Strophe C to its climax.[11]

Jewish poets in al-Andalus adapted Arabic poetic models to compose Hebrew language poems, so too, Jewish poets in Sepharad versified in Romance poetic forms. Paloma Díaz-Mas has identified the remnants of a rabbinic *mester de clerecía* genre in the *Coplas de Yosef,* the *Proverbios morales*, and other poems ("Un género casi perdido," 342). Our poem is an example of the Castilian *pregunta y respuesta* genre, amply represented in the *Cancionero de Baena* collection. It ultimately derives from the Provenzal *partimen*, a disjunctive question intended to elicit a response. In an exhaustive study of the *pregunta y respuesta* genre, Antonio Chas Aguión reports that it most often takes for its subject matter themes that are religious, didactic or doctrinal in nature, rather than sentimental. He observes that the challenger frequently justifies initiating the debate by citing a "need to know," that is to say, to be instructed by his opponent; in the present case the rationale is tinged with mockery. Ian MacPherson underscores that the *Cancionero* genre's rhetorical arsenal relies heavily on ambiguity, euphemism, and innuendo ("Courtly Codes," 54), and alludes to the "consciously and rigorously restricted" vocabulary that idealizes a "faceless and passive" (53) beloved from a "male-oriented" (55) perspective. Julian Weiss remarks on the "comic potential" of the genre for "amusing parodies of the scholastic method" (*The Poet's Art*, 23).

The public performance aspects of the debates staged at court— evident in the *Cancionero de Baena*—constitute an important dynamic for analysis of the poems' social implications. Yet, as John Cummins notes, the debate form eventually fell out of fashion and was withdrawn from the public arena to be installed in private spaces, becoming an "amusement for the participants themselves" ("Methods and Conventions," 309). The relatively lengthy contest concerning the pros and cons of the amatory senses between Juan Alfonso and Ferrant Manuel de Lando focuses attention on reciprocal, escalating efforts to defame the foe. Their poetic duel is heard in *public*, and concludes with the verdict given by Maestro Fray Diego de Valencia that the superior amatory sense is *visus*.[12] Its sexual tension is seemingly sited within the borders of *politesse* by euphemisms (*conquistar*, v*encer*, *cobrar*) that would disguise or ameliorate the same sexual violence that was always the final destination of our *alxamía* poem, a brief *private* colloquy that focalizes *factum* and is articulated in the absence of a judge.

It is well known that the *amor cortés* paradigm gives agency to the female partner, she is empowered to grant favors to her devotee.[13] The unchecked masculine ego that narrates this present act of sexual aggression subjugates his partner by rape, and reverses the polarities of power prescribed by courtly love precepts. Though our *alxamía* poem and its *Cancionero* counterpart share a common theme inherited from troubadour poetry, and though both are freighted with innuendo, less subtle differences in tenor, tone,[14] and setting separate them: one treats its question in a public performance with a certain measure of decorum (though the rival poets are less than polite to one another), while the other offers two voices (simulated by one poet?) in a private performance that culminates with a portrayal of rape that has from the outset been its principal destination.[15]

7. MEMORIAL BOOK

I began with a question: why is this debate poem worthy of our attention? I now essay an answer: In addition to whatever inherent artistic merit it possesses, it matters because there are no "Memorial Books" for Sepharad. Susan Slyomovics characterizes the genre as embodying attempts to memorialize a place that no longer exists, and to document its destruction by gathering testimonies from "oral literature, folk history, vernacular architecture, community photography, and sociocultural anthropology" (*The Object of Memory*, xiii). As a genre, the memorial book arose in the wake of the onslaught and cultural devastation wrought by modern political states and non-sovereign actors fulfilling their desire to eliminate real or imaginary rivals by wielding violence that traumatizes, displaces, and dispossess them, depressingly familiar human catastrophes. Memorial books have been compiled by Jews who survived the Holocaust, Armenian survivors of the 1915–17 massacres, Greeks and Turks displaced by population exchanges between 1914 and 1923, Germans exiled from post–World War II Eastern Europe, Palestinians after the establishment of the State of Israel in 1948, and Bosnians of any religion between 1992 and 1995. Historical Sepharad witnessed Christians in the medieval kingdoms of Leon, Castile, Aragon, and Navarra who treated, mistreated, and abused the Jews in their midst in accord with their own contingent self-interests; self-interest, it must be noted, played no lesser role in intra-communal Jewish community affairs.[16] Christians did not abjure participation in serial pogroms, and murder or forced conversion of Jewish neighbors were preludes to the definitive exile of the Jewish remnant. To my knowledge there is no Sephardic "memorial book" that would reconstruct the interior experiential history of any one of those destroyed communities. What is available is no more than the remaining fragments of the imagination of individuals once resident in, and members of, those communities, as is the case of this debate poem.[17] In this regard we do well to heed Roger Boase's observation that sociological factors shape an audience's expectations and these, in turn, constrain the poet's choices (*The Origin and Meaning*, 123). Here, then, is a unique expression of poetic imagination in Sepharad. Though disquieting, it is a product of the human imagination. If there are no physical consequences on a female body, the psychological trauma it implies is no less real. This depiction of sexual violence divulges attributes of the poetic imagination, as well as moral and ethical tendencies embedded in an identity forged by, and in tension with, the community. Identity, Tamar Alexander-Frizer reminds us, is formed in "the contradictory process of integration with other groups and segregation from them [that] set the ethnic boundaries of a group" (*The Heart is a Mirror*, 584). Wondering about the legitimacy of memorial books, whether they "create fictions, not actual villages but imaginary homelands," Susan Slyomovics broaches the question of the here-and-now when the then-and-there is accessible only by means of fragments: "Fragmentary memory turns trivial things into powerful symbols because, like archaeological artifacts, they are what remain" (23). So, too, this little poem.

APPENDIX A: TRANSCRIPTION OF HEBREW CHARACTERS

דימאנדה	רישפוישטה	אוטרה
ווש קי טאנטו שאביש	איל שאביר ווש לו טיניש	טאן פירפֿונדו טראסינדייש
אי ואליש	אי אינטינדייש /	קי מי טראיש
אין לה ארטי דיל אמאר	קיריישמי פריגונטאר	אין פונטו די פֿילאש טומשר
אקורדי די פריגונטאר	פור פרובאר איל מי שינטיד	אי פור אוטרה פארטי קאטאר
פור מי אבישאר /	קואל איש	אי קונשולאר
אלה קי מאש קיריייש	שי ירו אינמדשרייש	די אקי נון מי טראיריש
קואל דישטו אישקוגיריש	קי דיגו קי קיירו שין פֿאליא	נין מי קאנשאריש
אוואישטרה גישה טראטליא	דישיאליא	די קורילא
אי נון פֿאבלאליא	אי פֿאבלאליא	אי אלקאנסאליא
נין שולה מינטי מיראליא	אי נון טוקאליא	אי לואיגו פרישטו אינקלאבאליא
או ביין ביאיר אי פֿאבלאר	אי קיירו לה ב׳יר אי מיראר	אי שוברי איליא ריסימלאר
אי נונקה אאיליא לייגאר //	אי נונקה אאיליא ליגאר //	פֿאשטה לה ב׳ידה אפוקאר

APPENDIX B: *CANCIONERO DE BAENA* 369–372

369
Reqüesta de Juan Alfonso contra Ferrant Manuel
1. Al muy ilustrado, sotil, dominante,
   que saca las cosas fondo del abismo,
   al rímico pronto muy más que *Graçismo,*
   en todas las artes maestro bastante,
   al muy evidente, de noble semblante,
   purífico, casto, muy alto poeta,
   al lindo fidalgo, persona discreta,
   le fago pregunta por ser disputante.
   Finida
2. Dizidme, señor, gentil, emperante:
   ver mi amiga e nunca fablalla,
   o siempre fablalla e nunca miralla,
   de qué l'faga d'esto me dat consonante.

370
Respuesta de Ferrán Manuel contra Juan Alfonso
1. […]
Finida
2. E así respondo: non embargante
   que nunca querades, amigo, salvalla,
   veyéndola siempre podrá conquistalla
   el vuestro graçioso e lindo talante.

371
Replicaçión de Juan Alfonso contra Ferrán Manuel
1. […]
Finida
2. E assí concluyendo, gentil cavalgante,
   sostengo contrario de quaesta batalla:
   que nunca se vençe por mucho otealla
   ninguna fermosa sin ser demandante.

372
Respuesta de Ferrant Manuel contra Juan Alfonso
1. […]
Finida
2. Que vista de amor es causa mediante
   para qualquiera fermosa cobralla,

e todo lo ál es arte contralla,
segunt los actores Vergillo e *D'Amante*.

NOTES

1. For an introduction to the Debate genre, its history, forms, protean character, proclivity for multicultural environments, and consideration of whether its development (first testimonies on 2nd millennium BCE Sumerian cuneiform tablets) represents the linear evolution of a single genre or is the result of polygenesis, see G. J. Reinink and H. L. J. Vanstiphout, "Introduction" (Dispute Poems and Dialogues, 1–6).
2. See Hamilton 2010 for a photocopy of the text and another transcription and study. Michelle Hamilton concludes from codicological evidence that fol. 207v was originally bound between folios 198 and 199; see her article "Debating Love," 133, n. 15.
3. Reproduced from the edition by Brian Dutton and Joaquín González Cuenca, 644–51.
4. Consideration of that critical shibboleth lies outside the scope of this essay; I can only remark that the meticulous historiography practiced by scholars such as David Nirenberg (2002 and 2006) has illuminated questions of language, sociology, philosophy, and theology with which literary criticism has struggled.
5. Useful guidance regarding the question of *converso* identity may be had from Bruce Clark in his study of the exchange of Christian and Muslim populations between Greece and Turkey that was undertaken in the 1920s: "Between those two extremes—Anatolian Christians who felt entirely Greek and those who hardly felt Greek at all—there were an infinite number of points on a spectrum. That is how things really are in human affairs" (*Twice a Stranger*, 17). Note the emphasis on the dissimilarity of individual experiences that Susan Slyomovics reports in the words of a survivor of the Armenian genocide who compiled a memory book: "Thousands of women and men came to me. They spoke; they wrote down their stories, and no one's ordeal resembled that of another" (*The Object of Memory*, 5).
6. For an edition and study of this poem see Zemke 2008.
7. Michelle Hamilton is preparing a monograph study of the manuscript (private correspondence July 2014).
8. This transcription reflects the scribe's use of single *yod* for -és in *sabés*, *valés*, *eskogés*, *tenés*, *traés*, and *kansarés* and geminate *yod* for -éis in *keréis*, *traçendéis*, and *emendaréis*. For discussion of the historical evolution of second person verb forms see Dworkin (1998) and Rini (1996), who notes that poems collected in the *Cancionero general* (1511) document variants in the language of one and the same poet that vacillated between forms in –és and –éis (9) and argues the case that between 1450 and 1530 the forms *tú quieres, vos querés*, and *vos queréis* were allomorphs in the singular while *vos queréis* was the sole form of the plural (11).
9. The rubric *demanda* suggests the *demande d'Amour* that Jack Oruch characterizes as "a debate for deciding which lover, or kind of love, a person should prefer" which is "presented before a court […] presided over by Venus, Love, or Jove" (Nature's Limitations and the *Demande d'Amour*," 23). The question is consistent with that description, however the setting and the absence of a judge are not.
10. Certain features of the poem resist assignment to a specific genre. Martín de Riquer clarifies that debates in which the troubadors alternate in the composition of a single poem are known in five

forms, *la tensó, el partimen* (or *joc partit*), *el tornejamen, las coblas* and *la cobla tensonada*. The *tensó* may even be a simulated debate composed by one poet alone. In its extension this *alxamía* poem most resembles *la cobla* "un debate breve, en una o dos estrofas" (*Los trovadores*, I: 69). Its family resemblance to the *partimen* ("Juego al parecer eminentemente cortesano, el partimen se caracteriza por versar sobre puntos de casuística amorosa o cortés" [I: 68]) is marred by the absence of an appeal for judgment: "En los partimens, donde, como es natural, los dos contendientes no se ponen de acuerdo y cada uno se cree haber sido más convincente que el otro, los trovadores, al acabar la discusión, generalmente en las tornadas, designan jueces para que dictaminen quién ha sido el vencedor, imitando en esto, como en otras cosas, los usos de las justas caballerescas. Se trata de un mero juego cortesano y sin duda ocasional, bien reflejado en el *De amore* de Andrea CaplIanus," (I: 70). See further Cummins *passim*.
11. Keith Whinnom cautions against discounting the physical aspect of courtly love "Según la afortunada loución provenzal, el amante cortesano quiere poseerle a la dama "cor e cors", o sea, el corazón y el cuerpo." (*La poesía amatoria*, 27). My colleague Michael Solomon confirms that "*fasta la vida apokar*" is almost certainly a euphemistic phrase for ejaculation: "The idea that one can shorten his days or even bring on death by excessive copulation was common in medical writings on coitus from Ibn Jazzar to *Liber minor de coitu* to *El speculum al foderi* and many other texts written in the Galenic tradition" (personal correspondence July 25, 2014). Roger Boase places the Courtly Love preference for paradoxical expression directly in line with the Graeco-Arabic medical tradition: "European and Arabic court poets were justified in their use of figures of contradiction such as oxymora, hyperboles and dilemmas, by preconceptions about the nature of love itself" (*The Origins and Meaning*, 124).
12. The debates frequently appeal to a judge "to determine the winner—an interesting fact that seems to relate the poem to the *jeux-partis*, in which appeal to a judge is habitual" (John Cummins, "Methods and Conventions," 343). Notice, however, this *alxamía* version makes no appeal for judgment and so does not conform strictly to the *jeux-partis* form. Cummins characterizes Baena's debate with Manuel Ferrant as "short and trivial" (320).
13. Roger Boase notes that the fiction of Courtly Love "had a negligible effect on the status of women, which was never anything other than secondary. The woman raised on a pedestal by an admiring poet was scarcely more emancipated than the wife who was her husband's chattel, and she often fulfilled both roles simultaneously" (*The Origin and Meaning*, 128).
14. Discussing poems in the *Cancionero de Baena* that appear under the rubric *reqüesta* Antonio Chas Aguión writes "tan sólo dos piezas rubricadas como "reqüestas" formulan en sus versos una cuestión y en ambas predomina un tono mordaz" (*Juan Alfonso de Baena*, 99–100).
15. For further discussion of rape in medieval Iberian society see chapter seven of David Nirenberg's *Communities of Violence*.
16. The household accounts of the Kingdom of Navarra between 1093 and 1386 make patently clear the extent to which quotidian violence characterized inter- and intra-communal relations. For examples of the kinds of violence perpetrated, see Zemke 2014.
17. Tamar Alexander-Frizer warns against reading fictions as if they were sociological studies: "it is impossible to learn directly from the stories about the society that tells them. Relations between the story and reality are a multitiered, complex system that comprises reflections of reality, contradictions between the ideal and the actual, and expression of forbidden wishes. More than reflecting reality, the stories reflect the narrator's conception of reality and sometimes even create their *own* reality" (*The Heart is a Mirror*, 585).

REFERENCES

Alexander-Frizer, Tamar. Th*e Heart is a Mirror: The Sephardic Folktale.* Detroit, MI: Wayne State University Press, 2008.
Alonso, Álvaro, ed. *Carajicomedia*. Málaga: Ediciones Aljibe, 1995.
Alonso Hernández, José Luis. *Léxico del marginalismo del Siglo de Oro.* Salamanca: Universidad de Salamanca, 1976.
Alzieu, Pierre, Robert James and Yvan Lissorgues, eds. *Floresta de poesías eróticas del Siglo de Oro*. Toulouse: France-Ibérie Recherche, 1975.
Cantera Burgos, Francisco. "El Cancionero de Baena: judíos y conversos en él." Sefarad 27 (1967): 71–111.
Cela, Camilo José. *Enciclopedia del erotismo*, 4 vols. *Obras completa*, 14–17. Barcelona: Ediciones Destino, 1962.
Chas Aguión, Antonio. *Juan Alfonso de Baena y los diálogos poéticos de su cancionero*. Baena: Ayuntamiento de Baena, 2001.
Clark, Bruce. *Twice a Stranger: The Mass Expulsions that Forged Modern Greece and Turke*y. Cambridge, MA: Harvard University Press, 2006.
Cummins, John G. "Methods and Conventions in the 15th-Century Poetic Debate." *Hispanic Review* 31 (1963): 307–23.
Díaz-Mas, Paloma. "Un género casi perdido de la poesía castellana medieval: La clerecía rabínica." *Boletín de la Real Academia Española* 73 (1993): 329–46.
Dutton, Brian and Joaquín González Cuenca, eds. *Cancionero de Juan Alfonso de Baena*. Madrid: Visor Libros, 1993.
Dworkin, Steven N. "The Interaction of Phonological and Morphological Processes: The Evolution of the Old Spanish Second Person Plural Verb Endings." *Romance Philology* 42 (1988): 144–55.
Hamilton, Michelle. "Debating Love: A Fifteenth-Century Aljamiado Joc-Partit." *eHumanista* 14 (2010): 127–45.
Jeanroy, Alfred. *La poésie lyrique des troubadors*. 2 vols. Toulouse: Édouard Privat; Paris: Henri Didier, 1934.
Jensen, Frede. *Troubadour Lyrics: A Bilingual Anthology*. New York: Peter Lang, 1998.
Labrador Herraiz, José J. *Poesía dialogada medieval* (La 'pregunta' en el *Cancionero de Baena*). Madrid: Ediciones Maisal, 1974.
Le Gentil, Pierre. *La poésie lyrique espagnole et portugaise a la fin du moyen âge*. 2 vols. Genève: Slatkine, 1981.
MacPherson, Ian. "Secret Language in the Cancioneros: Some Courtly Codes." *Bulletin of Hispanic Studies* 62 (1985): 51–63.
Moliner, María. *Diccionario de uso del Español*, 2 vols. Madrid: Editorial Gredos, 1986.
Navè, Pnina. "Die romanisch-jüdischen Literaturbeziehungen im Mittelalter." *Grundiss der Romanischen Literaturen des Mittelalters,* I: 216–236. Heidelberg: Carl Winter, 1972.
Nelson Novoa, James W. "MS. Parma Pal. 2666 as a Document of Sephardi Literary and Philosophical Expression in Fifteenth-Century Spain." *European Judaism* 43 (2010): 20–36.
Nirenberg, David. "Conversion, Sex, and Segregation: Jews and Christians in Medieval Spain." *The American Historical Review* 107 (2002): 1065–93.
———. "Figures of Thought and Figures of Flesh: `Jews' and `Judaism' in Late-Medieval Spanish Poetry and Politics." S*peculum* 81 (2006): 398–426.

Oruch, Jack B. "Nature's Limitations and the Demande d'Amour of Chaucer's Parlement." *The Chaucer Review* 18 (1983): 23–37.

Pierrugues. *Glossarium eroticum linguae latinae.* Amsterdam: Adolf M. Hakkert, 1965 [Paris, 1826].

Reinink, G. J., and H. L. J. VanStiphout, eds. *Dispute Poems and Dialogues in the Ancient and Medieal Near East: Forms and Types of Literary Debates in Semitic and Related Literatures.* Leuven: Departement Oriëntalistiek; Uitgeverij Peeters, 1991.

Richler, Benjamin. *Hebrew Manuscripts in the Biblioteca Palatina in Parma: Catalogue.* Jerusalem: Hebrew University of Jerusalem, Jewish National and University Library, 2001.

Rini, Joel. "The Vocalic Formation of the Spanish Verbal Suffiex *–áis/-ás, -éis/-és, ís, -ois/-os*: A Case of Phonological or Morphological Change?" *Iberoramania* 44 (1996):

de Riquer Martín. *Los trovadores: Historia literaria y textos.* 2 vols. Barcelona: Planeta, 1975.

Slyomovics, Susan. *The Object of Memory: Arab and Jew Narrate the Palestinian Village.* Philadelphia: University of Pennsylvania Press, 1998.

Weiss, Julian. *The Poet's Art: Literary Theory in Castile c. 1400–60.* Medium Aevum Monographs, N.S. 14. Oxford: The Society for the Study of Mediaeval Languages and Literatures, 1990.

Whinnom, Keith. *La poesía amatoria de la época de los Reyes Católicos.* Durham: University of Durham, 1981.

Yovel, Yirmiyahu. "Converso Dualities in the First Generation: The *Cancioneros.*" *Jewish Social Studies* N.S. 4 (1996): 1–28.

Zemke, John. "In Memoriam Samuel Cook, Mentor of Samuel G. Armistead (Edition and study of Parma Biblioteca Palatina 2666)." In *Spain's Multicultural Legacies. Studies in Honor of Samuel G. Armistead*, 333–47. Eds. Adrienne L. Martin and Cristina Martínez-Carrazo. Newark, DEL: Juan de la Cuesta, 2008.

———. "'Et deue tener la paia enla mano & deue dezir yo jvro por aquel que fizo esta paia verde & sequa': Is convivencia operative in the medieval fueros?" In *Revisiting* Convivencia, 107–40. Ed. Connie Scarborough. Newark, DEL: Juan de la Cuesta, 2014.

CHAPTER THREE

How Old Is Ladino Literature?

OLGA BOROVAYA
Stanford University

ABSTRACT

Most scholars believe that Ladino (Judeo-Spanish) literature emerged in the eighteenth century, although it is well known that Ottoman Sephardim began to publish vernacular works in the early sixteenth century. As so far this assumption has not been questioned, the purpose of these notes is to problematize the criteria used for delineating the boundaries of Ladino literature and to demonstrate that the evidence alleged to prove a rupture in fact testifies to connections and continuity between sixteenth- and eighteenth-century authors.

1. LANGUAGE OR REGISTER?

Almost all histories and overviews of Ladino literature start in the eighteenth century, primarily because many scholars consider the fact that the Sephardi vernacular had reached its final shape only by that time sufficient reason not to regard earlier texts created by the same speech community in the same territory and in a language its members consider the same as part of this literature. This view has a detrimental effect on scholarship because, as a result, sixteenth-century Ladino literature has never been treated or even conceptualized as such, and some of its texts are seen as an extension of Spanish (Castilian) literature, while others have not even been studied by literary scholars. In the absence of vernacular works from the seventeenth century, it is generally assumed that, aside from a number of random texts in various Ibero-Romance varieties written in the sixteenth century, Sephardim did not produce a vernacular literature of their own during the first two hundred years of their residence in the Ottoman Empire.

Scholars of other literatures, as we know, do not use language standardization (whether formal or *de facto*) as a criterion of inclusion, which is why the study of Spanish literature, for example, begins with *El Cantar del Mío Cid*, written circa 1200 in an early Ibero-Romance variety. The history of Yiddish literature, according to its students, starts in the thirteenth century (see Frakes 2004: lviii–lix), despite the fact that this language went through an enormous evolution, and texts were produced in various parts of Europe. Although from a sociological standpoint it is obvious that in the Ottoman Empire Sephardi vernacular literature emerged in the sixteenth century,[1] literary scholars, following the linguists, but ignoring the opinions of Sephardim themselves, believe that this happened two centuries later.

Elena Romero, author of the most comprehensive and authoritative work on Sephardi vernacular literature, *Creación literaria en lengua sefardí* (Madrid, 1992), dedicates only a few lines in the introduction to the sixteenth-century works produced by Sephardim in the Ottoman lands, stating that they were written "in pure aljamiado but in a language which barely displays any features distinguishing it from the Spanish of its time and which can be described, at the most, as 'pre-Judeo-Spanish'" (Romero 1992: 18).[2]

Iacob Hassán starts his overview of Sephardi literature with the first volume of *Meam Loez*, a popular Bible commentary (begun in 1730), because, as he puts it, "the few Sephardi works that have survived from the sixteenth century" (Almosnino, compilations of religious precepts, and translations) "had not yet become independent from contemporaneous Spanish" (Hassan 1995: 320). This rather vague statement apparently means that in terms of language, those sixteenth-century works are closer to the literary texts produced in Spain than to *Meam Loez*. Does this mean that they should be considered part of Castilian literature and studied by scholars of Antonio de Guevara? Besides, while Hassán's comment may be relevant to Moses Almosnino's works, it certainly does not apply to the "compilations of religious precepts and translations," which use varieties (or, more precisely, registers) much less similar to Castilian.

In view of the stylistic heterogeneity of sixteenth-century vernacular texts, a number of linguists call the language of some of them "Judeo-Spanish," arguing that others were written in Spanish (i.e., Castilian). One of the most consistent proponents of this approach, Aldina Quintana, postulates the existence of a diglossic relationship within the Ottoman Sephardi community between two Romance varieties where Peninsular Spanish functions as the high variety and Judeo-Spanish as the low one (Quintana 2009: 226). Obviously, this Fergusonian diglossia (Ferguson 1959) would have existed within a broader relationship between two genealogically unrelated languages (defined as diglossic by Joshua Fishman 1989), namely, between Hebrew and the vernacular, where the high position is occupied by Hebrew. This means that Hebrew was the language of law, religion, and rabbinic literature, whereas "Spanish" served as the language of high secular and semi-religious production, leaving all other functions to Judeo-Spanish.

According to this view, only three authors whose works, all of them written or published in Salonica, used "Spanish." By far the most prominent among them was Moses Almosnino (1518–1580), a renowned scholar and prolific author of Hebrew and vernacular works. The best known in the latter category is his *Regimiento de la vida* (*RV*) (Salonica, 1564), a treatise largely based on Aristotle's *Nicomachean Ethics* (see Almosnino 2004). (The same volume included a shorter treatise, *Tratado de los suenyos*.) The other two writers are Daniel de Ávila Gallego, author of a medical treatise, *El Diálogo del Colorado* (Salonica, 1601, see de Ávila Gallego 2014) and the anonymous author of *Fuente clara* (Salonica, c. 1595, see Romeu Ferré 2011), a work of Jewish apologetics. The two authors, both of them ex-*conversos*, were physicians and philosophers.

Most other extant vernacular books published in Constantinople and Salonica in the sixteenth century are commonly considered to be written in Judeo-Spanish. They are mainly adaptations of Hebrew texts meant to serve as educational tools for those who were not fluent in Hebrew. Among them are an abridged adaptation of *Shulhan arukh* entitled *Mesa de el alma* (Salonica, 1568) and a translation of the Hebrew version of ibn Paquda's classic of ethical literature, *Hovot ha-Levavot*, entitled *Obligasion de los korazones* (Constantinople, 1569). Another small corpus of vernacular texts consists mainly of Bible translations, which used the so-called "Ladino-calque," considered by many scholars, including Hassán and Romeu, a functional style (see Hassán and Romeu 1992: 168).

Scholars who categorize "the literary language of the educated class of Salonican Jews in the mid-sixteenth century" (Quintana 2009: 226) as "Spanish" often cite Almosnino who once referred to the language of his writings as *romance castellano* (for instance, Romeu and Hassán 1992: 161). However, we have no evidence showing that he distinguished between the written and the oral forms (let alone between different varieties), since he referred to both as *romance* and *lengua ajena*. Moreover, at least in one case, he calls it *franco* (i.e., European) as opposed to Turkish (Almosnino 1998: 251). But if we are to accept the terms used by sixteenth-century speakers, we can also call the language of Ottoman Jews "Ladino," because Joseph Formon, the translator of *Obligasion de los korasones* says that Ladino is "the [language] most commonly used among us" (quoted in Molho 1960: 229). The same was said about "Spanish" (see Romero 1992: 37–38).

I believe that calling the language of the above-mentioned sixteenth-century works "Spanish" without any qualifications is incorrect, and not only because of the great number of interferences from other languages and varieties but, more important, because it is written in a non-Latin script incomprehensible to Spaniards, and thus explicitly meant for a different audience. Besides, while the use of two alphabets for one language does not have any effect on it, the same text written in different scripts is likely to have different messages for each target audience. This is why, for instance, languages of the Muslim majorities acquire new names when written by Christian minorities in their own scripts. Thus, Turkish written in Greek characters is called "Karamanli" and Arabic written in Syriac characters "Garshuni." Sephardim did not have a special name for their language that would distinguish it from Castilian (which in the Ottoman Empire was unnecessary anyway).[3] But they certainly did not call it "Judeo-Spanish," which is, nevertheless, a valid descriptive term used by many scholars.

It is also misleading to use the term "Spanish" to refer to the language of a few works, in opposition to the variety used in the rest of Sephardi vernacular texts, because it suggests that there is a fundamental cultural difference between the two corpuses. More precisely, it implies that the works of Almosnino and others are an extension of Castilian literature and thus are irrelevant for Sephardi culture and its study. It is, therefore, not surprising that based on Hassán's essay quoted above, historian Matthias Lehmann, among many others, believes that sixteenth-century Judeo-Spanish books were "isolated cases" and that Almosnino's works were "still written in Castilian Spanish" (Lehmann 2005: 34). Viewed as an extension of Spanish literature, they indeed appear to be "isolated cases" that were once produced but then somehow "disappeared from the life and cultural memory of the Sephardi Jews" (Quintana 2012: 703). However, as I will show in the next section, this was not the case.

The contradictions and misconceptions caused by the use of "Spanish" in reference to some sixteenth-century texts can be resolved if we adopt a somewhat different approach to Sephardim's linguistic practices and change the terminology correspondingly. If we describe the range of options available to them in terms of functions, the two-level diglossic situation postulated by Quintana becomes a one-level relationship. Since the Judeo-Spanish koiné resulting from contact between a number of mutually intelligible Ibero-Romance dialects was still far from being stabilized, and Castilian enjoyed the highest social prestige among these varieties,[4] the literary language used by the three Salonican authors, where Castilian elements were dominant, may be seen as a high register of Ladino.

As for the other two registers (or functional styles), they are effectively treated as such by Ora Schwartzwald in her analysis of the women's *siddur* (prayerbook) published in Salonica c. 1565). She describes the "Ladino" of the prayers and the "Judeo-Spanish" of the translator's instructions as a "written formal style" and one "reminiscent of speech," respectively (see Schwarzwald 2012).

Thus, all sixteenth-century vernacular texts produced in the Ottoman Empire can be divided into three groups in terms of register. The first includes most translations and explanations of religious precepts, such as *La mesa de el alma* or the instructions for prayers in the women's *siddur*. While their language contains a great number of Hebrew calques and loans, it is much closer to the spoken variety (known to us mainly from the testimonies included in the responsa) than the translations of the Bible and liturgical texts that form the second group. The third and smallest group is comprised only of original works, namely, *Fuente clara, Diálogo del colorado,* and the five extant vernacular works written by Almosnino.

Since sixteenth-century vernacular texts had different cultural statuses and targeted different audiences, they used different functional styles. Hence, like most other languages (including Yiddish), at least in some periods of its history, Ladino had more than one functional style (or register). When at the turn of the seventeenth century, due to the virtual end of the *converso* immigration, the genres requiring the high register of Ladino disappeared (Borovaya 2014: 258), so did the register itself. The same happened with the "calque" style in the 1740s, when Abraham Asá's versions of the Prophets and the Five Scrolls introduced a new principle of Bible translation. Thus, only one functional style, the one closest to the spoken language, had survived and was used by Jacob Huli for *Meam Loez*.[5]

2. RUPTURE OR CONTINUITY?

This does not mean, however, that sixteenth-century vernacular works were forgotten in less than two hundred years. In fact, *Fuente clara* was reprinted in 1740 by Jonah Ashkenazi, the publisher of Huli's *Meam Loez* (Yaari 1967: No. 384).

Nevertheless, it is often alleged that by the eighteenth century these books had become incomprehensible, which is often brought up as another argument against including them, and Almosnino's work in particular, in the corpus of Ladino literature. Unlike the theoretical objection related to the formation of the Judeo-Spanish koiné brought forth by some linguists, this claim, repeated by scholars in all fields of Sephardic Studies, is based on a single statement made by Jacob Huli, the meaning of which has never been put into question. In 1730, Huli famously declared Almosnino's work unintelligible for his readers: "the book written by our master and teacher Moses Almosnino of blessed memory, called *Regimyento de la vida,* is a very enlightening[6] book, but its idiom is incomprehensible" (Gonzalo Maeso and Pascual Recuero 1964: 147).

This statement appears in numerous works on Ladino language and literature and typically introduces discussions of *Meam Loez,* presumably explaining why Huli had to produce his Bible commentary. In addition, it has prompted all sorts of conclusions emphasizing discontinuity, for which it provides no grounds. For instance, Coloma Lleal writes, "The situation of rupture with the Spanish literary norm [...] was clearly captured by Huli in his introduction to Meam Loez [...]" (Lleal 1992: 27).

Although it is usually connected to an earlier sentence about two other sixteenth-century texts (*Mesa de el alma* and *Obligasion de los korazones*) that Huli declares useless for linguistic reasons, I am convinced that his statement about Almosnino's book cannot be taken as a comment on its language. To begin with, his linguistic expertise is questionable, which is obvious from his explanation that the Ladino translation of ibn Paquda's book is unintelligible for most readers, because it is written "in Spanish words." More important, Huli's argument is not about language per se.

The true purpose of this section of Huli's introduction is to prove to the rabbis, supporters and detractors alike, that the Ladino works of his predecessors are inadequate for mass education. He is particularly keen on proving the uselessness of Almosnino's *RV*. The first problem he mentions is a technical one, caused by the spelling (*solotreo* [sic]), which Huli considers correct but incomprehensible to his audience. The difficulty was probably caused not by the unstable orthography but, at least in Almosnino's case, had to do with the way of printing.

Unlike the other two books, *RV* was printed in unvocalized Rashi script with inconsistently used *matres lectionis*. John Zemke explains that in the sixteenth century neither the author nor the readers "required a consistent spelling system" and that "unpointed aljamía was read in the same fashion as unpointed Hebrew: a reader recognizes a known word form."[7] This means that reading *RV* required a vocabulary of philosophical and scientific terms far beyond that of the petty merchants and women who formed Huli's intended readership.

In fact, the second problem discussed by Huli is the lack of general understanding of the text, because the unlearned "do not understand his words to which they are not accustomed." Moreover, they do not understand "the meaning of what he says (*sus* ablas) which, being very short, require a lot of studying." Obviously, here *ablas* does not refer to words or the sentences (since one can describe Almosnino's sentences as very short only as a joke). Hence, this probably means that his ideas are not sufficiently explained. Huli indeed says that in order to "understand what he [Almosnino] wanted to say, one has to know how to study, as he intended to be short by conveying a lot of knowledge in few words."

The adjectives Huli uses to prove that the three Ladino books are incomprehensible for the masses (*karo, serado,* and *ondo*) appear in his introduction whenever he needs to explain why his predecessors had to produce new Bible commentaries. In every case, he says that the world had declined, and the words of the available commentary had become incomprehensible. But this evidently does not refer to linguistic problems, as such, since he tells us that Moses had to write the Torah in order to explain the Ten Commandments, because "the words of the Law are very sealed and short" (*las ablas de la ley son muy seradas i kortas*).

And it is precisely these words that Huli uses to describe Almosnino's *RV*: "sus ablas son muy seradas; las ablas, ke son muy kortas." Thus, his writing is too dense, which "is not useful for the common people, because they cannot spend a whole day trying to understand one thing." This last comment, in a way, contradicts what Huli considers the book's third problem, namely, that it is short and will be finished very quickly thus leaving the people without anything to read once again.

This lengthy discussion of *RV* and the fact that it is cited together with the adaptations of *Shulhan arukh*, the most authoritative legal code of Judaism, and *Hovot ha-Levavot*, described by Joseph Dan as "the most important and influential work of Jewish philosophical ethics" (Dan 1986: 25) is ample proof that it was still available and continued to be relevant for some readers, if only for the rabbis.

No doubt, *RV* was unintelligible to "the masses who do not study science" (Almosnino 2004: Fol. 10b) and were unfamiliar with Aristotle, Plato, and Maimonides, but this was also true at the time of its production, since it was intended for educated young men.[8] Moreover, Almosnino appended to *RV* a Ladino-Hebrew glossary containing 515 words that in his view would have been unknown to his readers. Hence, he expected them to know some Hebrew. Michael Molho explains why RV was inaccessible to the general public: "Judging by its literary structure and scholarly content filled with philosophical contemplations, this masterpiece was intended for educated people able to apprreciate the author's talent and his manner of writing" (Molho 1948: 99).

Finally, if this had been a purely linguistic problem, one of Huli's colleagues would have sooner or later adapted *RV*, as was done in its romanized edition (Amsterdam, 1729). In fact, In 1749, Abraham Asá produced a new translation of *Orah hayim*, the same section of *Shulhan arukh* that Meir Benveniste translated under the title *Mesa de el alma*. Yet *RV* and *Obligasion de los korasones*, complex ethical works that talked about abstract virtues and spiritual commandments and were intended for individual reading, were either not published in the Ottoman Empire again (the former) or not until 1898 (the latter). Instead, they were replaced with straightforward religious education and clear guidance provided by *Meam Loez,* which was appropriate for reading out loud in a group setting.

To sum up, the fact that Huli went to such lengths to prove the obvious, namely, that *RV* could not serve the purpose of mass education, testifies to Almosnino's high prestige among the rabbis, which made it impossible to reject his work without a thorough justification. To confirm that Almosnino's work was incomprehensible, Romero quotes a Salonican publisher and journalist, Saadi Halevy, who in 1871 announced his intention to "translate the famous book by the rabbi and philosopher Moses Almosnino called *Rules of Living*" (Quoted in Romero

1992: 84). While Romero emphasizes that Halevy felt that *RV* needed to be translated, I would stress the fact that three centuries after its publication the book was described as "famous" and deemd worth publishing.

As we have seen, Huli's statement does not tell us anything about the rupture with "the Spanish literary norm" (or about *any* rupture for that matter), but testifies to the immense differences between Huli's and Almosnino's intended audiences and, therefore, their educational projects. In this connectionn, it must be noted that those who read the 1740 edition of *Fuente clara* would have had no difficulty understanding *RV*. On the other hand, in 1898, the author of a new Ladino commentary on Exodus wrote, using the old rabbinical clichés and paraphrasing Huli in particular, that "for our sins, at this time, the minds of this generation are so weak" that they find *Meam Loez* incomprehensible; and when they return to their houses at night and take it in their hands, "reading without understanding" puts them to sleep (quoted in Romero 1992: 94–95).

Clearly, unintelligibility, especially for an audience for which the text in question was not intended, cannot be used as a criterion for exclusion, otherwise Chaucer, if not Shakespeare, might not be considered part of English literature. But if a given speech community considers a certain literary work part of its cultural heritage, scholars cannot ignore this, even if they have valid objections. Justifications of such claims are of particular importance for the study of the culture in question.

Starting in the 1890s, Sephardi intellectuals, including David Fresco, Moïse Franco, Abraham Danon, Joseph Nehama, Isaac Emmanuel, and Michael Molho, began to claim Almosnino as their first writer born in Turkey (Franco 1897: 76). Molho, the author of the first history of Ladino literature, starts with sixteenth-century texts and describes *RV* as the earliest work of ethical literature in Ladino (Molho 1960: 228). I am not sure that all of these literati read *RV* in full, but they would have had no difficulty understanding it. In any event, they were not only aware of Almosnino's "pure style," but this was the main reason why they insisted on continuity between his writings and what they called their own "corrupt Spanish." From the standpoint of these intellectuals, Almosnino's language, which had led some modern scholars to exclude his work from the corpus of Ladino literature, made him a particularly appealing figure for the Sephardi cultural canon.

Needless to say, a discussion of terminology alone is not enough to help us understand Ladino literature better, but it is a necessary step in identifying the corpus of texts we call by this name. This, in turn, brings up some questions regarding the criteria of inclusion. And, once we have defined what constitutes Ladino literature, we can move on to its new periodization and discuss its principles. In the process, we may discover numerous assumptions waiting to be reconsidered.

NOTES

1. The first known Ladino book, *Dinim de shehitah i bedikah* (The rules of ritual slaughter and inspection of animals), was printed in Constantinople *circa* 1510. (Yaari 1967, No. 29.) In transcribing Ladino, I use the system adopted by the periodical Aki Yerushalayim. However, in quotations from published texts, I keep the editors' transcriptions.
2. Later, she briefly discusses some sixteenth-century Bible translations, referring to their language as "Eastern Judeo-Spanish calque." (Romero 1992: 39.) All translations are mine.
3. Obviously, *aljamiado* is too broad a term, as it does not refer to a specific language but rather to the way of writing Romance languages that Jews and Muslims adopted in Iberia.
4. On this subject, see, for example, Minervini (1999).
5. Later, however, new social agendas called for new literary genres and new registers.
6. This is John Zemke's translation of *luzio* usually translated as "clear." "Enlightening" makes more sense in this context. (Zemke 2004: 1.)
7. Zemke, *op. cit.* 15.
8. On Almosnino's intended audience, see Borovaya (2014).

REFERENCES

Almosnino, Moshe ben Baruk. *Regimiento de la vida. Tratado de los suenyos*. Edited by John M. Zemke. Tempe: Arizona Center for Medieval and Renaissance Studies, 2004.

Almosnino, Moisés. *Crónica de los reyes otomanos*. Edited by Pilar Romeu Ferré. 251. Barcelona: Tirocinio, 1998.

Borovaya, Olga. "Moses Almosnino' Epistles: A Sixteenth-Century Genre of Sephardi Vernacular Literature." *Journal of Medieval Iberian Studies* 6, no. 5 (2014): 251–261.

de Ávila Gallego, Daniel. *Diálogo del colorado*. Edited and introduction by Pilar Romeu Ferré. Barcelona: Tirocinio, 2014.

Dan, Joseph. *Jewish Mysticism and Jewish Ethics*. Seattle and London: University of Washington Press, 1986.

Ferguson, Charles A. "Diglossia." *Word* 15 (1959): 325–340.

Fishman, Joshua. "Bilingualism and biculturalism as individual and as societal phenomena." In *Language and Ethnicity in Minority Sociolinguistic Perspective*. Edited by Joshua Fishman. 181–201. Clevedon: Multilingual Matters, 1989.

Frakes, Gerald C. "Introduction." In *Early Yiddish Texts 1100–1750*. Edited by Gerald C. Frakes, lviii–lix. New York: Oxford University Press, 2004.

Franco, Moise. *Essai sur l'Histoire des Israélites de l'Empire Ottoman depuis les origines jusqu'à nos Jours* (1897). repr.: New York: Georg Olms Verlag, 1973.

Gonzalo Maeso, David and Pascual Recuero, eds. *Me'am lo'ez: El Gran Comentario Bíblico Sefardí*. Madrid: Editorial Gredos, 1964

Hassán, Iacob M. "La literatura sefardí culta: sus principales escritores, obras y géneros." In *Judíos. Sefardíes. Conversos*. Edited by Angel Alcalá, 319–30. Valladolid: Ambito Ediciones, 1995.

Lehmann, Matthias. *Ladino Rabbinic Literature and Ottoman Sephardic Culture*. Bloomington: Indiana University Press, 2005.

Lleal, Coloma. *El Judezmo. El Dialecto Sefardí y Su Historia*. Barcelona: Universitat de Barcelona. 1992.

Minervini, Laura. "Formation of the Judeo-Spanish Koiné: Dialect Convergence in the Sixteenth Century." In *The Proceedings of the Tenth Conference on Judeo-Spanish Studies*. Edited by Annette Benaim. 41–53. London: Queen Mary and Westfield College, 1999.

Molho, Michael. "Dos obras maestras en ladino de Moisés Almosnino." In *Estudios y ensayos sobre tópicos judíos*, 95–102. Buenos Aires: Edición del Instituto Científico judío, 1948.

Molho, Michael. *Literatura sefardita de Oriente*. Madrid: CSIC, 1960.

Quintana. "Aportación lingüística de los romances aragonés y portugués a la coiné judeoespañola." In *Languages and Literatures of Sephardic and Oriental Jews: Proceedings of the Sixth International Congress for Research on the Sephardi and Oriental Jews*. Edited by David Bunis, 221–255. Jerusalem: Misgav Yerushalayim, 2009.

Quintana, Aldina. "From Linguistic Segregation outside the Common Framework of Hispanic Languages to a de facto Standard." In *Studies in Modern Hebrew and Jewish Languages Presented to Ora (Rodrigue) Schwarzwald*. Edited by Malka Muchnik and Tsvi Sadan. 697–714. Jerusalem: Carmel Publishing House, 2012.

Romero, Elena. *Creación literaria en lengua sefardí*. Madrid: MAPFRE, 1992

Romeu Ferré, Pilar, ed. *Fuente Clara*. Barcelona: Tirocinio, 2011.

Romeu, Pilar, and Iacob M. Hassán. "Apuntes sobre la lengua de la Crónica de los reyes otomanos de Moisés Almosnino según la edición del manuscrito aljamiado del siglo XVI." In *Actas del II Congreso Internacional de Historia de la Lengua Española. Vol. II.* 161–169. Madrid: Pabellón de España, 1992.

Schwarzwald, Ora (Rodrigue). "Linguistic Features of a Sixteenth-Century Women's Ladino Prayer Book: The Language Used for Instructions and Prayers." In *Selected Papers from the Fifteenth British Conference on Judeo-Spanish Studies*. Edited by Hilary Pomeroy, Chris J. Pountain and Elena Romero. 247–260. London: Department of Hispanic Studies, Queen Mary, University of London, 2012.

Yaari, Abraham. Hebrew Printing at Constantinople. Jerusalem: Hebrew University Press, 1967.

Zemke, John. "Introduction". In Almosnino, *Regimiento de la vida*, 2004.

CHAPTER FOUR

Historical Overview AND Outcome OF Three Portuguese Patterns IN Judeo-Spanish

quer(em)-se + PART. in Active Constructions, the wh-operator *o que*, and the Inflected Infinitive

ALDINA QUINTANA[1]
The Hebrew University of Jerusalem, Israel

ABSTRACT

Cultural and communal boundaries of the Sephardic communities emerged via hybridization and from the assimilation of elements of diverse cultural origin, in which the formation of Judeo-Spanish played a key role in the imaginative processes of developing Sephardic identity, and its preservation as the "language-of-power" within the communities gave meaning to their further existence. This chapter deals with language contact with Portuguese, variation and change in Judeo-Spanish. The intensity of this contact varied according to place and time, and the high degree of overlap in linguistic structure, which allowed significant *interlingual conflation*, will become obvious through the three patterns I shall address below.

1. HISTORICAL AND SOCIAL BACKGROUND

Sephardic communities as imagined[2] and diasporic communities are related to the profound changes experienced by Iberian Jews from the time of their settlement in the Ottoman Empire after 1492. In the process of self-fashioning a new collective identity and defining their boundaries, which emerged via hybridization and from the assimilation of elements of diverse cultural origin (Ray 2008: 18), the formation of Judeo-Spanish and its maintenance as "language-of-power"[3] not only played a key role but hybridity and heterogeneity as characteristics of a "diaspora experience"[4] will be especially evident at the level of language.

Within the broader process, which gave rise to mixed communities, dialectal contact and mixing led to the emergence of Judeo-Spanish. In this process, all the speakers groups belonging to different dialectal communities—including Portuguese speakers—shifted to Castilian. Through shifting, some language patterns of the shifted dialects were also transferred to Castilian, giving rise to the new language—Judeo-Spanish—separate from the source varieties spoken elsewhere (Penny 1992), which became the "language-of-power" of the new speech communities. This occurred because first Castilian became the "language-of-power" of the Iberian Jews immediately after their settlement in the localities of the Ottoman Empire, followed shortly thereafter by Judeo-Spanish[5] at the stage of a recognizable "naturalized pre-koine"[6] (according to Siegel's [1985: 373–376] classification in the developmental continuum of koines, this take place in the "first stage.")

As a printed language Castilian/Judeo-Spanish was the most successful and the only one that was able to create a "written representation" of the Sephardic imagined communities, thus also reaching people who were not able to read or write in Hebrew. Its role as language-of-power was reconfirmed in the first decades of the 18th century when Judeo-Spanish, as a fully "nativized koine," achieved a relative degree of standardization. Therefore, the use of Judeo-Spanish as a print language by the descendants of Spanish and Portuguese Jews and other Jews who were assimilated into them has not only been fundamental "for the development of a Sephardic identity," but the preservation of Sephardic identity was also very much dependent of the maintenance of a common vernacular language (Judeo-Spanish). This language has provided a particular and exclusive field of discourse which, in turn, has made Sephardic Jews aware of their membership of the group (Stechauner 2013: 31).

The elevation of the Judeo-Spanish language to the status of "language-of-power," where, in one sense it was a competitor with Hebrew, made its own contribution to the emergence and maintenance of the imagined Sephardic community as "a sub-ethnic group within the Jewish Diaspora" (Ray 2008). The auto-perception as an "imagined" Diaspora community and the role played by Judeo-Spanish as the essential expression of group affiliation to Sephardic identity is thrown into even sharper relief by the notion that the speakers themselves had of the term "Sepharad," understood now as the whole of "people who speak Judeo-Spanish," without reference to a specific location,[7] in contrast to its meaning at the time of the expulsion when it was used as a toponym referring to the Iberian Peninsula.[8]

The settlement of the expellees in different cities of the Ottoman Empire and the different mix of contributory dialects in each of them suggest a different result in the leveling of dialectal differences in each Judeo-Spanish community. As Penny

(1996: 56) proposed, new processes of dialectal leveling took place whenever Sephardim from existing communities created new communities in other locations (Quintana 2006a: 295). The development of two regional standards around the two great cultural centers—Salonica and Istanbul—did not lead to greater homogenization of Judeo-Spanish, especially in peripheral communities. Thus, the natural evolution of Judeo-Spanish continued with hardly any normative pressure.

A pluricentric language is always an imagining language, since

> the speakers of a pluricentric language [...] do not have a precise awareness of the general linguistic situation, i.e., of the historical language as a whole, because their perception of linguistic reality is influenced inevitably by interpretations and decisions, sometimes clearly ideological [...].[9]

In fact, hybridity and linguistic variations were often negatively interpreted by Sephardic leaders, especially since the mid-19th century, once the imaginations of Sephardic intellectuals were deeply influenced by the ideas of French centralism and, consequently, Judeo-Spanish which was imagined as being unworthy for a language. Comments such as the following were very often published in newspapers of the time:

> I es ke ya es byen savido ke *makað* <arov> la erida de la mestura kayó enla lingwa ke nozotros levan<tinos> pratikamos, mesklando munčo mas otras lingwas i avlando en kada <parte> una manera ke no topareš ǧente de una sivdad ke esté de <akod>ro enla avla, kon la de otra. Ke kada uno la pratika según la <kom>puzyeron en su sivdad. I la razón es ke dita lingwa espanyola ke nozotros pratikamos en Turkia no es deprendida no en gramátika no en vokabularyo otro ke es naxalað avotenu meolam ke del dia ke nwestros <an>tigos salyeron de la Espanya ronpyeron la vedradera lingwa espanyola <i> la fweron pratika<n>do kada uno según le venía [...].[10]

This chapter deals with language contact—in this case with the Portuguese—and variation in Judeo-Spanish, two issues directly related to mixing and differentiation. The intensity of this contact varied according to place and time, and the significance of their consequences may also vary as will become evident through the three patterns I will address below.

2. DIALECTAL CONTACT AMONG PORTUGUESE AND CASTILIAN/JUDEO-SPANISH SPEAKERS

Judeo-Spanish is the outcome of an immigrant koine resulting from the face-to-face dialect contact among speakers of Ibero-Romance languages which came together at the Iberian ports of departure bound for the Ottoman Empire or in the places of their establishment where their descendants continued the process of social integration aimed at creating a more homogeneous community. At the pre-koine stage, which was still far from conforming to the stabilized composite variety that would result from the process of koineization, Judeo-Spanish would be first spoken by the children of the expelled, who no longer would speak the dialects of their parents, and would become the vernacular of the new community (cf. Siegel 1985: 375–376; Kerswill 2013: 520).

Castilian was not learned in a formal way by the expellees who spoke other traditional dialects, or by their children, but was used in face-to-face interaction due to the high degree of intelligibility among them. This, as well as the subsequent lack of contact with peninsular Spanish, led to the formation of a new language on the basis of the colloquial varieties, many of whose features were rejected by the Castilian standard of the 16th century. In their desire to accommodate to Castilian speakers, Leonese, Aragonese, and also Catalan speakers, transferred linguistic features from their native dialects by shifting, as already evidenced in the first Sephardic texts written by the children of those expelled in the mid-16th century.[11]

Through these texts and through modern Judeo-Spanish, we can observe that the contribution of the traditional dialects to the Judeo-Spanish koine varies in extent: while features transferred from Catalan are limited to a short list of words (*dingun* 'nobody'; *mangrana* 'pomegranate'; *genera(n)sio* 'generation'; *unflar* 'to pump up, to swell (up)'; *kojeta* 'collecting contributions or donations'—employed by Catalan Jews even before the expulsion) or locutions such as *todos dos juntos* 'both' and *a pok a pok* 'slowly, bit by bit', Aragonese features are much richer and reach all the subsystems of Judeo-Spanish. Among them, it is worth mentioning some features rejected by the Spanish peninsular norm of the 16th century, such as the formation of participles, gerunds and subjunctive forms from the perfect stem (*tuvido* 'had'; *uvido* 'been'; *tuviendo* 'having'; *uviendo* 'having'; *supiendo* 'knowing') or the analog unification of the imperfect endings of the second and third conjugation, according to patterns of the first (*konveniva* 'it suited'; *komiva* 'he ate') in some varieties as well as a list of lexical items.[12]

Detecting Leonese features in Judeo-Spanish is more difficult, probably because the Leonese speaking areas, in which Jews lived in 1492, had already acquired a degree of advanced castilianization. *Luvia* 'rain'; *strelde* 'trivet' and *fegado* 'liver'—the two latter only found in some varieties of Judeo-Spanish—are some of the few words to which a Leonese provenance can be assigned. The relatively low presence of linguistic elements transferred from these traditional dialects—especially from Leonese and Catalan—into Judeo-Spanish dialects may be explained by the fact that the contact of their speakers with Castilian was short and not intense enough when one considers that their native languages ware marginalized to the family domain and to the interaction among congeners from the first moment that they stood face-to-face with the rest of the expelled. Therefore, with their deaths the three languages would cease to be spoken in the new community.

Although in Sephardic literature, one rarely finds references that indicate any relation of Judeo-Spanish to Portuguese,[13] dialectal contact of Castilian/Judeo-Spanish speakers with Portuguese speakers involved not only those who arrived in the Ottoman Empire shortly after the expulsion from Castile and Aragon in 1492 but also Crypto-Jews (i.e., Jews and their descendants who had been forced to convert to Christianity and who decided to return to the open practice of Judaism), especially those who, throughout the 16th, 17th and 18th centuries, emigrated from Portugal to the Ottoman Empire or settled in the port cities on the Adriatic Sea. Therefore, the contact between Judeo-Spanish and Portuguese speakers took place in different socio-historical contexts and in various ways. Obviously, the linguistic outcomes are also varied (Quintana 2014: 67).

Contact between Judeo-Spanish and Portuguese speakers led mainly to lexical loans, borrowing, interdialectalisms, among others, but the transfer of certain patterns stimulated also some structural changes in Judeo-Spanish morpho-syntax. The first pattern I will analyze concerns the outcome of a structural change which took place in Judeo-Spanish and which affected all dimensions of its variation. The second pattern is regionally marked because it can only be found in the speech of Judeo-Spanish speakers from the western Balkan communities. Finally, the third pattern should be considered as a localism, used by speakers of the nearly extinct variety of Bitola (Macedonia), a variety which, according to Luria (1930), Crews (1935) and Faingold (1996), should probably be more appropriately classified as a mixed language between Judeo-Spanish and Portuguese than a Spanish historical variety.

2.1. Se k(i)ere + participle (PART.) in Impersonal Constructions

Standard Judeo-Spanish shows a syntactic construction, which, no doubt, is a consequence of contact with Portuguese (Crews 1935: 233; Quintana 2004, 2009; Gabinsky 2008). This construction concerns one of the possible ways of expressing deontic modality in Judeo-Spanish in which the deontic value may be expressed by the impersonal phrasal *se k(i)ere* + PART. The impersonal verb *se k(i)ere*, which shows default 3.SG agreement, brings the modality together with the participle, and this carries the meaning to the action, and their perfective aspect and resultative value. A construction copied from Portuguese induced also the development of *se k(i)ere* to an epistemic verb and to a discourse marker of modal evidentiality.

2.1.1. The Impersonal Phrasal *se k(i)ere* + PART. as a Way of Expressing Directive Deontic Modality of Attenuate Obligation in Spoken Judeo-Spanish

This construction concerns one of the possible ways of expressing directive deontic modality[14] of attenuate obligation in which the directive value may be expressed by the impersonal phrasal verb *se k(i)ere* + PART. (1, 2, 3):

(1) Se kere   dicho.   JSp.
    Se require-3.SG said-MASC-SG
    Quer-se dito.   Port.
    Hay que decirlo.   Sp.
    It should be said.

(2) […] se kere   tashedeado   a otra kaza.[15]   JSp.
    […] se require-3.SG   moved-MASC-SG   to another house
    […] temos de mudar para outra casa.   Port.
    […] hay que mudarse a otra casa   Sp.
    […] one must move to another house

(3) Avrid   la shena, a la ovra!   se kere   avlado.[16] JSp.
    Open-IMP-PL   the scene! To the play!   Se require-3.SG   spoken-MASC-SG
    Levantai a cortina! Mãos a obra! Temos de falar!   Port.
    ¡Arriba el telón! ¡Manos a la obra! ¡Hay que hablarlo!   Sp.
    Raise the curtain! Let's start working! It should be talked about!

This construction (1, 2, 3) is characterized by being impersonal, both from the syntactic and the semantic standpoint: the verb shows default 3.SG agreement, and the pronoun *se*, which occupies the canonical position, is a minimal argument being assigned null case. The impersonal *se kere*—once emptied of its original semantic content ('s/he wants')—carries epistemic modality. However, along with the adjacent absolute participle, which, besides providing meaning to the action, gives it also a perfective-resultative value in the temporal posteriority, focused from the moment of enunciation, this discursive device is coded as a strong directive. On the other hand, the impersonalization of the construction—which also lacks an agentive argument—acts as a mitigating factor in the ilocutive force of the directive dictum to which the speaker of the utterance indirectly wants to involve the hearer. Fully grammaticalized as a locution, it is related to the impersonal construction consisting of the phrasal *se k(i)ere* + PART. + DO internal argument that I shall discuss below.

Well documented in the representations of dialogues in Sephardic texts from the 19th century, *se k(i)ere* + PART. has a very high frequency of use in spoken Judeo-Spanish. The compactness of modal impersonal expressions and their syntax enhances their diffusion (Aikhenvald 2006: 31), which may explain that these expressions have reached Judeo-Spanish.

2.1.2. *Se k(i)ere* Grammaticalized as a Verb of Epistemic Modality

The verb *k(i)erer* is a volitional verb which is used also as a modal auxiliary of other verbs to express volitional value. But the phrasal *se k(i)ere* is grammaticalized as a lexical mark to express epistemic modality, as can be shown in the following impersonal active construction (4, 5):

(4) […] beofen ke   *sekere*   18 komidas.[17]   JSp.
    […] so   that   *se need*-3.SG 18 meals-PL
    […] de modo que se necesita 18 comidas.   Sp.
    […] so that 18 meals are needed.

(5) *Se kere*   provas siguras!'[18]   JSp.
    Se need-3.SG secure evidence-PL!
    ¡Se necesita pruebas seguras!   Sp.
    It needs secure evidence!

In these sentences, all the elements occupy the canonical position that is characteristic for impersonal active transitive construction in Judeo-Spanish: impersonal-*se* + verb + DO.

2.1.3. The Linking Phrase *no se k(i)ere (ni) dicho* as Discourse Marker Describing Relationships of Modal Evidentiality

Negative construction with *se k(i)ere* + PART. gave rise to the linking phrase *no se k(i)ere (ni) dicho* 'needless to say; … not to mention …,' grammaticalized as a discourse marker of evidentiality (6, 7) in order to emphasize that a particular statement mentioned in the discourse considered absolutely evident or known to all, is not necessarily so obvious. Consequently, its use reveals a high degree of subjectivity.

(6) […] eskarvar non el orno non la ornaya por mano de los esklavos i   JSp.
    […] to rummage neither the oven nor the stove by hand of the slaves, and
    […] remover ni en el horno ni en la hornalla por medio de los esclavos y   Sp.
    […] The hands of slaves should not touch either the oven or the stove, and

    non se kere   *dicho* ke non pueden azer lunbre de muevo para azer kave[19]   JSp.
    not se require-3.SG *said* that [they] cannot make fire again to make coffee
    ni que decir tiene que no pueden hacer lumbre de nuevo para hacer café   Sp.
    needless to say they cannot make fire again to make coffee

(7) Un artikolo en la gazeta   tiene el nombre del eskritor,   JSp.
    An article in the newspaper bears the name of the writer,
    Un artículo en el periódico tiene el nombre del autor,   Sp.
    A newspaper article bears the author's name,

    kuadros de pintores *no se kere ni dicho*, i no es esto tuerto?[20]   JSp.
    painting-MASC-PL of painters *not se require*-3.SG *even said*, and not is this unfair?
    y, ni que decir tiene los cuadros de pintores, ¿no es injusto?   Sp.
    and needless to say artists' paintings also; isn't this unfair?

When this marker accompanies rhematic information, displays the variant *no se k(i)ere dicho* (6), and when it refers to thematic information, the variant *no se k(i) ere ni dicho* is used (7). This discourse mark is not necessarily interactive, so that it is frequently found in texts of written discourse that allow the subjectivity of the author. This favors its ironic use. It is the Judeo-Spanish discourse marker equivalent to the Spanish *ni que decir tiene* (cf. Torrent-Lenzen 2013).

2.1.4. *Se* + *k(i)ere* + PART. as a Way of Expressing Strong Suggestions in Spoken Judeo-Spanish

A similar construction—but with external argument instead of *se*-impersonal—may also be found in Judeo-Spanish (8) with the purpose of expressing strong suggestions, although it is considered non-standard:

(8) El oro   kere   martiyado.   JSp. (Informant)
    The gold-MASC-SG require-3.SG   hammered-MASC-SG
    El oro tiene que/debe ser martillado.   Sp.
    The gold has to be hammered.

This sentence is characterized by displaying a patient subject, which may never be animate, and the lack of an agentive argument (9). This is caused by the fact that animate subjects would automatically involve agentivity and semantic volitional value of the verb *kerer*, which would select a DO argument (10).

(9) *El mansevo   kere   komido.   JSp.
    The young-MASC-SG require-3.SG   eaten-MASC-SG
    ?El joven tiene que/debe ser comido.   Sp.
    ?The young [one] has to be eaten.

(10) El mansevo   kere   komida.   JSp.
     El joven   quiere   comida.   Sp.
     The young [one] wants food.

2.1.5. *Se* + *k(i)ere* + PART. as a Way of Expressing Epistemic Modality in the 18th Century

Already in texts written in the 18th century, it is possible to find sentences syntactically equivalent to (8). In (11), the main verb agrees also with an external argument that is placed in anaphoric relation to the preceding sentence (*las avlas*), and there is agreement between it and the participle:

(11) […] para entender la havana de las avlas […]   *keren* muncho
     estudiadas.[21]
     […] to understand the meaning of the quotations-FEM-PL […] [they]   *need*-3.PL
     carefully *studied*-FEM-PL
     […] para entender el sentido de las citas […] [éstas] necesitan ser muy estudiadas.
     […] to understand the meaning of the quotations, these things need to be carefully studied.

Its syntactic structure seems to have had its origin in the ambiguity caused by the interpretation of another construction of similar syntactic structure—but which was not passive—as a middle-passive periphrastic infinitival sentence (cf. 13, 14), despite the lack of auxiliary infinitive.

Mendikoetxea (2012: 486) argues that semantically, middle-passive sentences "attribute properties to entities; they are non-eventive (stative) statements and involve the modality factor of ability or possibility." Since, in Judeo-Spanish, *k(i)erer* as an auxiliary could only express volitional value, through the omission of the clitic *se*, the middle-passive periphrastic infinitival sentence was reanalyzed as a passive periphrastic constructions of *k(i)erer* + INF. of epistemic modality (12a). In this way, the problem is solved, at least in part. Evidence of this is that this construction is preserved in modern Judeo-Spanish. But, as with Spanish (Gómez Torrego 1999: 3364), Judeo-Spanish does not admit passive periphrastic constructions of *k(i)ere* + INF. because it is generally accepted that non-human agents display lack of willingness (12b).

(12) a. Las avlas *k(i)eren* ser estudiadas. JSp.
     The quotations-FEM-PL *need*-3.PL to be studied.
     Las citas necesitan ser estudiadas. Sp.
     The quotations need to be studied.

(12) b. ?Las avlas *k(i)eren* ser estudiadas (de/por mi). JSp.
     The quotations-FEM-PL *want*-3.PL to be studied-FEM-PL by me.
     ?Las citas quieren ser estudiadas por mí. Sp.
     ?The quotations want to be studied by me.

The construction in (11) shows substantially the same syntactic structure of Portuguese sentences with *querer-se* + PART., in which the modal verb expresses also necessity (13, 14): (a) the clitic *se*; (b) a preverbal subject (*Isto de mulheres, Estas cousas*); (c) the verb *querer* which has deontic modality, which agrees in number with the preverbal DP; (d) a postverbal participle which agrees in number and gender with the subject; and (e) a manner or adverbial expression which follows the participle. The only difference between the Portuguese construction (13, 14) and the Judeo-Spanish construction (8, 11) lies in the omission of *se* in the latter.

(13) Isto de mulheres *quer-se* tracdado com cuidado.[22] Port.
     This of women *need*-3.SG *se* treated-MASC-SG with care.
     This thing about women needs to be treated with care.

(14) Estas cousas *querem-se* tractadas com cuidado.[23] Port.
     These things-FEM-PL *need*-3.PL *se* treated-FEM-PL with care
     These things need to be treated with care.

In fact, bilingual speakers for whom Portuguese was their dominant language, or during the period of acquisition of Judeo-Spanish by Portuguese speakers copied this construction from Portuguese into Judeo-Spanish, most probably. Finally, it would spread to Judeo-Spanish speakers from the interlingua developed by bilingual speakers or students of Judeo-Spanish.

At this point, I should mention that, in the construction transferred from Portuguese, *querer* expresses clearly epistemic modality. Due to the lack of the verb *ser*, an auxiliary of the passive voice, this construction was interpreted as active in Portuguese.[24] The ambiguity caused by the verb *k(i)erer* in these sentences by the fact that they could also be read with volitional meaning, and the circumstance that Judeo-Spanish does not admit passive periphrastic constructions of *k(i)erer* + INF. occasioned that a sentence such as (11) might be interpreted as an unconventional agent-less passive (12) or as an active sentence without an indefinite (or generic) subject (15). This ambiguity by the interpreting of meaning smoothed the way once again for reanalysis of (11) and (15) as an SVO active sentence with the introduction of the clitic *se*. Whenever the reanalysis did not take place, we find clear indications of the switch from a (passive) NP-subject (11) to an (active) NP-object (15).

(15) […] ke sierto   kere   tenido   da 'át   muy ancho.[25]   JSp.
     […] that certainly *require*-3.SG had-MASC-SG *intelligence*-MASC-SG very wide-MASC-SG
     […] que ciertamente hay que tener una inteligencia muy grande.   Sp.
     […] that certainly one must have a very great intelligence.

2.1.6. Impersonal-*se* + *k(i)ere* on the Way to Becoming an Epistemic Verb

The difference of the syntactic structure of this construction (16, 17, 18) compared to that of the previous one (11), derives from the introduction of the clitic *se* which may be reanalyzed as the impersonal *se* or as the lexical *se*. However, the order and role of their constituents is retained.

(16) […] todo esto   *sekere*   *aparejado* de erev shabat.[26]   JSp.
     […] all this   *se require*-3.SG   *prepared*-MASC-SG from Erev Shabbat.
     […] Todo esto hay que prepararlo/tiene que ser preparado antes de Erev Shabbat.   Sp.
     […] all this must be prepared before Erev Shabbat.
(17) […] el agua […]   *sekere*   *traida* de erev shabat davka.[27]   JSp.
     […] the water-FEM-SG […]   *se require*-3.SG *brought*-FEM-SG from Erev Shabbat
                                                         precisely.
     […] el agua[…], hay que prepararla/tiene que ser traida antes Erev Shabat
     precisamente.   Sp.
     […] the water […] it should be brought/has to be brought precisely before
     Erev Shabbat.
(18) En la gordura […] ay en eya unas entranyas pretas […] y *sekere* muy *badkada*.[28] JSp.
     In the grease-FEM-SG […] there is in it black entrails […] and *se require*-3.SG
     very *examined*-FEM-SG

En la gordura […] hay en ella unas cavidades negras […] y tiene que/necesita ser   Sp.
examinada muy bien.
In the grease […] there are black cavities […] and it [the grease] should/need
to be examined very well.

If the sentence is interpreted as impersonal, *se* is taken to represent the subject. Therefore the verb may not agree with *todo esto* (16), *el agua* (17), and *la gordura* (18), which may play the role of internal arguments focalized and, therefore, placed pre-verbal. The replacement of the agent nominative that the verb *k(i)erer* selects by *se* "lowers transitivity, because it renders the subject of the clause indefinite and non-referential with an accompanying generic of habitual reading of the process denoted by the verb" (Clements 2006: 248–249). This may mitigate the strong suggestion expressed by the speaker in relation to the hearer.

The possibility of interpreting *se* as lexical—and consequently merged with *k(i)ere*[29]—would allow the identification of a subject-verb agreement in these sentences in which the information about its modality would also be lexical provided through the lexicalization of *sek(i)ere* as a single element. Therefore, only the context and the intonation might provide the hearer with their correct meaning. However, we observe that some sentences (16, 17), whether we interpret them as active or passive, admit only a deontic interpretation. They not only give information about a particular need, but the performance of an action ('to bring water') until a determined time point (always before Erev Shabbat) is required. The agent, who would carry out the action, is not described, but it is clear that only a human agent is able to do it. This ambiguity by the syntactic role of the nominal argument triggered new changes, whose motivation may be also in the surface similarity between the impersonal-*se* and the lexical-*se* sentences and, consequently, in the unclear syntactic role of *se*.

2.1.7. The Impersonal Phrasal *se k(i)ere* + PART. + DO Internal Argument as a Way of Expressing Directive Deontic Modality of Attenuate Obligation in Spoken Judeo-Spanish

In this construction (19, 20), the verb shows default 3.SG agreement with the non-agentive DO internal argument, and *se*, which now occupies the canonical subject position, is a "minimal argument" being assigned null case. The participle gives the action a perfective-resultative value in the temporal posteriority focused from the moment on the enunciation. The nominal argument occupies its unmarked position of DO, and the sentence may easily be read as impersonal and active. The possibility of alternating the participle with an adjective is excluded. Furthermore, the fixed order of the constituents is another characteristic of this construction in which the introduction of an element between the impersonal modal verb and the participle is not allowed. Thus, the possibility of a restrictive interpretation of the meaning of the DO—because of its agreement with the participle—is not possible, also through the fact that it does not form part of the same constituent.

(19) […] *se kiere*   *fecho*   todo.[30]   JSp.
     […] *se require*-3.SG   done-MASC-SG   all-MASC-SG
     […] hay que hacerlo todo.   Sp.
     […] all things have to be done.

(20) […] *se kere*   *estudiadas*   las lisiones.[31]   JSp.
     […] *se require*-3.SG   studied-FEM-PL   the lessons-FEM-PL
     […] hay que estudiar las lecciones.   Sp.
     […] one must study the lessons.

This means that the construction recovers the syntactic elements that the transitive verb *k(i)erer* ('wants') selects: subject and DO, and the meaning of the sentence is one of obligation. *Se kere* is grammaticalized as an epistemic verb,[32] and the participle—which agrees with the DO—provides the lexical meaning, with the perfective aspect and resultative value setting the action in the future. *Se* is taken to represent the subject (with indefinite meaning), while *todo* (19) and *las lisiones* (20) are direct objects. Therefore, the verb does not agree with the DO internal argument.

The concealment of the agent nominative—as shown in sentences (19) and (20)—occurs in syntax and semantics, but they are not impersonal from the pragmatic point of view. The characterization of this construction is recognized for its sense of impersonal obligation. But since the agent-hearer who is indirectly invited to be responsible for carrying out the action that the speaker encoded in the participle is of perfective aspect and of resultative value, the degree of involvement of the supposed agent-hearer does not decrease, although it is not made explicit through any lexical category.

The grammaticalization of this syntactic structure as a modal locution of deontic modality was facilitated by (a) the fixed constituents order—made manifest in the close relationship of dependency between *se k(i)ere* and the participle belonging to a single constituent; (b) the order of the constituents itself (*se k(i)ere* + PART. + DO (N/NP) + [non-mandatory] ADV.) which is also found in other periphrastic locutions; and (c) the conciseness of the sentence.

Returning to the first locution described at the beginning of this chapter (1, 2, 3), it must be said that it is a variant of the last (19, 20). Both are necessarily interactive, so they are commonly used in oral conversational speech. But they may also be found in written literature, especially in the representation of dialogues. From the syntactic point of view, the difference between them is determined by the context in discourse. Usually, when the DO has already been mentioned in the preceding sentence, its coreferentiality is expressed through the corresponding clitic. Because a participle does not support postponement of a clitic, and also it is not possible to prepend it to the impersonal-*se* or separate this from the verb, this possibility does not exist. Therefore, sentences introduced by *se k(i)ere* + PART. without DO always refer to rhematic information.

2.1.8. Conclusion

In this section, I have tried to show the documented changes followed by a construction copied from Portuguese by speakers of Judeo-Spanish and reanalyzed as a passive periphrastic infinitival construction switching to an active NP-object clause up to the development of (a) a new locution in Judeo-Spanish consisting of the impersonal phrasal *se k(i)ere* + PART. + DO and its contextual variant *se k(i)ere* + PART. as a way of expressing deontic modality; (b) an epistemic verb (*se k(i)ere*); and (c) a discourse marker of evidentiality (*no se k(i)ere dicho*). These outcomes are consequences of a gradual process of reanalysis and grammaticalization that was triggered not only because the syntactic structure of the sentence was copied from Portuguese—unknown in Judeo-Spanish—but also by the semantic ambiguity that arose from the different referential substance with which the heterophonic verb *querer* was loaded in each of the two related languages. As has been said above, this change has had an impact on Judeo-Spanish as a whole.

2.2. The *o que* wh-operator

The second case I shall address here concerns the *luke* [luʼke] wh-operator. A grammatical form calqued from Portuguese is the structural element *o que* wh-operator, first translated word-for-word through the heterophone *lu ke* (Sp. *lo que*) into Judeo-Spanish, whose function was that of a relative pronoun. The accommodation of this wh-operator involved other morpho-syntactical and semantical alterations which led to the reanalysis of the complex relative [lu][ki] to a gender unmarked and non-inflected allomorph [ʻluki] of the relative pronoun *ki* in Judeo-Spanish spoken in the Sephardic western communities of the Balkans (Quintana 2006a: 395; 2014: 86).

2.2.1. The *luke* wh-operator (Port. *o que*)

In Portuguese, *o que* [– human] and [± animate] introduces interrogative clauses in which the interrogative constituent bears the nuclear stress and may be classified as the expression of a type of narrow focus (Brito 2003: 464). Judeo-Spanish sentences (21, 22, 23, 24) are partially direct interrogatives introduced by *luke* [– human] and [– animate], in which it is a single morpheme,[33] discursively not linked, which is the focus of the interrogation, as in Portuguese.

(21) *Luke*   fazes?   JSp. (north & west)
     O que   fazes/estas fazendo?   Port.
     ¿Qué haces?   Sp.
     What are you doing?

(22) Eh, novia, *luke* pensas?[34]   JSp. (north & west)
     Ei, noiva, *o que* pensas?   Port.
     Eh, novia, *¿qué* piensas?   Sp.
     Hey bride, what do you think?

(23) Estu ki tengu a la manu,   *lu kue* es?[35]   JSp (Bitola)
     Isto que tenho na mão,   *o que* é?   Port.
     Esto que tengo en la mano, *¿qué* es?   Sp.
     This which I have in my hand, what is it?

(24) *Lukue* keri il rey di mi?[36]   JSp. (Bitola)
     O que deseja o rei de mim?   Port.
     ¿Qué quiere el rey de mí?   Sp.
     What does the king want of me?

In Spanish, this type of interrogative is expressed only by the wh-operator *qué*, which can also be followed by a noun phrase forming with it a constituent (Contreras 1999: 1937) in order to ask for an individual from a group. In Judeo-Spanish, *luke* does not admit any noun phrase, and therefore cannot be used as a deictic, also coinciding with the use of *o que* wh-operator in Portuguese.

As in Portuguese (Brito 2003: 475), in Judeo-Spanish partial direct interrogative clauses introduced by *luke* (21, 22, 23, 24) may also be interpreted as echo wh-interrogatives, in which the speaker reveals strangeness or surprise at information conveyed in the previous speech, or shows that he or she did not fully learn the information. These interpretations are associated with different intonation curves.

As a wh-operator *luke* emerges in Judeo-Spanish also in partial indirect interrogative clauses dependent on a transitive verb with unknown antecedents (25, 26, 27), in the same way that *o que* introduces this type of clause in Portuguese. This occurs because the partial indirect interrogative sentence is repeated in the free relative clause depending on the main verb.

(25) La kandela nun arilunbra, nun se *luke* ki aga …?[37]   JSp. (north & west)
     La vela no alumbra, no sé *qué* (es lo que) quiere que haga …   Sp.
     A vela não ilumina, eu não sei *o que* tu queres que eu faça … Port.
     The candle does not shine, (I) do not know what (you want) me to do?

(26) Save *luke* le vo arogar?[38]   JSp. (north & west)
     ¿Sabe (Usted) *qué* le voy a pedir?   Sp.
     Sabe *o que* é que eu lhe vou pedir?   Port.
     Do you know what I'm going to ask you?

(27) Yo li dimandi *luke* el dimandava?³⁹   JSp. (north & west)
    (Yo) le pregunté ¿*qué (era lo que)* preguntaba él?   Sp.
    Perguntei-lhe *o que* ele perguntou?   Port.
    I asked him, what did he ask?

It should be remembered that the syntactic structure of partial indirect interrogative clauses, such as in (26) and (27), may also be found in Spanish (28, 29), where *lo* should be interpreted as the antecedent of free or semi-free relative clauses introduced by *que*. Therefore, their meaning is not entirely equivalent to these Judeo-Spanish *luke* sentences since *lo* as determiner of *que* adds to the sentence a degree of determination on the queried matter (cf. Keniston 1937: 150; RAE 2010: 837, 848).

In Modern Judeo-Spanish, partial indirect interrogative and semi-free relative clauses with non-expressed subjects may have the same syntactic structure, and the only formal difference between them lies in the element that introduces the subordinate clause: the former are introduced by the wh-operator *luke* (26, 27), an indivisible morpheme after undergoing a process of reanalysis; the latter (28, 29) are introduced by the relative pronoun *ki* (unstressed) preceded by the demonstrative pronoun *lu* (unstressed). These forms are a consequence of the raising of [e] and [o] in unstressed syllables (Quintana 2014: 84–85). With this phonetic change, the ambiguity between the two constructions, which could have affected the activity of the hearer, would have been disposed of in Judeo-Spanish.

(28) ¿Sabe usted *lo que* le voy a pedir?   Sp.
    Savi *luki* li vo arogar?   JSp. (north & west)
    Sabes *o que*/que cousa eu lhe vou pedir?   Port.
    Do you know what I am going to ask him?

(29) Yo le pregunté *lo que* él preguntaba.   Sp.
    Yo li dimandi *luki* el dimandava.   JSp. (north & west)
    Perguntei-lhe *o que* ele perguntava?   Port.
    I asked him the same thing he asked.

The question is whether *lu* as an inflected element that acts as the antecedent of the relative *ki* or *ki*—in the presence of *lu*—has also undergone a process of reanalysis and become an uninflected single morpheme whose function is that of relative pronoun.

As in Castilian (Contreras 1999: 1950), Judeo-Spanish constructions such as (29) admit an interpretation in which "luki el dimandava" is a referential expression. But, contrary to Castilian—in which *lo* and *que* can be split by means of the words *mismo* and *único* (Contreras 1999: 1950; RAE 2010: 850), the splitting of *luki* seems not to be possible in Judeo-Spanish.⁴⁰

Luke as a wh-operator emerges even in pseudo-cleft interrogative sentences (30), especially when the verb of the main clause is *saver* or another verb belonging to *verba dicendi* and *sciendi*:

(30) Savi *luke* es ki li vo arogar? JSp. (north & west)
    ¿Sabe (usted) *qué* es lo que le voy a pedir? Sp.
    Do you know what it is that I'm going to ask you?

Precisely the Judeo-Spanish interrogative pseudo-cleft clause, which depends on an affirmative or negative main clause with the verb *saver*, coincides with the Portuguese construction (31). But when in the Portuguese equivalent construction the verb of the main clause is *perguntar* (JSp. *demandar*), *que* is not interchangeable with *o que* (32). It should be remembered that also Castilian allows only the morpheme *qué* in these subordinate interrogatives.

(31) [...] nu se *luke* es ki tjeni Mamiku.[41] JSp. (north & west)
    [...] no sé *qué* es lo que tiene M. Sp.
    [...] eu não sei *o que* é que a M. tem. Port.
    [...] I do not know what it is that M. has.

(32) Preguntei *que* é que os meus amigos fizeram.[42] Port.
    Dimandi *luke* es ki mis amigus fizierun. JSp. (north & west)
    Pregunté *qué* es lo que hicieron mis amigos. Sp.
    I asked what it is that my friends did.

As was already noted above, this shows that *luke* is an indivisible morpheme which, as a wh-operator, has replaced *ke* (Sp. *qué*) in discursively unlinked interrogative clauses, in which it is the focus of the interrogation. This fact is further supported by the inability to split up the *luke* sequence by the presence of a preposition, and by its emergence after prepositions in interrogative clauses (33, 34, 35):

(33) I por *luke* sera ke no kere (akordarse)?[43] JSp. (north & west)
    Y, ¿por *qué* será que no quiere (acordarse)? Sp.
    And why is it that he does not want (to remember)?

(34) In *lukue* travajatis ki ti kansatis?[44] JSp. (Bitola)
    ¿En *qué* trabajaste que te cansaste? Sp.
    At what did you work that you became [so] tired?

(35) Kun *lukue* keris ki ti mati?[45] JSp. (Bitola)
    ¿Con *qué* quieres, que te mate? Sp.
    With what do you want me to kill you?

2.2.2. *Luki* in Relative Constructions

Let us now see the behavior of *luki* in some relative constructions. In pseudo-cleft sentences, Judeo-Spanish shows also the same grammatical structure as Portuguese, both in wh-clefts (36) and it-clefts (37). As in Portuguese and Spanish, reduplication of the antecedent of the relative *ki* occurs when the relative is placed cataphorically, which should explain the lack of *lu* in it-clefts (37). Judeo-Spanish,

HISTORICAL OVERVIEW AND OUTCOME | 69

contrary to what occurs in Spanish, does not allow the reduplication of the antecedent of *ki* in it-cleft clauses. This is also the behavior of the relative pronoun in true it-clefts (38):

(36) *Lukue* vus arrogu es un kushiniku di dukadus [...][46]   JSp. (Bitola)
 Lo que te pido es un cojín pequeño (lleno) de ducados [...]   Sp.
 O que eu te peço é uma almofada pequena com ducados [...]   Port.
 What I ask you for is a small cushion (full) of ducats [...]

(37) Un kushiniku di dukadus [...] es *ki* vus arrogu.   JSp. (Bitola)
 Un cojín pequeño (lleno) de ducados [...] es *lo que* te pido.   Sp.
 Uma almofada pequena com ducados [...] é *que* eu te peço.   Port.
 A small cushion (full) of ducats [...] is what I ask you for.

(38) Es un kushiniku di dukadus [...] *ki* vus arrogu.   JSp. (Bitola)
 Es un cojín pequeño (lleno) de ducados [...] *lo que* te pido.   Sp.
 É uma almofada pequena com ducados [...] *que* eu te peço.   Port.
 It is a small cushion (full) of ducats [...] that I ask you for.

As in Spanish, the relative *ki* (Sp. *que*) preceded by *lu* (Sp. *lo*) appears also in relative clauses with an antecedent of low referential substance (*todu*, 39):

(39) Manyane ya vus kontu todu *lukue* mi paso oy.[47]   JSp. (Bitola)
 Mañana ya os cuento todo *lo que* me pasó hoy.   Sp.
 Tomorrow I'll already tell you everything that happened to me today.

But, as was shown above (38), true it-clefts do not allow an inflected element as an antecedent of *ki* when the correlative expressed antecedent consists of a nominal clause (see also 37, 38, 40a, 40b). However, when the relative pronoun is coreferential to an expressed postcedent (36), when its antecedent is not expressed (40c, 40d), or it is an element of low referential substance, such as *todu* (39), Judeo-Spanish requires *luki* as a relative pronoun.

(40) Las tres kozes son *ki*[40a] keru yo ki mi diges—la prime es
 une koze *ki*[40b] no tengu vistu. La sigunde es *lukue*[40c]
 no tengu kumidu. La di tres es lukue[40d] no tengu sintidu.[48]   JSp. (Bitola)

 Tres cosas son *las que* quiero yo que me digas: la primera es
 una cosa *que* no haya visto. La segunda es *algo que* no haya
 comido. La tercera es *algo que* no haya oído nunca.   Sp.

 Three things are what I want you to tell me—the first is
 one thing that I have not seen. The second is something that
 I have not eaten. The third is something I have never heard before.

That is, *luki* appears in complementary distribution to *ki* in relative clauses. These sentences show also that *ki* is an element that does not accept inflection. This is because, in the presence of the clitic *lu*, under the influence of the interrogative *luke* in sentences with the same or similar syntactic structure (semi-free relatives, especially when the verb of the main clause is *saver* or belongs to *verba dicendi* and *sciendi*, and wh-clefts), *ki* underwent also a process of reanalysis—namely, *luki* forms a continuous constituent in which *lu* is interpreted as an invariable element in Judeo-Spanish varieties spoken in the communities of the northern and western Balkans.

Ambiguity between partial indirect interrogative clauses dependent on a transitive verb with unknown antecedents (24) and free or semi-free relative clauses (41) takes place also in Portuguese (Brito and Duarte 2003: 678–680).

(24) *Lukue* keri il rey di mi?　　　　　　　　　　　　　　JSp. (Bitola)
　　　O que quer o rei de mim?　　　　　　　　　　　　　　Port.
　　　¿*Qué* quiere el rey de mí?　　　　　　　　　　　　　　Sp.
　　　What does the king want of me?

(41) Ombri, muzotrus nun savemus *lu kue* queri il rey di ti.[49]　　JSp. (Bitola)
　　　O homem, não sabemos *o que* o rei quer de ti.　　　　　Port.
　　　Hombre, nosotros no sabemos *qué* (es lo que) quiere el rey de ti.　Sp.
　　　Well, we do not know what the king wants from you.

In Portuguese *o que* is a single morpheme in interrogative clauses, which commutes with *que* in certain circumstances, but cannot happen when *o que* introduces a free finite relative clause (Brito and Duarte 2003: 682). It seems that when it is not an interrogative morpheme, in the presence of *o*, *que* may undergo a process of reanalysis—namely, *o que* may form a continuous constituent. If this happens, *o*, which is a clitic, is interpreted as an invariable neutral element. If reanalysis does not take place, *o*, being masculine and singular, may be interpreted as an element that admits flexion—that is, as a demonstrative pronoun and as the antecedent of the relative—followed by *que* (Brito and Duarte 2003: 682–683). By contrast, in Judeo-Spanish, *luke*, after undergoing reanalysis, became invariable in partial indirect interrogative clauses with unknown antecedents, and in relative clauses *luki* became a contextual allomorph of the relative *ki*.

2.2.3. Conclusion

In conclusion, this analysis has shown that contact with Portuguese speakers led to the replacement of the *ke* wh-mark *luke* in Judeo-Spanish spoken in the western communities of the Balkans. The calque of the Portuguese *o que* wh-operator[50] into Judeo-Spanish triggered some morphological and structural syntactic changes: *lu ke* reanalyzed to a single morpheme not only replaced the Judeo-Spanish *ke* wh-mark inherited from Castilian, but engendered also the reanalysis of the relative pronoun *ki*, preceded by the neutral determiner *lu*, giving rise to a new contextual variant of the relative pronoun.

The characteristics that the wh-operator *luke* ([– human] and [– animate], simple constituent, discursively not linked and null subject) in interrogative clauses shared with the neutral determiner *lu* ([– human] and [– animate] without antecedent or with elements carrying low information), followed by *ki* in relative clauses facilitated the reanalysis of *ki*. After the reanalysis, *ki* constitutes a single complex with *lu* ([lu] [ki] → [luki]), complementary to the morpheme *ki* (Sp. *que*) [± human] and [± animate]. In the distribution of their function as relative pronouns, *ki* seems to be the only one that may accept an antecedent consisting of a noun phrase, while *luki* may introduce semi-free relative clauses or relative clauses with an antecedent not expressed or loaded with low referential substance. The loss of gender by the neutral *lu* in this grammatical context seems to be related to the low frequency of use of the relative *ki* preceded by masculine and feminine determiners in Judeo-Spanish.

The phonic analogy of the Portuguese *o que* wh-operator to the complex element formed by the relative pronoun *ke* (stressed), preceded by the neutral determiner *lu*, not only facilitated the reanalysis of *ke* to a continuous constituent [luke], but also its diffusion into Judeo-Spanish as a wh-operator. As a result of this change, the syntactic structure of partial indirect interrogative clauses coincided with that of the semi-free relative clauses introduced by *ki* (unstressed) and preceded by the neutral element *lu*. This parallelism triggered new morpho-syntactical alterations through the reanalysis of the complex relative [lu][ki] to a gender unmarked and non-inflected morpheme ['luki], which seems to have become a contextual allomorph of the relative *ki*. This change was undoubtedly also facilitated by an internal tendency of the Judeo-Spanish spoken in the western communities of the Balkans, given the low frequency of use of the complex relative pronouns [il] [ki] and [la] [ki]. All this confirms that pre-existing structural similarity between languages in contact is "conducive to diffusion of both forms and patterns" (Aikhenvald 2006: 32).

2.3. The Inflected Infinitive

The last grammatical issue for discussion refers to the inflected infinitive, one of the several features that characterize the nearly extinct local variety of Bitola (also spoken in Pristina from 1863 until 1992).

Portuguese—with Galician and Mirandese (Jansegers and Vanderschueren 2010; Merlan 2007: 34)—has the characteristic of allowing a subject from inside the infinitive clauses, which may be preponed or postponed to the infinitive. In the so-called inflected infinitive, conjugated infinitive or "infinitivo pessoal," the subject is always postponed to the verb and it is manifested in inflected verbal morphemes carrying the categories of person and number, and occurs only in embedded clauses. Otherwise, its function is identical to non-inflected infinitives.

(Koptjevskaja-Tamm 1999: 146; Vincent 1999: 355). A sentence such as (42) would be unacceptable in Spanish:

(42) a.*El presidente afirmó ser*en* esas actividades útiles para el país.
    b. El presidente afirmó ser esas actividades útiles para el país.[51]

The difference between the two preceding sentences (42) is that the infinitive *ser* does not carry the person and number morpheme *-en* in the role of subject (42b), as occurs in (42a), and may occur in Portuguese (43):

(43) O presidente afirmou ser*em* essas actividades úteis para o país.[52]
    The president stated *to be*-3.PL these activities useful for the country.
    The president stated that these activities were useful for the country.

In Spanish, however, the subject of the infinitive can only be a lexical element (*esas actividades*), another way, which also allows Portuguese speakers to express the explicit internal subject of the infinitive (*essas actividades*), even if it is the only one in many infinitive clauses. According to Vanderschueren (2013: 116–123), this last possibility is mandatory when the verb refers strictly to verbal events, without reference to any participant, when the infinitive is in the passive sense or belongs to the so-called imperative infinitives. Inflection of the infinitive is always necessary (a) with a notional specified subject that is not indicated in its immediate context, (b) with generic subjects that defy interpretation, and (c), in modern Portuguese, even when the infinitive is combined with an explicit nominative subject (43). But, in most cases, one or the other pattern depends on lexical-semantic, discursive and morpho-syntactic factors (for example, in adverbial clauses the infinitive tends to be inflected).

The Judeo-Spanish infinitive lacks personal morphological markers, as in other Spanish varieties, however the inflected infinitive was detected in the variety spoken in Bitola and in this closely related variety of Pristina.[53] Sentences (44, 45, 46, 47) are examples of the Judeo-Spanish spoken in Bitola in the latter years of the twenties of the 20th century, in which the inflected infinitive is documented:

(44) Pur ser*is*   dis-hinadu, ti cayi il pantalón.[54]   Sp. (Bitola)
    By *to be*-2.SG careless in dress [you], drop your pants.
    Por ser descuidado en el vestir, te cae el pantalón.   Sp.
    Your pants are falling because you are careless in dress.

(45) Pur trayer*is*   pan, peshi trayis.[55]   JSp. (Bitola)
    By *to bring*-2.PL bread [you], fish bring.
    Por traer pan, traes pescado.   Sp.
    You bring fish instead of bread.

(46) Si stan maraviyandu di   ver*in*   el tipsin solu a la meze.[56]   JSp. (Bitola)
    They are amazing of   *to see*-3.PL   the tray alone on the table.

	Están asombrandos de ver solo la bandeja en la mesa.	Sp.
	They are amazed to see only the tray on the table.	

(47) Ke non me eches en olvido de me mandare*s* letras.[57]   JSp. (Bitola)
     Do not forget of me   *to send*-2.SG letters.
     Que no te olvides de mandarme cartas.   Sp.
     Do not forget to send me letters.

In Bitola's Judeo-Spanish, the inflected infinitive is restricted to infinitive clauses introduced by a preposition.[58] Therefore, the contextual conditions under which the personal inflections are added to the infinitive—which facilitate formally unveiling its internal subject—are much more limited in Bitola's Judeo-Spanish than in European Portuguese. Another limitation is that the inflected infinitive seems to be limited to intransitive verbs such as *ser*, *estar*, *salir*, *entrar*, etc.

The inflected infinitive in adverbial clauses is also documented in Bible translations of the 16th century (48):[59]

(48) […] 'ad hiʃʃāmedāx.   (Deut. 28, 24; 28, 51 [Heb.])
     […] hasta *seeres* destruido   (*Penta*, 1547)
     […] until *to be*-2.SG destroyed
     […] hasta que perezcas/hasta destruirte   (Biblia Valera, 1602 [Sp.])

Later Sephardic Bible translations always show a non-inflected infinitive inherited from Castilian in such reduced clauses, i.e. "asta destruirte"[60] [PREP. + INF. + *se*-2.SG-ACC.]. It is also documented in Sephardic texts written in the sixties of the 16th century by rabbis of the Sephardic elite (49, 50, 51).

(49) […] por   ser*en*   ambas açerca de cozas grandes.   (RV, 35)
     […] because   *to be*-3.PL both about great things.
     […] por tratar ambas de cosas importantes.   Sp.
     […] because they are both about important things.

(50) […] muchos ombres que por   ser*en* engratos […]   (HhL, 27)
     […] many humans, who because   *to be*-3.PL ungrateful […]
     […] muchos hombres que por ser ingratos […]   Sp.
     […] many men, who, because they are ungrateful […]

(51) […] ya se a espirmentado en muchas no   ser*en* platicas […]   (MA, 3)
     […] already been experienced in many not   *to be*-3.PL practical […]
     […] ya se ha experimentado en muchas que no son prácticas […]   Sp.
     […] it has already been experienced that many of them are not practical […]

Other documents show also that the inflected infinitive was a fairly common feature in the minutes of the rabbinical courts. Example (52) is part of a testimony given by a Sephardi man before 1589, and transcribed by the secretary of the rabbinical court of Salonica:[61]

(52) […] y que […] fall[a]ba por su escrito ser*en* las *qe(hillot)* Resp.
[…] and that […] [s/he] found by his writing *to be*-3.PL the holy
[…] y que […] hallaba por su escrito que las comunidades santas Sp.
[…] and that […] he found, according to his writing, that the holy

qe(došot) en débito a él más de tre(s) mil áspe(ros) […]
communities in debt to him for more than three thousand aspers […]
estaban en deuda con él por más de los tres mil ásperos […]
communities were in debt to him for more than three thousand aspers […]

Clauses (49, 50) are expressed without the verb inflection or as that-clauses [QUE porque + V$_{FINITO}$] in Spanish. Clauses (51, 52) are always susceptible to being commuted to [QUE + V$_{FINITO}$], and this possibility existed also in Judeo-Spanish in the 16th century:

(51′) […] ya se a espirmentado en muchas *que no son platicas* […]

(52′) […] que fallaba por su escrito *que las qe(hillot) qe(došot) eran en débito a él más de tre(s) mil áspe(ros)* […]

The use of the inflected infinitive seems to have been a fairly common feature among the Sephardim in the 16th century, and not only among the rabbis, as example (54) will show. This should induce us to raise the question about how long it continued to be used among the Sephardim, and, regarding the community of Bitola, whether the inflected infinitive continued to be used there from the 16th century or whether it was transferred from Portuguese speakers after 1740 when an important group of Portuguese Jews—who had previously lived in Valona and Berat (Albania)—moved to Bitola (Arbell 2002a, 2002b). In the absence of research on the matter, I have already suggested (Quintana 2015: 185) that

> the arrival of this group of Jews, numerically important and of a marked sociological nature, led to the levelling of dialectal differences, i.e., among the local Judeo-Spanish speakers and the Portuguese fugitives, who spoke Portuguese mixed with Castilian and Italian elements.

It seems obvious that the fact that this feature has had to compete with that inherited from Castilian—in which only a lexical subject is the way to express explicitly the internal argument of the infinitive—has had consequences for the formation of Judeo-Spanish, i.e., the variant with inflected infinitive was rejected in Judeo-Spanish. The fact that the eastern varieties allow only (pseudo)reflexive and reciprocal pronouns enclitics to the infinitive as in modern Spanish undoubtedly contributed to the rejection of the variant transferred from Portuguese. However, in the western varieties, Salonica included, the proclitic placement of the pronouns—as in medieval Spanish and modern Portuguese—coexisted with the other variant. The Bitola variety belongs to the second group.

Beyond this, in example (53), quoted from the same testimony, we find the word *-mos* (Sp. *nosotros*) linked to the infinitive *ir* in the clause [de + INF. + *se*] of the first sentence, and to *salir* in the clause [para + INFLECTED INF.] of the second sentence:

(53) […] determinamos junta mente de ir*mos* en caza de dito Reuvén y mirar su escrito,
[…] [we] determined together   to go *se*-1.PL to [the] home of Reuven and see his writing,
[…] determinamos irnos juntos a casa del fulano dicho y mirar su escrito,
[…] we determined to go together to the said fellow's home and look at his writing,

y ver si se averdaderían sus p[a]labra(s) para salir*mos* de su cargo,
and verify if one could confirm his words   to come-1.PL of his charge […]
y verificar si sus palabras eran ciertas con el fin de retirar nosotros los cargos contra él,
and to verify if his words may be confirmed in order to cancel our charges against him,

por lo cual fuimos en su caza   y   *nos* estregó el cuaderno […]
for which reason we went to his house, and he gave us the notebook […]
por lo cual fuimos a su casa   y   *nos* entregó el cuaderno […]
for which reason we went to his house, and he gave us the notebook […]

I am interpreting *mos* in the first sentence as a case of aspectual *se* because it is widely documented in Judeo-Spanish texts of the 16th century. In the second sentence, however, *salirmos* is a single unit in which *-mos* is the personal flexion of the verb.

My assumption is that the emergence of the verbal ending *-mos* in the same morpho-syntactical context in which the personal object pronoun *nos* may also be found might have led to an ambiguous interpretation between the two similar clauses. My suggestion is that the verbal inflection *-mos* was interpreted also as the clitic personal pronoun [INF. + nos] by a section of Judeo-Spanish speakers, giving rise to the replacement of the clitic form *nos* by *mos* in this syntactic context. Later, *mos* extended also to the clitic preverbal position, as it occurred in Mirandese.

The change of the clitic pronoun *nos* to *mos* has been usually explained as a phonetic change influenced by the possessive *muestro* in which the labialization of the nasal [n] in contact with [we] took place. My assumption is that the labialization of the nasal [n] in contact with [we] is the outcome of an independent phonetic change unrelated to the replacement of *nos* by *mos*:

a. Example (53) shows that *nos* was still the form of the preverbal clitic in 16th century Judeo-Spanish, and that this is the general norm in most texts written in this period.[62] However, it is virtually impossible to find the pronoun *nos* postponed to the infinitive, because *mos* already occupies that position.

b. The structural overlap between adverbial clauses with an inflected infinitive and an infinitive with the postponed clitic pronoun triggered by *mos* also occurred when the form bound to the verb—especially to *ser*—was *se* (54):

(54) [...] le truxeron una *zoná goyá*   para ser*se metam'é* con eya.[63]   Resp.
    [...] [they] brought him a whore non-Jewish   *to be*-3.SG impure with her.
    [...] le trajeron una prostituta no judía para que fuera impuro con ella.   Sp.
    [...] they brought him a non-Jewish whore for him to lie with her.

This example, extracted from a document written by members of a Portuguese family, shows the use of *se*-3.SG in the role of an inflectional personal morpheme of the infinitive, where Portuguese—and also Galician and Mirandese – has -Ø. Through this example we can see that the form of the clitic personal pronoun 3.SG has also acquired the function of infinitive personal mark instead of -Ø. This emphasizes once again the ambiguity that has arisen through the overlap of these adverbial constructions. The evidence of the last example suggests also that the structural overlap affected the speech of Portuguese speakers who had learned Judeo-Spanish.

Table 1. Inflected infinitive in Judeo-Spanish and Western Ibero-Romance languages

	Portuguese	Galician	Mirandese[64]	16th century written Judeo-Spanish; 20th Bitola
1. SG	*partir-Ø*	*partir-Ø*	*partir-Ø*	*partir-Ø*
2. SG	*partir-es*	*partir-es*	*partir-es*	*partir-es*
3. SG	*partir-Ø*	*partir-Ø*	*partir-Ø*	*partir-se*
1. PL	*partir-mos*	*partir-mos*	*partir-mos*	*partir-mos*
2. PL	(*partir-des*)	*partir-des*	*partir-des*	(*partir-[des/desh]*)
3. Pl	*partir-em*	*partir-en*	*partir-en*	*partir-en*

The ambiguous interpretation of the 3.SG and 1.PL persons of the infinitive paradigm should have caused its rejection in most varieties, and led only to the phonic replacement of the personal pronoun *nos* by *mos*. We should remember that in the Judeo-Spanish spoken in the Eastern communities such as Istanbul, Edirne or Izmir, the (pseudo)reflexive and reciprocal pronouns only support the enclitic position in adverbial infinitive clauses introduced by a preposition, a syntactic factor that should have contributed decisively to the rejection of the option that the inflected infinitive variant offered.

4. CONCLUSION

Returning to the questions posed at the beginning of this chapter, I can state that hybridity and heterogeneity are characteristic for Judeo-Spanish. The development of the three analyzed patterns stresses it clearly. The question that arises here is that of the transmission path of these patterns, which show specific examples of contact-induced language changes.

Thomason and Kaufman (1988: 44) argued that prestige seems to be irrelevant in cases of dialect transfer, and that as far as the social prestige of Portuguese is concerned, it seems not to have been relevant in selecting the material transferred to Judeo-Spanish. However, the prestige of Castilian among members of the first two generations of the expellees, and the Sephardic identity-defining role later assigned to Judeo-Spanish, makes it clear that the degree of prestige assigned by Iberian Jews to each language was an important factor in determining language shift.[65] Cultural pressure from the dominant Castilian group led to a rapid shift to the social dominant language, and consequently, the abandoned languages as spoken by the different groups died (Quintana 2015: 188). The transfers of patterns such as *querer-se* + PART. in active sentences and the inflected infinitive to Judeo-Spanish took place in this sociolinguistic context.

When Portuguese speakers shifted to Judeo-Spanish, they acquired the bulk of the target language's grammatical structure along with the vocabulary. In those situations of large-scale shift, the shift brought about change because it was imperfect (Ross 2001: 157–158), and several of the grammatical patterns and lexical items that were first transferred from the source language of the shifting speaker groups to the target language were eventually adopted by the whole speech community in its multiplex relationship links with one another.

Systematic similarities deriving from genetic relationship may play a role in facilitating contact-induced transfer. Law (2013: 271) argues that

> the *paradigmatic interchangeability* of particular elements of related languages without the need for adaptation or accommodation, which facilitated the borrowing of various kinds of linguistic material, particularly bound morphemes, that in other contexts have been found to be highly resistant to borrowing,

is particularly more frequent, and is made more important through contact between related languages because "structurally integrated features that are unlikely to be shared through contact in other situations are no more resistant to transfer than other, less structurally embedded features" (ibid. 296). The three analyzed patterns, which obviously belonged to language transfer, were later subjected to gradual processes of reanalysis as a result of the ambiguity arising from overlapping with similar morpho-syntactic structures in specific contexts. In the case of the first two patterns analyzed here, the processes of reanalysis led to gradual changes, while the latter were ultimately rejected.

Although morpho-syntactic changes induced by contact with Portuguese can be found in all varieties of Judeo-Spanish, the higher degree of hybridity as an outcome of long-term contact[66] is also evident in the varieties spoken in the western communities of the Balkan Peninsula, especially in the variety spoken in Bitola. This is related to the contact with the Portuguese Jews living in Venice and other cities of the Italian states, and especially in the cities of the Adriatic Sea until the beginning of the 19th century, who spoke a variety of mixed languages emanating from Castilian, Italian and Portuguese. The transfer of the *o que* wh-operator to the western varieties of Judeo-Spanish should have taken place in this social and linguistic context.

The three analyzed patterns give us also an idea about how Judeo-Spanish was forged, and about how the elements transferred from related languages—such as Portuguese—were imagined and experienced by Sephardim, due to the systematic similarities shared by the two languages. The high degree of overlap in linguistic structure allowed significant interlingual conflation, i.e. the collapsing of language boundaries at points of similarity between the languages (cf. Law 2013), up to the point that linguistic boundaries were fixed after processes of reanalysis and grammaticalization or by the rejection of the borrowings.

NOTES

1. The author is funded by grant 473/11 of the Israel Sciences Foundation (ISF). This work has been carried out within the framework of its project at The Hebrew University of Jerusalem.
2. Anderson (2006: 6) states that "[…] all communities larger than primordial villages of face-to-face contact (and perhaps even these) are imagined. Communities are to be distinguished, not by their falsity/genuineness, but by the style in which they are imagined." Although he primarily dealt with the mechanisms of building the modern nation-state and its emergence, he shows also that religious groups follow similar guidelines and mechanisms (ibid. 12–19).
3. According to Anderson (2006: 45), the creation of "languages-of-power" is a crucial consequence of the development of "print-capitalism"—the invention of printing technology and the distribution of printed books and media in vernacular languages instead of exclusive print languages (i.e., Latin, Arabic, Hebrew; ibid. 44) because it "laid the basis for national consciousness" (ibid. 44), insomuch as vernacular languages had the power, other than the traditional print languages, to create an exclusive and "particular language-field" of people to whom "only those" who were speaking the same kind of language, or at least a similar dialect, could belong. The media, such as books and newspapers, printed in the common vernacular suddenly made people aware of their fellow readers. This is the embryonic stage any imagined community had to go through in order to build an "image of antiquity" (ibid. 44). This, inevitably, progresses to distinguishing between the language of higher status and prestige and languages or dialects that have been "unsuccessful (or only relatively successful) in insisting on their own print-form" (ibid. 45). I use this term with reference only to the internal context of the Ottoman Sephardic communities, since—just as the printing of books in Castilian and other European vernaculars laid the basis for their national consciousness—printing works in the Sephardic vernacular, rather than only in Hebrew, played a crucial role in the creation of a Sephardic identity to which all Judeo-Spanish speakers belonged regardless of their Jewish origin.

HISTORICAL OVERVIEW AND OUTCOME | 79

4. According to Hall (1990: 235), the "diaspora experience" is defined "by the recognition of a necessary heterogeneity and diversity; by a conception of 'identity' which lives with and through, not despite, difference; by hybridity. Diaspora identities are those which are constantly producing and reproducing themselves anew, through transformation and difference."
5. From here on I shall use the term Judeo-Spanish, rather than Castilian, to refer to the language in which documents of Sephardic authors living in the Ottoman Empire are written, even in the 16th and 17th centuries, considering that a new, relatively stable, linguistic system is only observable first in the texts published after 1729.
6. A "koine" is a regional dialect or language that has arisen as a result of contact between two or more mutually intelligible varieties (dialects) of the same language.
7. Bunis (2008: 421) interprets the term "Sefarad" in the locution "lašon de Sefarad"—used in a Sephardic text published in 1775 in Salonica—as a locative: "Sephardim in the Ottoman Empire occasionally referred to their language as lašón de Sefaraδ [sic] 'language of Sefarad' without necessarily identifying Sefaraδ [sic] with 'Spain', since the term had come to denote any region inhabited by Sephardim, such as the Ottoman Empire." Stechauner (2014: 56) joins this interpretation. I find especially interesting the use of "lašón Sepharad" in Sephardic Hebrew sources from the Ottoman Empire, as well as "lašon de Sefarad" in Judeo-Spanish sources, in which "Sepharad" has no locative referent but an animated collective one, which refers to the people integrated into the communities that comprise the Sephardic Diaspora.
8. Stechauner (2014: 56–59) mentions some of the changes that the Hebrew toponym "Sepharad" underwent throughout history. For the semantic developments of it, see also the philological work by Aslanov (2014).
9. Oesterreicher (2002: 287–288; 2006: 3082–3083).
10. *Shaare Mizrah* 1(1) (29.12.1845), p. 1, apud Bunis (1993: 48). Translation: "And it is already well known that *makaδ <arov>*—the plague of the mixture—fell on the language that we Levantine speak, in which we mixed a lot things from other languages, and we speak differently in each place, so that you will not find speakers of a city that they will speak as in another one. Everyone speaks according to the language that emerged in his city. The reason is that this Spanish language that we speak in Turkey is not learned, neither the grammar nor the vocabulary, but it is ever an inheritance from our forefathers, because the day that our ancestors left Spain, they broke the true Spanish language, and since then everyone is speaking as it is coming to his mouth [...]." The locution "makaδ arov," lit. "plague of the mixture," is an allusion to the fourth of the Ten Plagues, during which, according to the Bible (Exodus 8: 17–20)—an episode also narrated in the Passover Haggadah—the Egyptians were punished by God because Pharaoh would not allow the Jews to leave his kingdom. According to the Jewish traditional interpretation, the *arov* (Heb. *'arov*) was a mixture of wild animals.
11. The high degree of similarity between Leonese, Aragonese and Castilian should be remembered, as well as the dialect continuum that these configured. Furthermore, the linguistic boundary between Castilian and Leonese and between Castilian and Aragonese was already very fuzzy in the late 15th century as a consequence of the rapid advance of Castilian. Because of all these conditions, to assign a concrete origin to each Judeo-Spanish form or pattern is not always easy.
12. Other patterns transferred from Aragonese, as well as a list of words, are available in Quintana (2009).
13. One of those rare references was formulated by R. Abraham Palachi (1809–1899) from Smyrna, who wrote "[...] i el espanyol ke avlamos ke el *shoresh* [roots] es de Portugal, lo tenemos mesklado de otros *leshonot* [languages] komo *italki, arami, sarfati, yevani, latino, sefaradi, aravi, parsi, ashuri, misri vexadome* [...]" ([...] and the Spanish that we speak, whose base is

Portuguese, is mixed with other languages such as Italian, Aramaic, French, Greek, Latin, Spanish, Arabic, Persian, Assyrian, Egyptian, etc. [...]) (Palachi 1862: 71).
14. The deontic modality is associated with social functions of obligation, depending on the directive interaction that the speaker proposes to the hearer through the contents of his or her statement. These statements are definable in terms of the intended perlocutionary effect, given that the request of the speaker is an attempt to get the hearer to do something (Austin 1962; Searle 1969).
15. Wagner (1930: 76).
16. Levi (1933: 2).
17. Papo (1873: 32).
18. Loria (1903: 53).
19. Papo (1873: 49).
20. Papo Bohoreta (1929).
21. Huli (1730).
22. Spitzer (1918: 13).
23. Ibid.; Crews (1935: 233); Wagner (1930: 76).
24. According to Martins (2005), the agreeing *se* construction was a passive construction in Old Portuguese, but it was reanalyzed as an active construction at the end of the Middle Ages.
25. Huli (1730).
26. Papo (1873: 159).
27. Ibid. 78.
28. Ibid. 317.
29. I have not succeeded in finding a single occurrence in modern Judeo-Spanish documents in which the verb *k(i)erer* with *se* may be inflected except in reflexive or reciprocal constructions. In these examples taken from a text written in the 19th century by a Sephardic rabbi of Sarajevo, *sekere* consists of a lexical unit completely lexicalized. The lexicalization of *kererse* with epistemic meaning may also be observed by other syntactic structures: *sekere el sofer que los aga pretos kon tintas kasher*, "It is necessary that the scribe makes them black with kosher ink" (Papo 1873: 128). It is interesting to note that the dictionary of Perez and Pimienta (2007: 243) includes the entry *kererse* with the meaning 'be necessary.' *K(i)ere* with a non-animate nominative expresses also epistemic value.
30. Crews (1979: 136).
31. Judeo-Spanish informant.
32. *Se* with the verb *k(i)erer* in plural retains the value of reflexive and reciprocal pronoun.
33. The lexicalization of *luke* was already mentioned by Schmid and Bürki (2000: 175).
34. Papo Bohoreta (1929).
35. Luria (1930: 29). *Lukue* is a diatopic variant of *luke* which was used in Bitola.
36. Ibid. 76.
37. Papo (1873: 22).
38. Papo Bohoreta (1929).
39. Molière (1903: 35).
40. It is important to mention the preference of Sephardic authors for writing *loke/luke* and *luki* as single words.
41. Buki Romano (1931).
42. This example is given by Brito (2003: 472).
43. Papo Bohoreta (1929).
44. Luria (1930: 72).
45. Ibid. 82.

46. Ibid. 30.
47. Ibid. 23.
48. Ibid. 56.
49. Ibid. 76.
50. This was also suggested by Wagner (1930: 94, note 4), Crews (1935: 184, note 47), Schmid and Bürki (2000: 175, note 40), and Quintana (2006a: 143; 2014: 85–86; 2015: 183–184). The possible relationship between the use of the interrogative pronoun *lo que* by some Argentinean speakers and the Portuguese interrogative *o que* was also mentioned by Kany (1969: 169). On the other hand, Stulic-Etchevers (2007), without taking into account this possibility, interpreted the development of the interrogative *luke* as an internal evolution of the Spanish starting with the relative pronoun.
51. Once corrected, sentence (42b) might only be used in a very formal context. The reason is that a Spanish speaker would usually construct a sentence with a finite verb.
52. This example is quoted in Mensching (2000: 158).
53. In 1863, a group of Sephardic Jews from Bitola moved to the city of Pristina, where this variety was still used by some speakers, at least in the family sphere, up to the virtual disappearance of the community in 1992 as a result of the war that ended with the former Yugoslavia.
54. This example—with another published spelling—comes from tales recorded by Luria (1930: 93).
55. Ibid. 55.
56. Published by Crews (1935: 107).
57. Ibid. 246, § 932).
58. The group of adverbial clauses introduced by a preposition [+ INFLECTED INF.]—semantically equivalent to the subordinating conjunction [CONJ+(QUE) +V$_{SUBJ/IND}$] – has a very high frequency of use in Portuguese (Vázquez 2011: 21).
59. Examples 48, 49, 50 and 51 are quoted in Quintana (2014: 73–74).
60. *Penta* (1739).
61. Examples 52 and 53 are quoted in Várvaro and Minervini (2007: 157). They are part of an oral testimony whose protocol was included in response 393 of Rabbi Medina (1595).
62. So far I have only found the clitic *mos*, both prepended and postponed to the infinitive, in texts written in the second half of the 16th century in the communities of Bitola and Gallipoli.
63. Example quoted in Quintana (2006b: 172), first published in R. Bassan (1737) response 92, though he lived from 1550 to 1625 (Shmuelevitz 1984: 190).
64. For Portuguese, Galician and Mirandese, see Merlan (2007: 34).
65. Ordinary language shift refers to the process whereby a group of persons that speaks a common language or the members of a language community are in contact with another language, and in this situation the target language as a whole is available to them and is, for the most part, already acquired.
66. According to Winford (2003: 11–12), "[…] greater intensity of contact generally means more borrowing, and long-term-contact facilitates the transfer of structural features from one language into the other."

PRIMARY JUDEO-SPANISH SOURCES

Bassan, Yehiel ben Hayim. *Sheelot u-Teshuvot*. Constantinople: Yona Eshkenazi, 5497 [1737].
Buki Romano, Abraham. "Tija Rahila." *Jevrejski Glas* 37–38 (11.09.1931): 8.
HhL: Paquda, Baḥye Ibn. *Sefer Ḥovat ha-Levavot belaaz*. Salonica: s.n., 5329 [1569].

Huli, Yaakov ben Meir. *Sefer Me'am Lo'ez. Bereshit.* Constantinople: Yona Eshkenazi, 5490 [1730].
Loria, Jak. *Dreifus. Drama en sinko aktos i un apoteoz.* Sofia: Tipografia Rahamim Shimon, 1903.
Levi, Moiz. *La ija del bankiero. Romanso de amor i ezmovyente.* Istanbul: Eliya Ğayus, 1933.
MA: Benveniste, Meir ben Shemuel. *Sefer Shulḥan ha-Panim y en ladino Meza de el alma.* Salonica: Yosef ben Ladoni, 5328 (1568).
Medina, Shemuel de. *Sheelot u-Teshuvot me-ha-Rashdam.* Choshen Mishpat section. Salonica: Abraham Migeza Batsheva, 5355 [1595].
Molière, Jean-Baptiste. *El hazino imajinado. Komedia en tres aktos.* Trezladado de el fransez por Sh. Benataf. Sofia: Tipografia Rahamim Shimon, 1903.
Palachi, Abraham. *Sefer Ve-Hoxiach Avraham.* Vol. 2. Salonica: Saadi Halevi Eshkenazi, 5626 [1862].
Papo, Eliezer ben Shem Tov. *Sefer Mesheq Beti.* Sarajevo: Defus Hadasha, 5633 [1873].
Papo Bohoreta, Laura. *Esterka.* [Sarajevo, ms.], 1929.
Penta 1547: *Constantinople Pentateuch.* Constantinople: Eliezer Soncino, 5307.
Penta 1739: *Heleq rishon me-ha-Arbaa ve-Esrim ve-hu-Hamisha Humshe Tora im laaz.* Constantinople: Yona Eshkenazi, 5499.
RV: Almosnino, Moshe ben Baruch. *Sefer Hanhagat Hahayim. Livro entitulado* Regimiento de la vida. Salonica: Yosef Yaabets, 5324 [1564].
Valera, Cypriano. *La Biblia, que es, los sacros del Vieio y Nvevo Testamento: Revista y conferida con los textos Hebreos Y Griegos y con diversas translaciones.* Amsterdam: Casa de Lorenço Iacobi, 1602.

REFERENCES

Aikhenwald, Alexandra Y. "Grammar in Contact: A Cross-Linguistic Perspective." In *Grammar in Contact: A Cross-Linguistic Typology.* Edited by Alexandra Y. Aikhenwald, and Robert M. W. Dixon, 1–66. Oxford, New York: Oxford University Press, 2006.
Anderson, Benedict. *Imagined Communities. Reflections on the Origins and Spread of Nationalism.* London, New York: Verso, 2006.
Arbell, Mordechai. "Los djudios de Avilona (Valona) en Albania." *Aki Yerushalayim* 69 (2002a): 13–14.
Arbell, Mordechai. "The Jewish Communities of Vlora (Valona, Avalona) and Its role in the Adriatic." Paper presented at the Fourth Conference Society and Culture of the Jews on the East of the Adriatic Coast, Dubrovnik, August 2002. 2002b. Unpublished manuscript (14 pp.)
Aslanov, Cyril. "Səfārad as an Alternative Name for *Hispania*: A Tentative Etymology." In *Between Edom and Kedar: Studies in Memory of Yom Tov Assis.* Part 1. Hispania Judaica Bulletin 10. Edited by Aldina Quintana et al. 239–249. Jerusalem: Hispania Judaica, Ben-Zvi Institute, 2014.
Austin, John L. *How to Do Things with Words.* Oxford: The Clarendon Press, 1962.
Brito, Ana Maria. "Frases interrogativas." In *Gramática da língua Portuguesa*, 7th ed. Edited by Maria Helena Mira Mateus et al. 460–479. Lisboa: Editorial Caminho, 2003.
Brito, Ana Maria, and Inês Duarte. "Orações relativas e construções aparentadas." In *Gramática da língua Portuguesa*, 7th ed. Edited by Maria Helena Mira Mateus et al. 653–694. Lisboa: Editorial Caminho, 2003.
Bunis, David M. "The Earliest Judezmo Newspapers: Sociolinguistic Reflections." *Mediterranean Language Review* 6 (1993): 7–66.

Bunis, David M. "The Names of Jewish Languages: A Taxonomy." In *Il mio cuore è a Oriente: studi di linguistica storica, filologia e ultura ebraica dedicati a Maria Luisa Mayer.* Edited by Francesco Aspesi. 415–434. Modena: Cisalpino, 2008.

Clements, J. Clancy. "Transitivity and Spanish Non-Anaphoric *se*." In *Functional Approaches to Spanish Syntax: Lexical Semantics, Discourse and Transitivity.* Edited by J. Clancy Clements, and Jiyoung Yoon. 236–264. New York: Palgrave Macmillan, 2006.

Contreras, Helles. "Relaciones entre las construcciones interrogativas, exclamativas y relativas." In *Gramática descriptiva de la lengua española.* Vol. 2. Edited by Ignacio Bosque, and Violeta Demonte. 1931–1963. Madrid: Real Academia Española, Espasa Calpe, 1999.

Crews, Cynthia M. *Recherches sur le Judéo-Espagnol dans les Pays Balkaniques.* Paris: Droz, 1935.

Crews, Cynthia M. "Textos judeo-españoles de Sálonica y Sarajevo con comentarios lingüísticos y glosario." *Estudios Sefaradies* 2. 91–258. Madrid: CSIC, 1979.

Faingold, Eduardo D. *Child Language, Creolization, and Historical Change: Spanish in Contact with Portuguese.* Tübingen: Gunter Narr, 1996.

Gabinsky, Marcos Alejandro. "Algunos enigmas de la especificidad lingüística común rumano-judeoespañola." *Revista de Filología Románica* 25 (2008): 157–163.

Gómez Torrego, Leonardo. "Los verbos auxiliares. Las perífrasis verbales de infinitivo." In *Gramática descriptiva de la lengua española.* Vol. 2. Edited by Ignacio Bosque, and Violeta Demonte. 3323–3389. Madrid: Real Academia Española, Espasa Calpe, 1999.

Hall, Stuard. "Cultural Identity and Diaspora." In *Identity, Community: Cultures, Difference.* Edited by Jonathan Rutherford. 222–237. London: Lawrence and Wishart, 1990.

Jansegers, Marlies, and Clara Vanderschueren. "El infinitivo flexionado gallego: ¿Entre portugués y castellano?" *Revue de linguistique romane* 295–296 (2010): 415–442.

Kany, Charles E. *Sintaxis Hispanoamericana (American-Spanish Syntax,* Chicago: The University of Chicago Press 1963). Madrid: Gredos, 1969.

Keniston, Hayward. *The Syntax of Castilian Prose. The Sixteenth Century.* Chicago: The University of Chicago Press, 1937.

Kerswill, Paul. "Koineization." In *The Handbook of Language Variation and Change.* 2nd ed. Edited by J[ack] K. Chambers, and Natalie Schilling. 519–536. Oxford: Wiley-Blackwell, 2013.

Koptjevskaja-Tamm, Maria. "Finiteness." In *Concise Encyclopedia of Grammatical Categories.* Edited by Keith Brown and Jim Miller. 146–149. Oxford: Elsevier, 1999.

Law, Danny. "Inherited Similarities and Contact-induced Change in Mayan Languages." *Journal of Language Contact* 6 (2013): 271–299.

Luria, Max A. *A Study of the Monastir Dialect of Judeo-Spanish Based on Oral Material Collected in Monastir, Yugo-Slavia.* New York: Instituto de las Españas, 1930.

Martins, Ana Maria. "Passive and Impersonal *se* in the History of Portuguese." On-line, <http://www.clul.ul.pt/files/ana_maria_martins/MartinsPassiveAnsImpersonal.pdf> [accessed May 30, 2015]. Published in *Romance Corpus Linguistics II: Corpora and Diachronic Linguistics.* Edited by Claus D. Pusch et al. 411–430. Tübingen: Gunter Narr, 2005.

Mendikoetxea, Amaya. "Passive and se Constructions." In *The Handbook of Hispanic Linguistics.* Edited by José Ignacio Hualde et al. 477–502. Malden, Oxford, West Sussex: Blackwell, 2012.

Mensching, Guido. *Infinitive Constructions with Specified Subjects: A Syntactic Analysis of the Romance Languages.* New York: Oxford University Press, 2000.

Merlan, Aurélia. "Las variedades lingüísticas del noroeste peninsular: convergencias y divergencias." *Lletres Asturianes* 96 (2007): 7–56.

Oesterreicher, Wulf. "El español, lengua pluricéntrica: perspectivas y límites de una autoafirmación lingüística nacional en Hispanoamérica. El caso mexicano." *Lexis,* o.s. 26.2 (2002): 275–304.

Oesterreicher, Wulf. "El pluricentrismo del español." In *Actas del VI Congreso Internacional de Historia de la Lengua Española, Madrid 29.9.-3.10.2003*. Vol. 3. Edited by José Jesús de Bustos Tovar, and José Luis Girón Alconchel. 3079–3087. Madrid: Arco/Libros, 2006.

Penny, Ralph. "Dialect Contact and Social Networks in Judeo-Spanish." *Romance Philology* 46.2 (1992): 125–140.

Penny, Ralph. "Judeo-Spanish varieties before and after the Expulsion." *Donaire* 6 (1996): 54–58.

Perez, Avner, and Gradys Pimienta. *Diksionario Amplio Djudeo-espanyol—Ebreo. Lashon me-Aspamia*. Maale Adumim: Sefarad—El Instituto Maale Adumim, La Autoridad Nasionala del Ladino i su Kultura, 2007.

Quintana, Aldina. 2004. "El sustrato y el adstrato portugueses en judeoespañol." (Neue Romania 31) *Judenspanisch* 8 (2004): 167–192.

Quintana, Aldina. *Geografía lingüística del judeoespañol: Estudio sincrónico y diacrónico* (Sephardica 3). Bern: Peter Lang, 2006a.

Quintana, Aldina. "Evolución de judeoespañol en el siglo XVII." (Neue Romania 35) *Judenspanisch* 10 (2006b): 157–181.

Quintana, Aldina. "Aportación lingüística de los romances aragonés y portugués a la coiné judeoespañola." In *Languages and Literatures of Sephardic and Oriental Jews*. Edited by David M. Bunis. 221–255. Jerusalem: Misgav Yerushalayim, Bialik Institute, 2009.

Quintana, Aldina. "Judeo-Spanish in Contact with Portuguese: A Historical Overview." In *Portuguese-Spanish Interfaces: Diachrony, Synchrony, and Contact* (Issues in Hispanic and Lusophone Linguistics 1). Edited by Patrícia Amaral, and Ana M. Carvalho. 65–94. Amsterdam, Philadelphia: John Benjamins, 2014.

Quintana, Aldina. "Judeo-Spanish in Contact with Portuguese: Linguistic Outcomes." In *In the Iberian Paninsula and Beyond: A History of Jews and Muslims (15th-17th Centuries)*. Vol. 2. Edited by José Alberto R. Silva Tavim et al. 165–196. Newcastle upon Tyne: Cambridge Scholars Publishing, 2015.

Ray, Jonathan. "New Approaches to the Jewish Diaspora: The Sephardim as a Sub-ethnic Group." *Jewish Social Studies*, o.s. 15.1 (2008): 10–31.

RAE. *Nueva gramática de la lengua española. Manual*. Madrid: Asociación de Academias de la Lengua Español, 2010.

Ross, Malcolm. "Contact-induced Change in Oceanic Languages in North-West Melanesia." In *Areal Diffusion and Genetic Inheritance: Problems in Comparative Linguistics*. Edited by Alexandra Y. Aikhenvald, and Robert M. W. Dixon. 134–166. Oxford: Oxford University Press, 2001.

Schmid, Beatrice, and Yvette Bürki. "El ḥaćino imaǵinado": *comedia de Molière en versión judeoespañola. Edición del texto aljamiado, estudio y glosario*. Acta Románica Basiliensia (ARBA) 11. Basel: Uni Basel, 2000.

Searle, John. *Speech Acts: An Essay in the Philosophy of Language*. Oxford: Cambridge University Press 1969.

Shmuelevitz, Arieh. *The Jews of the Ottoman Empire in the Late Fifteenth and the Sixteenth Centuries. Administrative, Economic, Legal, and Social Relations as Reflected in the Responsa*. Leiden: Brill, 1984.

Siegel, Jeff. *Koines and Koineization. Language in Society*, o.s. 14.3 (1985): 357–378.

Spitzer, Leo. "Frs. *Sa conversation ... ne sentait point son curé de village*—ptg. *seu burro*." In Leo Spitzer, *Aufsätze zur romanischen Syntax und Stilistik*. 5–14. Halle-on-the-Saal: Max Niemeyer, 1918.

Stechauner, Martin. "Imagining Sephardic Diaspora." M.A. Diplomarbeit, Institut für Religionswissenschaft, Universität Wien, 2013.

Stechauner, Martin. "Imagining the Sephardic Community of Vienna: A Discourse-Analytical Approach." In *Religion in Austria*. Vol. 2. Edited by Hans Gerald Hödl, and Lukas Pokorny. 49–91. Vienna: Praesens Verlag, 2014.

Stulic-Etchevers, Ana. "El desarrollo del pronombre interrogativo *loke* en judeoespañol." In *Cuatrocientos años de la lengua del Quijote: estudios de historiografía e historia de la lengua española: Actas del V Congreso Nacional de la Asociación de Jóvenes Investigadores de Historiografía e Historia de la Lengua Española (Sevilla, 31 de marzo, 1 y 2 de abril de 2005)*. Edited by Marta Fernández Alcaide, and Araceli López Serena. 585–598. Seville: Universidad de Sevilla, 2007.

Thomason, Sarah Grey, and Terrence Kaufman. *Language Contact, Creolization, and Genetic Linguistics*. Berkeley: University of California Press, 1988.

Torrent-Lenzen, Aina. "Estructura presuposicional e implicaturas de la locución marcadora evidencial "ni que decir tiene"." *Actas del XXVI Congreso Internacional de Lingüística y de Filología Románicas. 6–11 de septiembre de 2010 Valencia*. Vol. 4. Edited by Emili Casanova Herrero, and Cesáreo Calvo Rigual. 399–410. Berlin, Boston: Walter de Gruyter, 2013.

Vanderschueren, Clara. *Infinitivo y sujeto en portugués y español. Un estudio empírico de los infinitivos adverbiales con sujeto explícito*. Berlin, Boston: De Gruyter, 2013.

Várvaro, Alberto, and Laura Minervini. "Orígenes del Judeoespañol: textos." *Revista de Historia de la Lengua Española* 2 (2007): 147–172.

Vázquez, Ignacio. 2011. "Reflexiones sobre el infinitivo conjugado portugués desde la perspectiva española." *Exedra* 5 (2011): 9–26.

Vincent, Nigel. "Subordination and Complementation." In *Concise Encyclopedia of Grammatical Categories*. Edited by Keith Brown, and Jim Miller. 352–358. Oxford: Elsevier, 1999.

Wagner, Max Leopold. *Caracteres generales del judeoespañol de Oriente*. Madrid: Hernando, 1930.

Winford, Donald. *An Introduction to Contact Linguistics*. Oxford: Blackwell, 2003.

CHAPTER FIVE

The Syntactic Structure of Liturgical Ladino

Construct State Nominals, Multiple Determiners, and Verbless Sentences

MATTHEW MADDOX
University of Illinois at Urbana-Champaign

ABSTRACT

In this chapter, I analyze three syntactic constructions in Liturgical Ladino (LL) that have previously (Sephiha 1973, 1980, *et passim*; López-Morillas 1990) been labeled "calques," which typically occur in contact languages. I extend MacSwan's (1999) Minimalist bilingual language faculty model to LL. In this language, a single computational component has access to two lexicons, one Hebrew, the other Spanish. Lexical items with their formal features from either lexicon may be selected to enter into the syntactic derivation, thereby producing an apparent hybrid syntax.

1. INTRODUCTION

Liturgical Ladino,[1] a language described by Sephiha as a Hebrew-Spanish calque, displays syntactic constructions that are ungrammatical in Spanish, such as verbless sentences (1), construct state nominals (2), and multiple determiners (3).

(1) a. Este Ø el pan dela afriisyon. (Ladino)
       this   the bread of-the affliction
       "This is the bread of affliction."
    b. *Este Ø el pan de la aflicción. (Spanish)

(2) a. de presipyo sirvyentes Ø avoda zara. (Ladino)
from beginning servants worship foreign
"From the beginning servants of foreign worship."
b. *de principio servientes Ø alabanza extranjera. (Spanish)

(3) a. Kuanto fue demudada la noçe la esta mas ke todas las noçes. (Ladino)
how-much was changed the night the this more than all the nights
"How greatly changed was this night more than all other nights."
b. *Cuanto fue demudada la noche la esta más que todas las noches. (Spanish)

While these types of constructions have been analyzed by previous scholars (Sephiha 1973, 1980; López-Morillas 1990) as literal translations of Hebrew into Ladino, in this study a different approach is pursued, according to which the calques are instances of a phenomenon similar to bilingual code-switching. I propose, based on MacSwan (1999) that in LL the computational component has access to two different lexicons, Hebrew and Spanish. Calques of "Hebrew syntax" are due to the use of Hebrew lexical items, whereas "Spanish syntax" occurs when Spanish lexical items are selected.

Analyzing LL as a "calque language" raises several issues. While calques are often observed in the lexical domain, syntactic calquing is less widely attested. This type of calquing overlaps with another term, "structural borrowing," in which a syntactic construction from a source language is borrowed into a recipient language; i.e., preposition-stranding in some varieties of Canadian French being borrowed from English due to contact. However, extending this concept to explain LL calques is problematic because, as Winford (2003: 61–61) notes, "structural change is almost always mediated by lexical transfer." In other words, the so-called calques of LL are not borrowed wholesale from one language into another. Instead, they are syntactic configurations that are allowed to occur due to the use of certain lexical items from either language. King (2001: 135–149) demonstrated this type of phenomenon in her study of preposition-stranding, which she analyzes as being due to the borrowing of individual lexical-items, prepositions, along with their syntactic properties (formal features). The features that allow for preposition-stranding in English also allow for it in Prince Edward Island French.

The second problem with viewing the calques of LL as syntactic/structural borrowing is theory-internal and is related to how syntax is modelled within the framework of the Minimalist Program (MP). Within this framework the language faculty is taken to be an invariable system with which humans are biologically endowed; i.e., Universal Grammar. The differences that we find among languages are due to the primary linguistic data to which a child is exposed during the language acquisition process and the setting of parameters. LL calques, and language-mixture in general, can been thought to present a problem for a theory of UG because they appear to be examples of distinct syntactic systems, operating simultaneously. Within the MP, syntax is assumed to be uniform crosslinguistically; distinct syntactic/grammatical systems do not exist. Given that Spanish and Hebrew differ typologically and parametrically, how does syntax (the composition of linguistic structure) work with material from both? My hypothesis is that instances of calques can be reduced to the use of lexical items drawn from two different lexicons with specific formal features that allow for what superficially appears to be syntactic borrowing.

The third problem with the calque language view of LL is that the term suggests that there is a consistent one-to-one correspondence between the two languages involved. If this were true, then we should expect the same amount of words in the Hebrew text of the haggadah as in the LL. While this is often the case, it does not hold without exception. As is shown below, this inconsistency is explainable under my hypothesis. The calque language view of LL cannot explain systematically why some constructions are calqued but not others. One possible explanation under this view might be that the LL still has to be comprehensible to a non-Hebrew speaking audience. Consequently, the syntax of Spanish cannot be violated to the point of incomprehensibility. The problem with this is that what is calqued and what is not would be up to the judgement of the individual translator which should result in variation. While minor variation does occur from translation-to-translation, most versions tend to calque the same constructions. Consequently, this is not an adequate explanation.

While it is true that LL was used as a pedagogical tool, this does not negate its validity as an authentic language of interest to modern linguistics. Bunis (1996) gives a historical account of Ladino as an orally-transmitted system of spontaneous translation. He refers to it as primarily an oral tradition and only secondarily textual. Furthermore, this language was acquired as a child, in the context of school-instruction (Kohring 1996). The following analysis of three syntactic constructions in the text of the haggadah shows that LL operates in a manner consistent with our current understanding of the syntax of bilingualism. The remainder of this chapter is divided into four sections Section 2 presents the methodology and corpus, Section 3 introduces the theoretical framework, a Minimalist approach to code-switching, Section 4 is a formal analysis of the three types of constructions, and Section 5 is the conclusion.

2. METHODOLOGY AND CORPUS

2.1. The Haggadah

The Haggadah is the liturgical text used in Judaism for the celebration of the feast of Passover. The dating of its authorship is a matter of debate but it is generally given as sometime between 70 to 220 C.E. (Kulp 2005). Many of the rituals described in the text were practiced prior to an order actually being written down and, once compiled, the text was continually added to and amended over the centuries. One necessary assumption that has been made in this study is that all translations to LL are based on the same Hebrew text. Schwarzwald (1996) has pointed out the problems with comparing different Ladino translations of the haggadah.

For example, in the two versions she compares, she finds that one consistently has a monophthong where the other has a diphthong (366). However, since she focuses primarily on lexical and morphophonemic phenomena rather than syntax, the differences she has identified are not important here.

The primary language of the haggadah text is Rabbinic Hebrew. Aramaic also occurs, and can cooccur with Hebrew in the same sentence. While this may have implications for the LL translation, the issue is not explored in this study. The quantity of Aramaic in the text is limited and Aramaic and Hebrew are closely related, so it is not the kind of language-mixture between typologically distinct languages with which this study is concerned. Pérez-Fernández (1997: 5) briefly describes the amount of influence from Aramaic on Rabbinic Hebrew as being primarily lexical and morphological.

2.2. Corpus

The Hebrew versions of the relevant constructions are given below:

(4) devar Ø elohim   (Construct State Nominal)
    word   God
    "word of God"

(5) **ha**-layla **ha**-zeh   (Multiple Determiners)
    the-night the-this
    "this night"

(6) elohim Ø ba-shamayim   (Verbless Sentence)
    God   in-the-heavens
    "God is in the heavens."

A structural description of these constructions is given in Section 4; they were chosen for their typological dissimilarity. They are grammatical in Hebrew, but not in Spanish; the extent to which they are actually attested in the LL varies. Examples of these constructions were collected from a corpus comprised of five different LL translations of the Sephardic haggadah, as given below in Table 1:

Table 1. List of Haggadah Translations.

Name of Translator	Year of Publication	Place of Publication
Jacob Meldula	1812	Jerusalem
Shelomoh Alkaher	1946	Istanbul
Nisim Behar	1962	Istanbul
Isaac Azose, Sarah Benezra, Isaac Maimon	1995	Seattle
Zelda Ovadia	2002	Jerusalem

Five translations were chosen in order to determine whether the constructions under consideration were translated in the same manner. This attests to the extent to which LL can be considered a homogeneous linguistic system or not. These particular translations were used because they were easily accessible and all used Roman script for the Ladino, and sometimes the Hebrew, passages. Some minor, non-syntactic, differences were identified, which are discussed in the analysis below. As shown in Table 1, the corpus represents not only diachronic but geographical variation as well. In order to ensure that these constructions are limited to LL and not also present in modern Judeo-Spanish, the same constructions were searched for in the Judeo-Spanish translation of *Le Petit Prince* by Antoine de Saint-Exupéry, originally published in 1946, with the translation published in 2010. The results of this search were negative. Sephiha claims that LL syntax goes back to twelfth- or thirteenth-century Spanish syntax. A search in the *Corpus Diacrónico del Español* (CORDE) was carried out in order to determine whether there are parallels with Old Spanish syntax, which might mean that they were inherited. The results show that a construction similar to the double determiner construction did exist in earlier stages of Spanish[2], but parallels were not found for the other constructions.

3. THEORETICAL BACKGROUND

3.1. The Minimalist Program (MP) and the Modelling of Syntactic Architecture

The Minimalist Program (Chomsky 1995, *et seq.*) is a revised approach to the study of Universal Grammar in generative linguistics. It succeeded what had been known as the Principles and Parameters model. One of the motives behind the revision was to reduce the amount of assumptions that had been made during previous years; i.e., to make the minimal amount of assumptions, following Occam's Razor. It is not necessary to go into all the details of the MP's formulation here, but two important aspects need to be introduced.

First, within the MP, syntax is conceived of as being invariant crosslinguistically. Syntactic variation can be reduced to the setting of parameters, which are now thought of as formal features specified on functional items in the lexicon[3] (Roberts 2007). "Parameter" is a term that describes a point of optionality in Universal Grammar. When superficial differences are identified between two languages, it is due to a different feature present in the lexicon of one of those languages. For example, the most widely studied parameter is the Null Subject (or Pro-Drop) Parameter. This parameter is used to describe the fact that certain languages allow a null (phonologically unrealized) pronominal subject in finite clauses, like Spanish, while others do not. Holmberg (2005) claims that this parameter can be reduced to the featural makeup of the Tense node in the lexicon: if it has a referential D-feature, it will allow null subjects. The nature of parameters within Minimalism is a controversial topic even today and parameters are not the primary concern of this study. However, the assumption that syntax (UG) is invariant is important: it allows for the proposal that the "calques" that are observed in LL are nothing other than the syntactic effects of two different lexicons.

The second important aspect of the MP for what follows is how syntax is modelled; i.e., the manner in which syntactic structure is built up. Here I give a brief explanation (cf. Adger 2003), as a background for the analysis of each construction that follows in Section 4. Syntax first proceeds by drawing lexical items from the lexicon (Numeration) and then combining those items (Merge). Lexical items (LI) are bundles of formal features; they can be either function or content words or they can be phonologically unrealized. For example, the word *car* may have the following set of features: [+Noun, -Verb, -Animate, etc.]. Features may be either interpretable (semantically relevant) or uninterpretable (only formally relevant). The uninterpretable features have to be "checked" by an interpretable feature prior to Spell-Out, the point at which the structure built up is sent to the phonological and the semantic interface, known respectively as Phonological Form (PF) and Logical Form (LF). Checking of features is the operation Agree, which takes place via c-command. If uninterpretable features are not checked, the derivation will crash and it cannot be Spelled-Out, which takes place before features reach the interface, as illustrated below in Figure 1.

3.2. A Minimalist Model of the Bilingual Language Faculty

In MacSwan's (1999, 2000) study of Spanish and Nahuatl code-switching, the Minimalist model is applied to explain how speakers switch "between languages." The idea that a bilingual speaker has access to two distinct grammatical systems is problematic from the perspective of UG because grammar/syntax is assumed to be invariant. The variation that is seen on the surface is due to the lexicon or morphophonology. Do bilingual speakers use one grammar, or two grammars? What principle determines how two grammars may interact? In order to answer the second question, one must postulate a third bilingual grammar or some kind of control structure. As MacSwan (2000: 38) points out, this would violate the spirit of the MP, in which extra assumptions should be made "only if forced to do so by the data." This can be avoided if all speakers have only one syntactic component that may be fed by two lexicons. Importantly, this model of code-switching makes the prediction that all instances of switching can be attributed to formal features on lexical items in either one or the other lexicon. As is demonstrated in Section 4, this prediction holds true for the data taken from LL.

Code-switching can be modelled as syntax proceeding in the usual fashion, but being fed by two different lexicons. A representation of this model taken from MacSwan (2000: 52) is reproduced below:

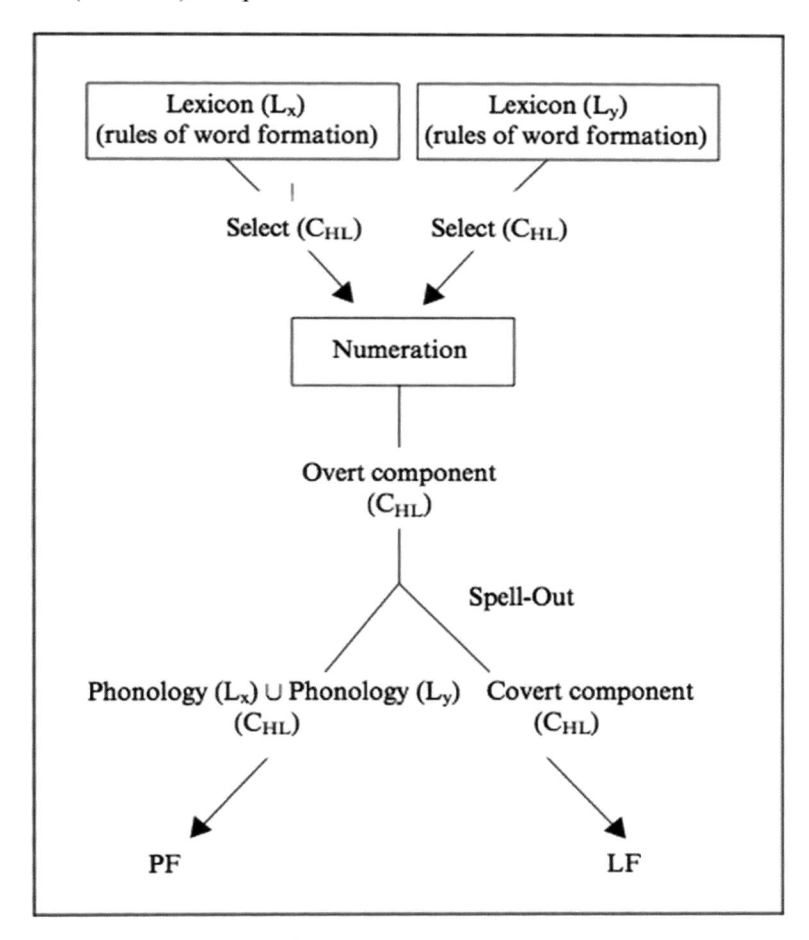

```
┌─────────────────────────────────────────────────────────────┐
│   ┌──────────────────────┐    ┌──────────────────────┐      │
│   │    Lexicon (Lₓ)      │    │    Lexicon (Lᵧ)      │      │
│   │ (rules of word       │    │ (rules of word       │      │
│   │  formation)          │    │  formation)          │      │
│   └──────────────────────┘    └──────────────────────┘      │
│              ↓                          ↓                   │
│         Select (C_HL)              Select (C_HL)            │
│                    ↘          ↙                             │
│              ┌──────────────────┐                           │
│              │   Numeration     │                           │
│              └──────────────────┘                           │
│                        │                                    │
│               Overt component                               │
│                   (C_HL)                                    │
│                        │                                    │
│                              Spell-Out                      │
│                      ╱  ╲                                   │
│   Phonology (Lₓ) ∪ Phonology (Lᵧ)   Covert component        │
│              (C_HL)                      (C_HL)             │
│             ↓                                ↘              │
│            PF                                 LF            │
└─────────────────────────────────────────────────────────────┘
```

Fig. 1. The Bilingual Language Faculty.

In Figure 1, structure is built up in the same way as presented in Section 3.1, the only difference being that there are two lexicons from which lexical items may be drawn. In LL, L_x would be Hebrew and L_y would be Spanish. LIs are selected and merged. If all the requirements of feature-checking are met, the derivation converges successfully.

4. EXTENSION OF THE BILINGUAL LANGUAGE FACULTY MODEL TO LL

In this section each of the three constructions is presented, with parallel instances from each translation. Its presence or absence in earlier phases of Spanish is discussed and a formal analysis demonstrates how the surface representation is derived from formal features of a lexical item.

4.1. Construct State Nominals (Gesenius 1910: 247; Seow 1995: 116)

In Hebrew and other Semitic languages, a dependency between one or more nouns, participles, or adjectives can be established via juxtaposition, without any intervening material. The relationship that results between the nouns can be one of possession or modification. Examples of simple Construct State Nominals (CSN) in Biblical Hebrew are provided below, where (7) is comprised of two nouns, (8) is a noun and an adjective, (9) is a participle and a noun:

(7) devar Ø elohim   (8) yefeh Ø   toar   (9) kholem Ø   khalom
    word   God   handsome form   dreamer.Part dream
    "word of God"   "handsome in form"   "a dreamer of a dream"

The final word in the construct chain is said to be in the Absolute State, while the initial word(s) are in the Construct State, in which it undergoes certain phonological modifications such as loss of stress, weakening, etc. Definiteness is also shared in the CC: the definiteness of the Absolute noun determines the definiteness of the Construct noun.

The CSN is used frequently in Rabbinic Hebrew, though the preposition *shel*, equivalent to English *of*, is also used (Pérez-Fernández 1997: 68). In the LL of the haggadot used for this study, the CSN does not occur, except for one example which is discussed below. All five translations use the canonical Spanish preposition *de* as seen in (10a-e) and (11a-e):

(10) Amar Ribi El'azar ben Azarya[4]   (11)   Terakh avi[5] Avraham va'avi Nakhor
     say.Perf.3S rabbi Elazar son Azaryah   Terah father Abraham and-father Nakhor
  a. Dixo R. Elhazar hijo **de** Azarya (1812)   a. Terah padre de Abraham y padre **de** Nahor (1812)
  b. Diṣo rebi Elazar ijo **de** Azarya (1946)   b. Terah padre de Avraam i padre **de** Nahor (1946)
  c. Diṣo Ribi Elazar ijo **de** Azaria (1962)   c. Terah pad're de Avraam i pad're **de** Nahor (1962)
  d. Disho Ribi Elazar ijo **de** Azaria (1995)   d. Terah padre de Avraam i padre **de** Nahor (1995)
  e. Disho Ribi Eliezer ijo **de** Azarya (2002)   e. Terah padre de Avraam i padre **de** Nahor (2002)

     "Rabbi Elazar, son of Azaryah, said ..."   "Terah father of Abraham and father of Nahor"

If the CSN were calqued in the LL we would observe examples such as *hijo Azarya* rather than *hijo de Azarya*, which do not occur. Instead, LL uses the "independent genitive," a prepositional phrase (Adger 2003: 265), just like Spanish. Based on the model discussed above, this is an instance where the preposition is taken from the Spanish lexicon and enters into the syntactic derivation. In formal terms, the noun has an interpretable [Case:_] feature that is valued as genitive when merged with the preposition which has an uninterpretable [genitive] feature. The preposition also has an uninterpretable D-feature, so it has to merge with an element that has an interpretable D-feature; i.e. the DP,[6] *Abraham*. This yields the structure below:

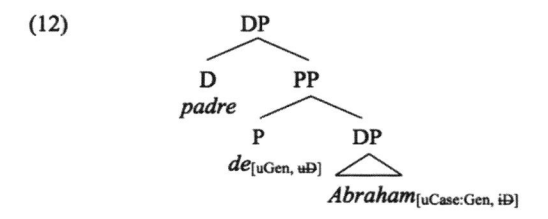

(12)

```
            DP
           /  \
          D    PP
        padre / \
             P   DP
        de[uGen, uD]  \
                    Abraham[uCase:Gen, iD]
```

Importantly, the Spanish noun *padre* (or the null determiner) is also used rather than a Hebrew noun. If the latter were the case, a CSN might be formed, assuming that nouns (determiners) in Hebrew have the required feature makeup.

As previously mentioned, there is a preposition in Hebrew, *shel*, equivalent to Spanish *de*, as in the name of the text: *Hagadah shel pesakh--Agada de Pesah*. LL uses the Spanish preposition *de* for both Hebrew CSNs as in (12) and *shel* genitive prepositional phrases as below:

(13) shema shel shakhrit   (Hebrew)
     Shema of morning
     Shema de la manyana (2002)[7]   (LL)
     "the morning Shema"

It appears that LL consistently draws the prepostion *de* from the Spanish lexicon in constructions of this type. However, if LL has access to two lexicons, it should be able to utilize both the Hebrew and the Spanish preposition in equal fashion. At this point I am unable to offer a complete explanation, but it may be that LL does not access the entire lexicon of each language but rather some items from one and other items from the other.

As alluded to above, there is one plausible example of a CSN in the LL text of the haggadah and it is the same in four of the five translations, the exception being the Meldula (1812) version, given in (14b):

(14) mittehillah   ovdey   avodah   zarah   (Hebrew)
     from-beginning   servants   worship   strange
     a. de presipyo sirvyentes avoda zara. (1946)   (LL)
     b. De principio servian nuestros padres idolatria. (1812)   (LL)
     "From the beginning they were servants of strange worship."

The phrase, "servants of strange worship," refers to idolatry or the worship of a foreign god, which is reflected in the less-literal English translations. The LL in (14a) does not use the Spanish preposition and has two Hebrew words: *avoda zara*. The fact that this is the only example of CSN in the LL and it is composed of two Hebrew words is likely not coincidental.

Previous analyses of Semitic CSNs, such as Ritter (1991), show that DPs are headed by a null determiner with the feature [genitive], not unlike the preposition *shel* as seen above. Ritter labels this null determiner D_{Gen}. Following the feature-checking model proposed above we can state that this determiner is present in the lexicon and its feature makeup contains an uninterpretable [genitive] feature. Ritter also demonstrates that DPs are composed of an additional functional projection, the Number Phrase (NumP), which is where a noun moves in order to have its Number features valued. Additionally, quantifiers are overt realizations of the Num head. The presence of this functional projection and the checking of features helps account for the constituent order within a CSN, where the possessed precedes the possessor: the possessor DP moves to NumP where its case feature is valued as [genitive] by D_{Gen}. The derivation of (14a) is represented below:

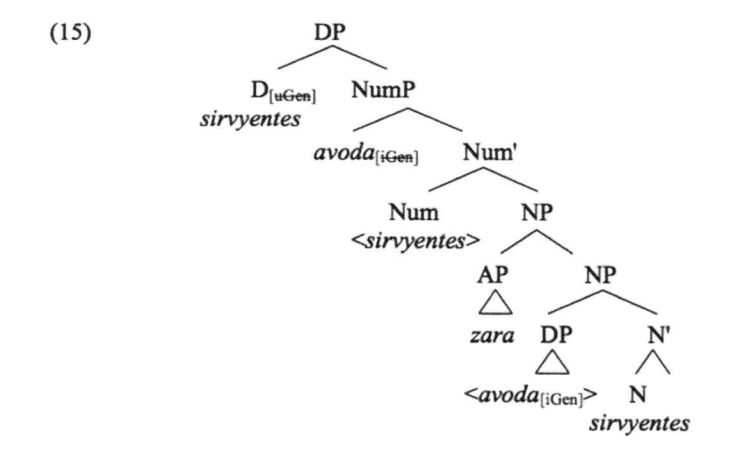

(15)
```
                    DP
                   /  \
           D[uGen]    NumP
          sirvyentes  /  \
                avoda[iGen]  Num'
                            /    \
                          Num     NP
                     <sirvyentes> /  \
                                AP    NP
                                △    /  \
                              zara  DP   N'
                                    △    \
                             <avoda[iGen]> N
                                          sirvyentes
```

A couple of questions arise given (15). First, why does N move to D? Ritter states that this occurs in order for D_{Gen} to be identified, but this concept may not necessarily be compatible with current MP theory. The second question has to do with morphophonology. As pointed out above, Hebrew words in the construct state undergo various morphophonological changes. In this case, the word that would regularly be in construct state is a Spanish word, *sirvyentes*. This word exists in standard varieties of Spanish (in standard spelling, *sirvientes*). What should be noted is that the morphophonological process that takes place in Hebrew CSNs does not occur here with the Spanish word. Whatever it is that triggers the change in Hebrew words in construct state does not apply to the Spanish. However, it is also true that some Hebrew nouns do not change their form when in construct state (Seow 1995: 117). This suggests that syntax may not be sensitive to this process.

Before ending this section the question of a common inheritance needs to be addressed. The CSN is not used frequently in LL and, to my knowledge, a similar construction never existed in any recorded varieties of Spanish. However, it is not out-of-the-question that it existed in earlier Romance given that it appears to have been present in Old French as discussed in Arteaga and Herschensohn (2010, 2012) and as seen in the data below:

(16) le   lit   son seignor
     the   bed   her husband
     "her husband's bed" (*Le Fresne*, Marie de France)

The same construction is also found in Ecclesiastical Latin, specifically in the Vulgate translation of the Bible:

(17) in tribu filiorum Isachar fuit   princeps Nathanahel filius Suar
                      Isachar was.3S   prince   Nathaniel   son   Suar
     "In the tribe of the sons of Isachar, the prince was Nathaniel son of Suar." (Num. 10: 15)

As with the the CSN, the possessed precedes the possessor, but there appears to be no phonological reduction of the first nominal. In Latin, the CSN only occurs when a non-Latin proper name is used as a possessor, while the Old French does not appear to be constrained in this way. The Latin may simply be a choice made on the part of the translator, St. Jerome, to signify a genitive relationship but without attempting to add Latin genitive case-endings to Hebrew names. Though interesting, a comparative analysis of these constructions is left for future work.

4.2. Multiple Determiners/Definiteness Agreement (DA) in DPs

As seen in (18), Hebrew attributive adjectives agree in definiteness with the noun they modify (Seow 1995: 72); the noun *yad* has a prefixed definite article, as does its adjective, *gadol*.

(18) **ha**-yyad **ha**-gdolah
     the-hand the-great

  a. **la** mano **la** grande (1812: 8)
  b. **la** maravia **la** grande (1946: 19)
  c. **la** maraviya **la** grande (1962: 20)
  d. **la** maraviya **la** grande (1995: 31)
  e. **la** mano **la** grande (2002: 22)

The same type of agreement occurs with demonstratives as well, as in (19), which behave syntactically like adjectives rather than determiners (Danon 2008: 876).

(19) Ma nishttannah **ha-layla** **ha-zeh** mi-kol ha-leylot?
why different the-night the-this from-all the-nights

   a. Quan diferente ésta noche masque todas las noches? (1812: 3)
   b. Kuanto fue demudada **la noçe la esta** mas ke todas las noçes. (1946: 6)
   c. Kuanto fue demud'ad'a **la noçe la esta**, mas ke tod'as las noçes. (1962: 5)
   d. Kuanto fue demudada **la noche la esta** mas ke todas las noches. (1995: 13)
   e. Kuanto fue demudada **la noche esta**, mas ke todas las noches. (2002: 10)

"Why is this night different from all other nights?"

DA can be analyzed as any other kind of agreement which takes place under c-command.[8] For example, when a noun and its modifier agree in gender, they are taken as having matching features which are then morphologically realized when checked. In Hebrew, it has been argued that nouns and adjectives have a definiteness feature, which has to be checked upon merging (Borer 1996, Siloni 1996, Shlonsky 2004). Danon (2008) claims that the definite article is not a head but rather the morphological realization of definiteness. However, there is not consensus in the literature and some maintain that the Hebrew definite article is a head and it takes an AP complement (Sichel 2002).

The Hebrew type of DA is not a property of Spanish. In contrast with what was seen in Section 4.1, this construction is paralleled in three out of five of the LL translations (19b-d), all of which follow the Hebrew pattern: Det + N + Det + Dem/Adj. The two translations that do not follow the Hebrew pattern, (19a,e), are acceptable in Spanish. (19a) is the canonical order of demonstrative adjective preceding a noun while (19e) is an instance of DP-internal movement.

There are several complicating factors that arise in attempting to analyze DA in LL. One of these is that the following assumption must be made:

(20) Given access to two different lexicons, L_x and L_y, lexical items drawn from either lexicon will have only those features for which they are specified in the lexicon from which they originate.

No explanation of a construction can be offered that involves attributing non-Spanish formal features to Hebrew LIs and vice versa. This means that the LL examples must be analyzed as either Hebrew DA or an instance of Spanish multiple determiners. The latter option may be optimal, since the only overt material in the construction is Spanish LIs. However, the former option is also viable if there is a null functional head, originating from the Hebrew lexicon, that is involved in DA.

THE SYNTACTIC STRUCTURE OF LITURGICAL LADINO | 99

Following this latter option, the feature [definiteness] is assigned by means of an agreement functional head. This has precedent in the AgrO node, object agreement, which Chomsky (1991) posited as responsible for assigning accusative case. An NP moves to SpecAgrO to be assigned accusative case. While AgrO is located in the Verb Phrase, the functional head being proposed for definiteness agreement, which has been proposed by others as well (Borer 1999; Shlonsky 2004), would be located in the DP domain. The posited functional head, which can be abbreviated as AgrD, exists in the Hebrew lexicon but not the Spanish lexicon. As with AgrO, we can assume that an NP moves up to SpecAgrD in order to be valued as definite. Below is the first DP of (19d) under this system:

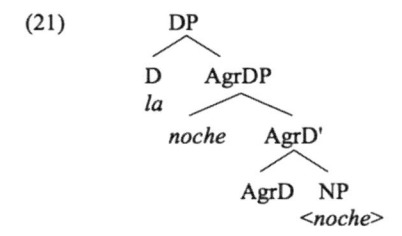

(21)
```
           DP
          /  \
         D   AgrDP
         la   /  \
           noche  AgrD'
                  /  \
               AgrD   NP
                    <noche>
```

A similar analysis is given in Androutsopoulou (1995) for multiple determiners in Greek. She proposes a functional head, Def, specified for the agreement features within the DP. She assumes, as do others (Cinque 1994, Bernstein 2001), that adjectives are merged prenominally and that postnominal orders are the result of movement. D is null and Def is spelled-out as the definite article. Thus, multiple definite articles imply multiple projections of Def within the DP. In order to account for word order, she also allows for DefPs to optionally move to the specifier of a higher Def. This can be applied to LL with the Spanish Def being present, in which case the derivation of (18a) is as below:

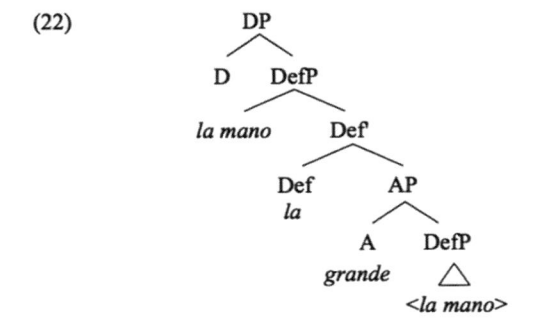

(22)
```
              DP
             /  \
            D   DefP
         la mano  /  \
                Def
                / \
              Def   AP
              la   /  \
                  A    DefP
                grande  △
                      <la mano>
```

This analysis can also explain (19) if we treat demonstratives as adjectives, in which case the derivation is the same as in (22). However, though Danon (2008: 876) does claim that Hebrew demonstratives "have the syntactic behavior of adjectives," this is not necessarily the case in Spanish and since the demonstrative under consideration is taken from the Spanish lexicon, it must behave, in accordance with the assumption in (20), as a Spanish demonstrative.

While demonstratives are generally taken to be determiners and thus D heads, Giusti (1992) claims that, based on word order evidence, determiners and demonstratives are categorically different. Furthermore, demonstratives head another DP-internal functional projection, Dem, which moves to D when no article is present, perhaps to check a definiteness feature. Adopting this model and combining it with Androutsopoulou's (1995) analysis results in the essentially the same structure, but allows us to dispense with the notion that demonstratives are adjectives. Thus, (19d) can be represented as below:

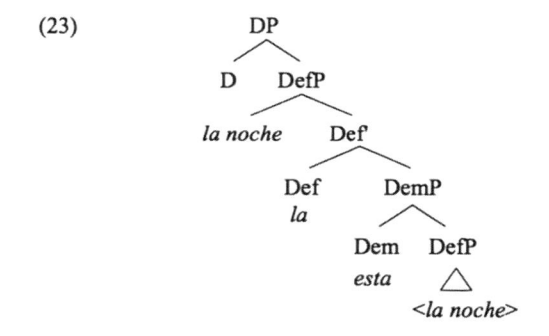

(23)
```
              DP
             /  \
            D    DefP
         la noche  /  \
                 Def   DemP
                  la   /  \
                     Dem   DefP
                     esta   △
                          <la noche>
```

Two analyses have been given above: the AgrDP analysis and DefP analysis. Both depend upon the presence of a functional projection and both have their drawbacks. The former is problematic because Agr nodes are generally not appealed to in the MP. Chomsky (1995) shows that the AgrS and AgrO nodes are not necessary, though he does not discuss the DP. Agreement is now modelled as feature-checking via c-command, an approach which presents its own problems for the LL data. With respect to the DefP analysis, the question still remains as to why multiple DefPs can be merged within LL but not within standard Spanish, though examples like the following do exist, both taken from Bernstein (2001: 15):

(24) a. el libro interesante este
         the book interesting this
         "THIS interesting book."
      b. ?el libro ese viejo
         the book that old
         "That book, the old one."

At first glance, (24a) looks similar to (18), if we take *este* to be a determiner. Note, however, that (24a) elicits a focus interpretation while (18) does not. Bernstein analyzes this focus construction as an instance of DP-internal movement, in which the the NP and its modifier scrambles to the left, where it receives main stress. On the other hand, (24b) looks even more like (18), but given the dubious judgements it elicits in speakers, it may not be grammatical.

4.3. Verbless Sentences

A verbless sentence is one in which there is no overt copula, as below:

(25) **Halachma anya** di achalu av'hatana b'ara d'mitsrayim.[9]
the.bread affliction that eat.PERF.3ComPl ancestors in-land of-Egypt

   a. **Este (es) el pan de aflicion** que comieron nuestros padres en tierra de Egypto. (1812)
   b. **Este Ø el pan dela afriisyon** ke komyeron noestros padres en tyera del ayifto. (1946)
   c. **Este Ø el pan dela, afriyision**, ke komieron nuestros pad'res en tierra de Ayifto. (1962)
   d. **Este es el plan de la afri-sion** ke comieron muestros padres in tierra de Ayifto. (1995)
   e. **Este Ø pan de l'afrision**, ke komerion muestros padres en tierra de Ayifto. (2002)

"**This is the bread of affliction** that our fathers ate in the land of Egypt."

In Hebrew, the copula is *hayah*; in Spanish it is *ser* or *estar*. In (25), the matrix clause is composed of two NPs and no copula. Three out of five LL translations also lack the copula (25b,c,e) while (25a) has a copula inserted in parentheses. Verbless sentences may also be adjectival as in (26), which has two verbless adjectival clauses:

(26) **Baruch shennatan** torah le-amo yisrael **baruch hu**.
blessed who-gave torah to people-his Israel blessed he

   a. **Bendito Ø el que dió** Ley a Israel, **Bendito Ø el**. (1812)
   b. **Bendiço Ø el ke dyo** ley a su poevlo yisrael, **bindiço Ø el**. (1946)
   c. **Bendiço Ø el ke dyo** ley a su puevlo Israel, **bendiço Ø el**. (1962)
   d. **Bendicho Ø ke dio** la ley a su puevlo Yisrael, **bendicho Ø El**. (1995)
   e. **Bendicho Ø el ke dio** la Ley a su puevlo Israel, **Bendicho Ø El**. (2002)

"Blessed is he who gave the Torah to his people Israel. Blessed is he."

In (26), all five LL translations also lack the copula. Verbless sentences are characteristic of Hebrew (27a), from the Biblical period up to modern-day, and of Semitic languages in general, but in Spanish (27b) it is ungrammatical; the copula is required.

(27) a. Dani Ø more.
       Dani teacher
       "Dani is a teacher."
    b. *Dani Ø profesor.
       "Dani is a teacher."

It is also present in Russian, African-American Vernacular English, etc.[10] In verbless sentences, there is no overt tense marker, unless an adverb is present; the word order can be changed without any difference in interpretation (Seow 1995: 59; Gesenius 1910: 453).[11]

Given that verbless sentence constructions (VSC) are ungrammatical in Spanish but not in Hebrew, how do we explain their presence in LL? The first step to answering this question is to determine what licenses VSCs in Hebrew; it is possible that the same element is at work in LL. Benmamoun (2008) argues that while there is no overt verb in these sentences, a Tense node is still projected. One property of VSCs that appears to be shared crosslinguistically is that they only occur in present tense, which traditional grammarians consider to be inferred from the wider discourse context. Using the notion of categorial features, Benmamoun argues that languages may differ as to whether a tense is specified to select a nominal complement or a verbal complement. In Hebrew (28), the present tense is only specified lexically to select a nominal complement; it may select a VP complement but it does not have to. On the other hand, past tense is specified to select a verbal and a nominal complement:

(28) Hebrew: a. Past [+V, +D]
     b. Present [+D]

(29) Spanish: a. Past [+V, +D]
     b. Present [+V, +D]

In Spanish (29) and languages that do not permit VSCs, both past and present tense are specified for verbal and nominal complements.

With respect to the minimalist model of feature checking, VSCs can be reduced to the presence of a D (nominal) or V (verbal) feature on [+Present] T. In Hebrew, present T need only check its D-feature; past T must check both its D- and V-feature. The structure of the VSC in (25e) is represented below:

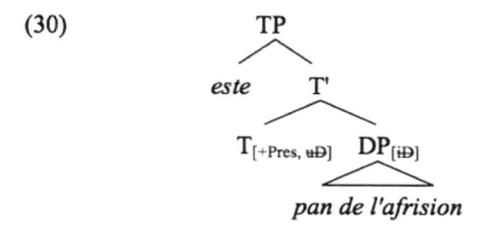

(30)

TP
├── este
└── T'
    ├── T[+Pres, uD]
    └── DP[iD]
        └── pan de l'afrision

In (30), T has an uninterpretable D-feature that is checked by the interpretable D-feature on the DP, which allows the derivation to converge. If T were [+Past] it would also have a V-feature that needs to be checked, but this is not the case here. As discussed in Section 3, these features are determined in the lexicon. Since LL uses two lexicons, it has access to different Ts. If the Hebrew T [+Present] is selected during numeration, a copula VP will not be needed. However, if a

Spanish T [+Present] is selected, a copula VP will be required in order to check the V-feature or the derivation will crash.

This analysis makes the prediction that LL will only display VSC in the present tense, since past tense VSC is ungrammatical in Hebrew. This seems to be contradicted by (19ab), repeated below in (31ab):

(31) a. Quan diferente **ésta noche** masque todas las noches? (1812: 3)
       how different this night more-than all the nights
    b. Kuanto fue demudada la noçe la esta mas ke todas las noçes. (1946)
       how-much was changed the night the this more than all the nights
       "Why is this night different from all other nights?"

(31a) has no copula while (31b) has an overt past-tense copula. (31a) appears to be an instance of past-tense VSC, which was predicted to be ungrammatical. However, the original Hebrew sentence is in present tense. This can be inferred because the sentence refers to "this night," the night of Passover, when the Haggadah is being recited. What we have in (31b) is a different interpretation of the Hebrew passage being reflected in these LL versions, which would be better translated as "How much was this night changed more than all other nights?" Steiner (2008: 166) explains that, due to the ambiguity of the Hebrew, the interpretation of this passage varies from community-to-community. This might be a case where interpretation overrides literalness in order to ensure that readers would understand what is being said. In linguistic terms, (31b) is still LL, but it is without VSC because the Spanish rather than the Hebrew T node was selected.

5. CONCLUSION

Three constructions that have been previously analyzed as calques are actually instances of the possibility in LL to access a Hebrew and a Spanish lexicon. Because lexical items have different featural specifications in each lexicon, syntactic effects will be observed in LL when a Spanish item is selected rather than a Hebrew item, and *vice versa*. Thus, it is not an entire frame-like structure that is being copied from one lexicon into LL with pieces from the other lexicon. Rather it is the use of a single lexical item, such as the Hebrew present Tense node, that allows for apparent Hebrew syntax despite cooccurrence with Spanish material.

While I have argued that these constructions are not calques, one way to make this concept amenable to my analysis is to redefine what is meant by "calque." Rather than defining it as the morpheme-by-morpheme copying of a word or structure from one language into another, we could reformulate it as the copying of a lexical item with all of its formal features (in the Minimalist sense) from language A into language B. This would be the typical case of language contact as in Prince Edward Island French where some prepositions, along with all of their formal features, were copied from the lexicon of English. LL is different because it continually has much greater access to both a Spanish and a Hebrew lexicon, as can be seen by the abundance of Hebrew- and Spanish-like syntactic configurations that are found in the LL translations of the Haggadah. In sum, LL is not a "calque language" but rather a bilingual register restricted to the religious sphere.

NOTES

1. I differentiate Liturgical Ladino (LL) from Judeo-Spanish (JS). LL is the traditional language used for translation of Hebrew sacred texts into Spanish, represented textually in Bible translations, commentaries, and haggadot. JS is the spoken (and written) vernacular.
2. Double determiners are possible in right-focusing constructions such as the following Modern Spanish, taken from Bernstein (2001): *el libro interesante este*. This Old Spanish example is taken from the "Obra sacada de las crónicas de San Isidro, de Don Lucas, Obispo de Tuy," dated by the CORDE from 1385 to 1396: *... e havie dado poder e senyoria en la tierra aquella e en toda Castiella a aquel mismo fillo suyo Fernando rey*. However, this is not quite the same as the LL data, where both the adjective and the noun agree in definiteness as shown by the double definite article.
3. The idea that all parameters are reducible to features on lexical items (LIs) in the lexicon is often referred to as the "Borer-Chomsky Conjecture," since they were the first to make this claim (Roberts and Holmberg 2010: 32).
4. In examples with multiple lines, the first line is the Hebrew; the second line is a parsing; (a-e) is LL.
5. The Hebrew nouns *ben* and *avi* are in the construct state. /ben/ has the vowel shortened from /e:/ to /e/; /av/ has an unpredictable construct state form, /avi/, as listed in dictionaries.
6. Following Abney (1987), the head of a Noun Phrase is actually a Determiner, hence DP. Strictly speaking, it is not the noun that originally has the D- and Gen-features, it is a null determiner. The noun moves to the head of the DP and picks up these features along the way.
7. For the sake of saving space, when all five versions of the haggadah have the same translation, only one is provided in the examples.
8. "Constituent-command" (c-command): α c-commands β iff (i) α is a sister of β or (ii) α is a sister of γ and γ dominates β.
9. This line is Aramaic.
10. Verbless sentences do occur in Latin and are also documented in at least one "creolized" variety of Spanish spoken in Caracas, Venezuela (Alvarez 1992). Whether verbless sentences were inherited in LL from Spanish remains an open question; further investigation is needed. Gildersleeve (1895: 147) suggests that copula omission was frequent in Latin. It would be a worthwhile to pursue copula variation in Latin, investigating when this property was lost and why it seems to be absent in current varieties of Romance. As for the case of verbless sentences in creolized Spanish spoken in the Venezuelan Caribbean, Alvarez (1992) suggests two sources: (1) it is an internal development or (2) it was adopted in Spanish due to contact. However, the author of that study does not go into any further detail on the matter.

11. There are two minor differences here: (26d), like the Hebrew, has no subject pronoun in conjunction with the wh-word; this would be ungrammatical in standard Spanish. And (26a) does not translate the pronominal suffix on the noun *amo/pueblo*, which the other versions give as *su*.

REFERENCES

Primary

Alkaher, Shelomoh. 1946. *Agada De Pesah: Hagadah Shel Pesah*. Istanbul: Basımevi Alkaher.
Azose, Isaac, Sarah Benezra, and Isaac Maimon. *Hagadah Shel Pesah: Passover Agada:Ağada De Pesah: in Hebrew, with Ladino and English Translation: According to the Custom of the Seattle Sephardic Community*. Seattle, Washington: s.n.
Behar, Nisim. 1962. *La Agada De Pesah: Hagadah Shel Pesah*. Istanbul: Güler Basımevi.
Meldula, Jacob. 1812. *Orden de la Agada de Pesah*. London: L. Alexander.
Ovadia, Zelda. 2002. *La Agada de luz-Agada de Pesah: segun las tradisiones de las komunidades djudias en los Balkanes, kon transkripsion fonetika i traduksion al Ladino*. Jerusalem: Erez.
de Sainte-Exupery, Antoine. 1946. *El Princhipiko*; (trans.) Avner Perez and Gladys Pimienta. Tintenfass: Neckarsteinach.

Secondary

Abney, Stephen P. 1987. *The English noun phrase in its sentential aspect*. Dissertation. Cambridge, MA: MIT.
Adger, David. 2003. *Core Syntax: A Minimalist Approach*. Oxford: UP.
Alvarez, A. 1992. Creole Interference in Venezuelan Spanish: The Absence of Ser/Estar. In P. Hirschbühler, K. Koerner (Eds.), *Romance Languages and Modern Linguistic Theory*, 1–10. Amsterdam: Benjamins.
Androutsopoulou, A., 1995. The licensing of adjectival modification. *Proceedings of the West Coast Conference on Formal Linguistics* 14. 17–31.
Arteaga, Deborah and J. Herschensohn. 2009. A Phase-Based Analysis of Old French Genitive Constructions. *Romance Linguistics 2009:* 285–299. Amsterdam, Netherlands: Benjamins, 2010. *MLA International Bibliography*. Web. 23 July 2015.
———. 2012. Diachronic View of Old French Genitive Constructions. In D. i. Arteaga (Ed.), *Research on Old French: The State of the Art*. Dordrecht, Netherlands: Springer. 19–44.
Benmamoun, Elabbas. 2008. Clause Structure and the Syntax of Verbless Sentences. In *Foundational Issues in Linguistic Theory*, eds. Robert Freidin, Carlos P. Otero and Maria Luisa Zubizarreta. Cambridge: MIT. 105–131.
Bernstein, Judy B. 2001. Focusing the "right" way in Romance determiner phrases. *Probus* 13: 1–29.
Borer, Hagit. 1996. The construct in review. In: Lecarme, J., Lowenstamm, J., Shlonsky, U. (Eds.), *Studies in Afroasiatic Grammar*. Holland Academic Graphics: The Hague, 30–61.
———. 1999. Deconstructing the Construct. In *Beyond Principles and Parameters*, K. Johnson and I. Roberts (Eds.). Netherlands: Kluwer.
Bunis, David Marc. 1996. Translating from the Head and from the Heart: The Essentially Oral Nature of the Ladino Bible-Translation Tradition. In W. Busse, M. Varol-Bornes (Eds.), *Sephardica: Hommage à Haïm Sephiha* (pp. 337–357). Bern, Switzerland: Peter Lang.

Chomsky, Noam. 1995. *The Minimalist Program*. Cambridge: MIT Press.
Danon, Gabi. 2008. Definiteness spreading in the Hebrew construct state. *Lingua* 118: 872–906.
Gesenius, Wilhelm. 1910. *Gesenius' Hebrew Grammar*. (A.E. Cowley, trans.; E. Kautzsch, ed.). Oxford: University Press.
Gildersleeve, Basil and G. Lodge. 1895. *Gildersleeve's Latin Grammar*. Wauconda, IL: Bolchazy-Carducci.
Giusti, G. 1992. *La sintassi dei determinanti*. Ph.D. dissertation. University of Padua.
Holmberg, Anders. 2005. Is There a Little pro? Evidence from Finnish. *Linguistic Inquiry* 36: 533–564
King, Ruth. 2000. *The Lexical Basis of Grammatical Borrowing*. Amsterdam: John Benjamins.
Kulp, Joshua. 2005. The Origins of the Seder and Haggadah. *Currents in Biblical Research* 4: 109–134.
López-Morillas, Consuelo. 1991. Hispano-Semitic Calques and the Context of Translation. *Bulletin of Hispanic Studies* 67: 111–128.
MacSwan, Jeff. 1999. *A Minimalist Approach to Intrasentential Code Switching*. New York: Garland.
———. 2000. The architecture of the bilingual language faculty: evidence from intrasentential code switching. *Bilingualism: Language and Cognition* 3: 37–54.
Pérez-Ferández, Miguel. 1997. *An Introductory Grammar of Rabbinic Hebrew*; (trans. John Elwolde). New York: Brill.
REAL ACADEMIA ESPAÑOLA: Banco de datos (CORDE) [on-line]. *Corpus diacrónico del español*. <http://www.rae.es> [May 12, 2014]
Ritter, E. 1991. Two Functional Categories in Noun Phrases: Evidence from Modern Hebrew. In S. Rothstein (Ed.), *Perspectives on Phrase Structure: Heads and Licensing* (pp. 37–62). San Diego: Academic.
Roberts, Ian. 2007. *Diachronic Syntax*. Oxford: UP.
Roberts, Ian and Anders Holmberg. 2010. Introduction: Parameters in Minimalist Theory. In *Parametric Variation: Null Subjects in Minimalist Theory*. Cambridge: UP. 1–57.
Schwarzwald, Ora. 1996. Methodological Problems in Comparing the Lexicon of the Ladino Haggadahs. In *Hommage à Haïm Vidal Sephiha*, (eds.) Winfried Busse, Heinrich Kohring and Moshe Shaul. 359–372.
Seow, C. L. 1995. *A Grammar for Biblical Hebrew*. Nashville: Abingdon Press.
Sephiha, Vidal Haïm. 1973. *Le Ladino: Judéo-Espagnol Calque*. Paris: Centre de Recherches Hispanique.
———. 1980. Le Ladino (Judéo-Espagnol Calque) ou l'emprunt à tous les niveaux. *Cahiers de l'Institut de Linguistique de Louvain* 6: 93–106.
Sichel, I. 2002. Phrasal movement in Hebrew adjectives and possessives. In: Alexiadou, A., Anagnostopoulou, E., Barbiers, S. (Eds.), *Remnant Movement, Feature Movement and the T-Model*. Benjamins: Amsterdam.
Siloni, T. 1996. Hebrew noun phrases: generalized noun raising. In: Belletti, A., Rizzi, L. (Eds.), *Parameters and Functional Heads*. Oxford UP: Oxford. 239–267.
Shlonsky, Ur. 2004. The Form of Semitic Noun Phrases. *Lingua* 114: 1465–1526.
Steiner, Richard C. 2008. On the Original Structure and Meaning of *Mah Nishtannah* and the History of Its Reinterpretation. *Jewish Studies, an Internet Journal* 7: 163–204.
Winford, Donald. 2003. *An Introduction to Contact Linguistics*. Oxford: Blackwell.

CHAPTER SIX

Ke Haber/Ne Haber

Linguistic Interference, Cross-Meaning, and Lexical Borrowing between Ottoman Turkish and Judeo-Spanish

PAMELA DORN SEZGIN
University of North Georgia

ABSTRACT

Judeo-Spanish/Ottoman Turkish language transfer is investigated within a historic context of multilingualism focusing on semantic categories. The Sapir-Whorf Hypothesis long postulated the importance of language in culture regarding the formation of conceptual categories. The hypothesis explored herein is that late Ottoman culture constituted a shared category of cultural knowledge and world view, despite the multilingualism that characterized the diverse Ottoman religious communities (*millet*). To investigate this problem, proverbs (Judeo-Spanish: *refranes*; Turkish: *atasözü*) are compared for shared meanings from nineteenth century published collections. The analysis also explores loan words and lexical registers of Ottoman Turkish words into Judeo-Spanish; Judeo-Spanish words into Ottoman Turkish; and Greek, French and Italian lexical registers in both languages.

1. INTRODUCTION

In the previous century, linguists Edward Sapir (1884–1939), and his student, Benjamin Whorf (1897–1941) were credited with the so-called "Sapir-Whorf Hypothesis": a philosophical statement encapsulating the close relationship between language and culture.[1] Language in this view, deriving from the work of the nineteenth century philosopher, Wilhelm von Humboldt (1767–1835), was said to be one of the defining aspects of peoplehood. Language shaped thought and was viewed as being in a reciprocal relationship with culture. Cultures simply were different ways of thinking. Human language made explicit human thought. Different focal vocabularies, for example, like those used by the Inuit with their many different words for snow, indicated important aspects of a culture, their priorities, and unique lifestyles. Unlike other animals, humans talk about culture and the words we use as well as other linguistic structures influence particular world views.[2]

The 'Sapir-Whorf Hypothesis" in recent years (1990s) was reformulated into the concept of linguistic relativity. While criticized by some scholars, it continues to serve as one of the foundational principles in anthropological studies of language and culture. In contrast, structural linguists like Noam Chomsky prefer to look for universals in human language and link them to neuroscience and grammatical structures. This chapter does neither. It does not investigate the uniqueness of a particular language in local culture nor search for broad species-characterizing, universal linguistic structures. Rather, it looks at the middle ground and poses the following questions: What can a language tell us about the social, cultural, and political interactions that its community had in a historic setting, in a multilingual, culturally pluralistic empire? What information can a language give us about relationships between cultural groups? What traces of these interactions are left, some ninety years after the empire's demise? And how do we study such a problem without contemporary fieldwork? What types of data remain in published sources that can help us reconstruct a language's vibrant, conversational rituals and help us understand the relationships between a particular group of people and their neighbors?

2. HYPOTHESIS AND RESEARCH DESIGN

This chapter presents a study of Judeo-Spanish/Ottoman Turkish language transfer in a historical context of multilingualism focusing on semantic and shared conceptual categories between the two languages. Language transfer, also called L1 interference and cross-meaning, generally operates in situations of bilingualism where speakers apply knowledge from their primary or native language to a second language. The interference or influence from their native language can be manifest in many aspects from grammar, vocabulary (loan words, registers), accent (including intonation, speech style), spelling (including orthography), to the transfer of structures.[3] Obviously, studying the interactions of these two languages in a pluralistic and multilingual setting is more complex than in the context of bilingualism. The historic dimension also thickens the plot: Judeo-Spanish is no longer spoken as a primary language on a daily basis. Its use, today, is restricted to internet list-serves like the *Ladino Komunitá,* in university classrooms, and through the performance of reconstructed folk songs.

2.1. Hypothesis

Late Ottoman culture constituted a shared category of cultural knowledge and worldview, although multilingualism characterized the diverse *millet* (Ottoman religious communities). Therefore, shared categories of meaning can be found in the Judeo-Spanish and Ottoman languages because of their long contact (circa 1492 to 1923) during the Ottoman Empire, even though the two languages are from very different language families and have few if any structural similarities (e.g., grammar, phonemes, morphemes, syntax, and the like).

2.2. Methodology

To investigate this problem, shared proverbs are compared between the Judeo-Spanish and Ottoman Turkish languages, and the use of loan words and lexical registers are investigated in both languages. Proverbs (Judeo-Spanish: *refranes*; Turkish: *atasözü*) are the focus instead of idioms/metaphors (Judeo-Spanish: *dichas*; Turkish: *deyim*). While metaphors are fascinating, they tend to be context specific and difficult to interpret. Proverbs, on the other hand, convey complete thoughts and were collected extensively in the nineteenth century. In Modern Turkish, many of the Ottoman proverbs are still used in daily speech.[4]

2.3. Sources

For the purposes of this preliminary study, two historic collections of proverbs were used. The collections are both from the nineteenth century. The collection used for the Judeo-Spanish proverbs was by Raimundo Foulché-Delbosc: *1313 Proverbios Judeo-Españoles* (reprint 2006). The proverbs were collected in 1888 in Constantinople/Istanbul. The publication utilized a distinctive orthography. The editor of the 2006 reprint notes: *"La presente edición conserva la ortografia empleada en el libro original francés, por lo que el modo en el que algunas palabras están escritas no responde a las reglas ortograficas del castellano actual."*[5] Foulché-Delbosc modified the standard Castilian orthography, often breaking its rules as necessary to reflect the Judeo-Spanish speech style that he was transcribing. Other collections of Judeo-Spanish proverbs were used as secondary sources, particularly those that were linked to the Eastern Mediterranean portion of the Ottoman Empire.[6]

The collection used to represent the Ottoman language proverbs was a book entitled, *Turkish Proverbs Translated Into English*, published by the Mechitarist (Catholic) Armenian Monastery of St. Lazarus in Venice in 1873, henceforth referred to as the *Armeno-Turkish Collection*.[7] An explanation about nomenclature is necessary regarding this collection. In nineteenth century European sources, the terms "Turkey," "Turks" and "Turkish" were used to describe the "Ottoman Empire," "Ottomans," and "*Osmanlıca*" (the Ottoman language). The *Armeno-Turkish Collection* does not specify where its proverbs were obtained. It is highly probable, though, that they were collected in Constantinople/Istanbul given the close ties of the Venetian Mechitarists with Armenians in that city, and the political, social, and cultural dominance of that community within the Armenian millet, especially during the development of the *Nizâmnâme-i Millet-i Ermeniyân* [Armenian Constitution] (1860–1863). Secondary sources used with the *Armeno-Turkish Collection* included Ottoman dictionaries and a contemporary collections of Turkish proverbs.[8]

The *Armeno-Turkish Collection* was published using the Western Armenian alphabet for the proverbs, rather than the modified Perso-Arabic script usually used for the Ottoman language, with the English translations appearing under them. [See Figure 1.] The Western Armenian alphabet contains thirty-eight letters of which thirty-one are used to render Ottoman Turkish and they can represent almost all of the sounds needed.[9] Such use of the Western Armenian alphabet for the Ottoman language is called "Armeno-Turkish." It was used by the Turkish-speaking Armenians of the Ottoman Empire in the nineteenth century to transliterate the vernacular version of the Ottoman language to make it more accessible to the Turkish-speaking Armenians. European school books in mathematics and the sciences were translated from French into Ottoman by Armenian publishers, rather than using the Perso-Arabic script. Armenian newspapers were also published using this script, it was used by Armenian actors in the Ottoman theatre, and American missionaries found it an easier vehicle for learning the Ottoman language.[10]

Armeno-Turkish was one of several alphabets used by non-Muslims to convey the Ottoman language.[11] For example, Orthodox Christians in central Anatolia wrote the Ottoman language using the Greek alphabet, Greek loan words and other linguistic features.[12] These texts were called *Karamanlidika*. Likewise the Greek language written in Smyrna/Izmir and Chios/Sakız Island changed script and used the Latin alphabet due to Italian influences on the Aegean coast. This version of the Greek language, which also used many Ottoman loan words, was known as *Smyrneika*.[13]

Jews, on the other hand, were rarely fluent Ottoman Turkish speakers, although the language was taught in the Alliance Israélite Universelle Schools from its beginnings (1860s). A few prominent Muslims attended Jewish schools and/or

— 10 —

18

Ամէն իլէն օլան աիյին պայրամ ըրր:
A calamity which befalls in public, is festivity and rejoicing.

19

Ճամիյէ լազըմ օլան մէշինէ հարամ ըրր:
That is not necessary to a chapel which belongs to a temple

20

Աջ այը օյնամազ:
The bear that is hungry never dances.

21

Հէր գուշուն էթի էէնմէզ:
The flesh of every bird cannot be eaten.

22

Սաղըր նէ քի իշիտիրսէ ույուտուրուր:
The deaf man forms of that which he understands a new sense.

23

Հէր շէյ ինճէլիքթէն, ինսան գալընլըղընտան,
գըրըլըր:
Every thing breaks because it is slender, man breaks because of his stoutness.

Fig. 1. An Example of the Armeno-Turkish Script from *Turkish Proverbs Translated into English* (The Armenian Monastery of St. Lazarus, 1873).

taught Ottoman Turkish, there, too.[14] Turkification came to the Jewish community in the twentieth century except for a few short-lived Judeo-Turkish publications in the 1890s.[15] Unlike the Turkish-speaking Armenians and Greeks in the Ottoman Empire, Jews used variations of the Hebrew alphabet for writing and publishing their own languages, Hebrew, Aramaic, liturgical Ladino, and Judeo-Spanish.[16] The *Solitreo* script was used for handwritten correspondence. The *Rashi* script was used for the content of newspaper articles with the headlines and titles in the square Hebrew *merubba* font.[17] Foreign researchers, like Foulché-Delbosc, though, used the modified or extended Latin alphabet for modern Castilian Spanish or French to record the Judeo-Spanish proverbs in the Ottoman context, rather than one of the indigenous Jewish writing systems.

3. HISTORIC AND SOCIOLINGUISTIC CONTEXT

In the case of Ottoman Turkish, the language started to be modernized during the *Tanzimat* in the nineteenth century, although the changes were not forced upon the masses, nor were they widespread. Urbanites and intellectuals from the various Ottoman ethnic groups were aware of these changes, as they were of the new laws and/or had participated limited forms of self-governance. Ottoman subjects were transformed into citizens through the legal and social changes mandated by the state, including two constitutional periods that were characterized by having elected parliaments.[18] Ottomanism was a mid-nineteenth century political ideology designed to save the empire from partition, and to compete with the growing Balkan nationalisms.

Language reform was part of the agenda to get everyone on the same page in state-building. Exiled Ottoman intellectuals in Paris participated in the *Société Asiatique* (1850s), searching for Turkic roots and folklore in their composite Ottoman language which also had Persian and Arabic components. Of course, Balkan nationalisms in the end, won, due in large measure to the meddling of the European Powers. Ottomanism was almost completely forgotten in European history books due to the stereotyped "Sick Man" image fostered by Great Britain from the late 1870s through the Great War (World War I), as well as by nationalistic historiography, views that until recently obscured our understandings of Ottoman modernity.[19] Nationalism views language and literature as essential features of the "soul of the people" but such a view found complex, cross-cultural Ottoman linguistic devices like Armeno-Turkish problematic. Armeno-Turkish did not fit the emerging Turkish nationalist paradigm of the early twentieth century, built from French revolutionary ideas of one nation, one language, one people.[20] For that matter, it was a bad fit for the emerging Armenian nationalist paradigm, too. Ottoman peoples were not homogenous and they were not living in silos, unexposed to the cultures and languages of their neighbors. Instead, they were part of a complex, cross-cultural sharing process, which also included languages, and which had been taking place for five or six centuries on three continents.

In the case of Judeo-Spanish, the late nineteenth and early twentieth centuries were periods of increasing recognition that the language the ancestors brought from Spain was in danger of becoming a dead language, replaced by the French and Italian languages that were associated with industrialization, education, and increasing business opportunities in a rapidly changing world.[21] Sephardic journalists in the Ottoman Empire embarked upon collecting projects, publishing folkloric texts to preserve their linguistic heritage.[22] Folklorists and linguists from Spain documented the language, notably Ramón Menéndez Pidal (1869–1968) and his students. Sephardic scholars like Maír José Benardete (1895–1989) continued this paradigm well into the 1970s, linking Eastern Sephardic culture and the Judeo-Spanish language to a lost Spain, part of a global Spanish-speaking diaspora.

The Judeo-Spanish language and its Sephardic culture in the Ottoman Empire did not exist in a time warp or vacuum. Within the Ottoman Jewish communities there was a high degree of internal diversity. Not everyone migrated from Spain, for example, at the same time; there were different waves of migration. There were regional differences in the Judeo-Spanish spoken in Iberia at the time of the expulsion. Some families went to Portugal and came at a later period, even a century later, to the Ottoman Empire. Byzantine Jewish communities continued after the Ottomans took control. In some cases, they remained as Greek-speakers, as in Yanya/Ioannina; and in other instances, eventually they were assimilated in the Judeo-Spanish world, as was the case in Constantinople/İstanbul.

4. LANGUAGE INTERFERENCE AND LEXICAL BORROWING

The story of language interference by French into Judeo-Spanish is well known via the history of the *Alliance Israélite Universelle* schools. French eventually replaced Judeo-Spanish as the language spoken at home, at least for several generations in middle-class and elite families, before the predominance of new, national languages in the twentieth century with the accompanying mandatory public education. The influence of Italian language, though, has not been really studied in the Ottoman Jewish communities. Italian Jews, though, called *Los Frankos*, became the elites in most of the Ottoman Jewish communities in the Balkans and Anatolia, as well as Egypt, during the late nineteenth and early twentieth centuries. The category "Italian Jews" did not necessarily imply that they were speaking Italian. Often, they were simply Ottoman Jews who bought Italian citizenship, which was for sale, as were aristocratic titles, during *Il Risorgimento* ("The Resurgence") in the 1860s when various Italian kingdoms unified into a modern nation state. On the other hand, there were examples of industrialists like the Allatini and Modiano families of Salonika/Thessaloniki or the Camondo family who were involved in banking and real estate development in Istanbul. These families held both Ottoman and Italian citizenship and maintained businesses in both the Austro-Hungarian and Ottoman Empires.

The Italian language, however, also made inroads into the Judeo-Spanish speech community in places like Alexandria, Izmir/Smyrna, and on a number of eastern Mediterranean islands, which from the thirteenth century onwards had communities of Genoese and Venetian merchants. The trade language called *Lingua Franca*, which was essentially Italian at its core, dominated in the Eastern Mediterranean for many centuries. Some Judeo-Spanish speakers would have had contact with it in the port cities and via their business interests. It was not modern Italian, but rather, had elements from the Florentine, Genoese, and Venetian dialects, plus many loan words from the local languages, including a predominance of Greek terms.[23] Indeed, prior to the development of Modern Turkish as a prime element of state-building in the 1920s and 1930s, many words connected to commerce and modernity were in lexical registers in both Ottoman Turkish and Judeo-Spanish borrowed from Italian and French. Even today, most of these registers still utilize these loan words, a domain untouched by the twentieth century language reform.

Examples of FRENCH loan words: abajur in Judeo-Spanish and panjur in Turkish (slatted shutters); otobüs (bus); büro (office); asansör (elevator); butik (boutique); atelye (workshop); broşür (brochure); bagaj (baggage); dekor (décor); gar (train station); plaj (beach); pasaj (passage: a shopping area); pardesü (overcoat or raincoat); motor (motor-boat); motosiklet (motorcycle).

Examples of ITALIAN loan words: banka (bank); balkón (balcony); gazeta in Judeo-Spanish and gazete in Turkish (newspaper); mobilya (furniture); bravo (bravo); bisikleta (bicycle); moderno (modern); moda (fashion, style).

Fig. 2. Lexical Borrowings from French and Italian used in both Ottoman Turkish and Judeo-Spanish (Constantinople Dialect) Rendered in Modern Turkish.

The idea of having specialized lexical registers, rather than just random loan words, characterized Ottoman Turkish. For example the names of fish and seafood, for the most part, were in a Greek register in Ottoman Turkish, a practice which has survived in Modern Turkish as well. (See Figure 3.)

Greek Name	English translation	Ottoman Turkish Names
ahtapódhi	octopus	ahtapot
antsoúles [also antzoúghies]	Aegean anchovy	ançüez
astakós	lobster	ıstakoz
bakaliáros ["Morina" is either a Judeo-Spanish or Italian name; Jews imported salt cod into the Ottoman Empire from Great Britain]	salt-cod	morina*
barboúni	red mullet	barbunya
gharides	shrimp	karides
ghlósa [Both the Greek and Turkish words translate as "tongue."]	sole	dil*
hamsi	Black Sea anchovy	hamsi
kalamari [also kéfalos]	squid	kalamar
lakérdha	bonito or tuna cured in salt	lâkerda
levréki [also lavráki]	sea bass	levrek
louféri [also ghofári]	bluefish	lüfer
mídhia	mussels	midye
orfós [also orofós]	dusky grouper	orfoz
palamidha [also palamida in Judeo-Spanish]	bonito	palamut
rénga	herring	ringa
sardéles [also, sardhéles]	sardines	sardalya
sinarída [also sinaghridha]	dentex	sinarit
skoumbrí	mackerel	uskumru
soupiá	cuttlefish	supya
tónos	tuna	tonbalığı
trántsa	pink dentex	trance
tsipoúra	gilthead or sea bream [dorade]	çipura
tsíros	dried mackerel	çiroz

Fig. 3. Seafood and Fish Names.

Lexical borrowing was also something that characterized the relationship between Judeo-Spanish and Ottoman Turkish. Harris (1996), Varol-Bornes (1996), and Romero (2012) analyzed the vowel changes in Turkish words that were borrowed into Judeo-Spanish.[24] Regarding the published collections of proverbs in which these words were used, that change is not necessarily apparent; the vowel changes are more noticeable in speech. Rather, the consistency of semantic categories was manifest in many of the proverbs: categories that seemed to be shared between the two languages, Judeo-Spanish and Ottoman Turkish.

The meanings of the loan words varied in their adaptation from Ottoman Turkish into Judeo-Spanish. In some cases, the Ottoman meaning was retained in Judeo-Spanish, and in other cases, the Ottoman words took on a completely new meaning. Abraham Danon (1903) provided a selection of short, religious narratives, perhaps from rabbinical responsa, that were translated into Turkish by the Jews in the eighteenth century, as well as proverbs, sayings, phrases and expressions from Ottoman Turkish used in the Judeo-Spanish speech of his contemporaries. He remarked that even the elder, illiterate women in Adrianople/Edirne used the difficult Persian and Arabic words found in Ottoman in these borrowed items, particularly the proverbs.[25] Danon hypothesized that these Ottoman Turkish loan words replaced forgotten Castilian Spanish words. As well, French and Italian words that sounded like Spanish were also substituted.[26] Lexical borrowing was extensive. Raymond Reynard cites some 2000 loan words from Ottoman and/or Modern Turkish into Judeo-Spanish. Danon published three glossaries of these loan words in the early twentieth century.[27] These words were also seen in published dictionaries of Judeo-Spanish and in the secondary proverb collections.[28] [See Figure 4 for Ottoman loan words in Judeo-Spanish.]

Of course, lexical borrowing was not the only result of the contact between Ottoman Turkish and Judeo-Spanish. As Sarah Thomason summarized, there are at least seven different mechanisms of contact-induced language change. These include code-switching, code alternation, passive familiarity, negotiation, second-language acquisition strategies, bilingual first-language acquisition, and deliberate decision.[29] The processes of code-switching, code alternation, passive familiarity, and deliberate decision all seem possible as explanatory devices for describing why whole phrases from Ottoman Turkish as identified by Abraham Danon are borrowed into Judeo-Spanish. Linguistic fieldwork by researchers in the twentieth century have identified linguistic transformations beyond just borrowed vocabularies such as Judeo-Spanish words with Hebrew and Turkish suffixes, calques or word-for-word translations from other languages copied into Judeo-Spanish, importation of Turkish verbs; phonological changes; and vowel replacement.[30] These changes were rather similar to the linguistic interference of Turkish in contemporary Balkan languages about which Thomason observed: "most of the Turkish loanwords are nouns, but there are also quite a few verbs and, in the most affected languages, many adverbs, prepositions, and conjunctions as well" (2001: 108).

The lexical borrowing of Ottoman Turkish words into Judeo-Spanish as illustrated in Figure 4 is not restricted to a particular register, as it was with the fish and seafood names taken from Greek into Ottoman Turkish.[31] Some categories of words, though, seem to predominate. For example, Ottoman words are used for many professions or occupational categories: e.g., *basmacı* (fabric merchant); *hamal* (porter); *kasap* (butcher); *kuyumcu* (jeweler); *kunduracı* (shoemaker); *çoban* (shepherd). Ottoman words are also used for everyday objects and conditions: *chadir* (umbrella – a provincial meaning in Ottoman); *chanak* (an earthenware bowl); *findjan* (from *fincan*) (porcelain cup); *kazan* (a large basin or cooking pot); *buz* (ice or ice cold); *bayat* (stale); *çark* (wheel); *charuka* (from çarık) (a kind of sandals); *bostan* or *bustan* (garden); *bodrum* (basement); *boy* (height or size). Of course, some food names have been adapted from Ottoman Turkish, too: e.g., *borekas* (from *börek*, a filled savory pastry); *chicolata* (from çukulata) (chocolate); *chay* (from çay) (tea).

One of the most interesting loan words is *buchúkes* (from *buçuk*) which in Turkish means "half" but in Judeo-Spanish meant "twins."[32] The word for twins in both Ottoman and Modern Turkish is *ikiz*.[33] This example illustrates the condition of loan words taking on a completely new meaning in Judeo-Spanish that is different than their original Ottoman meaning.

---

ankéta/anket = inquiry
araba = araba: car or carriage
bakal = greengrocer
basmacı = merchant who sells cloth
bazár = Ottoman: pazar meaning "market"
bayát = stale
bodrum = basement
boston (bostan, bustan) = garden; Ottoman: bustan
boy = height or size
borekas/börek = a kind of filled pastry or turnover
buchúkes = twins; in Modern Turkish, buçuk means "half" and in Ottoman, "twins" are ikiz
buz = ice or ice cold
chadir = umbrella; in Ottoman: çadır means "tent" and can also have the provincial meaning as "umbrella"
chanaka = chanak/çanak = earthenware pot or bowl
chanta/çanta = purse or handbag

chark/çark = wheel; also chárke in J-S
charúka = leather sandals; Ottoman: çarıkı
chay/çay = tea
chicolata = chocolate; Ottoman: çukulata
chobán/çoban = shepherd
dar uti = to iron; Ottoman: "uti" from ütü "pressing iron," ütülemek being derivative, a verb made from a noun
findjan/fincan = cup of porcelain
halis = pure
hamál/hamal = porter
ishalla/inşallah = G-d willing
kalabalik = crowded. As in "Con calabaliq [buena companiya], se abre la gana (el apetito viene comiendo)" (Foulché-Delbosc, p. 21, #164)
karar = decision
kasap = butcher
kofté/köfte = patties usually made of meat but also they can be made from vegetables
kunduradje/kunduraci = shoemaker
kuyumcu = jeweler
bilibiz /leblebi = roasted chickpeas
musafir = guest; Ottoman: misafir
patladear/patlamak = to break; as in "La piedra patladea, la persona no" (Foulché-Delbosc, p.48, #579)
paras = money; in Ottoman: para
peshtimál/peştemal (also destmal) = bath towel
sachma/saçma = nonsense or insignificant chatter; as in "Corta la chema [Shema] y di la satchma [cuchufleta]" (Foulché-Delbosc, p. 21, #179)
saklayıcı = concealing, secretive. As in "El Corazon lo save el saklaiji." (Foulché-Delbosc, p. 80, #322)
shaka/şaka = joke
shasheo = to become dizzy and bewildered, surprised; Ottoman Turkish: şaşkın olmak
shukur/şükur and sükr = thanks (as in "Thanks be to G-d")
sirá/sıra = order, sequence, series
tefter/defter = notebook or ledger
tepsi = tray
zor = difficult

Fig. 4. Examples of Ottoman Turkish Words in Judeo-Spanish.[34] *Examples taken from words used in Foulché-Delbosc (2006/1888) and in the online Diksionario de Djudeo-Espanyol a Turko (Ladinokomunita).*

In comparative perspective, the Armenian and Greek languages of Anatolia and of the Balkan and Middle Eastern Armenian and Greek communities under Ottoman rule are also full of Ottoman Turkish loan words. For example, when I was learning Modern Greek, whenever I could not remember a word, I just substituted a Turkish noun, added a Greek ending. Often my clumsy use of *linguistic productivity* was correct and the selected word had the same meaning in Greek as it does in Turkish. Listen to selections of Western Armenian folk music on YouTube from Armenian-American performers, and even if you do not speak Armenian, you can recognize many Turkish loan words, if you are a Turkish-speaker. The *longue durée*, to borrow Braudel's term, of Ottoman rule in the Eastern Mediterranean is present in loan words and borrowed lexical registers, still used in many diverse, contemporary languages in the area, today.

What about the reciprocal situation? Are there Judeo-Spanish loan words in Ottoman Turkish? The obvious ones have to do with Jewish religious practice and are Hebrew in their origin in both Judeo-Spanish and Ottoman Turkish: *haham* (rabbi) and *havra* (a small synagogue or congregation). Others are from the business world: *haver* (business partner), a word found in the Charles Wells' Redhouse Dictionary of Ottoman Turkish (1880: 464). In both Ottoman and Modern Turkish, though, the preferred word is *ortak*. The word *haver* appears in Judeo-Spanish from the Hebrew. Another Hebrew word used in Judeo-Spanish is the word for kosher: *kaşer*. In the Jewish folklore of Thrace, the claim was made that the name of a famous Turkish cheese, *kaşar peyniri*, was derived from the Judeo-Spanish word for kosher but its Turkish version employs vowel harmony. The second vowel changed in Turkish so that *kaşer* became *kaşar*. The cultural evidence for the derivation was that Jews were famous cheese-makers and dairy-shop owners in places like Silivri and Çorlu.[35]

Hebrew and Ottoman Turkish are from very different language families which makes it easy to feel secure in attributing the aforementioned etymologies. But words from the Spanish part of the Judeo-Spanish lexicon are almost impossible to attribute in Ottoman Turkish due to the similarity of the modern Romance languages. Spanish, Portuguese, Italian and Romanian share Latin roots for many words. For example, we might want to attribute a Judeo-Spanish origin for the Ottoman word, *kasa*. This word accumulated a number of different meanings: as a commercial crate, as a cash box, safe box, or cash register. It might derive from the Judeo-Spanish word: *kasha,* and similarly, the word for cashier in Judeo-Spanish is *kashera*. But who is to say that *kasa* did not enter Ottoman Turkish from one of the Italian dialects used in the Eastern Mediterranean, from the word *cassa,* or from the Portuguese *caixa*. One of the most famous words in Ottoman Turkish attributed to Judeo-Spanish was *masa* (table); in Judeo-Spanish, the word is *méza*. In this case, the Italian word is *tavola,* so one might at first think that indeed, the word is from Judeo-Spanish. Sevan Nişanyan's etymological dictionary for

Turkish, attributes the similarities of this word in the modern Romance languages to its shared Latin root, *mensa*.[36] Obviously, though, it was borrowed from either Spanish or Portuguese, which in both languages it appears as *mesa*, with a vowel change from "e" to "a" in Turkish, since Latin-speakers were long gone from Constantinople by the Ottoman conquest in 1453. The similarity of these words in the Romance languages, though, complicates attribution for the sources of these lexical borrowings.

5. PROVERBS AND SHARED MEANINGS

As Goldberg observed: "proverbs … have both a synchronic and a diachronic trajectory—that is, they are transmitted geographically within a single period and are passed down from one generation to another." (Goldberg 1993: 106) Proverbs are embedded in the conversational rituals of everyday life. Proverb collections, on the other hand, to some extent decontextualize them. In this study, though, the fact that many of the Ottoman Turkish examples found in the *Armeno-Turkish Collection* (1873) are still used today by Turkish speakers and oddly enough, on Facebook and the internet, where the geographic transmission gives way to a transnational space. So, their continued usage makes discerning their meaning possible. The survival of these proverbs provides an example of multigenerational continuity, despite the fact that the Turkish language underwent a serious transformation from its Ottoman form, particularly during the early years of the Turkish Republic (1920s and 1930s).

My research methodology was to try to match proverbs from the two collections, whenever possible, or if I could find the proverb in one of the historic collections, then I assumed I could date it. In other words, Foulché-Delbosc from 1888 and the *Armeno-Turkish Collection* from 1873, represent a time period before nationalism. If there are proverbs held in common between the two collections, that is, between Judeo-Spanish and Ottoman Turkish languages, then perhaps this sharing can tell us something about the Ottoman culture and intergroup relations. In contrast, we would expect non-Muslims to have knowledge of Turkish proverbs after 1924, because of mandatory education in the Turkish language which accompanied nation-building. Following the creation of the Turkish Republic by the Treaty of Lausanne, the comprehensive work of modern nation-building ensued. In Modern Turkey, this meant a great deal of linguistic and educational change. The slogan, *"Vatandaş Türkçe konuş"* ("Citizen, speak Turkish") (1928–1930s) marked the beginning of a long campaign to have a standardized language that all ethnic groups within the country would share.[37] The modern Turkish nation-state, like its French and other European antecedents, mandated elementary school education in the national language. People who wanted their children to learn foreign languages had to send them to afterschool programs and to special foreign-language high schools and universities. All public uses of language in broadcasting, for example, and advertising, were in Turkish until the early 1990s.

The Judeo-Spanish proverb tradition is indeed rich and the shared proverbs that I have begun to identify [Figure 5] from these two nineteenth century collections are only one category of Judeo-Spanish proverb. Other categories include proverbs that are shared with other Spanish-speaking communities in the world, e.g., *"En boca cerrada no entra mosca."* ["A fly cannot enter a closed mouth," which means you need to keep an open mind (Foulché-Delbosc, p. 35, #407). And proverbs that have particular Jewish or Biblical referents: *"Rovar pites calientes y besar mesusoth."* Also rendered as *"Arrovar pites y besa el Mezuzah,"* which refers to someone who has false piety. That person is kissing the *mezuzah* per the Biblical commandment but they are a thief (Foulché-Delbosc, p. 79, #1121).[38]

Turkish: "Havlayan köpek ısırmaz."
Judeo-Spanish: "Perro ladrador, nunca mordedor" [or "nunca bien mordedor"]
Also: "Perro que mucho [muncho] ladra no modre."
English translation: "The dog that barks does not bite."
Sources: Foulché-Delbosc, p.65, #873 and #875; Turkish version from Turkish Culture Portal http://www.turkishculture.org/literature/literature/turkish-proverbs-133.htm?type=1

Turkish: "Kenarına bak bezini al, anasına bak kızını al."
Judeo-Spanish: "Mira la madre, toma la hija."
English translation: The Turkish version has an additional phrase at the beginning: "Observe the edge, if it is pleasing, take the linen; observe the mother and take the daughter." [The meaning of the first part of the proverb implies to check the quality of the fabric.] The Judeo-Spanish version just has the second part: "Observe the mother, take the daughter."
Sources: Foulché-Delbosc, p.56, #716; Armeno-Turkish Collection, p. 32, #156; Yurtbaşı, p. 387.

Turkish: "Her koyun kendi bacağından asılır."
Judeo-Spanish: "Cada cordero de su pacha lo colgan." Also: "Cada carnero por su pie se encolga."
English translation: "Every sheep is hung by its leg." Meaning: Everyone is responsible for his or her own actions. [Also: "Every ram is hung by its foot."]
Sources: Foulché-Delbosc, p. 18, #113 and #114; Armeno-Turkish Collection, p. 26, #119.

Turkish: "Pire için yorgan yakmak."
J-S: "Por una pulga quemar una colcha."
English translation: "Burning a quilt for a louse."
Sources: Foulché-Delbosc, p. 67, #902; Turkish version from the Turkish Culture Portal http://www.turkishculture.org/literature/literature/turkish-proverbs-133.htm?type=1

Turkish: "Tatlı yeyip tatlı söyleşelim."
J-S: "Come dulce, que hables bien."
English translation: "Eat sweets, speak sweetly or well."
Sources: Foulché-Delbosc, p. 20, #158; Yurtbaşı, p. 693, "tatlı."

Turkish: "Yalancının mumu yatsıya kadar yanar."
Judeo-Spanish: "La candela del mentiroso no dura largo."
English translation: "The liar's candle will burn only until bedtime." "The liar's candle will not last long."
Meaning: Lies only work for a limited time.
Sources: Foulché-Delbosc, p. 44, #525; Turkish version from the Turkish Culture Portal. http://www.turkishculture.org/literature/literature/turkish-proverbs-133.htm?type=1

Turkish: "Denize düşen yılana sarılır."
Judeo-Spanish: "Quien la mar se caye, y de la culevra se engancha."
English translation: "The one who falls in the sea grabs [even] a snake."
Sources: Foulché-Delbosc, p. 68, #916; Turkish version from the Turkish Culture Portal and from the Armeno-Turkish Collection, p. 7, #4.

Turkish: "İki ayağını bir pabuca sokmak."
Judeo-Spanish: "Dos pies y un zapato." Or: "Dos pies en un zapato."
English translation: "Two feet in [inserted into] one shoe."
Meaning: Trying to do everything at once, being overwhelmed or so overworked that you are paralyzed.
Sources: Foulché-Delbosc, p. 28, #294; Armeno-Turkish Collection, p. 35, #175.

Turkish: "Kızım sana söylerim, gelinim sen anla."
Judeo-Spanish: "Vo lo digo a vos mi ija, para ke lo siente mi ermuera."
English translation: "I am telling you my daughter so that my daughter-in-law can hear it." Or: "I tell it to my daughter for my daughter-in-law to understand."
Meaning: Sometimes a message is intended for someone other than the actual recipient.
Sources: Judeo-Spanish in Bardavid and Ender, Trezoro, p. 59; Turkish version from the Turkish Culture Portal http://www.turkishculture.org/literature/literature/turkish-proverbs-133.htm?type=1

Turkish: "Kesemediğiniz eli şevkle öpünüz."
Judeo-Spanish: "Besa mano que queres ver cortada." Also: "Mano que queras ver herida, bésala."
English translation: "Kiss [ardently] the hands which you cannot cut off [or wound]."
Meaning: The meaning in of the Turkish proverb is one of subordination: go along with the situation because there is nothing else that you can do but submit. The Judeo-Spanish proverb in contrast, in its contemporary usage, implies a slyness, to feign subordination in order to get the upper hand.
Sources: Foulché-Delbosc, p. 16, #86 and p. 52, #655; Armeno-Turkish Collection, p. 9, #15.

Turkish: "Bana arkadaşını söyle, sana kim olduğunu söyleyeyim."
Judeo-Spanish: "Dime con quien conozcas, te dire quien eras." [Contemporary Judeo-Spanish usage is in the familiar second person: "Dime quien conoses, te dire quien sos;" The proverb is given as rendered in the Foulché-Delbosc collection which in this case seems to employ a hybrid of Castilian Spanish and Judeo-Spanish.]
English translation: "Tell me who your friends are [tell me who you know] and I will tell you who you are."
Sources: Foulché-Delbosc, p. 27, #287; Turkish version from Panagiotis Georgalas' "Greek-Turkish Proverbs Page"< http://learnturkish.pgeorgalas.gr/ProverbsSetEn.asp>.

Turkish: "Sütten ağzı yanan, yoğurdu üfleyerek ver."
Judeo-Spanish: "Quien se quema en la chorba, asopla en el yogurt."
English translation: "The one who burned his mouth on milk [or soup in the J-S version], blows on the yogurt."
Sources: Foulché-Delbosc, p. 76 #1067; Turkish version from the Turkish Culture Portal.

Fig. 5. Examples of Shared Proverbs in Ottoman Turkish and Judeo-Spanish.

6. CONCLUSIONS

In this chapter, the preliminary results of a comparative study have been presented, a study that looked at shared meaning in proverbs and lexical borrowing between the Judeo-Spanish and Ottoman Turkish languages. This study was framed in a context of multilingualism in the late Ottoman Empire and also, in a period of intense experimentation with orthographies. Languages in contact in the Ottoman Empire shared many of the same specialized registers, such as the Greek names for fish, or French and Italian loan words that represent the nuts and bolts of a modern life. The geographic focus of this paper has primarily been Constantinople/Istanbul, but secondarily, information from Smyrna/Izmir and its special version of Greek have been used to try to illustrate patterns of linguistic interaction among the Ottoman communities.

In terms of the methodology used, the study of shared proverbs provides a deeper level of analysis than does the demonstrated lexical borrowing. It is easy in any two languages in the world to find some shared or similar words, which may or may not tell us about historical relationships between the speakers of those languages. Proverbs, though, because of their link as an expression of world view, as a kind of verbal folklore, provide a more profound territory for the exploration of intergroup relations. More data is needed in order to strongly make the case for a shared Ottoman culture via similarities in semantics between the dominant, elite Ottoman Turkish language, and the languages of other ethnic and religious groups in the empire. The comparative work demonstrated between Judeo-Spanish and Ottoman Turkish in this paper may provide a technique for looking at hidden cultural clues in different languages that shared the same cultural space during a specific but rather long period of history. The culture of empires is much different than that of the nation-state, particularly in the area of multilingualism. Polyglots were cosmopolitans who were able to not only survive in empires, but thrive in them. Proverbs and lexical borrowing are a window into a very different cultural system and world view than the one we ourselves have experienced growing up in the nation-state, with its emphasis on the dominance of one national language.

NOTES

1. The "Sapir-Whorf Hypothesis" was not an actual hypothesis in terms of its testability nor did Sapir and Whorf actually collaborate on its formation. See E. F. K. Koerner (2002: 39–62).
2. Whorf became aware of the important relationship between language and culture while pursuing his day job as an industrial fire inspector. He noticed that accidents occurred because barrels marked "empty" that formerly held dangerous chemicals exploded when workers flicked cigarettes near them. The concept "empty" indicated to the workers that the barrels were not dangerous; they did not realize that the vapor left inside of the containers could ignite. For more about this example, see Whorf's collected works edited by John B. Carroll (1998).
3. For more on language contact, see Winfried Busse and Michäel Studemund-Halévy (2011), Yaron Matras (2009), and Sarah Grey Thomason (2001).
4. Ottoman proverbs frequently appear on the internet in places like the Turkish Culture Portal (http://www.turkishculture.org/literature/literature/turkish-proverbs-133.htm?type=1), and on the Greek/Turkish Proverb page of Panagiotis Georgalas' website (http://learnturkish.pgeorgalas.gr/ProverbsSetEn.asp).
5. See Raimundo Foulché-Delbosc (2006: 10; reprint; original in French, 1888).

6. These collections included the following sources: Beki Bardavid and Fani Ender (2006); Henry V. Besso (1935: 209–219) and (1948: 370–387); Abraham Galante (1902: 440–454); M. Kayserling (1889); and Isaac Jack Levy (1969).
7. This work was released as "a reproduction of an important historical work" by ULAN Press in 2014. An original copy is housed in the University of Oxford's Bodleian Library. Other editions of this work (1844, 1880, and 1907) are available online under a Creative Commons use license via the Hathi Trust Digital Library (www.hathitrust.org).
8. The Ottoman dictionaries were by J. P. Kieffer and T. X. Bianchi (1835), the Redhouse (1880) as edited by Charles Wells, and that of Ferit Devellioğlu (1990). The proverb collection was that published by Metin Yurtbaşı (2013).
9. See Andrew T. Pratt (1866). Reverend Pratt advocated the use of Armeno-Turkish to teach Western missionaries the Ottoman language. He thought it was easier and more efficient than using the Perso-Arabic script.
10. See Johann Strauss (2003) regarding the importance of Turkish-speaking Greeks and Armenians in translating works of European literature and science for use in their schools and as a business opportunity for a rising middle class who were hungry for this knowledge. Armenian publishers in Constantinople/Istanbul, Venice and Trieste were at the forefront of this trend, printing books that were distributed in the Ottoman Empire. The work of Murat Cankara (2015) is ground-breaking on the use of Armeno-Turkish by non-Armenians. For more on the importance of Armeno-Turkish newspapers, see Bedros Der Matossian (2014: 11) and regarding the use in the theatre, see Agop J. Hacikyan et al. (2005: Vol. III, 58–60). To learn more about the role of Armenians in the emerging Turkish literature of the nineteenth century, see Sagaster (2011).
11. For more about the complex interrelationship between religions and languages in the Ottoman Empire, and additional examples of how Armenian and Greek scripts were used for Ottoman Turkish, see Evangelia Balta and Mehmet Ölmez (2011).
12. Sarah Thomason gives examples of the various ways that Ottoman Turkish influenced the Greek spoken by Asia Minor Greeks (2001: 74, 86–87).
13. For more information about *Smyrneika,* see Alex Baltazzi, George Galdies, and George Poulimenos (2012).
14. Aron Rodrigue (1990: 86) mentions that Ottoman Turkish was in the curriculum of these schools, and Mehmed Talaat Pasha (1874–1921) taught at one of the schools in Edirne. In my own research, sources suggest that Rıza Tevfik (after, 1934, Bölükbaşı) (1869–1949), the famous Ottoman polymath, philosopher, poet, and head of the public health system, attended either an Armenian (in his daughter's accounts) or a Jewish school in Edirne (Rodrigue, ibid., 125).
15. Laurent Mignon (2011a) discusses linguistic Turkification of the Jewish community in the early twentieth century and Judeo-Turkish literary publications beginning in the 1890s. A few of these short-lived publications used the *Rashi* script for Ottoman Turkish.
16. Mahir Şaul (2013) discusses contextual and semantic differences of words and expressions that native speakers used to refer to their speech over time and the political ideologies lying behind today's scholars preferences for some of these as a label for a language that I am calling "Judeo-Spanish," the vernacular spoken at home and in the community, as opposed to the languages used by Jews in the synagogue liturgy and/or for translation of Biblical literature.
17. Mahir Şaul (ibid., 192–195) also discusses the typefaces, fonts and variations of Hebrew script used to publish Judeo-Spanish in the Ottoman Empire.

18. The First Constitutional Period (*Birinci Meşrutiyet*) was from 1876 through 1878. The Second Constitutional Period (*İkinci Meşrutiyet*) is broken into four terms because the process was disrupted due to wars and coups: 1908–1909, 1912–1913, 1914, and 1919.
19. For an overview regarding Ottoman modernity, see M. Şükrü Hanioğlu (2008). Nazan Çiçek's (2010) work on the Young Ottomans provides a good contextual analysis regarding Ottoman intellectuals dealing with nineteenth century ideas of modernity, including language reform. Roderic H. Davidson's "The *Millets* as Agents of Change in the Nineteenth Century Ottoman Empire" (reprinted 2014) is a classic article on this subject.
20. Johann Strauss (op. cit.) pioneered a non-nationalist discourse about the multilingualism of empire and the strange phenomenon that although Ottoman subjects were speaking and reading different languages, they were all reading the same great works of European literature in the nineteenth century.
21. The language death of Judeo-Spanish continues to be a preoccupation. See Rey Romero (2012), Mary Altabev (2003) and Tracey Harris (1994).
22. See Nesim Benbanaste (1988) who remarks on these trends and whose own work in the Jewish newspapers of Istanbul often was focused on preserving cultural, linguistic, and folkloric materials.
23. See the study on Greek and Italian navigation terms as a *Lingua Franca* used in Ottoman Turkish and elsewhere in the Mediterranean by Henry Kahane, Renée Kahane and Andreas Tietze (1958).
24. See Tracy K. Harris (1996: 73–87); Marie-Christine Varol-Bornes (1996: 213–237); and Rey Romero (2012).
25. See Abraham Danon (1903: 221) for his explanation in French regarding the wholesale importation of these Ottoman Turkish phrases into Judeo-Spanish speech.
26. Danon (ibid., 220).
27. Glossaries of Turkish terms, lexical categories, and expressions used in Judeo-Spanish appear in Abraham Danon's articles (1903), (1904), and (1913). See also Raymond Renard (1966: 132) for other examples.
28. See the dictionary currently used by Ladino Komunita, an online list-serve of Judeo-Spanish speakers worldwide: G. Orgun, G., R. Portal, and A. R. Tinoco, (2003–2014); an Istanbul-based dictionary by Klara Perahya and Karen Gerson Şarhon (2012).; the dictionary by Eli Kohen and Dahlia Kohen-Gordon (2000); that of Joseph Nehama (1977) based upon his earlier work (pre-World War II) in Salonika, and that of Pascual Pascual Recuero (1977).
29. For more on the process and mechanisms of language contact, see Sarah Thomason (2001: 129–156).
30. Marie-Christine Varol-Bornes analyzed these changes in her articles (2013), (2011), (2008), and (1996). Tracey Harris also wrote about lexical borrowings and Turkish influences in Judeo-Spanish: (2001), (1996), and (1994).
31. Note, though, that Judeo-Spanish also borrowed from Greek, and Abraham Danon (1922) identified some of these Greek loan words.
32. *Buchukes* (bučúkes) is found in Nehama (1977: 100) as well as the other Judeo-Spanish dictionaries used in this study and in Danon's glosseries (op. cit.).
33. *İkiz* appears in the Ottoman dictionaries consulted for this project: that of J. D. Kieffer and T. X. Bianchi (1835), as well as in Charles Wells' Redhouse (1880).
34. The orthography for Judeo-Spanish words in this section follows the *Ladino Komunita* dictionary of Orgun et al, op. cit., which is based upon the current orthography standardized by the Israeli publication, *Aki Yerushalayim*, published by the Kol Yisrael, the Voice of Israel National Radio.

See http://www.twirpx.com/file/1427775/ Modern Turkish orthography is used, herein, for the Ottoman words simply as a practical device.
35. See Mahir Şaul (2011: 185–186) for a discussion of this word and further permutations it has undergone in the contemporary context.
36. See Sevan Nişanyan (2010) for the etymologies of these words: *havra, kasa, masa,* and *kaşar.* http://www.nisanyansozluk.com/
37. For the chronology of the mandating of Turkish language by Jewish educational institutions, see Esther Benbassa and Aron Rodrigue (1995: 102–103). In 1928, there was a movement for Jews to learn and speak Turkish. In 1931, it became forbidden to attend foreign-language primary schools; primary education was conducted only in Turkish.
38. For a comprehensive overview of Judeo-Spanish proverb traditions, see Levy (1969), op. cit.

REFERENCES

———. *Turkish Proverbs Translated into English.* Venice: The Armenian Monastery of St. Lazarus, 1844 [Harvard University Library]. Online at The Hathi Trust: www.hathitrust.org

———. *Turkish Proverbs Translated into English.* Venice: The Armenian Monastery of St. Lazarus, 1873 [Bodleian Library, Oxford University: old catalogue #3828 /permalink #014633614].

———. *Turkish Proverbs Translated into English.* Venice: The Armenian Monastery of St. Lazarus, 1880 [University of California Library] Online at The Hathi Trust: www.hathitrust.org

———. *Turkish Proverbs Translated into English.* Venice: The Armenian Monastery of St. Lazarus, 1907 [Cornell University Library]. Online at The Hathi Trust: www.hathitrust.org

Altabé, David F. Erhan Atay, and Israel J. Katz, eds. *Studies on Turkish-Jewish History, Political and Social Relations, Literature and Linguistics: The Quincentennial Papers.* New York: Sepher-Hermon Press, 1996: 73–87.

Altabev, Mary. *Judeo-Spanish in the Turkish Social Context: Language Death, Swang Song, Revival or New Arrival?* Istanbul: The Isis Press, 2003.

Balta, Evangelia and Mehmet Ölmez, eds. *Between Religion and Language: Turkish-Speaking Christians, Jews, and Greek-Speaking Muslims and Catholics in the Ottoman Empire.* Istanbul: Eren, 2011.

Baltazzi, Alex, George Galdies, and George Poulimenos. *A Lexicon of Smyrneika: İzmir Rumcası Sözlüğü /Smyrneikes Kouvedes.* Istanbul: Tarih Vakfı Yurt Yayınları, 2012.

Bardavid, Beki and Fani Ender. *Trezoro Sefaradi.* In two volumes: *Folklore de la Famiya Djudiya* and *De Punta Pie a Kavesa.* Istanbul: Gözlem Gazetecilik Basın ve Yayın A. Ş., 2006.

Benbanaste, Nesim. *Örneklerle Türk Musevi Basınının Tarihçesi.* Istanbul: Sümbül Basımevi, 1988.

Benbassa, Esther and Aron Rodrigue. *The Jews of the Balkans: The Judeo-Spanish Community Fifteenth to Twentieth Centuries.* Cambridge, MA: Blackwell Publishers, 1995.

Besso, Henry V. "A Further Contribution to the Refranero Judéo-Espangol," *Revue Hispanique* 36 (1935): 209–219.

Besso, Henry V. "Judéo-Spanish Proverbs: Their Philosophy and Their Teaching," *Bulletin Hispanique* 49 (1948): 370–387.

Busse, Winfried and Marie-Christine Varol-Bornes, eds. *Hommage à Haïm Vidal Sephiha.* Bern: Peter Lang, 1996.

Busse, Winfried, and M. Studemund-Halévy, *Lexicología y lexicografía judeoespañoles.* Bern: Peter Lang, 2011.

Cankara, Murat. "Rethinking Ottoman Cross-Cultural Encounters: Turks and the Armenian Alphabet." *Middle Eastern Studies* 51(1) (2015): 1–16.

Carroll, John B. (ed.). *Language, Thought, and Reality: Selected Writings of Benjamin Lee Whorf.* Cambridge, Mass.: Massachusetts Institute of Technology Press, 1998. 24th printing; original, 1956.

Danon, Abraham. "Essai sur les vocables turcs dans le judéo-espagnol." *Keleti Szemle* 4 (1903): 215–229 and 5 (1904): 111–126.

Danon, Abraham. "Le turc dans le judéo-espagnol." *Revue Hispanique* 29 (1913): 5–12.

Danon, Abraham. "Les elements grecs dans le judéo-espagnol." *Revue des Études Juives* 75 (1922): 211–216.

Davidson, Roderic H. "The *Millets* as Agents of Change in the Nineteenth Century Ottoman Empire." In Braude, Benjamin, *Christians and Jews in the Ottoman Empire: The Abridged Edition with a New Introduction.* Boulder: Lynne Rienner Publishers, 2014.

Der Matossian, Bedross. *Shattered Dreams of Revolution: From Liberty to Violence in the Late Ottoman Empire.* Stanford: Stanford University Press, 2014.

Devellioğlu, Ferit. *Osmanlıca-Türkçe Ansiklopedik Lûgatt.* Ankara: Aydın Kitabevi, 1990.

Foulché-Delbosc, Raimundo. *1313 Proverbios Judeo-Españoles.* Buenos Aires: Ediciones Obelisco S.L., 2006 (reprint); original from 1888.

Galante, Abraham. "Proverbs judéo-espagnols." *Revue Hispanique* 9 (1902): 440–454.

Goldberg, Harriet H. "The Judeo-Spanish Proverb and Its Narrative Context." *PMLA Publications of the Modern Language Association of America*, 108.1 (1993): 106–120.

Hacikyan, Agop J., Gabriel Basmajian, Edward S. Franchuk, and Nourhan Ouzounian (eds). *The Heritage of Armenian Literature. Volume III: From the Eighteenth Century toModern Times.* Detroit: Wayne State University Press, 2005.

Hanioğlu, M. Şükrü. *A Brief History of the Late Ottoman Empire.* Princeton: Princeton University Press, 2008.

Harris, Tracy K. *Death of a Language: The History of Judeo-Spanish.* Newark: University of Delaware Press, 1994.

Harris, Tracy K. "Turkish Elements in Judeo-Spanish." In *Studies on Turkish-Jewish History, Political and Social Relations, Literature and Linguistics: The Quincentennial Papers.* Edited by David F. Altabé et al., 73–87. New York: Sepher-Hermon Press, 1996.

Harris, Tracy K. "The Incorporation of Non-Spanish Elements into Judeo-Spanish." In *Proceedings of the Twelfth British Conference on Judeo-Spanish Studies, 24–26 June, 2001.* Edited by Pomeroy, Hilary and Michael Alpert, 13–22. Leiden: Brill, 2004.

Kahane, Henry, Renée Kahane, and Andreas Tietze. *The Lingua Franca in the Levant: Turkish Nautical Terms of Italian and Greek Origin.* Urbana: The University of Illinois, 1958.

Kayserling, M. *Refranero provebios españoles de los judíos españoles.* Budapest Posner, 1889.

Kieffer, J. D., and T. X. Bianchi. *Dictionnaire Turc-Français.* Two volumes. Paris: L'Imprimerie Royale, 1835.

Koerner, E. F. K. "On the Sources of the 'Sapir-Whorf Hypothesis'" In *Toward a History of American Linguistics*, 39–62 [Chapter 3:]. Oxfordshire: Taylor and Francis, 2002.

Kohen, Elli and Dahlia Kohen-Gordon. *Ladino-English, English-Ladino Concise Encyclopedic Dictionary (Judeo-Spanish).* New York: Hippocrene Books, 2000.

Levy, Isaac Jack. *Prolegomena to the Study of the Refranero Sefardi.* New York: Las Americas, 1969.

Matras, Yaron. *Language Contact.* Cambridge: Cambridge University Press, 2009.

Mignon, Laurent. "Avram, İsak and the Others: Notes on the Genesis of Judeo-Turkish Literature." In *Between Religion and Language: Turkish-Speaking Christians, Jews, and Greek-Speaking Muslims and Catholics in the Ottoman Empire*. Edited by Evangelia Balta and Mehmet Ölmez, 71–83. Istanbul: Eren, 2011a.

Mignon, Laurent. "Lost in Transliteration: A Few Remarks on the Armeno-Turkish Novel and Turkish Literary Historiography." In *Between Religion and Language: Turkish-Speaking Christians, Jews, and Greek-Speaking Muslims and Catholics in the Ottoman Empire*. Edited by Evangelia Balta and Mehmet Ölmez, 111–123. Istanbul: Eren, 2011b.

Nehama, Joseph. *Dictionnaire du judéo-espagnol*. Madrid: Instituto Benito Arias Montano, 1977.

Nişanyan, Sevan. *Nişanyan Sözlük Çağdaş Türkçenin Etimolojisi, 2010*. <http://www.nisanyansozluk.com/?s=yeni-uye>.

Orgun, G., R. Portal and A. R. Tinoco. *Diksionario de Djudeo-Espanyol a Turko*. Used by the online *Ladino Komunitá*, an international Judeo-Spanish speech community. Manuscript, 2003–2014. < http://www.twirpx.com/file/1427775/>

Pascual Recuero, Pascual. *Diccionario Básico Ladino-Español*. Barcelona: Ameller Ediciones, 1977.

Perahya, Klara with Karen Gerson Şarhon. *Diksyonaryo Judeo-Espanyol Turko/Ladino-Türkçe Sözlük*. Second edition, expanded. Istanbul: Sentro de Investigasiones sovre la Kultura Sefardi Otomana-Turka and Gözlem Gazetecilik Basın ve Yayın A. Ş., 2012.

Pratt, Andrew T. "On the Armeno-Turkish Alphabet." *Journal of the American Oriental Society*. 8 (1866): 374–376.

Renard, Raymond. *Sepharad: Le monde et la langue judéo-espagnol des Séphardim*. Mons, Belgium: Annales universitaires de Mons, 1966.

Rodrigue, Aron. *French Jews, Turkish Jews: The Alliance Israélite Universelle and the Politics of Jewish Schooling in Turkey, 1860–1925*. Bloomington: Indiana University Press, 1990.

Romero, Rey. *Spanish in the Bosphorus: A Sociolinguistic Study on the Judeo-Spanish Dialect Spoken in Istanbul*. Istanbul: Libra Kitapçılık ve Yayıncılık, 2012.

Sagaster, Börte. "The Role of Turcophone Armenians as Literary Innovators and Mediators of Culture in the Early Days of Modern Turkish Literature." In *Between Religion and Language: Turkish-Speaking Christians, Jews, and Greek-Speaking Muslims and Catholics in the Ottoman Empire*. Edited by Evangelia Balta and Mehmet Ölmez, 101–110. Istanbul: Eren, 2011.

Şaul, Mahir. "What's In a Name? Ladino, Espanyol, Djudyo, Judeoespañol, Sefardi." In *Judeo-Spanish in the Time of Clamoring Nationalisms*. Edited by Mahir Şaul, 179–253. Istanbul: Libra Kitapçılık ve Yayıncılık, 2013.

Şaul, Mahir, ed. *Judeo-Spanish in the Time of Clamoring Nationalisms*. Istanbul: Libra Kitapçılık ve Yayıncılık, 2013.

Strauss, Johann. "Who Read What in the Ottoman Empire (Nineteenth and Twentieth Centuries)?" *Arabic Middle Eastern Literatures* 6.1 (2003): 39–76.

Thomason, Sarah Grey. *Language Contact: An Introduction*. Edinburgh: U. P. Marston, 2001.

Varol-Bornes, Marie-Christine. "Influencia del turco en el judéo-espagnol de Turquía." In *Hommage à Haïm Vidal Sephiha*. Edited by Winfried Busse and Marie-Christine Varol-Bornes, Bern: Peter Lang, 1996: 213–237.

Varol-Bornes, Marie-Christine. *Manual of Judeo-Spanish: Language and Culture*. Translated by Ralph Tarica. Bethesda: University of Maryland Press, 2008.

Varol-Bornes, Marie-Christine. "Les verbes empruntés au turc en judéo-espagnol (Bulgarie)." In *Lexicología y lexicografía judeoespañoles*. Edited by Winfried Busse and Michael Studemund-Halévy, 87–105. Bern: Peter Lang, 2011.

Varol-Bornes, Marie-Christine. "Langue et identité judéo-espagnoles, trois scenarios pour une disparition." In *Judeo-Spanish in the Time of Clamoring Nationalisms.* Edited by Mahir Şaul, 13–35. Istanbul: Libra Kitapçılık ve Yayıncılık, 2013.

Wells, Charles (ed.). *Redhouse Turkish Dictionary in Two Parts, English and Turkish, and Turkish and English.* Second edition. London: Bernard Quaritch, 1880.

Yurtbaşı, Metin. *Sınıfandırılmış Atasözleri Sözlüğü.* Istanbul: Excellence Publishing, 2013.

PART TWO

Fin de siècle Judeo-Spanish Language, Literature AND Culture

CHAPTER SEVEN

Networks OF Patronage AND THE Making OF Two Ladino Newspapers

MATTHIAS B. LEHMANN
University of California, Irvine

ABSTRACT

This article looks at Saadi Halevi and Elijah Carmona as representatives of two generations of modern Ladino print culture. It suggests that we need to look beyond the rhetoric of modernization and enlightenment, so pervasive in both contemporary accounts and in modern historiography, and focus on the importance of social class and the dynamics of networks of patronage in order to understand the rise of modern Ladino letters and, in particular, the Ladino press.

1. INTRODUCTION

Between September 1907 and March 1908, the long-running Ladino newspaper *La Epoca,* which had appeared in Salonika since 1875, published a series of 28 installments with excerpts from the memoirs of its late founder, Saadi Halevi. The serialized version of Saadi's memoirs carried the subtitle "Como nació La Epoca,"[1] presenting the biography of the author and the story of his newspaper as closely intertwined. The autobiography of another well-known Ladino publicist, Elijah Carmona, appeared in 1926; the title of this text, too, suggested a close connection between the life story of the author and his newspaper: *Cómo nació Eliyah Carmona, cómo se engradeció y cómo se hizo director del "Juguetón."*[2] Saadi Halevi (1820–1903) and Elijah Carmona (1869–1931) represent two different generations of Ladino publicists. Halevi was among the pioneers who established a Ladino newspaper culture in the last quarter of the nineteenth century, whereas Carmona was active during the years when Ladino culture was at its most vibrant, first as the author of numerous short novels and, after 1908, as the editor of the satirical magazine *El Juguetón*. The two autobiographies reflect, then, a generational shift. As Saadi Halevi himself marveled in the prologue to his memoir, presumably written in the early 1900s and looking back to the establishment of his newspaper a quarter century before: "How much the times have changed! How much the customs have been transformed!" (*Mis memorias*, #3)[3]

As Gabriele Jancke has demonstrated in the case of sixteenth century German scholarly autobiographies, the authors of these texts presented themselves not as isolated and autonomous individuals but rather as embedded in complex social and communicative networks. Among those, relations of patronage were particularly important. Patronage ties in these texts do not appear as dyadic, binary relations between two individuals, but are always inscribed within far-flung networks that highlight the unequal distribution of resources and power within contemporary society (see Jancke 2002, esp. 1–16, 75–82). Such network-embeddedness is an important feature of Saadi Halevi's and Elijah Carmona's autobiographies as well. Both authors situate themselves within the wider context of the local, Jewish, and Ottoman world. In both accounts, a vast gulf separates the wealthy Jewish elite from the lower classes, and Ladino publicists like Saadi and Carmona inhabit a somewhat precarious place in between. In forging a path that leads them towards the establishment of their respective newspapers, they depend on networks of patronage that belie any simple juxtaposition of "traditional" versus "modern," Jewish versus Ottoman, or Ottoman versus European.

2. TWO LADINO AUTOBIOGRAPHIES

In his study of Jewish autobiographical writing, Michael Stanislawski has warned against the positivistic tendency to mine "ego-documents" for historical data without appreciating the literary constructedness of these texts (Stanislawski 2004). He suggests that any analysis of such documents needs to begin with an understanding of the overall literary "design" of the narrative, rather than taking the text as a depository of (more or less) accurate recollections of historical facts. Such caution is certainly warranted for the two Ladino memoirs discussed here. Robyn Lowenthal long ago described *Como nació Eliyah Carmona* as both a "quasi-picaresque autobiography" and a "novelized memoir," which for all the historical information it contains also needs to be appreciated as part of Carmona's extensive fictional literary oeuvre (Lowenthal 1984).[4] It was written a full eighteen years after the foundation of *El Juguetón*, which marks the end point in Carmona's narrative, and it is obvious that the detailed dialogues that appear in the text are embellished if not entirely fictional.

At least there is no doubt that Carmona was the author of his own life-narrative, which was produced at his *Juguetón* printing press. Saadi Halevi's memoir—especially the version that appeared posthumously in *La Epoca* in 1907–8—is another matter. Aron Rodrigue and Sarah Stein have recently published the manuscript of a much longer version of Saadi's memoir. What was printed in *La Epoca* was not simply an excerpt from the longer text discovered by Rodrigue in the National Library of Israel, but rather a significantly more detailed account of the part of Saadi's memoir that deals with the events that led up to the foundation of his newspaper (Rodrigue and Stein 2012).[5] Unfortunately, the relation between the two versions[6] is not entirely clear, but the text that appeared in the pages of *La Epoca* had likely undergone extensive editing by Saadi's sons, especially Shmuel (Sam) Lévy, who had succeeded his father as the editor of *La Epoca* in 1898, as well as of its French counterpart, *Le Journal de Salonique*.

Sam Lévy mentions the existence of three different manuscripts of the memoirs in 1946. While it is plausible that the document published by Rodrigue and Stein was one of those three versions, we do not know who produced it and how it relates to the other manuscripts that apparently did not survive, or how any of these are related to the version in *La Epoca*. A close look at the manuscript published by Rodrigue and Stein suggests that it was not the original written by Saadi Halevi over a period of several years beginning in 1881, but that it too was copied well after it had been completed. Thus Saadi writes in this version (and this is not a later addition or alteration in the manuscript): "As I write this biography that took nine years to finish, I still remember that dark and cursed day ..."[7]—obviously he could not have said this until after concluding work on his memoir in 1890. Another example is Saadi's reference to Maurice de Hirsch, whom he describes as "the philanthropist and king of charity, *y de bendicha memoria* (and of blessed memory)," again without any indication of a later alteration of the text.[8] Hirsch passed away in April 1896, so the memoir must have been reworked and this manuscript must have been written after that date.

The basic facts recounted about the foundation of *La Epoca* are the same in Rodrigue and Stein's version and in that published by *La Epoca* in 1907–8. The additional material that appeared in the latter may come from another version of the memoirs that is no longer extant but could have been written by Saadi Halevi himself, or, just as possibly, it may represent the heavy editorial hand of Sam Lévy. What does distinguish the account in *La Epoca*, however, and what suggests that it underwent extensive editing, is that it presents a much more artfully designed narrative. Suspense and expectation are built up from one installment to the next, and the significance of details provided earlier in the text only becomes apparent as the story unfolds. As in Carmona's book, autobiography and founding story of the newspaper overlap. In fact, the purpose of Saadi's and Carmona's narratives is to celebrate and promote their respective periodicals and to highlight their role in public Ottoman Sephardic culture. Both stories culminate with the establishment of the newspaper against all odds, overcoming all kinds of adversities, from the hostility of a conservative rabbinic establishment faced by Halevi to the financial woes of a young Carmona wandering the Sephardic communities of the Eastern Mediterranean in search of an opportunity.

3. PLOTLINES

A crucial moment in Saadi's life and the starting point of his narrative is a series of events in the year preceding the founding of *La Epoca* in 1874, when his eldest son Haim is accused of publicly violating the Sabbath, Saadi Halevi defends him and is consequently placed under a ban of excommunication *(herem)* by the rabbinate, and Saadi's family suffers the attack of a violent mob of what he describes as religious fanatics: "I remember the thousands of fists raised against my oldest son and myself; I remember the fury and rage of the mass who were destroying without knowing why … hearing the shouts, the frightful yells and high-pitched screams of the people, the sound of the breaking glass and the doors they broke down violently …" (*Mis memorias,* #4). In Saadi's telling, he escapes the violence thanks to the help of the wealthy industrialist and philanthropist Moïse Allatini and goes into hiding. But even when he returns home, the *herem*, which excludes him from the Jewish community, threatens to destroy his printing business, which is now shunned by its former clientele and abandoned by its former workers (*Mis memorias,* #8).

Saadi Halevi presents himself as being driven by a commitment to "enlightenment" and "progress" (he never quite explains what that means). In Salonika, Halevi gains the support of Allatini and of the young members of the Cercle des Intimes, a Francophile association established in 1874. Preparing to launch his newspaper, Halevi travels to Vienna to purchase a new set of Rashi characters for his printing business. Meanwhile, his friends from the Cercle des Intimes set out to assemble an archive of material for publication: "They had already begun to organize the newsroom," he notes upon his return from Vienna. "Many novels *(romansos)* had already been translated. All the issues of the *Indépendance*[9] were stored in a cupboard fully annotated. A box had been filled with Jewish news" (*Mis memorias,* installment #20). The anecdote incidentally reveals something about the operation of the early Ladino press, which relied heavily on material drawn from other, often European, publications and on non-news items such as serialized novels, often translated from European languages. "Telegrams arrive every day," the members of the Cercle des Intimes noted as they plotted the establishment of a Ladino newspaper with Halevi as chief editor, "the *Indépendence* and other newspapers provide us with the political news. A bit from here, a bit from there, novels, news from the city, and a newspaper is filled each week" (*Mis memorias*, #15).

The serendipitous events that allow for obtaining the Ottoman government's publication license for *La Epoca* are a key element in Halevi's narrative. In the wake of the accusations against his son, the confrontation with the rabbinate and the excommunication, and the subsequent attack on his family, Saadi decides to send Haim away for a while, to Constantinople. There, Haim Halevi spends his evenings in some of the grand cafés of the capital, where prominent members of the Ottoman elites are regular guests. On one occasion, he makes the acquaintance of a Turkish-speaking Muslim and the two engage in a conversation, which prompts the Muslim to commend Haim on his fluency in the Turkish language and to inquire whether he reads the language as well as he speaks it. Haim admits that he does not know the Ottoman-Arabic alphabet, but he convinces his new friend that he can teach him "Spanish" characters (i.e. *soletreo*), which he insists are much easier to learn than Ottoman. They continue to correspond through letters written in Turkish with *soletreo* letters after Haim returns to Salonika (*Mis memorias*, #12–14).

The importance of this episode only emerges several installments later. Because of his trouble with the Salonikan rabbinate, Saadi Halevi cannot hope to obtain a publication permit for his newspaper from the local authorities, which will inquire about his bone fides among the local rabbinate, so instead he goes to Constantinople in quest of a license from the imperial administration. Saadi is well received by his friend Yehezkel Gabai, who holds an influential position in the Jewish community of Constantinople and who introduces him to the Empire's acting chief rabbi, Moshe Halevi, who promises his support. Eventually Saadi presents himself in the Ottoman government office to petition for his publication license. The Ottoman functionary is sympathetic, but mentions to Saadi that he has a Jewish friend in Salonika and, given his political problems with the rabbinate and his being an outcast placed under a *herem*, Saadi is worried that his Salonikan troubles are coming back to hurt him when he is so close to obtaining his permit. As it turns out, the functionary is none other than the Turkish friend of Saadi's son Haim, and sure enough the imperial license for *La Epoca* is issued a mere three weeks later (*Mis memorias*, #26).[10]

Elijah Carmona's autobiography presents a rather different narrative. There is no linear story leading to the establishment of a newspaper, and, unlike Saadi Halevi, Carmona nowhere claims any ideological commitment to progress and enlightenment driving him to the foundation of *El Juguetón*. Instead, Carmona's life seems to evolve in fits and starts and his story is capricious and full of—often self-inflicted—setbacks. He tries himself at various jobs and inevitably fails, but slowly, though haphazardly, he ends up in the printing business. Carmona begins to work in the printing house of *El Tiempo*, the longest-running Ladino periodical of the Ottoman capital.[11] After only a few months, there is a shakeup in the Ladino publishing scene in Constantinople when David Fresco, editor of *El Telégrafo*, is removed from his position by government decree following his publication of a critical article about the acting chief rabbi. This ends up creating an opportunity for Carmona to be the head typographer for *El Tiempo*, but he is dissatisfied with the salary he is offered, leaves his employment, and unsuccessfully tries to raise money for establishing his own printing business (Carmona 1926: 12–14).

A turning point in Carmona's story comes about half-way into the autobiography when his mother has an idea: "I am going to tell you stories *(consejicas)* and you can have them printed and sell them for 10 paras each" (Carmona 1926: 43). This marks the beginning of Carmona's career as one of the most prolific authors of popular literature in Ladino.[12] He purchases a set of Rashi characters from an Armenian printer and sets up inside a Greek-owned printing shop, and he starts quite successfully to write and sell novels in Ladino—as he explains, for a popular audience of those who read neither Turkish nor French (Carmona 1926: 44). According to Carmona's account, his novels are at first based on the stories his mother tells him, but he also goes to the theater and uses the material to create his own novels: "I saw the plays, took the stock from one and the whiff from another, and thus came up with a novel" (Carmona 1926: 45). After three years, Carmona has his first run-in with the Ottoman censor but finds a way to continue publishing his novels, until the censors finally instruct Carmona "in the future not to write in the novels anything involving murder, robbery, or love," which effectively puts an end to the enterprise (Carmona 1926: 47).

Further travails ensue when Carmona goes to Alexandria and Cairo in Egypt, which at the time, as an autonomous province within the Empire, attracted many Ottoman publishers who sought to circumvent the ever more stringent—and arbitrary—censorship of the Hamidian regime in Constantinople (Yosmaoğlu 2003: 15–49). Once again, Carmona fails, with the Ladino market in Egypt too small to sustain his business and squandering capital that he raises from a wealthy philanthropist on an ill-advised business dealing in fake jewelry (Carmona 1926: 47–77). Upon his return to Constantinople, Carmona works in the printing house of David Fresco and resumes the writing of novels, which he publishes in Jerusalem because of the lighter censorship in that provincial city (Carmona 1926: 88). The autobiography ends, somewhat abruptly, with Carmona claiming that he vows a full eight years before the Young Turk Revolution that, if censorship in the Empire is ever lifted, he will establish his own newspaper, a humoristic journal—and in 1908, after the revolution creates expectations of greater freedom, Carmona, like hundreds of other Ottomans from different ethno-religious groups, seeks and obtains a license to begin publishing a new newspaper—*El Juguetón* (Carmona 1926: 91–93).

At the end of his autobiography, Carmona maintains that his only intention in founding *El Juguetón* was to sell his writing—a business idea, that is, not a political project. And yet, he says, the periodical ultimately secured its success when the new chief rabbi, Haim Nahum, decided to sue the newspaper because of its satirical portrayal of the rabbinate. The incident, Carmona claims, gained the newspaper "within four months a renown that it otherwise could not have achieved in twenty years" (Carmona 1926: 93). Thus, while Saadi Halevi portrayed his anti-clericalism as the starting point of the journey that led to the establishment of *La Epoca*, in Carmona's telling his confrontation with the rabbinate appears as an opportune incident at the very end of the narrative.

4. FROM SAADI'S ANTICLERICALISM TO CARMONA'S SECULARISM

As Rodrigue and Stein point out, the excommunication of 1874 was "the central trauma in Sa'adi's life"[13]—or, at any rate, the central motif in his autobiography. It is therefore not surprising that Saadi's memoirs engage in a sustained polemic against the rabbinic establishment, forging the image of a culture war between the forces of backwardness and ignorance against those of progress and enlightenment. He takes great pride in his own role as an ally of the Westernizing commercial elite in Salonika, and he emphasizes the long tradition of his family's printing house in shaping Jewish culture in the city, beginning with his great-grandfather who had arrived in Salonika from Amsterdam in 1731. "If the Halevi press served to publish the works of many Eastern Jewish sages," Saadi notes, "later the journal *La Epoca* served the moral interests of the Jews of these lands and helped the progress of the people" (*Mis memorias*, #11).

Saadi Halevi's memoir constructs a clear dichotomy between the world of rabbinic tradition and that of Western-style modernity. He frequently refers to individuals he sees as representatives of the former as "fanatics," and his references to traditional beliefs and practices are hostile and often sarcastic. At the same time, he celebrates the beneficial influence of the modernizers and completely identifies with the agenda of Moïse Allatini, the founder of the Alliance school in Salonika in 1873 and an ardent advocate of Westernization. Saadi identifies backwardness and superstition not only with the rabbinic scholars, however, but also with the Jewish lower classes, such as the dockworkers who, Saadi explains, "at the time were all Jews and very backward and fanatical people," and whose ire he only barely escapes when they try to assault him one fine afternoon when he is taking a walk by the sea (*Mis memorias*, #20).

It is worth looking beyond the language of culture war that informs so much of Saadi Halevi's memoirs. Saadi himself was much more part of the traditional world of Ottoman Jewish society than he cared to admit, and for all his opposition to rabbinic superstition, he never suggests an alternative vision of what Judaism might look like and never embraces an agenda of reform similar to that of the *maskilim*, or advocates of a Jewish enlightenment, in Northern or Eastern Europe. In his memoirs, Saadi describes his encounter with the acting Chief Rabbi in Constantinople, Moshe Halevi, in terms that are remarkably deferential—"the people must be considered fortunate to have such a leader"—for someone who cultivates the image of being an anti-rabbinic rebel (*Mis memorias*, #25). Saadi's own religious practice suggests that he is engaged in a struggle against the rabbinic establishment, not against Jewish tradition as such. When the *herem* keeps him from attending synagogue, he continues to pray by himself at home (*Mis memorias*, #22), and describing his own religious identity he notes: "The truth is that I was never very religious. But I always believed in the one God, and I always had faith in the greatness of the people of Israel, the law of Moses, and the Ten Commandments, which are the basis of all religion" (*Mis memorias*, #23). This is the closest Saadi comes in his memoir to spelling out his own vision of a Judaism compatible with progress—but there isn't really anything particularly novel or modern about it.

There is a striking difference between Saadi Halevi's militant anti-clericalism and Carmona's matter-of-fact secularism. Halevi presents himself a rebel engaged in a fight against fanaticism and for enlightenment, fully embracing, it appears, the European Orientalist view of the Ottoman Empire (and its Jews).[14] In Carmona's narrative, in contrast, there is nothing of this antagonism against religious tradition or the rabbinate. During his early travels to Salonika and Izmir and later to Alexandria and Cairo, he turns to the local rabbinate for help, just as he turns to representatives of the Alliance Israélite Universelle or to relatives and family friends. During his first trip, when Carmona arrives in Salonika in 1896, he goes directly to the home of Chief Rabbi Covo, carrying a recommendation from the Chief Rabbi of Constantinople. Years later, in Cairo, he also turns first to the Chief Rabbi for assistance when he tries to raise money for establishing a Ladino newspaper in the city (Carmona 1926: 33, 57).

Carmona clearly moves within overlapping networks, and the irreconcilable dichotomy between traditionalists and modernists that appears a generation before in Saadi's writing is gone. At the same time, Carmona presents himself as leading very much a secular life and fully in tune with modern urban Ottoman culture, traveling on Yom Kippur, not obeying dietary restrictions, and delighting when he happens upon a Turkish-speaker in a bar in Cairo, "because I had great pleasure in speaking the language of my fatherland" (Carmona 1926: 70–1). All of this comes across matter-of-factly, not as an act of rebellion against Jewish tradition. For Carmona—and many other Sephardic Jews of the early years of the twentieth century—secularism is already a lived experience, not an ideological agenda. Saadi Halevi's self-representation in *Mis memorias* interprets the world around him, as well as more specifically the events that lead to the founding of *La Epoca*, through the language of an anti-clerical culture war. Carmona, writing as a representative of the next generation, is more sanguine about these ideological fault lines as he presents the image of an Ottoman Jewish society where rabbinic, Alliancist, as well as kinship and economic networks overlap and complement one another.

5. NETWORKS OF PATRONAGE

The crisis in the wake of his excommunication presented an opportunity for Saadi Halevi to enter into a relation of patronage with Moïse Allatini, the prominent industrialist and philanthropist who had long been critical of the circumstances of the Jewish community in Salonika. In a report furnished to a Jewish visitor from Germany, Ludwig August Frankl, Allatini had written that "the chief cause of the miserable condition of the Jews, is to be found in the hostile spirit of the prevalent religion [Islam], and the hatred of the [Ottoman] Government." "Besides these causes," he added,

> I find that the Jews … who find their way here, possess only a superficial civilization. They propagate among the masses the belief, that schools, instruction, reforms, are a desecration of religion, and thus there has arisen, if not a feeling of hatred against western improvements, at least a feeling of distrust, and a great amount of indifference.[15]

By the time Saadi Halevi encountered Allatini, the latter had been steadily advancing the cause of Westernization, founding the Alliance school in Salonika in 1873 (Rodrigue 1990: 39–40). On occasion of their first meeting, Allatini explained to Saadi: "Our city cannot remain in its state of moral backwardness," and flattering Saadi he added: "Knowing that you possess an enlightened mind that is open to progress, I have placed you by my side to serve as an intermediary between me and the people" (*Mis memorias*, #6).[16] Thus a relation of patronage was established between Saadi and Allatini. Allatini would protect Halevi in his confrontation with the rabbinate, whereas his newspaper *La Epoca*, established with the support of Allatini and other likeminded individuals, was to give voice to the Westernizing agenda propagated by the wealthy philanthropist.[17]

The rhetoric of a culture war pitting traditionalists against modernizers that permeates Saadi's memoir cannot obscure the fact that this ideological battle was fought within the context of economic inequality and class division—his juxtaposition of Allatini and the wealthy members of the Cercle des Intimes against the working-class Jewish dockworkers was mentioned above.[18] The socio-economic inequality of Jewish Salonika that lurks behind the confrontation of "progress" against "tradition" is illustrated well when Saadi describes how one of Allatini's associates, Shmuel ben Rubi, rescues him from a Jewish mob following his excommunication. As Ben Rubi takes him to his mansion in the upper city neighborhood of Chavush Manastir, Saadi admires the beautiful vista over the entire city, down to the sea and up to the mountains, "something that few Salonikans will have ever seen" (*Mis memorias,* #4). Thus, the topography of the city itself illustrates how far the wealthy elite in Salonika is removed from the world of the average Salonikan Jews, and how the clash of cultures in Saadi's memoir is also a clash of social classes.

Saadi Halevi himself, of course, is faced with descent into poverty when his printing press is shuttered as a result of his excommunication. He thus seeks allies in the upper classes and embraces their cause of modernization from above, distancing himself rhetorically in his memoir from the lower, working class Salonikan Jews and their rabbinic leaders. It is not only an ideological idea of modernization that he embraces: for him, championing the cause of Westernization is also a matter of economic survival. In fact, Halevi's own narrative offers an indication that there are more prosaic, economic considerations behind the foundation of *La Epoca* and his alliance with Allatini, beyond a lofty commitment to progress and enlightenment. In a dialogue that appears in the memoirs—fictional, of course, but not therefore less telling—a member of the Cercle des Intimes is the first to suggest the establishment of a newspaper: "'What if we had a newspaper,' Señor Yosef Sulam said one day. 'That would be the best way to ensure a livelihood for Han Saadi' … If the newspaper grows, then his income is secured, apart from its service to the nation" (*Mis memorias,* #15). There is an important, if unintended, admission here: after his troubles with the local rabbinate, Saadi Halevi has lost much of his printing business, his workers have quit lest they be associated with an outcast, and the Torah scholars who once printed their books at Halevi's publishing house are turning elsewhere. Establishing the newspaper *La Epoca*, therefore, is a pragmatic business decision based on the assumption that there is a market for a Ladino periodical in Salonika. After all, another member of the Cercle chimes in, "everyone is [already] reading the newspaper from Vienna [i.e., the Judeo-Spanish *Coreo de Viena*] and *El Nacional* from Constantinople" (*Mis memorias,* #15).[19]

Carmona describes his entrance into the world of printing, writing, and publishing as the result of a quest to reverse the declining economic fortunes of his family, which has fallen on hard times. Along the way, he finds himself sharing a dingy hotel room in Izmir with a Jewish man who turns out to be a murderer on the run and living rough on the streets of Cairo for a while, and it is only at the end, through his work as a Ladino publicist, that he restores his standing as part of the middle class. Writing novels and publishing for Carmona is a way to make a living, not a civilizing mission—an important realization because scholars of Ladino culture have mostly emphasized the Westernizing agenda and educational nature of nineteenth century Judeo-Spanish print culture. Individuals from middle class families like Halevi and Carmona may once have become a part of the class of Torah scholars, a traditional kind of learned elite in Ottoman Jewish society. As this traditional world was giving way to a new reality, with the growing encroachment of European ideas, goods, and capital in a semi-colonized Ottoman economy and rapidly changing society, members of the middle class and, in particular, the Sephardic *hommes de lettres*, needed to find a new place for themselves. They were vulnerable to the changes that swept away the traditional social order and descent into poverty was a real threat. Carmona's autobiography can be understood as a commentary on such middle class anxieties.

Like Saadi Halevi, Carmona portrays his life story within a context of different networks of patronage. A case in point is when he first ventures outside Constantinople in order to find work in Salonika, in 1896. "I went straight to the house of the Chief Rabbi there, Rabbi Covo, to show him a letter of recommendation from the Chief Rabbi of Constantinople." Nothing comes of Carmona's hope for a job referral, however, other than that the Chief Rabbi promises him room and board until the end of the month. The next day, he seeks out Carlo Allatini, the son of Saadi's benefactor Moïse, equipped with a letter by a member of the notable Fernández family of Constantinople,[20] and another letter for Allatini's secretary Leon Carmona, a distant relative of Elijah's. He is not much more successful, leaving his meeting with ten *liras* for the rest of the month, "and after that God may help you." Finally, Carmona makes his way to see a certain Jacques Pasha, "an old friend of the family," who tries to get him a job as an inspector for the local tram, again without success (Carmona 1926: 33–4).

The simultaneous appeal to different networks of patronage repeats itself throughout Carmona's autobiography, including the rabbinate in different cities, teachers and benefactors of the Alliance Israélite Universelle, and relatives and family friends. When Carmona finally does obtains substantial support from a Muslim friend of his father's in Cairo, a certain Ahmed Sherif Pasha (Carmona 1926: 66–7), he ends up losing the capital after he lets himself be talked into peddling fake jewels in Alexandria. It is only upon his return to Constantinople that he enters into a business contract with a Greek printer, paying a rental fee to use the latter's printing shop and slowly establishing a reputation and earning business for himself (Carmona 1926: 78).

One way to read Carmona's account of his travails in search for a supporter is as a critique of the networks of patronage that permeated Ottoman and Ottoman Sephardic society, and of the glaring inequalities that lay at its foundation. Unlike Saadi Halevi who takes great pride in his association with Allatini, which he describes as a partnership of like-minded allies, Carmona always appears as the underdog asking for handouts. The—obviously fictionalized—dialogues between himself and his reluctant sponsors are ironic and irreverent. What Halevi and Carmona have in common is their precarious economic situation as part of the urban middle class in a rapidly changing Ottoman Empire. They depend on establishing relations of patronage with a benefactor, something that Saadi Halevi accomplishes in the wake of his confrontation with the Salonikan rabbinate as an ally of Moïse

Allatini's civilizing mission and Carmona fails to do for the better part of his autobiography. For both, the path into Ladino publishing is a way to stabilize their economic position and to ward off (or reverse) social descent.

As Saadi Halevi's and Elijah Carmona's autobiographies suggest, it is important to look beyond the tropes of secularization and Westernization that have long dominated the historiography on modern Ladino print culture, and on modern Ottoman Sephardic society more generally. Ladino publicists like Saadi Halevi presented themselves as engaged in an epic struggle against a traditionalist and corrupt rabbinate, and the French-based Alliance and its local Ottoman supporters likewise painted their own educational project as a civilizing mission, fighting the religious leaders and overcoming the superstition of the masses. Behind the Orientalizing language and the image of a culture war between rabbinic tradition and European modernity, however, we can appreciate how the old social cleavage of Ottoman Sephardic society in many ways simply appeared in a new key. The civilizing mission of notables like Moïse Allatini in Salonika was a way for a new economic elite that owed its prowess to the integration of the Ottoman into a European-dominated economy to assert political power within Jewish society. At the same time, a group of Ladino publicists emerged to compete with the rabbinic scholars of old over access to patronage, each making their own claims to cultural capital and ideological leadership within the Jewish community. But despite the rise of new elites and a realignment of economic, political, and cultural power within the Jewish community, there was also a great deal of continuity. The history of Ladino print culture, like that of rabbinic scholarship of earlier centuries,[21] is a history of the formation and negotiation of relations of patronage. These relations of patronage were embedded in various networks that crisscrossed the cities of the Eastern Mediterranean, extending from Salonika and Constantinople to Vienna and Cairo, and they continued to straddle the divide between old (rabbinic) and new (Westernizing) elites, belying the imagined dichotomy between Sephardic tradition and European modernity in the closing decades of the nineteenth century.

NOTES

1. "How *La Epoca* was born."
2. "How Elijah Carmona was born, how he grew up, and how he became the editor of *El Juguetón*."
3. Saadi Halevi's *Mis memorias* appeared in *La Epoca* in 28 installments between September 1907 and March 1908. The in-text citations refer to the number of the installment. I have used the collection of cut-outs from *La Epoca* with the complete series of *Mis memorias* held in the Ben Zvi Institute Library, Jerusalem, 1107.5 ל / H88.
4. On Carmona's newspaper, see also García Moreno (2010, 2013).
5. On the foundation of *La Epoca* and on Saadi Halevi see Borovaya (2012: 81–97).
6. Another selection of excerpts from Saadi Halevi's memoirs appeared in the 1930s in the Ladino newspaper *La Acción*, but only parts of the series are still extant. Saadi's son, Sam Lévy, published

a French translation of fragments of his father's memoirs in *Le Judaïsme Sépharadi* in Paris, in 1933. See Rodrigue and Stein (2012: liv–lv).
7. Rodrigue and Stein (2012), 97 (English), 245 (Ladino), 56a in the original manuscript. Images of the original Ladino manuscript at http://www.sup.org/ladino/.
8. Rodrigue and Stein (2012), 80 (English), 227 (Ladino), 45b in the original manuscript.
9. Halevi is likely referring here to *L'Indépendance Belge*, which appeared in Brussels from 1831 to 1940. In 1873, the newspaper's masthead listed the contact information for subscribers in Constantinople and Izmir, so it obviously had a readership in major Ottoman cities.
10. These events also appears in the version published by Rodrigue and Stein, though in somewhat different form (Rodrigue and Stein, 97–110).
11. Stein (2004) explores the significance of *El Tiempo* in the rise of the Ladino press and its role in urban Ottoman Sephardic society.
12. On Ladino novels, including those by Carmona, see Romero (1992: 221–263); on the serialized novel in the Ladino press, see Borovaya (2012: 139–165).
13. Rodrigue and Stein, *A Jewish Voice*, xx.
14. On the Orientalist view of Ottoman Jews—what he calls the "Eastern Jewish Question"—see Rodrigue (1990: 1–24).
15. Cited in Frankl (1859: vol. 1, 198–9).
16. It was probably intended by Saadi to invoke here the image of the Biblical Moses, availing himself of his brother Aaron to act as an intermediary between him and the people (Exodus 4: 10–17).
17. The dichotomy of rabbinic tradition versus modernity is complicated, however, by Saadi's own description of his visit to Constantinople, where he goes in order to request a publishing license for *La Epoca*. He goes to the imperial capital as an envoy of Moïse Allatini, which opens many doors for him and allows him to meet with the acting chief rabbi. But it is a letter of introduction from the Salonikan rabbi Gattegno, "the only religious man" in Salonika who still supported Saadi, that really sways the chief rabbi, Moshe Halevi, who in turn connects him with the right person in the Ottoman administration to obtain his permit (*Mis memorias*, #23, 25).
18. Minna Rozen describes the conflict between rabbinate and Westernizing notables in Salonika as being primarily a struggle for political power and suggests that the juxtaposition between "traditionalists" and "modernizers" fails to capture what was at stake. See Rozen (2005: 142–151).
19. Just how successful as an economic enterprise *La Epoca* turned out to be is another question. Olga Borovaya has cautioned against exaggerated assumptions about the print run and reach of Ladino newspapers, certainly before the 1890s, when the circulation of *La Epoca* was about 750. See Borovaya (2012: 53). At the time, *El Tiempo* of Constantinople sold 900 copies, *El Telegrafo*, also of Constantinople, 500 copies. See Fesch (1971: 68).
20. Salomon and Isaac Fernandez were the heads of the Alliance's regional committee in Constantinople.
21. See the discussion in Bregoli (2014).

REFERENCES

Borovaya, Olga. *Modern Ladino Culture*. Bloomington: Indiana University Press, 2012.
Bregoli, Francesca. "Printing, Fundraising, and Jewish Patronage in Eighteenth-Century Livorno." In *Jewish Culture in Early Modern Europe: Essays in Honor of David B. Ruderman*, Edited by Richard Cohen, Natalie Dohrman, Adam Shear and Elchanan Reiner, 250–259. Pittsburgh and Cincinnati: University of Pittsburgh Press, 2014.

Carmona, Elijah. *Cómo nació Eliyah Carmona, cómo se engradeció y cómo se hizo director del "Juguetón"*. Constantinople: El Jughetón, 1926.
Fesch, Paul. *Constantinople aux derniers jour d'Abdul Hamid*, 1907. Reprint New York: Burt Franklin, 1971.
Frankl, Ludwig August. *The Jews in the East*, transl. P. Beaton, 2 vols. London: Hurst and Blackett, 1859.
García Moreno, Aitor. "El humor gráfico en la prensa sefardí: el caso de *El Juguetón* de Constantinopla," *Sefarad* 70 (2010): 195–240.
García Moreno, Aitor. "Juegos de palabras: palabras de *El Juguetón*." In *Judeo-Spanish in the Time of Clamoring Nationalisms*. Edited by Mahir Şaul, 37–59. Istanbul: Libra, 2013.
Jancke, Gabriele. *Autobiographie als soziale Praxis.* Cologne: Böhlau, 2002.
Loewenthal, Robyn. "Elia Carmona's Autobiography: Judeo-Spanish Popular Press and Novel Publishing Milieu in Constantinople, Ottoman Empire, Circa 1860–1932," unpublished Ph.D. dissertation, University of Nebraska, 1984.
Rodrigue, Aron. *French Jews, Turkish Jews*. Bloomington: Indiana University Press, 1990.
Rodrigue, Aron and Sarah Abrevaya Stein. *A Jewish Voice from Ottoman Salonica: The Ladino Memoir of Sa'adi Besalel a-Levi*. Stanford: Stanford University Press, 2012.
Romero, Elena. *La creación literaria en lengua sefardí*. Madrid: Ediciones Mapfre, 1992.
Rozen, Minna. *The Last Ottoman Century and Beyond: The Jews in Turkey and the Balkans 1808–1945*. Tel Aviv: Tel Aviv University, 2005.
Stein, Sarah Abrevaya. *Making Jews Modern*. Bloomington: Indiana University Press, 2004.
Stanislawski, Michael. *Autobiographical Jews: Essays in Jewish Self-Fashioning*. Seattle: University of Washington Press, 2004.
Yosmaoğlu, İpek K. "Chasing the Printed Word: Press Censorship in the Ottoman Empire, 1876–1913," *Turkish Studies Association Journal* 27 (2003): 15–49.

CHAPTER EIGHT

Itzhak Benveniste AND Reina Hakohén

Narrative and Essay for Sephardic Youth[1]

ELISA MARTÍN ORTEGA
Universidad Autónoma de Madrid

ABSTRACT

The changing role of women in Sephardic communities in the end of the 19th century generates a social debate which is reflected in Judeo-Spanish literature, especially in the so-called 'adopted genres' (novel, essay, theater, journalism). In this chapter we analyze two opposed examples of this polemic: the essay *Las muchachas modernas*, by Reina Hakohén, who attacks the Westernization, and the romantic novel *Konfidensyas de un amigo*, by Izhak Benveniste, which defends enthusiastic the new customs.

1. INTRODUCTION

Towards the end of the 19th century and the beginning of the 20th, there are important changes in the Eastern Sephardic communities—those located in the Turkish-Balkan region and the countries that were born from the dismemberment of the Ottoman Empire—that were motivated by the rise of nationalism and the arrival of new ideas that promoted a Westernization of customs. These changes were especially noticeable in the area of the changing role of women.[2]

The expansion of the *Alliance Israélite Universelle*,[3] a network of schools that provided an education featuring instruction in French, with a Western perspective, played an important role in promoting girls' literacy and general education, particularly those of the better educated upper social classes. The Alliance provided these women with access to written culture—first as readers and eventually also as writers. It also opened up their access to public life, especially through their participation in charity societies and through gainful employment, domains that had previously been limited only to men. These changes gave rise to a vivid polemic within Sephardic society, between those who defended traditional ways of life and warned of the dangers of assimilation and those who defended the adoption of the new customs.[4]

At the same time, during this period we see a flourishing of the so-called 'adopted genres' of Sephardic literature,' that is, those genres, including theater, journalistic writing, essay and novel, that were not typical of traditional Judeo-Spanish literature and that adopted Western works as their models.[5] Newspapers played an important role in the diffusion of these genres, and provided a way for women to participate in written culture not only as readers, but also as authors. In many of the novels, plays, essays and pieces of journalistic writing that have survived, we can sense an ever-increasing presence of a female readership. Amelia Barquín, who has researched the Sephardic novel, provides some information that explains the interest of women in this new literary genre:

> El más difícil acceso de estas a la educación y la cultura y sus mayores limitaciones en cuanto a sus posibilidades de realizar diferentes actividades en comparación con los hombres, su situación constreñida a un espacio social más reducido (sobre todo para las pertenecientes a una clase social inferior) las coloca en la situación más a propósito para disfrutar de un género literario que no se caracteriza por su alta calidad y buena factura y que proporciona evasión y consolación. (Barquín 1997: 176)[6]

The debate on the consequences of modern life and the new role of women occupies an important place in Sephardic literature from the turn of the 19th and 20th centuries. This is so not only in essays (Ayala 2006, 2008) and journalistic writing (Romero 2007, Quintana 2009), but also in fictional writing: novels (Barquín 1997, 1999, 2005; Cimeli 2007, 2013; Alpert 2010), theater (Valentín 2008, 2010, 2012) and even poetry. In particular, satirical poetry often satirizes the new customs and fashions and women's new way of life (Romero 2008, 2009a, 2009b).

Here we investigate these issues through the study and comparison of two texts that, although related in their genesis and content, are written in different literary genres and defend opposing ideas: the manifesto *Las muchachas modernas* ["modern girls"] by Reina Hakohén, one of the first Sephardic women writers of which we are aware, and *Konfidensyas de un amigo* ["Confidences of a friend"], by Itzhak Benveniste, a romantic story that we will analyze in more detail, since it has not been studied or collected in any other previous work.

2. REINA HAKOHÉN AND IZHAK BENVENISTE

Reina Hakohén, from Salonika, is, along with Rosa Gabay, from Istanbul, one of the first known women writers in Judeo-Spanish. The first mention of Reina Hakohén in the research literature appears in Romero (1992: 104). Later, Aldina Quintana referred to her as "la intelectual sefardí más importante de principios del siglo XX" ["the most important female Sephardic intellectual of the beginning of the 20th century"] (Quintana 2009: 125).

We do not have much information about her life, but we do know that she lived in Salonika, where she published all of her writing, and that she is the author of an important religious work, the *Comentario a Daniel* (Salonika, Ets Hayim, 1901). As is clear from the title, this work is a commentary on the Biblical Book of Daniel. It is written in the style used in the last books of the series *Me'am Lo'ez*, the great biblical commentary in Judeo-Spanish. Reina Hakohén shows great erudition regarding Judaism, which indicates that she received religious education. Her strong religious background also illuminates some fundamental aspects of her ideology, which are reflected in her vision of the role of women in society and of changes in traditional Sephardic life.

Reina Hakohén is also the author of an unpublished autobiography. This manuscript is housed in the holdings of the library of the Hebrew University of Jerusalem and is being researched by Professor Gila Hadar of the University of Haifa. In this work, Hakohén narrates a number of mystical experiences and shows an ascetic type of religiosity.

In addition, Reina Hakohén published two short texts, which we can place within the genre of essayistic prose, where she polemicizes on the changes that were taking place in Sephardic society. In these essays, she appeals to young people to go back to tradition and not to be seduced by the new customs or by the *esprito moderno*, in her own words, for this will end up destroying the Judeo-Spanish communities and their life. The two short texts are entitled *Por los modernos: Un razonamiento contra la mansevez de muestra époka* ["For the modern ones: Thoughts against our time's youth"] (Salonika, Ets Hayim, 1899) and *Las muchachas modernas: Una buena lisyón a syertas muchachas de muestra époka por kitarlas del kamino yerado* ["A good lesson for certain contemporary young women to lead them away from the wrong path"] (Salonika, Ets Hayim, 1898). Both texts have been edited and commented in Martín Ortega (2013: 145–175). Here we will focus on the second text, *Las muchachas modernas*, which is twelve pages long.

From an ideological point of view, the author places herself in this text within a school of thought that defends Jewish religion and is critical of modern life, which is often described as superficial, materialistic and destructive of the traditions and values of the Jewish people. The main idea in the text is one that has a strong paradoxical character; namely, that women in the past were strong without showing it: the reality was that women controlled men with their skills ('artes'), got what they wanted from them, and always ended up influencing their decision. Instead, with the arrival of modern life and the new customs, women have lost all their power and are controlled by men.[7] The first lines of the text are illustrative:

> Es a vozotras, senyoritas modernas, ke me adreso. El esprito moderno trokó enteramente vuestras naturas. Si los savyos antiguos, ke avlavan tanto por la maravioza fuersa de la mujer enverso el ombre, se toparían en esta época i verían vuestra floshura de korasón, kómo vos estásh deshando sombayer de los ombres i estásh cayendo en sus redes, ivan a dezir: ¿es esto posivle? ¿Puede ser ke el fiero se abolte por kalay, i el kalay por fiero? ¿Kómo la mujer, la krianza la más fuerte ke egziste en el mundo, devenir agora tanto flosha? (Martín Ortega 2013: 156–157)[8]

The author is very critical regarding both the new role of women and men who, according to her, trick women and take advantage of them, disguising as love what in reality is nothing but self-interest and passion for money. At the same time, however, Hakohén gives evidence that something has changed substantially: she herself, a woman, writes and publishes texts with her ideas, which was unthinkable just a few decades before. In addition, she shows that she is in possession of a considerable cultural background, both regarding religious matters—she makes abundant use of biblical quotation, in particular the stories of Samson and Delilah, Judith and Holofernes, the love narratives of King Solomon and the prophecies of Haggai and Jeremiah—as well as of profane literature, including her knowledge of *Don Quixote*, which she mentions explicitly (Martín Ortega 2013: 149). The text is addressed to modern young ladies. That is, she writes for a female readership that she wants to warn against the new habits and the terrible consequences they may bring to them. It is thus a conservative and moralistic work.

A few months later, in the same year of 1898, another text was published also in Salonika, *Konfidensyas de un amigo: Rakonto para la djuventud*. This text is signed by Itzhak Benveniste, about whom we have not been able to find any bibliographical information. We do not know of any other publications by this author either. At the beginning of the prologue he declares that this is the first text he publishes.

The copy that we have consulted, in electronic version, is found in the U.S. Library of Congress, and has not been transcribed or edited yet. It is a text of 26 pages, containing a short story with both aesthetic and propagandistic aims. The book is written in Hebrew letters and has punctuation marks, although in the fragments that we transcribe here we have altered the punctuation to make them easier to read. There are question and exclamation marks, periods, commas, quotation marks and long dashes in the dialogues between characters.[9]

In the prologue, the author explains that he wrote this story with the intention of countering the ideas that Reina Hakohén had exposed some months earlier in *Las muchachas modernas*, a text that, therefore, must have circulated in the Sephardic community of Salonika. In a classical *captatio benevolentiae*, Itzhak Benveniste explains why he has written the text and to whom it is addressed and asks the reader for forgiveness for its poor quality, justifying its publication by the necessity of spreading his ideas:

PRÓLOGO

Espero ke me permitirésh, por una primera vez, servirme de mi flaka péndola, no por dar una lisyón a las demuazeles de esta époka, komo pretendyó azerlo la autora de la broshura "Las muchachas modernas", aparesida el anyo pasado i ke muchas de entre vozotras ternerían meldado por pura kuryozidad. Londje de mí una idea semejante. Si akea bos atakó –¡o ándjeles de buendad, de ermozura i delikadesa!– ke tantos poetas kantaron vuestras divinas kualidades, si eya djimió por vuestros sea-dizyentos yeros i trató los djóvenes modernos de amadores del oro i falsadores, vuestro servidor no vino ke por azer embarar la impresyón ke vos kavzaría la lektura de sus avlas, kon un chiko rakonto ande verésh los veros sentimyentos de un djóvene verso una ninya, i la reserva, la delikadesa i la onestidad de la demuazel de klasa moderna de este tyempo. Tambyén i los motivos ke azen mankar la unión de los amorozos.[10]

Itzhak Benveniste says that he writes to defend the honor of women and the noble sentiments of modern young men. For this purpose he does not offer an argumentative text, like Reina Hakohén's, but a short story. The text can thus be considered a didactic or exemplary narrative. The end of the prologue is full of clearly rhetorical formulae:

Si la puvlikasyón de "Las konfidensyas de un amigo" tadró asta agora, es por lo ke vuestro muy umilde servidor esperaba ke un eskrivano más delikado i más capache ke él tomara vuestra difeza en una mejor forma. Ma komo desde su aparisyón nada fue eskrito asta oy, espero ke toparésh de gusto ke mejor vale tadre ke nunka.[11]

It does not seem that the author took a very long time to finish his story, since, as mentioned, its publication took place just a few months after that of Reina Hakohén's text, which Benveniste himself identifies as the reason that induced him to write. There is no reason to suppose that the text had been written beforehand either. In any case, Itzhak Benveniste justifies his daring to write by the need to preserve the honor of modern young women, which had been attacked. He presents himself as defender of a true idea held by a minority, with a penchant towards feeling victimized.

The intended readership of Itzhak Benveniste's reply were the same *muchachas modernas* to whom Reina Hakohén wrote. But the writer, in order to connect with them, employs the genre of the romantic novel, which was popular among female readers. The message is transmitted through a story of impossible love.

Amelia Barquín (1997) points out that the intended readers of these stories were in general the less educated lower classes, since more educated readers generally preferred to read in Western languages, instead of reading Judeo-Spanish stories, which usually had less literary quality and often were translations or adaptations of European works. At the same time, the Sephardic novel played a very important role in the spreading of Western ideas among the lower classes, who found there secular entertainment and models of modern life. Women were an important part of this readership. Barquín explains how the topics discussed in popular novels had an impact on society and how these novels reflect the tastes of those readers:

> Concedamos que el destinatario de la novela popular determina la obra en el sentido de que ésta ha de darle lo que él desea ver repetido sin cansarse nunca: final justiciero y triunfo de los débiles, emociones fuertes y grandes pasiones, etc.; sin embargo, en otro nivel, la novela popular influye en la evolución de las mentalidades, las costumbres y los gustos. Hay, pues, una corriente de influencia en doble dirección: obra-público y público-obra. La novela es un factor más de la modernización en que paulatinamente entra la sociedad sefardí, modernización que crea, a su vez, la situación y las circunstancias para que el público se interese por la novela y la disfrute. (Barquín 1997: 171)[12]

3. NARRATIVE, IDEOLOGICAL AND LINGUISTIC FEATURES OF *KONFIDENSYAS DE UN AMIGO*

A preliminary analysis of the narrative features of Itzhak Benveniste's text shows us that the narrative makes use of the story-within-a-story strategy. Two friends meet: Itzhak, the author's alter ego, and Alberto, who is the true narrator. Alberto appears as a desperate young man who tells Itzhak the story of his life. Their meeting takes place in a café and from the beginning Alberto's exaggeratedly emotional character is evident:

> En el invyerno del anyo a la franka 1896 tenía yo de uzo después del lavoro del día de renderme a_la Olimpya por traer a_mi esprito fatigado un poko de repozo. Una tadre enkontrí en dito kafé un amigo de mi chikés, el kual estava solo. Asentado alrededor de una mezika, arimado sobre su kaveza, i paresía pensativo i melankóliko.[13]

The conversation continues with topoi of romantic literature: the lover cannot eat or sleep and even wishes for death to arrive. Alberto uses Itzhak as his confidant; hence the title of the story.

The story is the following: Alberto falls madly in love with his neighbor, Lucha. He observes her, looks at her, but does not dare to speak to her. He becomes lovesick, since he does not know how to express his feelings. One day, a catastrophe takes place: there is a fire that destroys their houses. In the middle of this desperate situation, he declares his love for Lucha, who accepts it, as well as his promise to get married.

Their houses having been destroyed, they are not neighbors any longer and Alberto does not see Lucha anymore. He misses her so much that he is not able to focus on anything. He makes no progress in his studies because of his lovesickness. One day, Alberto sees Lucha by chance in a park and restarts his contact with her. He begins to spy on her, following her to her house and observing all her movements, this becoming an evergrowing obsession. However, he does not want to marry her at this point, because he first needs to find a good job that would allow him to make a living and provide for her.

Alberto, who has already abandoned his studies can only find very low paying jobs. Time goes on until one day Lucha gets angry, reproaches him for his lack of commitment and accuses him of infidelity. Alberto defends himself, reaffirming his love for her, but he also tells her that he cannot offer her a dignified existence and asks her to look for another husband. Even though he loves her, he cannot give her what she needs. Becoming aware of the situation, Lucha says goodbye with much sorrow. Her last words are "do not forget me".

The characters are completely flat and do not show any evolution. Lucha is a modest woman and Alberto a man in love, even lovesick, who, nevertheless, is not able to keep his love because of his lack of practical sense and his poor capacity to express his feelings. They both belong to the group of modern youth: they study and speak French.

The style is remarkable for its syrupy character. There are many descriptions of nature that reflect the feelings of the character and there is an abundance of topics of romantic literature, such as leaning out of a window and remaining speechless. This is shown here with a few examples. The following fragment describes Alberto's feelings when he felt in love with Lucha:

> Era mi balkón ande yo pasava todas las tadres a aregar, a plantar, a sentir la golor de las flores, la kultura de las kualas era estonses el más karo de mis divertimyentos. ¡Kuántas vezes en medyo de estas distraksyones amadas, mientras el enzerar del sol en el alma de la natura me deshava yr delizyiosamente en lungos i dulces penseríos![14]

Alberto's interest in gardening, which is frequently mentioned in the story, is a topos that shows his special sensibility, which, in some respects, could be considered feminine, according to traditional schemas. In any case, this hobby reinforces the extreme sentimentality that permeates the text. Consider the description that Alberto makes of the object of his love:

> Mi vezinika era muy ermoza, figúrate, amigo, una fizyonomía de ándjel, kolor roza, ojos klaros, kaveos byondos, perlas por dyentes, un dulsor i una delikadeza en su avlar ke me enkantavan syempre. En un byervo eya asemejava a una de estas divinitas ke mos pintan los autores gregos antikos en sus beyas obras trezladadas en fransés.[15]

The text reflects familiarity with Western literary models, especially the Romantic novel. Recurrent themes such as the image of the unhappy lover and the absolute idealization of women are found in the text, in an exaggerated fashion. This is how Alberto describes his enormous difficulty to express his secret love:

> Una tadre armado de koraje, malgrado mi emosyón, esperé el retorno de Lucha ke tadrava de venir de la eskola, kon la intensyón de ofrirle un chiko buketo de mis mejores flores kon dezirle dos byervos. Figúrate mi situasyón kuando eya ariva: plantado sobre mi balkón kon un fuerte batimiento de kore, pálido, no tuve la ozadía ni pude pronunsyar su nombre por yamarla, tanto mi espanto era grande.[16]

Alberto's inhibition is a fundamental element to understand the tragic end of the story. He is presented as a passionate young man who does not have the necessary skills to make his dreams come true. He is naive and disinterested.

The author shows skillfulness in the construction of dialogue which displays a certain dynamism. The following example is taken from the moment of the house fire, one of the most dramatic events in this story:

> —¡Alberto, Alberto! ¡No me deshes, sálvame de akí!—me dize eya rogándome. Todo mi kuerpo fue elektrizado al abrasar por kombinasyón su beya figura. Mi meoyo se trubló i no pude más retenerme:
> —Lucha, mi byen amada Lucha—le dishe—¿ké te espantas? Un riko puede abandonar sus rikezas por presto salvarse en el perikolo, ¿ma un amorozo puede abandonar a la ke ama?[17]

Here we find a direct reference to Reina Hakohén's text, where she warns young women that Westernized young men are only preoccupied with money, and put money above love:

> Komportavos komo las verdaderas ijas de Israel i no vayásh más detrás de luksos i de afeites i de ermozuras falsas, ke ya vos dishe ke los mansevos modernos no se sombayen ni de afeites, ni de luksos, ni de ermozura, salvo del oro. Akea pasyón ke tenían los ombres antiguos por las mujeres, la tyenen agora por el oro, este metal presyado. En el tyempo antiguo no era konsiderado por nada enfrente al amor de la mujer. (Martín Ortega 2013: 160)[18]

Alberto is, thus, constructed as a character that is the antithesis of everything that Reina Hakohén attributes to Westernized Sephardic young men. His main defects are naiveté, excessive love and a lack of practical sense. His sincere devotion towards his beloved is never questioned.

Even a cursory linguistic analysis of Itzhak Benveniste's Judeo-Spanish text shows a clear influence of Western languages. There are almost no Hebrew words, but the text is full of Italian words (*dunke, esteso*) and, especially French borrowings (*mersi, elevo, kuartier*). Sometimes it is difficult to determine their exact origin, as with the word *kore* 'heart' (cf. Standard Italian *cuore*), which alternates with *korasón*. The dialogue uses a colloquial register, although without any proverbs or idiomatic expressions. These linguistic features are identified by Amelia Barquín as typical of the Sephardic novel, as a way to reinforce its didactic function:

> La novela servía a las élites instruidas en las escuelas modernas y en el francés como instrumento para intentar inculcar los modelos de la cultura occidental en los sectores populares que no habían recibido esta formación (…). Hemos observado ya su interés por dignificar la lengua acercándola a otras occidentales de más prestigio, mediante el procedimiento de adoptar préstamos de todo tipo que se supone que el lector acabará aprendiendo e incorporando a su expresión. Pero hay aún una segunda intención didáctica, que se entiende bien teniendo en cuenta que nos hallamos en el mundo judío de Oriente de principios de siglo: las novelas proporcionan a los sectores menos favorecidos (entre ellos las mujeres de clase modesta) un medio para llenar su ocio con un entretenimiento de raíz occidental y sobre todo profano, rasgos que para los nuevos ilustrados suponen elementos de progreso. (Barquín 1997: 166)[19]

Nevertheless, we also find in *Konfidensyas de un amigo* some references to religion and the Jewish milieu, although they are not many: There are allusions to the story of Noah and to the biblical command to take a wife. A particularly significative passage is one narrating a scene in the rabbinical school that Alberto attended. He hadn't seen Lucha for some time, after the fire, and while he was *ladinando*— that is, translating the Hebrew Bible to Judeo-Spanish aloud—he expressed his feelings in the following manner:

> Un día, el livro delante de mí, yo ladinava a alta boz, según komandó el maestro, lo ke trata de la arka de Noah, ke es por seguro el más interesante de esta maravioza istoria. Yo ladinava ansí:
> "I el senyor disho a Noah: yo kyero azer alianza kon te. Tú entrarás en la arka kon tu mujer, tus ijos i las mujeres de tus ijos. Toma un par de kada sorta de animales ke están sobre la tyera i ke abolan al syelo."
>
> I yo, dezgrasyado de mí, mediante el gran alterío de mi meoyo, tuvyendo syempre mi tino en mi byen amada, adresándome a eya pronunsyé sin sezo, sin saver lo ke yo dezía esto ke sige:
> —Toma antes de todo a Lucha i azle el mejor lugar en tu nave. I eya es la más ermoza de todas las kriansas ke tú arás entrar en la barka. Sus ojos klaros te aklararon en los días de luvyas. Va bushkarla. Tú la fayarás a la ventana de su kaza arimada komo una flor, esperando tu arivo. Tú la kuvrirás de kaentes vestidos porke no se esfríe i no se kale, syendo va aver mucha umedad.[20]

Such a speech caused the hilarious reaction of his classmates and his teacher's anger. The scene comes close to being ridiculous, and underlines Alberto's incapacity to concentrate on anything other than worshipping his beloved Lucha. He abandons his studies because of his constant distraction and finds work in trade, but this is a precarious job, that does not provide enough income to allow him to get married. It is at this moment when a biblical quotation comes to his mind, while he is still thinking exclusively about his love:

> Estonses de ves en ves me venía a la idea esta frase tan sakra: "no es bueno ke el ombre esté solo, agámole kompanya". La kompanya ya estava pronta. (…) Ma Lucha ya era devenida demuazel byen formada i en idea de no poder más tyempo esperar. Por la ora ande está en toda su splendor deve ser destakada de la rama, por azer sentir la suave golor i dekorar la bononyera de un kavalyero, syendo se un o dos días pasan eya se amorcha i no más tyene la mizma valor de antes.[21]

In this fragment, a strong traditionalism is evident, in spite of Alberto and Lucha being symbols of the evolution in customs. At the end, it is social conventions that ruin their relationship: their impossibility to talk or get close to each other spontaneously and without hiding; the idea that the man must work to provide for his wife; the need for a woman to get married within a specific age range.

It is thus important to contextualize the modernity of the text. From an ideological point of view, a remarkable aspect of the text is the absolute celebration of modern young people, their sincerity, their feelings and their way of life. They are defended from their detractors. The young women are honest and modest. The young men are not the selfish opportunists that Reina Hakohén describes, but, rather, they are shown to be sincere, modest, dedicated, even capable of the greatest sacrifice, renouncing their love in order to obtain what is best for their beloved. Alberto does not find a good job, does not get an appropriate social position, and it is for this reason that he renounces Lucha's love.

The tragic end of the story is somewhat surprising. In principle it would seem that it would be more didactic to have a happy ending in order to encourage young people to be led by love and to accept the Western way of life; but this does not seem to be the author's intention. On the one hand, the author is influenced by the models of Romantic literature, with its propensity towards unhappy love. On the other hand, he wants to present the life of two people who, in a way, are victims of the society in which they live. Their love does not prosper because of multiple complications. Nevertheless, there is no social denunciation of this situation. The author accepts it, and so do his characters. Itzhak Benveniste focuses on defending, above all, the sincerity of young people and the honesty of their feelings. In this way, he attempts, after all, to exalt romantic love, to propose it as an ideal, even if it is an unreachable one, and to praise people who devote themselves to it, defending the authenticity of their passions and the value of their total and absolute sacrifice.

4. CONCLUSION

The two texts that we have examined in this chapter contribute, without a doubt, to the polemic regarding Sephardic youth in which many of that period's major figures participated and which is reflected in speeches and argumentative articles in the Sephardic press, as well as in literary fiction, from different points of view.

We may conclude that Itzhak Benveniste's story, in spite of having been written by a man, connects better with feminine ideology: by allowing the reader to identify with the tragedies of the main characters, it offers young women who are unhappy with their lives the possibility of immersing themselves in compensatory fantasies. On the other hand, Reina Hakohén's text, which is an essay written by a woman, seems to be addressed to the social élites, since it employs other cultural and religious referents. Her essay does not have the catchiness of the popular novel. The comparison of both texts gives us an example of the paradoxical character of certain social discourses—the woman who attacks modern young women and the man who defends them—as well as of their complexity—the woman who criticizes the new role of women so harshly is one of the first exponents of the access of Sephardic women to public life and written culture.

NOTES

1. This chapter has been written within the framework of the research project "Los sefardíes ante sí mismos y sus relaciones con España III: hacia la recuperación de un patrimonio cultural en peligro" (Spain, Ministerio de Economía y Competitividad).
2. For more information on the role of women as preservers and transmitters of Sephardic culture until the 20th century, see Seroussi (2003: 195–214); Cohen (1995: 181–200); Díaz Mas (2009: 81–101; 2008: 255–266; 2007: 187–200). On Sephardic women and changes in their traditional roles, see Díaz-Mas, Ayala and Barquín (2009: 22–39); Ayala (2006: 45–67; 2008: 144–155); Quintana (2009: 113–139).
3. For further details on changes in education, see Rodrigue (1983: 263–286; 1990); Benbassa (1991: 529–569).
4. For other examples of texts inscribed in this polemic, see Ayala (2008: 144–155); Rodríguez Ramírez and Rivlin (2009: 181–212).
5. For a panoramic view of the history of literature in Judeo-Spanish, see Romero (1992).
6. "Women's more restricted access to education and culture, the limitations that they found for engaging in different activities, compared to men, and their confinement to a reduced social space (particularly in the case of women belonging to the lower social classes) place them in a situation conducive to enjoying a literary genre characterized not by its high quality and craftsmanship but providing evasion and consolation" (Barquín 1997: 177).
7. This was a fairly widespread idea at the time. Some years later it was theorized by an Ashkenazi rabbi, Semah Rabiner, in his book *Las madres judías de la época bíblica* (Istanbul, 1913). For more details, see Rodríguez Ramírez and Rivlin (2009: 181–212) and Tina Rivlin's doctoral dissertation *Judeo-Spanish (Ladino) Ethic and Rabbinic Literature during the Westernalization of the Bulgarian Sephardic Communities: A Generic and Thematic Study on* Las Madres Judias de la época bíblica *by Rabbi Dr. Zemach Rabiner (Istambul, 1913)*, which was defended in 2012 at the University of Bar-Ilán (Israel) under the direction of Professor Shmuel Refael.
8. "It is to you, modern young ladies, that I address myself. The modern spirit has completely changed your nature. If the old learned men, who said so much about the prodigious force of women towards men, found themselves at the present time and saw your feebleness of heart, how you are letting yourselves be tricked by men and are falling into their nets, they would say: Is this

possible? Can iron become tin and tin iron? How could women, the strongest beings that exist in the world, have become so weak now?" (Martín Ortega 2013: 156–157)

9. For the transcription of the text we have followed the following correspondences between phonemes and graphemes: *b* voiced bilabial plosive /b/; *v* voiced bilabial fricative /β/; *ch* voiceless prepalatal affricate /ʧ/; *dj* voiced prepalatal affricate /ʤ/; *h* voiceless (post-)velar fricative /χ/ or voiceless laryngeal fricative /h/; *j* voiced prepalatal fricative /ʒ/; *ny* palatal nasal /ɲ/; *s* voiceless alveolar fricative /s/; *z* voiced alveolar fricative /z/; *sh* voiceless prepalatal fricative /ʃ/; *ts* voiceless alveolar fricative /ts/. The digraphs lamed+yod and lamed+yod+yod have been transcribed as *y* everywhere, given that the Judeo-Spanish pronunciation is always /j/ regardless of spelling.

10. "I hope you will allow me to make use of my clumsy pen for the first time, not to give a lesson to today's young ladies, as was the intention of the author of the brochure *Las muchachas modernas*, which appeared last year and many of you may have read out of mere curiosity. Far from me such an idea. If she attacked you—oh angels of goodness, of beauty and of delicacy!—when so many poets sang your divine qualities, if she bemoaned your alleged errors and treated modern young men as lovers of gold and dishonest, I, your servant, came here only to stop the impression that reading her words would have caused on you, which a little story where you will see the true feelings of a young man towards a girl, and the reservation, delicacy and honesty of a modern young lady of this day. And also the reasons that make the union of lovers fail."

11. "If the publication of *Las konfidensyas de un amigo* was delayed until now it is because this humble servant of yours was hoping that a more capable writer would undertake your defense more skillfully that he could. But since nothing has been written until today, I hope you will agree that it is better late than never."

12. "Let us agree that the intended readership of the popular novel determines the work in the sense that the novel must give it what it wants to see again and again: a just ending and the triumph of the weak, strong emotions and great passions, etc. However, at a different level, the popular novel has an effect on the evolution of mentalities, customs and tastes. There is thus a bidirectional influence: work-readership and readership-work. The novel is one more factor in the modernization that progressively affects Sephardic society and this modernization creates, in its turn, the situation and circumstances for the reading people to be interested in the novel and enjoy it" (Barquín 1997: 171).

13. "In the winter of the year 1896, according to the Western calendar, my habit was to go to Olimpya after the day's work, to give my tired spirit a little relaxation. One day I met in said café a childhood friend, who was alone. He was sitting at a small table, leaning on his head, and he looked pensive and melancholic."

14. "I was on my balcony where I spent every evening watering, planting, smelling the flowers, whose cultivation was my favorite entertainment. How many times, in the middle of these beloved distractions, as the sun was setting, I allowed myself to go delightfully in the soul of nature in long and sweet thoughts!"

15. "My young neighbor lady was very pretty; imagine it, my friend, a countenance like an angel, pinkish color, light eyes, blond hair, pearls for teeth, a sweetness and delicacy in her talk that always enchanted me. In one word, she resembled one of those deities that the ancient Greek authors depict in their beautiful works translated into French."

16. "One evening, armed with courage, in spite of my emotion, I awaited the return of Lucha, who was late coming back from school, with the intention of offering her a small bouquet of my best flowerings and telling her a few words. Imagine my situation when she arrived: standing in my balcony, my heart beating strongly, colorless, I did not dare or could pronounce her name to call her, so great was my fear."

17. "- Alberto, Alberto!, do not leave me, save me from here!—she was pleading to me. All my body became electrified when I held her beautiful body. My brain was troubled and I couldn't restrain myself any longer:

>—Lucha, my beloved Lucha—I said to her—what frightens you? A rich man can abandon his riches in order to save himself from danger quickly, but can a lover abandon her who he loves?"

18. "Behave like true daughters of Israel and do not pursue luxury, cosmetics or false beauty, since, as I already told you, modern young men do not care about cosmetics, luxury or beauty; only about gold. That passion that in the old times men used to have for women now they have it for gold, that precious metal. In the old days, it was considered as nothing compared to the love of a woman."

19. "The novel served the élites who had been educated in modern schools and in French as a tool to try to inculcate Western cultural models in the lower classes, which had not received this educational training [...] We have already noticed their interest in dignifying the language by bringing it closer to other Western languages with greater prestige, through the procedure of adopting all types of borrowings, which presumably readers will end up learning and incorporating into their own expression. But there is a second didactic intention, which makes perfect sense when we take into account the fact that we are in the Eastern Jewish world of the beginning of the 20th century: the novels give the least favored sectors of society (among them lower class women) a means to fill their free time with an entertainment that has Western roots and, importantly, is secular; these are features that for the new enlightened élites are elements of progress."

20. "One day, with the book in front of me, I was translating into Ladino aloud, as the teacher had commanded, the passage that deals with Noah's ark, which is without a doubt the most interesting part of this story. I was translating like this:

>'And the Lord said to Noah: I want to make an alliance with you. You will get on the ark with your wife, your sons, and your sons' wives. Take a pair of each sort of animals that walk on the ground and fly in the sky.'

And I, wretch that I am, through a great confusion of my mind, thinking always about my beloved, spoke without sense, without knowing what I was saying, the following:

>—Before anything else, take Lucha and give her the best place on your boat. And she is the most beautiful of all the creatures that you will take onto your boat. Her clear eyes will enlighten you in the days of rain. Go look for her. You will find her on the window of her house, leaning like a flower, waiting for your arrival. You should cover her with warm clothes, so that she does not get a cold and does not get wet, since there is going to be a lot of humidity."

21. "Then from time to time this holy phrase came to my mind: 'It is not good for man to be alone, let us make a companion for him'. The companion was ready. [...] But Lucha had become already a fully grown young lady who could not wait any longer. For the flower when it is in its full splendor must be cut from the branch, so that its sweet odor can be smelled and it can decorate the lapel of a gentleman, being it the case that if one or two days pass, it withers and does not have the same value as before."

REFERENCES

Alpert, Michael. "The Ladino novel". *European Judaism. A Journal for the New Europe* 43.2 (2010): 52–62.
Ayala, Amor. "La instruksion es el mas ermozo afeite por la mujer. Una conferencia de David Fresco sobre la nueva mujer sefardí (Estambul, 1929)". *Sefárdica* 17 (2008): 45–155.
Ayala, Amor. "La mujer moderna por Y. A. Basat (La Alvorada, Ruse 1899): la mujer sefardí y sus deberes en la nueva sociedad". *Miscelánea de estudios árabes y hebraicos. Sección Hebreo* 55 (2006): 45–67.
Barquín, Amelia. "La vie moderne dans le roman sépharade du XX siècle". In *Les Sépharades en littérature. Un parcours millénaire*. Ed. Esther Benbassa, 81–105. Paris: PUPS, 2005.
Barquín, Amelia. "La aventura de la novela sefardí". *Neue Romania* 22 (1999): 9–24.
Barquín, Amelia. *Edición y estudio de doce novelas aljamiadas sefardíes de principios del siglo XX*. Leioa: Universidad del País Vasco, 1997.
Benbassa, Esther. "L'éducation féminine en Orient: l'école des filles de l'Alliance Israélite Universelle à Galata, Istambul (1879–1912). *Histoire, économie et société* 4 (1991): 529–569.
Cimeli, Manuela. "Encuentros literarios entre Ashkenaz y Sefarad: la recepción en la literatura judeo-española de la obra narrativa de los hermanos Philippson y de Marcus Lehman", Tesis doctoral, Universität Basel, 2013.
Cimeli, Manuela. "La nueva vida 'a la franca'—algunas observaciones acerca de la novela judeo-española de principios del siglo XX". *Acta Romanica Basiliensia* 19 (2007): 55–63.
Cohen, Judith R. "Women's role in Judeo-Spanish song traditions". In *Active Voices. Women in Jewish Culture*. Ed. Maurice Sacks, 181–200. Chicago: The University of Chicago Press, 1995.
Díaz-Mas, Paloma. "Folk Literature among Sephardic Bourgeois Women at the Beginning of the Twentieth Century". *European Journal of Jewish Studies* vol. 3–1 (2009): 81–102.
Díaz-Mas, Paloma, Ayala, Amor y Barquín, Amelia. "La incorporación de las mujeres sefardíes a la esfera pública en el paso del siglo XIX al XX". In *Actas del primer congreso internacional Las mujeres en la esfera pública. Filosofía e historia contemporánea*, 22–39. Madrid: C.E.R.S.A., 2009.
Díaz-Mas, Paloma. "Las mujeres sefardíes del Norte de Marruecos en el ocaso de la tradición oral". *El Presente. Studies in Sephardic Culture* 2 (2008): 255–266.
Díaz-Mas, Paloma. "Cuadernos de mujeres: el cuaderno de Clara Benoudis y otras colecciones manuscritas de cantares tradicionales sefardíes". In *Romances de Alcácer Quibir*. Ed. Kelly Benoudis, 187–200. Lisboa: Ediçoes Colibri-Centro de Estudos Comparatistas, 2007.
Martín Ortega, Elisa. "Las primeras escritoras sefardíes, entre tradición y modernidad: dos textos de Reina Hakohén de Salónica". *Miscelánea de Estudios Árabes y Hebraicos. Sección Hebreo* 62 (2013): 145–175.
Quintana, Aldina. "La mujer sefardí ante sí misma y ante ellos: una lectura por las páginas de la *Alborada* (Sarajevo 1900–1901). *El Presente. Studies in Sephardic Culture* 3 (2009): 113–139.
Rivlin, Tina. "Judeo-Spanish (Ladino) Ethic and Rabbinic Literature during the Westernalization of the Bulgarian Sephardic Communities: A Generic and Thematic Study on *Las Madres Judias de la epoca biblica* by Rabbi Dr. Zemach Rabiner (Istambul, 1913), Tesis doctoral, University of Bar-Ilan, 2012.
Rodrigue, Aron. *French Jews, Turkish Jews. The Alliance Israélite Universelle and the Politics of Jewish Schooling in Turkey, 1860–1925*. Bloomington: Indiana University Press, 1990.
Rodrigue, Aron. "Jewish Society and Schooling in a Thracian Town: The Alliance Israélite Universelle in Demotica, 1897–1924". *Jewish Social Studies* vol. 45, 3/4 (1983): 263–286.

Rodríguez Ramírez, Eva Belén y Rivlin, Tina. "El legado sefardí de Semah Rabiner". *Miscelánea de Estudios Árabes y Hebraicos. Sección Hebreo* 58 (2009): 181–212.

Romero, Elena. "Textos poéticos sobre la emancipación de la mujer sefardí en el mundo de los Balcanes (I)". *Sefarad: Revista de Estudios Hebraicos y Sefardíes* 69,1 (2009a): 173–227.

Romero, Elena. "Textos poéticos sobre la emancipación de la mujer sefardí en el mundo de los Balcanes (Final)". *Sefarad: Revista de Estudios Hebraicos y Sefardíes* 69, 2 (2009b): 427–476.

Romero, Elena. *Entre dos (o más) fuegos: Fuentes poéticas para la historia de los sefardíes de los Balcanes.* Madrid: CSIC, 2008.

Romero, Elena. "La prensa judeoespañola contra los recelos, la burocracia y la censura". In *Ayer y hoy de la prensa en judeoespañol.* Ed. Pablo Martín Asuero and Karen Gerson Sarhon, 11–38. Estambul: Isis, 2007.

Romero, Elena. *La creación literaria en lengua sefardí.* Madrid: Mapfre, 1992.

Seroussi, Edwin. "Archivists of Memory: Written Folksong Collections of Twentieth-Century Sephardi Women". In *Music and Gender: Perspectives from the Mediterranean.* Ed. Tullia Magrini, 195–214. Chicago-London: The University of Chicago Press, 2003.

Valentín del Barrio, Carmen. "Comportamientos lingüísticos de la mujer moderna en el teatro costumbrista sefardí (1990–1930)". *eHumanista: Journal of Iberian Studies* 20 (2012): 384–401.

Valentín del Barrio, Carmen. "La mujer moderna en el teatro costumbrista sefardí (1990–1930)". In *Los sefardíes ante los retos del mundo contemporáneo: identidad y mentalidades.* Ed. Paloma Díaz-Mas and María Sánchez Pérez, 293–303. Madrid: CSIC, 2010.

Valentín del Barrio, Carmen. "El retrato femenino en el teatro sefardí costumbrista". In *Proceedings of the Fourteenth British Conference on Judeo-Spanish Studies.* Ed. Hilary Pomeroy, Christopher J. Pountain and Elena Romero, 253–264. London: Department of Hispanic Studies Queen Mary, University of London, 2008.

CHAPTER NINE

The Invention OF Eastern Judeo-Spanish

The Betrayals of Spanish in the Re-romanization Process (End of 19th Century) and Its Consequences

MARIE-CHRISTINE BORNES VAROL
Institut National des Langues et Civilisations Orientales

ABSTRACT

At the end of the 19th century Eastern Judeo-Spanish was re-romanized through contact with French, modern Iberian Spanish and Italian. The main argument developed in this chapter is that Italian and French had a much smaller effect on the Judeo-Spanish language than Iberian Spanish did. Contact with modern Iberian Spanish caused a great amount of linguistic insecurity on the part of Judeo-Spanish speakers, for sociolinguistic and linguistic reasons. In the case of Italian, knowledge of this language was limited. French, on the other hand, was sufficiently different from Judeo-Spanish to make massive interference unlikely. In addition, it was systematicaly taught as a foreign language in order to become a medium for instruction. Although the Judeo-Spanish writers had a limted knowledge of modern Spanish, they considered it as a model for Judeo-Spanish and tried to re-hispanize Judeo-Spanish in a rather chaotic way. The focus of the chapter is on the effects of this language policy on verbal morphology, in particular the fluctuation of infinitive forms and the transformations of the diphthongization rules, where these effects are particularly evident.

1. INTRODUCTION

In this article I shall use the term "Judeo-Spanish" to refer to the language spoken and written by the Sephardic Jews of the ex-Ottoman Empire, which is called by its speakers *djidyó* or *djudyó, djudezmo, espanyoliko* and here and there *ladino*[1] (Şaul, 2013).

What I want to show is how the sudden re-romanization of Eastern Judeo-Spanish through the contact with French, modern Spanish (or Castilian) and Italian at the end of the nineteenth century affected the representation of the language in the mind of its speakers and the language itself. I shall focus on the difference between the type of influence that French and Spanish had and their effects on the language, limiting my demonstration to some aspects of verbal morphology: the infinitive form and diphthongization.

My point is that Italian and French produced less damage to the language than modern Spanish did, for sociolinguistic and linguistic reasons: Italian because its influence was limited, and French because it was sufficiently different from Judeo-Spanish and systematically taught as a foreign language in order to became a medium for instruction, while the influence of Spanish, much more similar to Judeo-Spanish than Italian and French are, was indirect and only written. French and modern Spanish were both presented as model languages but the weight of Spanish as a norm of prestige was much bigger because it was evident for all the people and not only for a westernized elite.

2. CHANGES IN JUDEO-SPANISH LANGUAGE AND LANGUAGE CONTACTS

As Aldina Quintana recently explained (Madrid, 2014) Judeo-Spanish went through a first process of koineization during the 16th century which led to a shared norm at the beginning of the 17th century.

The language underwent a new koineization period at the end of the 19th century as a consequence of the modernisation of the Ottoman Empire. The Judeo-Spanish press developed from 1860 onwards, and the new schools opened from 1870 by the Alliance Israelite Universelle taught French massively to the Jewish children of the Empire. As a consequence of the modernisation process, the Sephardic Jews established intellectual contacts with Spanish progressive elites who began to show interest for the lost part of Hispania formed by the descendants of the Expulsion and their "old fashioned language." This movement is well documented in the writings of the Spanish Senator Angel Pulido Fernández (1904, 1905).

These new language contacts changed the way the speakers were considering their language and culture.

Much has been said on the influence of French on Judeo-Spanish. Thanks to Sephiha (1986), Nahum (1992), Harris (1994), Bunis (1996; 2013), Busse (1996), Ayala (2006), Díaz-Mas and Barquin (2007), Schmid and Bürki (2010) and others, many articles have been written about the linguistic ideas of the Judeo-Spanish elites and the ideological positions debated in the press during the last years of the Ottoman Empire. During this "guerre des langues" to paraphrase the French sociolinguist Louis-Jean Calvet, the position of the Alliancists has been the most spread. Their prejudice against Judeo-Spanish was the same as the French prejudice against regional languages like Provençal or Breton. The Alliance pointed out the modernity of the French language, but the most important thing for Alliancists was the appropriateness of a nation to a language (Bornes Varol 2013b).

In the case of the multilingual Ottoman Jews it was an invitation to choose one language, as their national one, representing their identity. The 19th century ideologists and largely 20th century ones despised multilingualism and language mixture. "Unfortunately," the Judeo-Spanish people were a multilingual and culturally multi-referenced people. Their linguistic identity consisted of speaking (more or less) three to four languages and to be able to mix them in a very creative way. As I have shown before when studying the influence of Turkish on Judeo-Spanish (Bornes Varol, 2008), it is no mean achievement to be able to notice the convergences between a Semitic language, a Turkic one and a Romance base (at least), especially concerning syntax, morphology and phonetics. It is even more remarkable that they are able to notice the divergences between the languages and to solve them (Bornes Varol 2011). In spite of this shared linguistic ability they could have been proud of, the Judeo-Spanish polemicists in their majority did not defend multilingualism as their linguistic identity,[2] because of the prevailing ideology of their time. They just supported different languages as candidates for their "national language": French for the Alliancists, Turkish for the Ottomanists, Hebrew for the Zionists. Judeo-Spanish was defended as an identity and traditional language, by Sam Levi in the Salonikan newspaper *La Epoka* for example (Guillon, 2013a), but only provided that it was purified, getting rid of its mixed character. That meant that the only way to save the Judeo-Spanish "jargon," *el espanyol muestro*, 'our Spanish' was to convert it to *el espanyol halis de la Spanya*,[3] 'the true Spanish of Spain'. The position of the Jewish elite was the same in Turkey in the 1880s as it is today.[4]

3. THE RE-ROMANIZATION PROCESS

During the process of re-romanization of the end of the 19th century, the impact of the three Romance languages in contact with Judeo-Spanish (leaving aside Rumanian because its influence was regional and unshared) was unbalanced because of their different symbolic weight, the respective quantitative importance of the contacts, the vectors of the contact, and the way children learnt them.

The influence of Italian was limited. It was more significant in Salonika than elsewhere because of the important presence of an Italianized elite, *los Frankos*. In Istanbul they were proportionally less present and influential. The Italian schools of Salonika and Istanbul had lesser possibilities than French teaching schools (Catholic private schools and of course Jewish schools of the Alliance Israelite Universelle).[5] Jewish children were massively educated in French schools, whereas Italian schools were attended by an elegant minority. In Istanbul a popular satirical text makes fun of italianized "bourgeoisie": *Roberto, metete kolleto; los guantes? en el büró; el papá? Ande Samanó; la mamá? Ande Lazaró; Ayá van a azer Shabad? Ay, sí, perke/porke no?!* (Varol Bornes, 2008: 378 note 174)

The Alliance schools were attended by nearly all social classes and especially girls, who were cut off from the traditional education. In these schools, French was taught as a foreign language. Its learning was guided and standardized with spelling, conjugation and grammar lessons. It was a prestige language in the community, but it was considered inappropriate for everyday exchanges. Like Italian, it was clearly seen as a foreign language added to a multilingual baggage. Nevertheless, the relatedness of French to Judeo-Spanish was overexploited, providing many new words and concepts. Haïm Vidal Sephiha (1986) even spoke of the development of an inter-language he calls *judeo-fragnol*.

The Spanish language, on the other hand, had a different position. Contact with Spain and the Spanish language at the end of the 19th century was limited to a few Sephardic personalities in touch with the Spanish progressive intellectuals, academics and politicians. Their knowledge of Spanish was essentially written (as we can see with the pronunciation of [w] in verbs like *trankuilizar, seguir*). The hispanophile Judeo-Spanish intellectuals asked for newspapers, books, and dictionaries. Spain did not have schools in the Eastern Mediterranean. Finally, Judeo-Spanish suffered from the prejudice that Judeo-Spanish language was nothing more than Spanish: a corrupted, degenerated dialect of Spanish, but Spanish and only Spanish. The symbolic weight of modern Spanish was inversely proportional to the knowledge the Sephardim had of it. If the idea of French as a national language for Levantine Jews looked unnatural to the people, Spanish made sense for everybody. Hebrew was the language of the first exile, Spanish was the language of the second. At least, the linguistic relatedness of the two languages was evident.

Now, in the dynamics of linguistic contacts we know that it is easier to assimilate a marked and foreign element than an unmarked and almost identical one (Bornes Varol, 2011: 466; Lagarde, 1996: 52[6]). French, Hebrew and Turkish verbs were easely judeo-hispanized as borrowings by means of the inflectional endings *-ear, -iyar* and *-ar* (*aranjar, darshar, kizdrear/kizdriyar*). French verbs were easily re-analyzed (*rendre > render, prendre > prender, comprendre > comprender; débarrasser > des-baras-ar, embarrasser > em-baras-ar*, and so on) and adapted. On the contrary, Spanish verbs were not considered as borrowings but as correct forms. The discrepancy between Spanish and Judeo-Spanish conjugation was often misunderstood and interpreted in terms of corruption and mistakes of the latter by its speakers. This discrepancy generated confusion and linguistic insecurity among them and confirmed Judeo-Spanish speakers' negative opinion of their patrimonial language.

4. CORPUS AND SAMPLES

In the corpus that I have chosen for the demonstration, French elements are very present and all the authors show a moderate to intensive use of a Spanish dictionary. The influence of Italian is limited to the success of the verbs *reushir* 'to be successful' and *dechidir* 'to decide' and the variant *diridjir* 'to run/manage'. It seems reasonable to conclude that the Spanish verbs *decidir* and *dirigir* drew the

Italian *decidere* and *dirigere* and the French borrowing *desidar* < *décider* to the third group (*-ir*). Multicausal effects are frequent in this re-romanization process.

I selected the verbs in a series of texts from the end of 19th century and the beginning of the 20th, from authors who were trying to promote a new standard, closer to Spanish and, in the process, inventing at least a special language which is not Modern Spanish, nor Medieval Spanish, nor Judeo-Spanish, but something like a re-romanized interlanguage.[7] The texts that I have chosen are the following:

1. The memoirs written by Saadi Betsalel Halevy at the end of the 19th century, edited by Aron Rodrigue and Sarah Abrevaya Stein (2012), transliterated by Isaac Jerusalmi, *A Jewish voice from Ottoman Salonica*. This text is representative of the intellectual elite of Salonika, whose language is influenced by Italian more than other Judeo-Spanish varieties. This text is also influenced by French and shows here and there the use of a Spanish dictionary.
2. The booklet *Istorya de Alexandros el Grande*[8], published in Vienna en 5650 (1889–1890). This work was translated from German and shows an overuse of a Spanish dictionary (Bornes Varol 2013a).
3. The manuscript introduction to a book of proverbs from the Judeo-Spanish polyglot Great-Rabbi Hayim ben Moshe Bejerano. He corresponded with many Spanish intellectuals such as Unamuno and Ortega, sent articles to Spanish reviews, as Paloma Díaz-Mas pointed out (2001), took part in the polemics on the language and supported a re-castilianization of Judeo-Spanish, which led him to write in a curious semi-Spanish. (Bornes Varol 2010)
4. The memoirs of Rafael Çikurel, *Mis memorias—Una vida yena de drama i perikolos*, published in 1911 in the paper *La boz del Pueblo* in Izmir, transliterated from Rashi script and edited by Henri Nahum (2002). At first sight the language of the memoirs looks a lot like the "Judeo-Fragnol" described by Sephiha. Nahum (2002: 99) describes it as "the elegant variety of the vernacular judeo-spanish of the enlightened class."[9] It has a lot of borrowings from French and many Castilian words and expressions.
5. I used also the transcribed texts from a choice of articles dealing with a variety of subjects printed in the Judeo-Spanish press and written between 1888 and 1914. These articles have been transliterated and have glossaries and translations to Turkish and English made in 2006 by present-day Judeo-Spanish speakers in Istanbul (Birmizrahi *et alii*, 2006).
6. I added some data scattered in the scientific works of my colleagues: text editions and linguistic studies[10].

The transliterated texts give us information not only about the language at the end of the 19th century but also about its actual interpretations and doubts, since the Hebrew graphical system used to write Judeo-Spanish leaves much room for variation. That is the reason why I chose texts transliterated by native Judeo-Spanish speakers like Isaac Jerusalmi (1), Henri Nahum (4), or the Gözlem édition team (5).

To complete the analysis of the consequences of 19th century disruptions, I took as a point of comparison several other sources:

- the contemporaneous oral corpora I collected myself in Turkey in the 1990s,
- the proverb-book of Mrs. Flore Gueron Yeschua from Bulgaria (Bornes Varol 2010)
- a recent letter from Izmir (reproduced in Annexe, *cf. infra*)
- J. Nehama's Judeo-Spanish/French dictionary (1977).[11]

5. GRAPHICAL PROBLEMS

The manuscripts analyzed here were written in *solitreo*, the Eastern Hebrew cursive style, and the printed texts are in Rashi script, which is a special form of Hebrew characters. Bejerano's prologue is written in Latin characters, a way to bring Judeo-Spanish closer to Spanish in order to attract Spanish readers. As *yod* can represent [i] or [e], and no more than two *yod* can be used in a sequence, it is difficult to note verbs like *reyir/riyir* … when there is a dieresis we have frequently an *aleph* separating [e] and [i] like in *reír* or *kreer* (קריאיר) but not always, and we find also forms written like *kreyer* (קרייר). So קריי can be read as *kree, kreye, kreí, kreyí*:

Table 1. The fluctuation of *kreer* 'to believe'

French	Spanish	Judeo-Spanish	
		19th c. authors	20th c. authors & transliterators
croire	creer	creeron/creendo; (HB) no kree un kredo, kreder/kredyer/kredir < kredyendo/kreer < kre(i)ya (?) (*IA*); kreer kreyes; kreea, kreendo kreesh; kreemos; kreendo (kreyendo?); kreerme; kreevos; kreo (*MNP*); kreia; kreian; era kreendo; kreygo; kreeron (kreyeron?) (RÇ); kreer (?) kreendo (?) kreer (?); No kree kreia; (SHL)	creyo, creyes/créer, creendo, creed, creo … (*Hazino*) kreygo/kreyo, kreye, kreyer(se) kreyendo (Ist) kreer, kreo, kréete, kreído (Nehama)

Abbreviations of sources: *MNP* = *Lo ke Meldavan Nuestros Padres*, transliterated by Gözlem Kitabevi team; HB = Hayim Bejerano, in Latin characters; RÇ = Rafael Çikurel, transliterated by Henri Nahum; SHL = Saadi Ha Levi, transliterated by Isaac Jerusalmi; FGY = Flore Gueron Yeshua, in Latin characters; *IA* = *Istorya de Aleksandros*, transliterated by M. C. Varol; (others: Ist = Istanbul; Nehama = dictionary; *Hazino* = Schmid and Bürki).

The ambiguity of Hebrew characters and their inadaptability to the Judeo-Spanish language became an argument for some of the Judeo-Spanish intellectuals that wanted to change the language, including the alphabet in which it was written. Among them were Hayim Bejerano and his friend Eliya Krispin, editor of *Luzero de la pasiensia*, the first Judeo-Spanish paper printed in Latin characters (Díaz-Mas and Barquín, 2007).

It is a possibility that the morphological fluctuation that we find between verbs of the second group in *-er* and third group in *-ir* was encouraged by the graphical ambiguity. Today it is difficult to know if the infinitive of the usual verb 'to fill up' is *inchir* or *incher*. One reason is that in some forms there is no morphological difference between the second and the third conjugation. Forms like the imperative *inche* and *incheron* 'they filled up' (*inche Moshón, ke la noche es larga!, incheron las kupas*) are ambiguous as belonging to a second or a third conjugation verb. This is putting aside the fluctuation of this verb with *inchar* (like in Spanish *henchir* and *hinchar*).

For those reasons I left aside a great number of verbs. I also left aside the semantic aspects of the contact of Romance languages with Judeo-Spanish and I focused on French versus Spanish influence, their contradictions and their effects on these Judeo-Spanish texts.

6. COMPLICATING RE-ANALYSES: THE CASE OF FRENCH *-DUIRE* VERBS

Consider the data in Table 2, which show the adaptation of French verbs ending in *-duir* in 19th and 20th century texts by Judeo-Spanish authors:

Table 2. Complicated re-analyses (1): The case of French *-duire* & Spanish *-ducir* verbs

French	Spanish	Judeo-Spanish		
		19th c. authors	20th authors & transliterators	
produire	producir	**produsyó** (HB) produsen, produsida; (*MNP*) *produsir*, no se produsió; *se produzkan*; (RÇ)	produkto (FGY) produizir (prodwizir) (Nehama)	X
conduire	conducir	konduizir, konduizido (RÇ)	kondukta; (FGY) kondokta konduktor (Nehama)	
traduire	traducir	tradució (HB) *tradusido* (RÇ); traduizar; *trazuizado* (Papo);	tradüizir, tradüizido *cf* tresladar (Nehama)	X
introduire	introducir	*introduizir*, fui entroduizido, introduizirme; (RÇ)	entroduzgamos (Perahya); introduzir (Nehama)	X

Abbreviations of sources: *MNP = Lo ke Meldavan Nuestros Padres,* transliterated by Gözlem Kitabevi team; HB = Hayim Bejerano, in Latin characters; RÇ = Rafael Çikurel, transliterated by Henri Nahum; FGY = Flore Gueron Yeshua, in Latin characters; (others: Ist = Istanbul; Nehama = dictionary; Perahya = Gruss, 2010; Papo = *Pele Yo'ets,* transliterated by myself).

As mentioned before, Judeo-Spanish speakers are very accustomed to identifying verbal paradigms in foreign languages. They borrowed a list of verbs ended by *-duire* from French (< latin DUCERE) and adapted them first as *-duizar: conduire > konduizar, introduire > introduizar, produire > produizar, traduire > traduizar*. It is also possible that they adapted them spontaneaously in *–duizir*, due to the similarity with the very frequent verb *dizir*, 'to say' (in French *dire*): *dire > dizir, konduire > konduizir* …

Here we can see that the regularity of the process is disrupted by Spanish. Forms with [-duθir] may be reinterpreted as [-dusir] because of French graphical usage. Rafael Çikurel for example uses *konduizir, konduizido, introduizir, introduizido* but *produsir* and *tradusir, tradusido*. Bejerano who wanted to improve Judeo-Spanish by keeping it as close as he could to Spanish, failed in this endeavor because he did not know how to conjugate past tenses of this very irregular verb: *produsió, tradució*[12] (modern Spanish *tradujo, produjo*). This disruption produces variability with effects of discontinuity today *-duzir/-duizir/-dusir*, and also irregular forms like *introduzgamos*. Some verbs have disappeared, including *konduizar* or *konduizir* (today replaced by *kulanear*, from Turkish, in Istanbul).

7. *PONER, METER* AND *POZAR*

The verb *poner* 'to put', and its derivations, which was commonly used until the 18th century,[13] was about to leave the system at the end of the 19th, replaced by *meter*, which has the double advantage of converging with the French verb *mettre* and its derivations and to have a regular conjugation which is more economical. Another replacement was the verb *pozar* < French *poser*, 'to put; to alight', which is also regular.

With *meter* we find *admeter* 'to admit', *remeter(se)* 'to put back; to recover', *kometer* 'to perpetrate', *komprometer(se)* 'to compromise oneself', *entremeterse* 'to intervene', and last but not least *permeter* 'to allow' and *prometer* 'to promiss', very common in Judeo-Spanish.

Here the confrontation with modern Spanish *permitir, admitir, remitir/ prometer, comprometer, someter, cometer/reponer(se)* jeopardize the re-analysis of the verbs, their adaptation from French to Judeo-Spanish and the process of regularization, leading to the hesitations of the Judeo-Spanish speakers of the second half of the 20th century.

Mrs. Flore Gueron writes *komprometen, se entremeten, kometyeron*, but hesitates between *permeter* and *permitir*: *permeten/permitían, permitido*.

Henri Nahum, who tranliterates Çikurel's text, writes *remeter, remetí, someterse* and *sotometerse* but *somitidvos; admeter, admetería* but *admitidos; kometer* but also *kometir*. See Table 3.

Table 3. Complicated re-analyses (2): French -*mettre* & Spanish -*meter*, -*mitir*, *poner*

French	Spanish	Judeo-Spanish		
		19th c. authors	20th c. authors & transliterators	
promettre	prometer	prometer (*MNP*); prometer; aprometyeron; la prometa (SHL) aprometer; promete (HB);	aprometen, aprometyó aprometen, la prometa (FGY) prometer (Nehama)	
compromettre	comprometer	komprometer (SHL); aprometer (Kalwo/Semo)	komprometer, se kompromete (FGY) komprometerse (Nehama)	
soumettre (se)	someter(se)	sumeter; sumeterse; sumetida (*MNP*); someterse/sotometerse (RÇ); sotometer; sotometyó (SHL); someterse (HB)	sumeter, se sumeten (FGY); someterse/somitidvos (Nahum); sotometerse (Nehama)	X
commettre	cometer	kometer; kometí; kometidos (RÇ); comete, que cometan (HB)	kometer, kometen, kometyeron (FGY) kometer/kometir (Nahum); Ø (Nehama)	X
s'entremettre	Ø	entremeterse; entremetedores (SHL); se entremetería, se entremeta (Kalwo/Semo)	entremeterse, se entremeten, entremetidos; entremeterse (Nehama)	
admettre	admitir	admetervos (MP); admetemos, admitido (HB)	admeter, se admete (FGY); admeter/admitidos (Nahum); Ø (Nehama)	X
permettre	permitir	permitido, permitirlo (*IA*); permeter; permetermos; permete; permetido; permeteriya; (*MNP*); permetemos, se permete, permeten, permetido, me permito (HB); premeter; premetía, ke me premetan (SHL)	permeten/permitían; permitido (FGY); permeso/permiso (*MNP*); se permetieron (L. Izmir) permeter (Nehama)	X
transmettre	transmitir	transmitidos (HB)	transmeter (Nehama)	

(Continued)

Table 3. (Continued)

remettre	remitir	remeter; remetí; remetidos (*MNP*); remeter; remetí; (RÇ)	remeterse, remetyéndose (FGY) remeter (Nehama)	
remettre (se) mettre	reponer(se) poner	metyeronse, metidos?, mete, metan (*IA*); meter; ke meta; metia; metiyan; metidas; metí (*MNP*); 0se pone, poner, ponen, ponían, ponga, pongamos, ponete; mete, meter (HB); meter, metimos, metyeron (Kalwo/Semo)	meter, metyendo, metite, metimos, metyeron (FGY) se metevan (L.Izmir) meter (Nehama)	
Ø	Ø	akometer (SHL);		

Abbreviations of sources: *MNP* = *Lo ke Meldavan Nuestros Padres,* transliterated by Gözlem Kitabevi team; HB = Hayim Bejerano, in Latin characters; RÇ = Rafael Çikurel, transliterated by Henri Nahum); SHL = Saadi Ha Levi, transliterated by Isaac Jerusalmi; FGY = Flore Gueron Yeshua, in Latin characters; *IA* = *Istorya de Aleksandros,* transliterated by M. C. Varol; (others: Ist = Istanbul; Nehama = dictionary; Kalwo/Semo = articles tranliterated by David Bunis, 2013; L. Izmir = letter from Izmir annexed; Nahum = transliteration of Rafael Çikurel's memories).

There is no problem with *prometer, komprometer, entremeterse, remeter, meter* but there is variation among authors with *admeter/admitir, permeter/permitir, someter/somitir/sumeter/sotometer* (< Italian); *transmitir/transmeter* and internal variation in Bejerano's system: *transmitir, admeter/admitir, kometer, permeter, someter* sometimes on the same page. Bejerano also eliminates *meter* to re-establish *poner*.

The same situation occurs with *pozar*, the other substitute of *poner,* as shown in Table 4.

Table 4. Complicated re-analyses (3): French – *poser* & Spanish -*poner*

French	Spanish	Judeo-Spanish		
		19th c. authors	20th c. authors & transliterators	
poser (se)	poner(se)	pozar: pozadas (RÇ); apoza (*MNP*); apodzar, apodzaron (Kalwo/Semo)	apoza (FGY) apozar (Nehama) pozar (Ist)	

THE INVENTION OF EASTERN JUDEO-SPANISH | 173

composer	componer	*kompozar; kompozó/ komponyeron; kompuesto (SHL)*; kompuesto (*MNP*); kompuesto (*IA*); compuestas (HB);	kompuesto; se kompone (Perahya); *komponer/kompozar* (Nehama) kompozar, kompozaron (Ist)	X
exposer	exponer	me eksponí (RÇ); expuesto; exponerse (HB)	ekspozar, ekspoza, ekspozando,(FGY) eksponer/ekspozar (Nehama) ekspozar (Ist)	
supposer	suponer		soupozan (Perahya) *suponer/supozar, supuesto* (Nehama)	
indisposer	indisponer		indispuesto (FGY); *endispozar endisposto* (Nehama) e/indispozar, e/indispozado (Ist)	
disposer	disponer	dispuestas; dispone (HB)	dispoza, dispozas, dispozan, *dispozado/dispuesto* (FGY) disponer/dispozar (Nehama)	
imposer	imponer	imposó; impone (HB);	impozar/empozar, empoza (FGY) imponer/impozar (Nehama) empozar (Ist)	
opposer	oponer	oponerse (HB)	oponer/opuesto (Nehama)	
proposer	proponer	propone (HB)	propoza, propozas, propozando, propozisyón (FGY) proponer(se) (with conjugation), propuesto/propozar (Nehama) propozar (Ist)	
reposer (se)	reponer(se) reposar	repozando, arepozar (SHL); el reposo/repozo (HB); repozar (Kalwo/ Semo)	Ø repoza, se repozan, repozándose, repozado (FGY) repozar, repozado (Nehama & Ist)	

(Continued)

Table 4. (Continued)

déposer > dépôt deponer (Law) > déposition	depositar >depósito	fueron depozitando (SHL);	depozar/depozitar (Nehama) Ø	

Abbreviations of sources: *MNP* = *Lo ke Meldavan Nuestros Padres,* transliterated by Gözlem Kitabevi team; HB = Hayim Bejerano, in Latin characters; RÇ = Rafael Çikurel, transliterated by Henri Nahum; SHL = Saadi Ha Levi, transliterated by Isaac Jerusalmi; FGY = Flore Gueron Yeshua, in Latin characters; (others: Ist = Istanbul; Nehama = dictionary; Kalwo/Semo = articles tranliterated by David Bunis, 2013; Perahya = Gruss, 2010).

There is no continuity in the formal analysis nor harmonization of the paradigms. *Repozar* and *apozar* look stable, leaving aside dialectal features. Some authors use *poner*, others use *pozar*. Betsalel Ha Levi hesitates between *kompozó* and *komponyeron* and we can see that the irregularities of the verb have disappeared. Çikurel (or Henri Nahum?) hesitates between *imposó* and *impone*, but one could have read *impuso*. Nehama fluctuates a lot and gives the two forms *imponer/impozar, proponer/propozar, suponer/supozar, exponer/expozar, komponer/kompozar, disponer/dispozar,* but he chose *depozar* versus *oponer*. He also chose *indispozar*, but the past participle fluctuates: *endisposto* from *poner* and *endispozado* from *pozar*.

8. CONFUSING INFINITIVE FORMS, PARADIGMS AND GROUPS OF CONJUGATION

Borrowings from French or Turkish belong preferentially to first group in *-(e)ar*, the most frequent and regular one in Judeo-Spanish. We saw that the interference with Spanish was confusing and complicated the process of integration of the borrowings.

Even the useful and frequent verb *dizir* 'to say', rather stable in spite of the variation *dizer/dezir/dizir* was disrupted by contact with Spanish. Bejerano, for example, introduces *desir* < Spanish *decir* and makes a preterite *dicieron* (sic), that is to say a hypercorrected form, to replace the Judeo-Spanish preterite *disheron*. In the 1960s, Perahya writes *dizir* in a letter to Ben Rubi and Ben Rubi answers using *desir* (Gruss, 2010: 135).

An outlook of the linguistic chaos that ensued, authors using one, two or even more forms on the same page and even in the same sentence, is given in Table 5:

Table 5. Paradigm hesitation: French -er /Spanish -ir > Judeo-Spanish -ar, -er, -ir ?

French	Spanish	Judeo-Spanish	
		19th c. authors	20th c. authors & transliterators
consommer	consumir	konsome (*MNP*); konsumyendo, konsumir (SHL); konzumir/er < se konzume (*IA*); konsumir (Kalwo/Semo)	konsumir, konsomasyón (Nehama)
corriger	corregir	corregir, corigir (HB),	korijar (FGY); korijar (Ist) korijar (Harris)
décider + It. decidere	decidir	desidar/desidían, desidyó/ desididó 'decided'(*MNP*); se desidió, me desidí; desidir/ dechizó, me dechizí (RÇ)	desidar, desida, desidava, desidates, desidó, desidarán (FGY) decidieron (L. Izmir) desidaron (Ist)
différer	diferir	difera, diferan (HB);	
diriger + fr. régir	dirigir + JE rijir / rejir	dirijir, diridjir, dirijar (*MNP*); dirigendosen (HB); se dirijeron/dirijadores/diridjirlos, dirijendo (SHL); dirigó (*IA*)	el rijo (FGY) diridjir (Nehama); dirijar/rijir, rije (Ist)
distinguer	distinguir	distinguir (SHL);	distingir, distingido (Nehama)
exiger	exigir	exijir, tinía exigido (RÇ);	egzijen (FGY) egzijir (Nehama) egzijaron (Ist)
exister	existir	egziste (*MNP*); existia (RÇ); eksistensya (Kalwo/Semo)	egzistir, egziste, egzisten (FGY); egzistiya (Ist) egzistir (Nehama)
insister	insistir	ensistyó (*MNP*); insistir/ insistó (RÇ); ensistyó, ensistir, ensistyeron (SHL)	ensistas (2nd Prest) (FGY) ensistir (Nehama)
opprimer	oprimir	oprimantes (HB); oprimir (Kalwo/Semo)	opremir (Nehama)
persuader	persuadir	persuadir (*IA*);	
posséder	poseer	posedía; posedar (*MNP*)	posedan (FGY); posedar (Nehama) poseder/posedar (Ist)
préférer	preferir	prefere (HB);	preferavan (Ist); preferar, se preferan, prefera (FGY) preferir *cf* preferar (Nehama) preferar (Harris)
prohiber	prohibir	prohibar (HB); proibisyones, proibitó (*IA*);	

(Continued)

Table 5. (Continued)

protéger	proteger	protejer ou protejir, protejido (*IA*); protejarme (SHL); porte-jar (Kalwo/Semo)	protejan, protejado, ke proteje (FGY); protejar (Ist)
répéter	repetir	repetar (RÇ); repetamos (*La Epoka*)	repetando (FGY); repetar (Nehama) repetar (Harris)
résider	residir	rezidar/reziendo, me rezidí (RÇ);	rezidir (Nehama)
restituer	restituir	restituir (*IA*);	
exprimer	*exprimir	eksprimir (SHL); exprim**ir**, exprim**i**das (HB)	eksprime (FGY); eksprimir (Jerusalmi)
imprimer	imprimir	imprimaron (HB);	imprimir, imprimidor (Nehama) emprimar (Ist)
déprimer	deprimir	deprimar (*IA*)	
supprimer	suprimir	suprimir, suprimian (RÇ);	supremir (Nehama)
primer	*primar	primir, prime, primia (RÇ);	prime (FGY); primir/premir (Nehama)
*primer	premiar	aprimido 'gratified'[12] (SHL);	
infliger	infligir	inflijarme/inflijido (RÇ)	inflijir (Nehama)
expédier	expedir	ekspidir (*MNP*); ekspedir, fueron ekspedidos (RÇ)	
extirper	extirpar	extirpir (*IA*)	

Abbreviations of sources: *MNP* = *Lo ke Meldavan Nuestros Padres,* transliterated by Gözlem Kitabevi team; HB= Hayim Bejerano, in Latin characters; RÇ = Rafael Çikurel, transliterated by Henri Nahum); SHL = Saadi Ha Levi, transliterated by Isaac Jerusalmi; FGY = Flore Gueron Yeshua, in Latin characters; *IA* = *Istorya de Aleksandros,* transliterated by M. C. Varol; (others: Ist = Istanbul; Nehama = dictionary; Kalwo/Semo = articles tranliterated by David Bunis, 2013; L. Izmir = letter from Izmir annexed; Jerusalmi = transliteration of Saadi Betsalel Ha Levi's memories; Harris = *Death of a Language*, 1994; *La Epoka* = Saadi Ha Levi's salonician newspaper).

As a consequence, Judeo-Spanish speakers still hesitate between *englutir/englutar* 'to swallow' *render/rendir* 'to give back'; *raer/rayer/rayar* 'to grate'; *imprimir/imprimar* 'to print'; *entinyir/entinyar* 'to dye, to spoil'; *poseder/posedar* 'to possess'; *kovrar/kovrer* 'to get back a debt', and many other verbs.

9. THE WORRIES OF DIPHTHONGIZATION

Diphthongization and vowel alternations are the most difficult problems that Judeo-Spanish speakers have to deal with when they are in contact with Spanish.

They do not have a command of the rules of verbal diphthongization in modern Mainstream Spanish, as a historical process of regularization (with or without diphthong) has taken place on in many Judeo-Spanish verbs.

Laura Minervini (2011) who studied merchants' letters of the end of 16th century notes that *rogar, querer, mostrar* do not diphthongize, unlike in Standard Spanish. She explains this fact by the pressure of the infinitive form in the case of *querer* and *rogar*. Minervini (2006) also points out, as a characteristic of the classical period, the paradigms without diphthongization of verbs *contar, dormir, meldar, mostrar, pensar, querer, rogar, temblar* wich I consider here *infra*.

There are substantial differences among our authors concerning these verbs. *Querer* looks chaotic in 19th century but recovered its regular form of the 16th century, without diphthongization, in the 20th. With *akodrarse* we can notice the confusion with the French verb *accorder*, which has a different meaning, and the corresponding Spanish Gallicism *acordar* 'to give, grant, agree, harmonize' ...

We can see in Table 6 that speakers tend to separate the form with metathesis *akodrarse,* for the verb meaning 'to remember', and the form without metathesis *akordar,* for 'to agree'. The diphthong has disappeared again after a period of confusion.

We can also point out the fanciful form *akordyeron* in Aleksandros, and Bejerano's hesitation between the forms with and without diphthong and with and without metathesis for the verb meaning 'to give, agree ...': *acuedrar/acordar, acordo/acuerdo*. Betsalel Ha Levi also hesitates between *akodro* and *de kordo* in the same paragraph. Today, if I consider my own lists, the question of the metathesis remains unsolved but there is no more diphthongization for *akodrar* nor *akordar.* This is shown in Table 6.

Table 6. The worries of diphthongization: over-, under-, hypercorrection & inversion processes

Spanish	Judeo-Spanish	
	19th C. authors	20th authors & transliterators
acordarse > me acuerdo, se acuerda, se acuerdan, se acordaron, se acordó, acordándose	el recuerdo; [acuerdar Bejerano in Havassy][14] (HB) *akodrar*, akodro, 'I remember'; akodra, se akodró (*MNP*), el rekuerdo, *se akordyeron* (a) 'they remembered' (*IA*); se akodran (RÇ); akodrandome; se akodra (SHL); akodrarse, akodrándosen, rekodrar, rekordar, rekodra (Kalwo/Semo);	akodrarse, te akodras, se akodra, mos akodramos, te akodrates, ke se akodren; acordar (Algazi in Havassy)[15] akodrarse, me akodro, te akodras, se akodran (Ist. & Nehama)

(Continued)

Table 6. (Continued)

acordar (<Fr.), concordar, meterse de acuerdo > concuerdo, concuerdan; acorde; de acuerdo (Fr. accorder, s'accorder)	*acuedrar* (hipcc); *acordar*, acorda, de común acordo; de acuerdo (HB); se akordaron (Ist 1908)[15]; akordará, *akordar*, fue akordado, me akordaron mais (42) todo el mundo *se akodra* sovre los insidentes (*MNP*); de komun akodro (280) de kordo (279); se metian de akodro (SHL);	se akordaron, meterse d'akodro/d'akordo (Ist) akordar, de akodro (Nehama) el akordo (FGY)
(en)colgar > cuelgo, culgas, cuelga, colgamos	enkolga (*el Burlón*)	enkolgar, enkolgando (FGY) enkolgando, enkolgo (Nehama)
despertar > despierto, despiertan, despierto, se despertó, despertaron,	*se despiertó* (hipcc) (HB); el dezespyerto (*IA*); despertan (288); *desperto/despyerto* 'awake', despyertaron 'they wake up'(the 3 forms p. 344 from *el Burlón*) (*MNP*); *despyerte*, ke *despertes*, me *despertí*, se *despyertó*, despertava, despertar (Kalwo/Semo)	espertar, esperta, espertan, espyerto (FGY) aspertar(se); (me) asperto, (te) aspertas … se despertó, despertaron (Ist) despértate/despyerto (Nehama)
dormir > duermo, que duerma, duerme! dormían, durmiendo + fr. dormir, dormons, dorment, dormirent	que duerma;(HB); durmir; durmiya durmyendo (*MNP*); durmiyan (SHL); *duermir*, dormían (Kalwo/Semo)	durmir, durme, durmido, durmyendo (FGY); dormir/durmir, durmo, durmes, durme! (Ist) dormir, *durme/duerme*, durmamos, dormid, durma dormido/durmido, (Nehama)
empezar > empiezo, empezamos	empieza, empiezan (HB); empesando, empesó, empesaron, reempese (*IA*); empesa, empesamos (*MNP*); empesas (Kalwo/Semo)	ampesar/empesar? ampesa, empesan empesates (FGY) empesar, empesa (Nehama & Ist)

entender > entienden	entenden (RÇ); entyenden (Kalwo/Semo)	entender, entyende, entyenden, entyende!, entendites, entendyó, entendido.(FGY) entyendo, se entyende, entendites, entyenden, mos entendimos (Ist & Nehama)
morir > muero, moriría, muriendo, murió, muerto, morían, muere!,	murir murería (graphy u/o?); murir/murería; muryendo; muryó; muerto (*MNP*); muerir *(IA)*; morir/murir, murido; *murian*; muryeron; de murir y *mueria* 189 *murir; muerir* 248 (SHL); mueren (*La Epoka*)	**murir: muere, mueren, muérete!; muerto** (FGY)
(de)mostrar > muestro muestras muestra, demostramos	demuestró, muestraron (*IA*); mostra, demostrar (314), demonstrimos (316, *El Telegrafo*), mostratesh, mostró mostrandose, mostrava (*MNP*); mostrar, monstrando (SHL); demostrar (Kalwo/Semo); mostra, amóstrame (*Hazino*)	**amostrar**: amosta, amostran; amostrando; (FGY) **demostrar;** (FGY) amostrar, amosta, amostrando (Ist & Nehama)
pensar > pienso, piensan, piensa, que piense, pensaré + Fr. penser	pensamos pensais pensando pensar [en piensando in Havassy] (HB); pensando (*IA*); pensan, pensa, pensaré, pensavamos (*MNP*); pensa (RÇ); pensar, pensó, ke pense (Kalwo/Semo)	penso, pensas, pensa pensan (*Hazino*) **pensar**: pensas, pensa, pensan; ke pense, pensando (FGY); penso i arepenso i del penseryo salgo loco (Ist, proverb) pensar, pensava, me lo penso (Nehama)
perder > pierde	perderse, *perde* [pierder voy in Havassy] (HB); pyerde (*IA*); pedrer; peryeron, perdyó, pyedre (*MNP*); perdí, pedrites (RÇ); depedrer, depyedra, depedriera, pedria, pedriendo, pedrites, pedriyó, pedrieron (SHL); pedrer, pedrí, pedrida, ke pyedra, pedryó (Kalwo/Semo)	pedrí (Algazi in Havassy) **pedrer**/pidrir?: pyedres, pyedre, pyedren; pedryó, pidrimos, pedryeron; pidría; pedrido/pidrido (FGY);. pyedrer > pyedro, pyedre, pyedryó … (Ist)

(Continued)

180 | MARIE-CHRISTINE BORNES VAROL

Table 6. (Continued)

preferir > prefiere Fr. préférer	prefere (HB);	preferavan (Ist); preferar, se preferan (FGY)
prender > prende (aprender, comprender) Fr. prendre apprendre comprendre	priende (HB); prende, prendyó (Kalwo /Semo)	Ø, prendear < prenda (Nehama)
querer > quiero, quiere, queréis, quería, quise, quiso, queriendo	quiero, *quiere*, queria, queríamos; [no quieres in Havassy] (HB) kizyeron/kijyeron (*IA*); *kere*, kerer, kererían, keridos; *keren*; kije, kería, kijo; kijyendo; kijo kero; keresh (*MNP*); kijo, kijeron (RÇ); kerer, *kyere*, *kyeren*, kyije, kijo, kijendo, k**e**ria, k**ye**ria *(SHL); kero,* keres, *kere*, keremos, keren, kería, kerían (Kalwo/Semo)	quero, queres, quere, queren (*Hazino* …) **kerer**: keres, kere, keremos, keresh, keren; kijites, kijo; kerían; kerá; ke se kera, keramos, sin ke keran; si no kijeres; kerido/kirido (FGY) kyerer, kyere, kyero, kyered (Nehama) kerer, kero, keres … (Ist)
sentir > siente, sintieron, sintió	Sentir (HB); syente, sintyeron, sintóse (*IA*); sintir/sentir, syente, sintid, sintyendo, sintyó (*MNP*); sintir, sintí, sintía, resentiamos (RÇ); sintir, sintitesh, sintyeron, sintido, konsintir (SHL) sentir, syento, konsyente (Kalwo/Semo)	**sintir**: syenten; sintyeron; sintían; ke syenta; en sintyendo (FGY). **konsintir/konsentir,:**te konsyentes, se konsyente, se konsyenten, ke (te) konsyentas; konsintyendose (FGY) sintir; sintyeron (L. Izmir)
servir > sirvo sirves sirve servimos sirven, servia, sirvieron,	servir, syerven (*IA*); servir, syerve; syerven (*MNP*); servir, se sirvieron, sirvió; serviendosen (RÇ); sirvir, sirvidos (SHL); servir, syerve, sirvyendo (Kalwo/Semo)	servir: sirves/syerves, no *syerve*, servimos, syerven; sirvyó/servyó, se servyeron; se servían; servido, ke se syerva; en sirvyéndosen/servyendo. (FGY); servir, no *sirve*, sirvyó (Ist) servir, syervo *syerve*, serví, servimos servyó, servamos, servid, ke servyera (Nehama)

verter > vierto convertir > convierte	vertir? 'to shed' (*MNP*); vertyeron (SHL) convierten (HB);	verter; konvertir (Nehama)
volar > vuelo, vuelan	volan (HB); embolada (SHL)	bolar, bolando (FGY); bolar, bolo, bolan (Ist)
volver > vuelve, volvió envolvieron, se revolvió	*volve*, volvieron (HB); boltó 'returned', boltan, aboltan, aboltar; revolver (*MNP*); volver, volveronse, envolveron, *revueltóse*, aboltóse, envolvido (*IA*);	aboltar, aboltan, abolta!, la buelta (Ist) abolta! abolta, aboltar, aboltan, aboltó; revoltar (FGY)

Abbreviations of sources: *MNP* = *Lo ke Meldavan Nuestros Padres*, transliterated by Gözlem Kitabevi team; HB= Hayim Bejerano, in Latin characters; RÇ= Rafael Çikurel, transliterated by Henri Nahum); SHL = Saadi Ha Levi, transliterated by Isaac Jerusalmi; FGY = Flore Gueron Yeshua, in Latin characters; *IA* = *Istorya de Aleksandros*, transliterated by M. C. Varol; (others: Ist = Istanbul; Nehama= dictionary; Kalwo/Semo = articles tranliterated by David Bunis, 2013; L. Izmir = letter from Izmir annexed; *El Telegrafo* = articles transliterated by Birmizrahi *et alii*, 2006).

Variation affects the verbs *servir, sentir, querer, mostrar, murir*; while *pensar, dormir, kolgar* look stable, as does *mostrar* if we exclude the odd exception of *Aleksandros*. If we recall that *querer, mostrar, pensar, durmir* already had no diphthongization in the preceding "classical period" (*cf. supra* Minervini 2006) we can see that the evolution of these verbs suffered a partial reversion.

In his attempt to write in correct (Judeo?)-Spanish Bejerano overdiphthongizes *prender, despertar* and underdiphthongizes *volar, volver, preferir, perder, entender*, often contradicting usual Judeo-Spanish. He curiously seems to avoid the diphthongizing present persons of verb *pensar*, resorting to the substantives *la pensada, los pensamyentos, el pensar*.

Volver and *volar* have been rejected by modern speakers and the traditional forms *aboltar* i *bolar* reestablished. *Verter* is given by Nehama as a synonym of *echar* and, in his dictionary, the entry for *konvertir* is as brief as the ones for French borrowings used to be, that is to say limited to one word without examples or conjugation models.

The fluctuation in the infinitive form *poder/pueder* 'to be able', a very useful and frequent verb and a modal one, is still ongoing nowadays. Examples are given in Table 7. The irregular forms strengthened by Spanish are still competing with the tendency to regularize the paradigm. The irregularity of the preterite resists, but showing much fluctuation. In Istanbul today *pueder* dominates, but the preterite forms *pude, pudo*, etc., resist beside marginal forms like *podyó, pudyó*. We seldom find *puedyó*. In spite of this disorder a regular form based on the diphthongated infinitive paradigm *pueder* was developing when I wrote my *Manual of Judeo-Spanish* (1[rst] ed. in French, 1998).

Table 7. The worries of diphthongization (2): The trials and tribulations of *poder* 'to be able'

Spanish	Judeo-Spanish	
	19th c. authors	20th c.authors & transliterators
poder > puedo, puedes, puede, podemos, pueden; podía; pude, pudimos, pudieron, podiendo, podré, podría, pudiera	poder, puede, podemos, podían, pude, podres (2e pl. fut.); poderoso (HB); puedo, puede, puedemos, pueden, *podiya/podía/puedía*, pudo, pudimos?, pudyeron, pueda; poderozo (*IA*); pueder, puede, puedemos, puedesh, puedía/puediya pude, pudo, pudimos pudyendo, podyera (*MNP*); poder, se puede, pueden, puedrán; pudía? pude, pudo, pudimos, aver pudido? (RÇ) *poder/pueder,* puedo, puede, pueden, *podia/puedia/pudia,* podian, pudo, pudyeron, pudyendo, puedresh, ke no puedan, pudyeran, **si yo *pudia* deskuvrir/en ke manera lo *puedia* yo deskuvrir** (209) los **po**derozos (208) un **poe**derozo (209) (SHL); poder, puedo, puedes, puede, puedemos, pueden, podía, puedas, podrán (Kalwo/Semo)	poder: puedes, puede, podemos, podesh, pueden; *podyeron/ pudyeron*; *pudía/podía*, pudían; *puedrás; pudría, pudrían*; ke se pueda, puedas, ke no puedan; *pudyendo/podyendo (FGY)*. pudía, aver pudido (Nahum) podia/pudia (Jerusalmi) podyera (*MMP*) **poder, verb cf. pueder**; puedo, puede, pueden, puedía, puedían, pude, *puedré/podré* ke pudyera, pudyendo, puedido (Nehama) el poder; poderozo;(Nehama) **pueder** regularized (Harris); **pueder,** puedemos, puedía pude, pudo/podyó, pudyó/ puedyó (Ist) ke puedgas (S. Natan)[17]

Abbreviations of sources: *MNP* = *Lo ke Meldavan Nuestros Padres*, transliterated by Gözlem Kitabevi team; HB= Hayim Bejerano, in Latin characters); RÇ= Rafael Çikurel, transliterated by Henri Nahum; SHL = Saadi Ha Levi, transliterated by Isaac Jerusalmi; FGY = Flore Gueron Yeshua, in Latin characters; *IA* = *Istorya de Aleksandros*, transliterated by M. C. Varol; (others: Ist = Istanbul; Nehama= dictionary; Kalwo/Semo = articles tranliterated by David Bunis, 2013; Jerusalmi = transliteration of Saadi Betsalel Ha Levi's memories; Nahum = transliteration of Rafael Çikurel's memories; Harris = *Death of a Language*, 1994).

10. CONCLUSION

It is difficult to analyze the contact between Spanish and Judeo-Spanish, because we have to deal at the same time with diachronic and synchronic phenomena. One complication is the verbal polymorphism that existed in Medieval Spanish. I have mentioned the case of *henchir/hinchar*, but A. Quintana (2009) shows that the early competition between Aragonese and Portuguese Romance forms led to variation between *bater* and *batir* in Judeo-Spanish. The resulting picture would have been still more complex if I had considered here the variation in future forms, with the introduction of the French-like forms *vyendrá* and *tyendrá* beside *verná, venrá, venirá, vendrá* and *tenrá terná tenerá tendrá*. How should we analyze them? Are these new forms a direct influence of French? An extension of diphthongization? An internal attempt to regularize the paradigm and solve the extreme synchronic variation? I lean towards considering it a multicausal phenomenon.

In language contact, the diachrony of the main language (here Judeo-Spanish) in contact plays an important role (Varol, 2001). The problem is that an important part of this diachrony is objectively shared by Spanish and Judeo-Spanish. But if we consider the early 17th century as the first koineization period of Judeo-Spanish language, then we can consider that Spanish had a very reduced importance for the later evolution of Judeo-Spanish.

The other convergence criteria, like the frequency of the interactions with Spanish speakers, the extension of the knowledge of Spanish among Judeo-Spanish speakers, the number of speakers, are insignificant and could not have any noticeable influence.

It is the ideological position defended by both Spanish and Judeo-Spanish intellectuals which played an immoderate role. The wrong/mistaken assumption that Spanish was true Judeo-Spanish and Judeo-Spanish a corrupted peripheral dialect of Spanish gave an immoderate importance to the odd inventions of journalists and authors. They thought that there was no necessity to learn Spanish as a related foreign language (as it was the case with French or Italian), so everybody could invent what he judged to be true or elegant Spanish. This belief was sustained by the French Alliancists who considered, contrary to all evidence, the different languages spoken in France as corrupted dialects of French. The press spread these ideas and their inventions, and they were well received by the readers of Judeo-Spanish books and papers, who mostly belonged to the middle class, the most numerous and influential one, because it made sense for them.

Unfortunately, that was enough to contradict the regular integration of French borrowings, to stigmatize Judeo-Spanish archaïsms and creative innovations and to reject well integrated borrowings from Hebrew, Turkish and French. Because they were marking the insuperable divorce between the two languages, they had to disappear.

Even more, what could have been an inventive and innocent phenomenon if limited to lexical items like substantives, adjectives and adverbs, which does not affect the system as much, and even to verbs if phonetically and morphologicaly integrated, became very destructive when reaching the verbal morphological system itself. Doubts with respect to conjugation deeply affected writers, creating excessive variation and causing linguistic insecurity. The discrepancy between French and Spanish grammar and forms, added to their partial similarity, worsened the situation.

Judeo-Spanish writers could have resisted, and eliminated some forms, chosen pertinent paradigms, gone back to the process of regularization, but they lacked time. The fragmentation of the Empire, the nationalist ideals of monolingualism, the death of thousands of speakers murdered during the Shoah and the subsequent diaspora, reduced the number of speakers in such a way that only Spanish seems today to be their sole recourse even if it means their total disappearance as Judeo-Spanish speakers. As we all know, the fiction goes on, as the Sephardim are invited to "come back" to Spain as if nothing had happened during five centuries.

Here we can see that historical, cultural and linguistic knowledge do not have any weight against ideology.

Agora si me permetesh/permitish/permetash, premetesh, (a)serro/(a)syerro mi artikolo.Vos rengrasyo la pasensya/pasyensa/pasyensya i vos rogo ke me pedronéch/perdonéch ... los yerros en lo ke kije/kyije/kerí/kise/kisye espyegar a unos i explikar a otros.

APPENDIX

Letter from Izmir in Judeo-Spanish without signature, dated December 20th 2000
Otobiografia 1er capitolo: Izmir

> Yo nasí en Izmir, agora ay mas de 60 anios. Me fui a la escola « Béné Bérith » (serca de caza) ke era menos emportante de l'Aliansa ande **avio (sic) estudiado** mi padre. Las lesiones eran quaje todas en Turco, y un poco en Ebreo, con el mismo profesor, León Danon, ke tuvo mi madre en su manseves.
>
> En Izmir los Djoudios bivian muy bueno desde 4 sieclos y medio. Ma mi padre, que era comersante, soufria de los dasios que eran mouy pesgados. Y tambien, en los anios 1933/34 empeso un cierto nasionalismo: entre otros, los estudiantes **se metevan a dizir** a los Djoudios, en la caleja o en el tranvay: "Türkçe konuş" (Avla en Turco). Mismo, una notche se **permetieron** de aharvar a muestra puerta y de dizir que mos sintieron avlar en Espagnol que era una verguensa (ou verguersa?)!
>
> Y ansi, mi padre con su haver **decidieron** de emigrar en Egipto ande, en aquel tiempo, no avia dasios del todo. **Me acodro** que durante la Hagadah (que esmemora la salida del Egipto) en lugar de "lecchana abáá bééretz Yisrael" cantavamos "lechana abáá Bééretz Misraïm."

A una proxima ocazion, si vos aze plazer, vosvo **pueder** kontar ciertos aspectos de muestra vida en Alexandra que era una sivdad grande, maraviyoza y muntcho mas moderna de Izmir.

NOTES

1. I shall use the term *ladino* only to refer to the calquing of Hebrew in religious texts like Torah and Passover Haggadah or prayers translated word by word from Hebrew.
2. Excepting the original ideas of Sam Levi in the french paper *Le Journal de Salonique*, who celebrates the multilingualism as a modern ottoman linguistic identity giving evidence to his concept of "*union des races*," 'union of races' in the Ottoman Empire (Guillon, 2013b: 110). See also the original position of Moïse Sullam en *la Vara*, in New York, as recently observed Rosa Sanchez (paper read at the UCLA ladino conference, March 3, 2015)
3. Concerning the presence of the article before countries names see (Varol (Bornes) 2008: 293)
4. Rivka Behar showed during the 18th conference on ladino studies in Madrid (July 2014) that the only allusion to sephardic culture tolerated by the Jewish Community of Istanbul today in its private High school in Istanbul was the possibility to take (in the limit of two hours a week) optional lessons of modern Spanish.
5. Christian schools in Istanbul: N[tre] Dame de Sion for girls was founded in 1856; St Benoît first appeared in 1583, passed to Lazarists in 1783 and new schools for girls and boys opened in 1839; Ste Puchérie for girls opened in 1836; St Joseph and St Michel for boys at the end of the 19th. The first Alliance school for Jewish children was founded in Edirne (Andrinople) in 1867, Larissa (Grèce) 1868, Chumla (Bulgaria) 1870 et Vidin (Bulgaria) 1872, Salonique et Izmir (Smyrne) in 1873, Istanbul 1875. In Istanbul were also Üsküdar American Academy for girls, 1876; Roberts College, 1863; the German school, 1868; St Georg Austrian College, 1882; the Italian College, was founded at the beginning of 19th. An Italian school, built by the jewish banker A. Camondo, was founded in 1888.
6. C. Lagarde's analysis relies on William F. Mackey's book *Bilinguisme et contact des langues*, Paris: Klincksieck, 1976.
7. Presenting in 1883 Hayim Bejerano's article to be published in *El Boletín de la Institución de la Libre Enseñanza* Saturnino Jiménés writes:

> *El español que emplea no es el anticuado que está en uso entre las clases inferiores del pueblo israelita sino que lo adultera con giros y vocablos exóticos procedentes de las varias lenguas que [le] son familiares; por esto he vertido su carta al español moderno* (n° 140, p. 116)

In a recent article Stephanie von Schmädel (2011: 168) writes about the kind of Judeo-Spanish written in the novel *El Konde i el Djidio:*

> *[...] el léxico de la novela no se caracteriza por ser una reproducción del habla de Viena ni de ningún otro dialecto sefardí. Más bien es un reflejo del intento del autor de crear un estilo nuevo para textos literarios cuya base sigue siendo un judeoespañol vernáculo pero muy influenciado por los mecanismos de la modernización lingüística.*

8. *Istorya de Aleksandros el grande rey de M[a]kdonya. Lektura muy interesante i provechoza. Edisyon i propyedad de la libreriya editorial del Si" Yosef Shlezinger a Vyenah/Histoire d'Alexandre le Grand, Vienna/Autriche 5650.*
9. "Le langage qu'il écrit est le langage élégant qu'utilisaient les Juifs de la "classe éclairée", c'est à dire un judéo-espagnol mêlé de mots français hispanisés et de tournures françaises, mais aussi de mots et de tournures d'espagnol castillan".
10. In the tables (*hazino*) refers to Schmid and Bürki, 2000; (Kalwo/Semo) refers to Yosef Kalwo and Shem Tov Semo, two famous journalists of the Judeo-Spanish press in Vienna towards 1864–1875 (Bunis, 2013); *La Epoka*, to Saadi Ha Levi's Salonika newspaper; *El Burlón*, to articles from the satirical newspaper, transcribed in R. Birmizrahi *et alii* 2006; *El Telegrafo*, to articles from Yehezkel Gabay's newspaper (Istanbul, 1878–1931) transcribed in R. Birmizrahi *et alii*, 2006.
11. In the tables (Ist) refers to oral corpora from Istanbul; (Nehama) to the dictionary; (Perahya) to Perahya, Yehuda Haim, 1886–1970 in S. Gruss, "una lengua materna por adopción" (2010); (L. Izmir) refers to a contemporary letter from Izmir (*cf. annexe*); (Algazi in Havassy) to R. Havassy, 2011; (*MNP*) to R. Birmizrahi *et alii*, 2006; (Harris) to T. K. Harris, 1994; Papo to Papo, Yehuda ben Elyezer (trezladado en ladino por mano de), *Pele Yo'ets*, Vienna: Schlesinger, 1872, transliterated by myself; (Jerusalmi) to the transliteration of Saadi Betsale Ha levi's memories by Isaac Jerusalmi (Rodrique and Stein, 2012); (Nahum) to the transliteration of Rafael Çikurel's memories by Henri Nahum, 2002);
12. Note the Spanish graphy of *traducio*.
13. O. Schwartzwald (2011: 58) comments the presence of *apremidos* 'oppressed' < verb *apremi(a)r* (note the group variation) in a prayerbook of the end of the 16th century which is also present in the Ferrara Bible.
14. Reporting a song in an article sent to the *Boletín de la Libre Enseñanza* of Madrid in 1885, Bejerano writes *acuerdar, te ruego, en piensan*do, *pierder voy el repozo, no quieres* whereas Algazi in 1925 writes in the same song *acodrar, te rogo, pedrí* and *no queres* (R. Havassy, 2011).
15. A little song about 1908 Young Turks' Revolution says: *Niyazi kon Enver,* d*iskutyeron kon el rey, pronto se akordaron, Hürriyet mos tomaron* (Rika Varol, Ist).
16. Cf.supra note 12.
17. Shem Tov Natan, born in Salonika is a fluent speaker of Judeo-Spanish and an active member of the association *Aki Estamos*, in Paris.

REFERENCES

Ayala, Amor. "Por nuestra lingua (Sofía 1924): un artículo periodístico sobre la lengua y la identidad entre los sefardíes en la Bulgaria de entreguerras." *Neue Romania* Judenspanisch 35 (2006): 83–98.

Bejerano, Hayim. Colección de refranes maximas expresiones, conservadas por la tradición oral y recogidos de labios de ancianos sefardies de Bulgaria, Palestina, Rumania, Rodes, Salonica, Grecia, Turquia, Yougoslavia, Precedidos de un Prologo. Andrinople, 1913 (manuscript).

Birmizrahi, Rifat, ed. *Lo ke Meldavan Nuestros Padres–Babalarımızın Gazetelerinden—From Our Father's Newspapers.* Translated by Ninet Bivas and Leon Keribar. Istanbul: Gözlem, 2006.

Bornes Varol, Marie-Christine. "Qui a 'traduit' Istorya de Aleksandros el Grande Rey de Makdonya (Vienne, 1889–1890)? Ou l'invention du judéo-espagnol." In *Sefarad an der Donau. La lengua y literatura de los sefardíes en tierras de los Habsburgo*. Edited by Michaël Studemund-Halevy, Christian Liebl and Ivana Vucina Simóvic, 221-238. Barcelona: Tirocinio, 2013a.

Bornes Varol, Marie-Christine. "Langue et identité judéo-espagnoles: trois scenarios pour une disparition." In *Judeo-Spanish in the Time of Clamouring Nationalisms*. Edited by Mahir Şaul, 13–35. Istanbul: Libra, 2013b.

Bornes Varol, Marie-Christine. "De l'identité dans la langue à l'identification d'équivalences interlinguistiques en situation de contact. Les processus et les limites de l'emprunt en judéo-espagnol (Turquie)." In *Chocs de langues et de cultures? Un discours de la méthode*. Edited by Marie-Christine Bornes Varol, 77–109. St. Denis: PUV, 2011.

Bornes Varol, Marie-Christine. "Un erudito entre dos lenguas: el 'castellano' de Hayim Bejerano en el prólogo a su refranero glosado (1913)." In *Los Sefardíes ante los retos del mundo contemporáneo: Identidad y mentalidades*. Edited by Paloma Díaz-Mas and María Sánchez Pérez, 113–128. Madrid: CSIC, 2010.

Bornes Varol, Marie-Christine. *Le proverbier glosé de Madame Flore Guerón Yeschua (Judéo-espagnol—Bulgarie)*. Paris: Geuthner, 2010.

Bornes Varol, Marie-Christine. "Pour une définition du judéo-espagnol: les bornes de la langue." In *Linguistique des langues juives et linguistique générale*. Edited by Frank Alvarez-Péreyre et Jean Baumgarten, 113–142. Paris: CNRS, 2003. See also infra Varol (Bornes).

Bunis, David, M. "Shem Tov Semo, Yosef Kalwo, and Judezmo Fiction in Nineteenth Century Vienna." In *Sefarad an der Donau. La lengua y literatura de los sefardíes en tierras de los Habsburgo*. Edited by Michaël Studemund-Halevy, Christian Liebl and Ivana Vucina Simóvic, 39–146. Barcelona: Tirocinio, 2013.

Bunis, David M. "Modernization and the language question among Judezmo-speaking Sephardim of the Ottoman Empire." In *Sephardi and Middle Eastern Jewries: History and Culture in the Modern Era*. Edited by Harvey Goldberg, 226–239. Bloomington, IN: Indiana University Press, 1996.

Bunis, David, M. ed. *Languages and Literatures of Sephardic and Oriental Jews*. Jerusalem: Misgav Yerushalayim, 2009.

Busse, Winfried and Michael Studemund-Halevy, eds. *Lexicología y lexicografía judeoespañolas*. Bern: Peter Lang, 2011.

Busse, Winfried. "Le judéo-espagnol: un jargon?" In *Hommage à Haïm Vidal Sephiha*. Edited by Winfried Busse et Marie-Christine Varol Bornes, 239–246. Berne: Peter Lang, 1996.

Diáz-Mas, Paloma. "Corresponsales de Angel Pulido e informantes de Menendez Pidal: Dos mundos sefardíes." In *Los trigos ya van en flores. Studia in Honorem Michelle Débax*. Edited by Jean Alsina and Vincent Ozanam, 103–115. Toulouse: Université de Toulouse-CNRS, 2001.

Diáz-Mas, Paloma and Amelia Barquín. Relaciones entre la prensa española y la prensa sefardí a finales del siglo XIX: el caso de *El Luzero de la Pasensia*." In *Ayer i hoy de la prensa en Judeoespañol*. Edited by Pablo Asuero Martín and Karen Gerson Şarhon, 37–46. Istanbul: Isis, 2007.

Diáz-Mas, Paloma and María Sánchez Pérez, eds. *Los sefardíes ante los retos del mundo contemporáneo. Identidad y mentalidades*. Madrid: CSIC, 2010.

García Moreno, Aitor. "Innovación y arcaísmo en la morfosintaxis del judeoespañol clásico." *Revista Internacional de Lingüística Iberoamericana* 4.2 (2006): 35–51.

Gruss, Susy. "Una Lengua materna por adopción." In *Los sefardíes ante los retos del mundo contemporáneo. Identidad y mentalidades*. Edited by Paloma Diaz-Mas and María Sánchez Pérez, 129–138. Madrid: CSIC, 2010.

Guillon Hélène. *Le Journal de Salonique. Un périodique juif dans l'Empire ottoman (1895–1911)*. Paris: Presses Universitaires de Paris-Sorbonne, 2013a.

Guillon, Hélène. "*Le Journal de Salonique*, outil de formation d'une opinion publique dans une communauté juive ottoman." In *La Presse judéo-espagnole, support et vecteur de la modernité*. Edited by Rosa Sánchez and Marie-Christine Bornes Varol, 103–112. Istanbul: Libra, 2013b.

Harris, Tracy K. *Death of a Language: The History of Judeo-Spanish*. Newark: University of Delaware Press, 1994.

Havassy, Rivka. "From Written Text to Folk-Song: On Some Aspects of the Judeospanish (ladino) Cancionero on the Eve of Modern Era." In *Estudios Sefardíes dedicados a la memoria de Iacob M. Hassán (Z"L)*. Edited by Elena Romero, 261–273. Madrid: CSIC, 2011.

International Journal of the Sociology of Language 37, 1982.

Istorya de Aleksandros el grande rey de M[a]kdonya. Lektura muy interesante i provechoza. Edisyon i propyedad de la libreriya editorial del Si" Yosef Shlezinger a Vyenah. Vienna: Schlesinger, 5650 (1889–1890).

Lagarde Christian. *Le parler "Melandjao" des immigrés de langue espagnole en Roussillon*. Perpignan: Presses Universitaires de Perpignan—CRILAUP, 1996.

Minervini, Laura. "El desarrollo histórico del judeoespañol." *Revista Internacional de Lingüística Iberoamericana* 8 (2006): 13–34.

Minervini, Laura. "Tres cartas en judeoespañol: edición crítica y comentario lingüístico." In *Estudios Sefardíes dedicados a la memoria de Iacob M. Hassán (Z"L)*. Edited by Elena Romero, 331–350. Madrid: CSIC, 2011.

Nahum, Henri, transliteration and critical edition. *Mis memorias: Una vida yena de drama i perikolos—Un commissaire de police ottoman d'origine juive à Izmir au début du XXe siècle: Les mémoires de Rafael* Çikurel. Istanbul: Isis, 2002.

Nahum, Henri. "La guerre des langues à Smyrne." *Yod* 35, Domaine judéo-espagnol II, 1992, addenda.

Nehama, Joseph. *Dictionnaire du Judéo-Espagnol* (avec la collaboration de Jesús Cantera). Madrid: CSIC, 1977.

Pulido Fernandez, Angel. *Los Israelitas españoles y el idioma castellano*. Madrid: Suc. de Rivadeneyra, 1904 [Reissued: Barcelona: Riopiedras, 1992].

Pulido Fernandez, Angel. *Españoles sin patria y la raza Sefardí*. Madrid: E. Teodoro, 1905. [Reissued: Granada: Universidad de Granada, 1993].

Quintana, Aldina. "Variación diatópica en Judeoespañol." *Revista Internacional de Lingüística Iberoamericana* 8 (2006a): 77–98.

Quintana, Aldina. *Geografía lingüística del Judeoespañol. Estudio sincrónico y diacrónico*. Bern: Peter Lang, 2006b.

Quintana, Aldina. "Aportación lingüística de los romances aragonés y portugués a la coiné judeoespañola."In *Languages and Literatures of Sephardic and Oriental Jews*. Edited by David Bunis, 221–255. Jerusalem: Misgav Yerushalayim and The Bialik Institute 2009.

Quintana, Aldina. "La pré-koiné judeoespañola en la segunda mitad del siglo XVI: descripción y clasificación del grado de nivelación vs. variación lingüística." Paper read at the 18° Congreso de Estudios Sefardíes, Madrid: CSIC, June 30, 2014.

Rodrigue, Aron and Sarah Abrevaya Stein. *A Jewish Voice from Ottoman Salonica: The Ladino Memoir of Sa'adi Besalel a-Levi*. Translation, Transliteration and Glossary by Isaac Jerusalmi. Stanford: Stanford University Press, 2012.

Rodrigue, Aron. *De l'instruction à l'émancipation: Les enseignants de l'Alliance israélite et les Juifs d'Orient, 1860–1939*. Paris: Calmann-Lévy,1989.

Romero, Elena. "La polémica sobre el judeoespañol en la prensa sefardí del imperio otomano: materiales para su estudio." In *Los sefardíes ante los retos del mundo contemporáneo. Identidad y mentalidades*. Edited by Paloma Díaz-Mas and María Sánchez Pérez, 55–64. Madrid: CSIC, 2010.

Sánchez, Rosa. Paper read at the UCLA Ladino conference, March 3, 2015.

Sánchez, Rosa. "Un personaje prototípico del teatro sefardí oriental: acerca de la galiparla del franquito." In *Los sefardíes ante los retos del mundo contemporáneo. Identidad y mentalidades*. Edited by Paloma Díaz-Mas and María Sanchez Pérez, 87–97. Madrid: CSIC, 2010.

Şaul, Mahir, ed. *Judeo-Spanish in the Time of Clamoring Nationalisms*. Istanbul: Libra, 2013.

Schmaedel, Stephanie von. "El léxico en El Konde i el Djidyo de Shem Tov Semo (Viena) y la modernización del judeoespañol." In *Lexicología y lexicografía judeoespañolas*. Edited by Winfried Busse and Michael Studemund-Halevy, 167–180. Bern: Peter Lang, 2011.

Schmid, Beatrice and Yvette Bürki. *"El hacino imaginado": comedia de Molière en versión judeoespañola. Edición del texto aljamiado, estudio y glosario*. Basel: Romanisches Seminar [= ARBA 11], 2000.

Schmid, Béatrice. "Por el adelantamiento de la nación. Las ideas lingüísticas de Abraham A. Cappon." In *Los sefardíes ante los retos del mundo contemporáneo. Identidad y mentalidades*. Edited by Paloma Díaz-Mas and María Sánchez Pérez, 99–112. Madrid: CSIC, 2010.

Schwartzwald (Rodrigue), Ora. "Lexical Variations in Two Ladino Prayer Books for Women." In *Lexicología y lexicografía judeoespañolas*. Edited by Winfried Busse and Michael Studemund-Halevy, 53–86. Bern: Peter Lang, 2011.

Selinker, Larry and Lakshmanan Usha. "Language Transfer and Fossilization: The 'Multiple Effects Principle'." In *Language Transfer in Language Learning*. Edited by Susan M. Gass and Larry Selinker, 197–216. Amsterdam and Philadelphia: John Benjamins, 1992.

Sephiha, Haïm-Vidal. *Le judéo-espagnol*. Paris: Entente, 1986.

Stein, Sarah Abrevaya. "Language Politics and the First Judeo-Spanish Daily of the Ottoman Empire." In *Languages & Literatures of Sephardic and Oriental Jews*. Edited by David Bunis, 386–397. Jerusalem: Misgav Yerushalayim, 2009.

Studemund-Halevy, Michael. "Shem Tov Semo, Sefardi Vienna and the Cradle of Judezmo Philology." In *Los sefardíes ante los retos del mundo contemporáneo. Identidad y mentalidades*. Edited by Paloma Díaz-Mas and María Sánchez Pérez, 317–331. Madrid: CSIC, 2010

Studemund-Halevy, Michaël, Christian Liebl, and Ivana Vucina Simóvic, eds. *Sefarad an der Donau. La lengua y literatura de los sefardíes en tierras de los Habsburgo*. Barcelona: Tirocinio, 2013.

Varol (Bornes), Marie-Christine. *Le judéo-espagnol vernaculaire d'Istanbul: Etude Linguistique*. Bern: Peter Lang, 2008.

Varol (Bornes), Marie-Christine. "Calques morphosyntaxiques du turc en judéo-espagnol: mécanisme et limites." *Faits de Langues—Langues de diaspora, langues en contact*, 18, 85–100. Paris: Ophrys, 2001.

Varol (Bornes), Marie-Christine. *Manuel de Judéo-espagnol—Langue & Culture*. Paris: L'Asiathèque, 1998 (first edition).

CHAPTER TEN

Salomon Israel Cherezli's *Nuevo chico diccionario judeo-español–francés* (Jerusalem 1898–1899) as a Judeo-Spanish Monolingual Dictionary

AITOR GARCÍA MORENO
ILC-Consejo Superior de Investigaciones Científicas, Madrid, Spain. Instituto Universitario Menéndez Pidal—Universidad Complutense, Madrid, Spain

ABSTRACT

Although conceived as a bilingual Judeo-Spanish–French dictionary, the *Nuevo chico diccionario judeo-español–francés* (Jerusalem 1898–1899) composed by Salomon Israel Cherezli includes a large amount of explanatory notes written in Judeo-Spanish added to the Judeo-Spanish lemmas contained in it. This study dedicates to the description and characterization of this kind of paraphrases, which, to a certain extent, convert Cherezli's work into some kind of Judeo-Spanish monolingual dictionary.

1. INTRODUCTION

As it sometimes happens, the story of this paper begins with a false clue. While preparing the critical edition of some of *Solombra*'s satirical articles entitled *La pita de noche de šabat* ('The pita-bread of Shabbat's night'), published for years on Fridays in the Sephardic diary newspaper *Acción* (Thessaloniki, 1929–1940),[1] I chanced upon the following enigmatic fragment:[2]

> Arreglada «Acción»:
> Para no vaćiarme los celebros en dando a entender a_los meldadores de_la «Acción» la habaná de ḥovardá, abrí el diccioner ĵudeo-español que tengo yatic en el almario de mis libros y meldí:
> ḥovardá – ŷomert: persona que asolta la pará; gastador.
> Esta espiegación no afarta; se quiere declarado con cantablina, que el verdadero ḥovardá no es lo_que diće el diccioner.

Which might have been that *diccioner ĵudeo-español* that Solombra took in his hands looking for the definition of *ḥovardá*? After looking carefully in all Judeo-Spanish dictionaries and glossaries written to the date of Solombra's text within our reach—including, in chronological order, William Schauffler's *Otsar divre lashon hakodesh* (Constantinople, 1854); Daniel Mefanov's *Little French-Bulgarian-Hebrew Dictionary* (Sofia, 1896 [title in Bulgarian]); Salomon Israel Cherezli's *Nuevo chico diccionario judeo-español–francés* (Jerusalem, 1898–99); Albert D. Pipano's *Diccionario judeo-español–búlgaro* (Sofia, 1913), and Menahem Moshe's *Millon kis yehudi-sefaradi-'ivri* ([Thessaloniki], 1934)—,[3] I came to the conclusion that Solombra's quotation was more than probably a fake.

Actually, the solution for this riddle—as it many times happens, too—had been given by Solombra himself in the previous issue of *La pita de noche de šabat*, entitled "¿Cuálo es ḥovardalic?" of 18th June 1937 where we can read:

> —Si quiereš saber mi sebará—les diĵe yo a_los dos litigantes—, ella es la mišma de_la que puedríaš topar en un diccioner ĵudeo-español, si existía.

Nevertheless, our search served to realize the high number of times that some authors use Judeo-Spanish language to define Judeo-Spanish lemmas, even when their purpose is to write a bilingual (or trilingual) dictionary. This paper is devoted to the analysis and study of those samples of monolingual Judeo-Spanish vocabulary that can be found in the aforementioned Cherezli's work.

2. JUDEO-SPANISH MONOLINGUAL DICTIONARIES

Judeo-Spanish Lexicography had a certain flourishing in the last decades of 19th century, especially thanks to the production of texts focused on the learning of foreign languages (Hebrew, Bulgarian, German, French, Turkish, English,

Yiddish …).[4] But, probably because of the same reason, up to the date there is not even one dictionary in which Judeo-Spanish is used to explain the Judeo-Spanish Lexicon, excepting the still unpublished work of Nissim de Yehuda Pardo, *El consultor o panléxico: vocabulario del ĵerigonza ĵudeo-español* of the first decades of the 20th century, whose edition is being prepared by David. M. Bunis.

In spite of this, as it has been shown by David M. Bunis (2002) regarding Yehuda Alkalay's *Quntres darkhe no'am* (Belgrade, 1839), and by Aldina Quintana (2013) relating to Yisrael Bajar Hayim's *Sefer Otsar Hahayim* (Vienna, 1823), some scattered definitions in Judeo-Spanish of Judeo-Spanish words can be found in certain Sephardic texts.

Also, in the last two pages (63–64) of Joseph Nehama's *La correspondencia: libro de cartas diversas y de comercho* ([Thessaloniki], 1906), recently edited and studied by Paloma Díaz-Mas and Teresa Madrid Álvarez-Piñer (2014) there is a brief vocabulary in two columns, containing 104 Judeo-Spanish lemmas together with their explanation in Judeo-Spanish.

Lastly, I also have pointed out (2013b) the existence of a bunch of short monolingual Judeo-Spanish vocabularies in Alexander Thompson's *El catecismo menor, o una corta declaración de lo que creen los protestantes cristianos …* (Constantinople, 1854), with 131 entries in total, apart from several humoristic dictionaries[5] published in some satirical Sephardic newspapers.

Let's consider some samples taken from those two texts, in order to show what we mean when talking of Judeo-Spanish monolingual dictionaries or vocabularies. Thus, at the beginning of the "Léxico" included in *La correspondencia* (p. 63a) we read:

> **imitar**.–haćer lo que haće otro.
> **imprevisto**.–que non se esperaba.
> **engajamiento**.–empeño.
> **intentar**.–haćer davá.
> **expresión**.–la manera, las palabras con las cualas una cośa es dicha.[6]

And this is the short words list that follows to the first question of the *Catecismo menor* (p. 5):

> **principal**.–el más importante.
> **fin**.–una cosa [*sic*] buščada y deseada.[7]

Also, it is to note that, even when in the vocabularies included in the *Catecismo menor* and in *La correspondencia*—as we have already mentioned—only 131 and 104 words, respectively, are defined, there are three lemmas (*ćelo, providencia* and *relaciones*) shared by both texts. The definition in each case is not the same at all:

Word defined	Definition in the *Catecismo menor*	Definition in *La correspondencia*
ćelo	fuerte amor para alguna cosa y aborrición de todo lo que es contrario a ella.	ḥibá, calientor.
providencia	la potencia de ver de avante lo que acontecerá; goberno, reǧimiento.	el Dio.
relaciones	ataduras como las de marido y muǰer, padre y hijo, maestro y siervo, rey y súbdito, vecinos uno con otro, y de todos los hombres uno con otro.	raportos; ataderos de hecho.

In the same way, in the text focusing our attention here, Cherezli's *Chico diccionario ǰudeo-español–francés*—although it is, as shown in the title itself, a bilingual Judeo-Spanish–French dictionary—such kind of definitions/explanations of Judeo-Spanish lemmas can be found for around 250 times. These are some of the samples that we will discuss below:[8]

    encadenar (: atar con cadenas)   enchaîner. [p. 29]
    gorgojo (: guśanico que daña el trigo)   charançon *m.* [p. 83]
    olivar (: lugar plantado de árboles de aćeitunas)   olivette *f.* [p. 11]
    mosto (: el zumo esprimido de la uva antes de haćerse vino)   moût *m.* [p. 140]

3. *NUEVO CHICO DICCIONARIO ǰUDEO-ESPAÑOL–FRANCÉS* BRIEF DESCRIPTION

Cherezli's *Nuevo chico diccionario ǰudeo-español–francés/Nouveau Petit Dictionnaire Judéo-Espagnol-Francais* was published in two volumes (1st volume "Parte Primera/Première Partie, א - י" Jerusalem: A. M. Lunez, 1898; 2nd volumen "Parte segunda, ל - ש", Jerusalem: S. Haleví Zuckerman: 1899/5659), and printed both in square Hebrew characters (corresponding to Judeo-Spanish text) and in Latin characters (corresponding to French text).

After a brief Introduction (pp. [I]–VIII), the dictionary is spread over 232 pages and comprises 5348 alphabetically-arranged Judeo-Spanish lemmas and sub-lemmas: 2771 in the first volume and 2577 in the second volume. Each lemma and sub-lemma is accompanied by equivalents in French, but in 20 cases, instead of the French equivalents, we find internal remissions to other lemmas present in the text by means of the expression *véase*, as follows:

    avedradear   véase *averdadear.* [p. 4]
    agüelo   véase *aḃuelo.* [p. 6]
    [aŷilé]   véase *prisa.* [p. 7]

huérfano, na   véase *güérfano.* [p. 9]
[odá]   véase *camareta.* [p. 10]

As pointed out in the Introduction (p. V), lemmas corresponding to words of Turkish or Arabic origin—including Judeo-Spanish derivatives—appear between brackets ("medios cuadrados"),[9] as we see in:

[utiyar], dar utí [Tk. *ütü* 'iron']   repasser le linge. [p. 11]
[ilic [Tk. *ilik*]], ojal   boutonnière *f.* [p. 20]
[dir [Ar. *dayr*]]   couvent *m.* [p. 102]
[šacalear [*cf.* Tk. *şaka* 'mockery']]   plaisanter. [p. 232]

Lemmas (and sometimes also sub-lemmas) are very often followed by lexical glosses in parentheses, or separated by comma. These glosses may correspond to:

a) Up to two (phonetic, graphical, morphological) variants, like in:
   escola (escuela, ešcola)   école *f.* [p. 37]
   herir (ferir)   blesser. [p. 39]
   arrojar (arojar, arronĵar)   lancer. [p. 52]
   garón <גאָרון> (garón <גָּרוֹן>)   gosier *m.* [p. 77]
   devanar (endevanar)   dévider. [p. 91]
   nicochirio, nicochiricio   ménage. [p. 151]
   foya <פ'ויה> (foya <פ'וליה>)   fosse *f.* [p. 174]
   carcarear (cacarear)   caqueter. [p. 204]

b) Up to two synonyms, like in:
   [damlear], gotear   couler goutte à goutte. [p. 88]
   diluvio (mabul)   déluge *m.* [p. 96]
   necio, ia (torpe; bobo, ḃa)   sot, sotte. [p. 151]

c) One variant and one synonym, like in:
   hipo (himpo, saluzo)   *hoquet *m.* [p. 38]

And, what is more important for our study:

d) A short paraphrase or explanation, sometimes together with a synonym, like in:
   dormilón, lona (: que durme muncho)   dormeur, euse. [p. 90]
   enćina (balut: modo de árḃol)   chêne *m.* [p. 25]
   ollada (: lo que contiene una olla)   potée *f.* [p. 12]

Sub-lemmas, 487 in total, mainly consist of expressions incorporating the lemma, and do not necessarily correspond to lexical units in Judeo-Spanish, as we see in:

diente   dent *f.* [p. 95]
   dientes hechos de mano   dents artificielles. [p. 95]
   dientes de leche   dents de lait. [p. 95]

> **los 4 dientes de delantre** dents incisives. [p. 96]
> **los 2 dientes que se topan entre los 4 dientes de delantre y las muelas, colmíos** dents canines. [p. 96]
> **escarba-dientes** cure-dent *m.* [p. 96]
> **dolor de dientes** mal de dents. [p. 96]
> **diente buracado** dent cariée. [p. 96]
> **hinchir de plomo, de plata, un diente buracado** plomber une dent. [p. 96]
> **quitar los dientes** arracher les dents. [p. 96]
> **diente de ajo** gousse d'ail *f.* [p. 96]

Actually, in some cases, sub-lemmas do not even contain the lemma, and they just refer to concepts related to it, as in:

> **enprestador, dera** prêteur, euse. [p. 29]
> **el que toma enprestado** enprunteur, euse. [p. 29]

or in:

> **estamparía** imprimerie *f.* [p. 32]
> **letra de estamparía** caractère *m.* [p. 32]
> **el que arresenta las letras** compositeur *m.* [p. 32]

French equivalents—mainly infinitives of verbs, adverbs, masculine and feminine of adjectives, and substantives—can be up to three, as we see in:

> **afamado, da** renommé, ée; fameux, euse; célèbre. [p. 47]
> **arrevés** au contraire, à l'envers, de travers. [p. 53]
> **deśeo** désir *m.*, envie *f.*, souhait *m.* [p. 94]
> **llamar** appeler, nommer, invoquer. [p. 119]

But in some cases, what we find is a French explanation or definition of the Judeo-Spanish lemma, as in:

> **vianda (cumaña)** provisions pour le chemin *fpl.* [p. 65]
> **saḃidor, dera** celui, celle qui sait. [p. 152]
> **consuegra** les deux belles-mères qui ont marié leurs enfants ensemble.[10] [p. 214]

Last, as seen in all these samples, grammatical information (*m.*, *f.*, *mpl.* and *fpl.*) only appears after those French equivalents corresponding to substantives.

4. MONOLINGUAL DEFINITIONS IN THE TEXT

The presence of all those aforementioned variants, synonyms and paraphrases accompanying the lemmas (and sub-lemmas) seems to reflect the need to clarify the meaning of certain terms difficult to understand, as explained by Cherezli himself in his Introduction (p. [IV]) where we read: "A los yierbos difíciles (yuch) ajuntimos a sus lado un corto declaro". However, in our study we will only pay attention to those expressions which consist of a kind of more or less elaborated definition in Judeo-Spanish.

4.1. Delimitation Problems

Excluding all those parenthetical contents made up by one or more single words that clearly correspond to variants or synonyms (or a combination of both), it is not always easy to make a difference between paraphrases/definitions on the one hand, and fixed analytic structures which act in Judeo-Spanish as lexical units, on the other. This fact is especially common in samples like:

atestiguar [here for 'testify'] **(dar 'edut** [Hb. עדות 'testimony'])   témoigner. [p. 17]
interrogar (hacer istindac [Tk. *istintak* 'interrogation')   interroger. [p. 26]
encachar (hacer kerijá [Hb. כריכה 'bookbinding'])   relier. [p. 29]
vender al encante (hacer meźad [Tk *mezat* 'auction')   vendre à l'encan, aux enchères. [p. 29]
encuadernar (encachar, hacer kerijá)   relier. [p. 30]
dudar (tener dubio [It. *dubio*], **safec** [Hb. ספק 'doubt'])   douter, soupçonner. [p. 89]

where the parenthetical expression contains verbal phrases made up of a verb of general semantics like *dar*, *hacer* or *tener* together with a Hebrew or Turkish noun. In those cases we consider that what we find in parentheses is not a definition but a complex lexical unit that, of course can serve to "better understand" the lemma.

The same thing happens in other samples like *"**nievar (hacer nieve)** neiger.* (p. 150)", where the analytic structure seems to be much more frequent in Judeo-Spanish than the verbal derivative itself, according to Nehama's dictionary;[11] or in

deśmigajar (hacer migajas)   émietter. [p. 95]
deśmigar (hacer migas)   [émietter]. [p. 95]
despedazar (hacer pedazos)   dépecer. [p. 100]

even when nor the derivatives or the verbal phrases are included in Nehama's work.

Last, also compound nouns can be found as amplifiers of the lemmas, as we see in:

escarba-orejas (escarbador del oydo)   cure-oreille *m.* [p. 15]
vid (pie de viña)   cep *m.*, pied de vigne. [p. 65]
[sedef [Tk. *sedef* 'nacre']], **raíź de perla**   nacre *f.* [p. 161]

Obviously, in these cases we cannot talk of monolingual definitions either.

4.2. Recurring Patterns

As we have been able to observe in some of the samples already presented, there are many different manners to carry out those Judeo-Spanish monolingual definitions, and any lemma is susceptible to receive a paraphrase. Nevertheless and despite the general lack of systematicity in Cherezli's work, we can establish different lexical-semantic groups which are recursively defined in Judeo-Spanish, and in many cases, following the same pattern in the definition.

4.2.1. That is what happens with the names of months as in:
enero (: el primer mes del año; **teḃet** [Hb. טבת]) janvier *m.* [p. 27]
febrero, febrayo (: el segundo mes del año) février *m.* [p. 179]
marzo (: trecer meś del año; **adar** [Hb. אדר]) mars *m.* [p. 136]
aḃril (: el cuartén mes del año; **nisán** [Hb. ניסן]) avril. [p. 6]
mayo (: cinquén meś del año; **iyar** [Hb. אייר]) mai *m.* [p. 132]
ĵunio (: el se)én mes del año; **siván** [Hb. סיון]) juin. [p. 81]
ĵulio (: el setén mes del año; **tamuź** [Hb. תמוז]) juillet *m.* [p. 81]
agosto (: el ochén mes del año; **aḃ** [Hb. אב]) août *m.* **[ú]**[12] [p. 7]
septemḃre (: nuevén mes del año; **elul** [Hb. אלול]) septembre *m.* [p. 165]
octuḃre (: el diećén mes del año; **tišrí** [Hb. תשרי]) octobre *m.* [p. 14]
novemḃro (: el oncén mes del año; **ḥešván** [Hb. חשון]) novembre *m.* [p. 149]
decemḃre (: el doćén mes del año; **kislev** [Hb. כסלו]) décembre *m.* [p. 99]

4.2.2. The names of trees are always defined in the same way,[13] as we see in:
almendro (: árḃol de almendras) amandier *m.* [p. 42]
alviano (: árḃol de alvianas) noisetier *m.* [p. 40]
azofaifo (: árḃol de zofaifas) jujubier *m.* [p. 46]
banano (: árḃol de muź) bananier *m.* [p. 57]
castaño (: árḃol de castaña) châtaignier *m.* [p. 200]
limonero (: árḃol de limón) limonier *m.*, citronnier *m.* [p. 129]
manzano (: árḃol de manzana) pommier *m.* [p. 135]
nogal (: árḃol de nueź) noyer *m.* [p. 149]
olivo (aćeitunar, árḃol de aćeituna) olivier *m.* [p. 12]
peral (: árḃol de peras) poirior *m.* [p. 185]
prunal (: árḃol de prunas) prunier *m.* [p. 190]

4.2.3. Also demonyms[14] included in the text as lemmas are always defined, and they present in all cases a parallel-scheme definition by means of a relative phrase, as we see in:
africano, na (: que es de_la África) africain, ne. [p. 50]
alemano, na (: que es de_la Alemania) allemand, de. [p. 42]
americano, na (: que es de la América) américain, aine. [p. 44]
araḃo, ḃa (: que es de la Arabia) arabe. [p. 51]
austriaco, ca (: que es de la Austria, Nemsía) autrichien, enne. [p. 2]
búlgaro, ra (: que es de la Bulgaria) bulgare. [p. 62]
español, ñola (: que es de la España) espagnol, ole. [p. 34]

SALOMON ISRAEL CHEREZLI'S *NUEVO CHICO DICCIONARIO ǰUDEO-ESPAÑOL–FRANCÉS* | 199

      evropeo, a (: que es de la **Evropa**)   européen, enne. [p. 18]
      grego, ga (: que es de la **Grecia**)   grèc, grecque. [p. 86]
      holandés, śa (: que es de la **Holanda**)   *hollandais, aise. [p. 11]
      indiano, na (: que es de la **India**)   indien, enne. [p. 24]
      inglés, śa (: que es de la **Ingletierra**)   anglais, se. [p. 23]
      italiano, na (: que es de la **Italia**)   italien, ienne. [p. 19]
      ruso, sa (: que es de la **Rusía**)   russe. [p. 225]
      turco, ca (: que es de_la **Turquía**)   turc, turque. [p. 111]

4.2.4. All measure units of the text are always defined. In these cases, the definition/explanation consists on the equivalence with other measure units, as we see in:

      centímetro (: uno de cien del metro)   centimètre *m.* [p. 164]
      céntimo, centiśmo (: uno de cien del franco)   centime *m.* [p. 164]
      decámetro (: meśura de diez metros)   décamètre *m.* [p. 102]
      decímetro (: uno de diez del metro)   décimètre *m.* [p. 99]
      [deste [Tk. *deste*]], mano de papel; 25 pligos   main de papier. [p. 98]
      drama (: caśi tres gramos)   drachme *f.* [p. 103]
      grosa (deste; doće dośenas)   grosse. [p. 86]
      legua (: 4000 metros)   lieue *f.* [p. 128]
      [ocá [Tk. *oka*]]: 400 dramas   ocque *f.* [p. 14]
      onza (: 75 dramas)   once turque. [p. 13]
      quilogramo (: mil gramos)   kilogramme *m.* [p. 218]
      quilómetro (: mil metros)   kilomètre *m.* [p. 218]
      reśma (: 500 pligos de papel)   rame *f.* [p. 227]
      sieclo (dor [Hb. דור 'epoch, century']; tiempo de 100 años)   siècle *m.* [p. 162]
      soldo (: 5 centiśmos)   sou *m.* [p. 158]
      yarda (: 91 zantímetros)   yard *m.* [p. 119]

Also partitive numerals (fractions) are defined in a similar way, more than probably to avoid their interpretation as ordinals:

      décimo (: uno de diez)   dixième *m.* [p. 99]
      ochavo, va (: uno, una de ocho)   huitième. [p. 9]
      onźavo, va (: uno, una de onće)   onzième. [p. 13]

And in the case of the names of coins, some encyclopedic information is usually included too:

      dolar (: moneda de plata de los Estados Unidos que vale cinco francos)   dollar *m.* [p. 89]
      duro (: moneda de plata española que vale cinco francos)   douro *m.* [p. 90]
      rubla (: moneda rusa)   rouble *m.* [p. 224]

4.2.5. Personal derivatives in *-ero* do not always receive a Judeo-Spanish definition in the text[15] but, when they do, it has most of the times the same scheme:

      armero (: vendedor de armas)   armurier *m.* [p. 55]
      botonero (: vendedor de botones)   boutonnier *m.* [p. 61]

cuchillero (: vendedor de cuchillos)   coutelier *m.* [p. 207]
droguero (: vendedor de drogas)   droguiste *m.* [p. 103]
entojero (: vendedor de entojos)   lunetier *m.* [p. 25]
esterero (: vendedor de esteras)   nattier *m.* [p. 33]
espejero (: vendedor de espejos)   miroitier *m.* [p. 35]
galechero (: vendedor de galechas)   sabotier *m.* [p. 75]
güevero (: vendedor de güevos, aves)   coquetier *m.* [p. 78]
harinero (: vendedor de harina)   farinier *m.* [p. 54]
leñero (: vendedor de leña)   marchand de bois *m.* [p. 130]
librero (: vendedor de libros)   libraire *m.* [p. 128]
mantequero (: vendedor de manteca)   beurrier *m.* [p. 134]
triguero (: vendedor de trigo)   blatier *m.* [p. 117]
vidriero (: vendedor de cośas de vidro)   vitrier *m.* [p. 66]

Only "**baulero** (: el que haće baúles) bahutier *m.*" (p. 55) has a different form. And in the case of "[gallinero] **(: vendedor de gallinas, de aves, de güevos)** coquetier *m.*" (p. 75), it is to note that the Judeo-Spanish paraphrase comes to establish a difference with the previous lemma "**gallinero** poulailler *m.*" (p. 75), which refers to the 'chicken-coop'.

4.2.6. Other derivatives containing certain prefixes usually tend to receive a similar definition. That is what we see, on the one hand, in those adjectives containing *in-*:

imposible (: que no es posible)   impossible. [p. 21]
inconveniente (: que no conviene)   inconvenant, te. [p. 30]
indiferente (: que no hay diferencia)   indifférent, te. [p. 24]
inĵusto, ta (: que no es ĵusto)   injuste. [p. 23]

and, on the other hand, in some verbs containing *des-*:[16]

desgoźnar (: quitar las reźés [Tk. sing. *reze*])   otter les gonds. [p. 93]
desgüesar (: quitar los güesos)   désosser. [p. 98]
desplumar (: quitar las plumas)   (dé)plumer. [p. 100]
despolvar (: quitar el polvo)   épousseter. [p. 99]
despiojar (: quitar los piojos)   épouiller. [p. 99]
destocar (: quitar, deśhaćer el tocado)   décoiffer. [p. 98]

4.2.7. Lastly, we can group another set of examples corresponding to common nouns, whose definition begins in all the cases with the expression *modo/sorte de ...* ('sort of …'):

ajedrez (sandrach [Tk. *satranç*]**: modo de ĵugo** [It. *gioco*])   jeu d' échecs. [p. 16]
almireź (: modo de mortero)   égrugeoir *m.* [p. 42]
[**bilbil** [Tk. *bülbül*]: modo de páĵaro)   rossignol *m.* [p. 68]
avena (: un modo de cebada que dan a comer a_los caballos)   avoine *f.* [p. 4]
comadreja (: modo de cuatropea)   belette *f.* [p. 209]

culantro (: modo de planta)   coriandre *f.* [p. 208]
enćina (balut [Ar. *bal·lut*]**: modo de árḃol)**   chêne *m.* [p. 25]
endidia (: modo de planta de comer)   chicorée *f.* [p. 24]
gavilán (: modo de ave)   épervier *m.* [p. 73]
gaś (: modo de ropa de seda delgada)   gaze *f.* [p. 74]
gota (: modo de ḥaćinura)   apoplexie *f.*, goutte *f.* [p. 80]
golondrina (: modo de páǰaro)   hirondelle *f.* [p. 81]
onso, sa (: modo de cuatropea; **lonso**)   ours, se. [p. 13]
paitón [Fr.] (: modo de carroza)   phaéton *m.* [p. 168]
rum [Fr.] (: modo de raquí)   rhum *m.* [p. 224]
romana (: modo de peśo)   romaine *f.* [p. 224]

As we can see, many of them are referred to animals and plants, but in some cases (*aǰedrez*, *almireź*, *gaś*, *paitón*, *rum*, and *romana*) refer to diverse samples of *realia*.

4.3. Special Examples

Sometimes, the French equivalent provided is not exactly a French word or complex expression, but some kind of explanation or definition that, curiously, is written in the same terms that the Judeo-Spanish definition accompanying the lemma. That is what we find in:

calostro (: primera leche de la muǰer después de parida)   premier lait qui vient aux femmes après leurs couches. [p. 197]
castañeta (: sonido que se haće //con el dedo pulgar y el de enmedio)   bruit qu'on fait en //frottant fortement le pouce contre le doigt du milieu. [pp. 201–202]
empapelar (: emburujar con papel)   envelopper avec, dans du papier. [p. 21]
enǰundia (: la godrura de las aves)   graisse de volaille. [p. 31]
malograrse (: morir a la flor de su edad)   mourir à la fleur de son âge. [p. 132]
malparado (: en negro estado)   en mauvais **état**. [p. 133]
sofreír (: freír livianamente)   frire légèrement. [p. 159]

Given the fact that we do not know whether Cherezli helped himself with any specific previous Spanish-French dictionary, or whether he just made use of his own knowledge of the French language, we cannot know which definition came first. Nevertheless, the truth is that some of the aforementioned French formulations can be found in some bilingual Spanish-French dictionaries which Cherezli might have known.

This is a comparison with some of the most important bilingual Spanish-French dictionaries:[17]

Table 1.

Cherezli **1898–99**	Sejournant **1759**	Núñez de Taboada [7]**1833**	Salvá **1862**
calostro ... premier lait qui vient aux femmes après leurs couches	CALOSTRO, *f. m.* Premier lait qui vient aux femmes après leurs couches, qui s'épaillit & ſe caille. [...]	CALOSTRO, *s. m.* Calostre: le premier lait aqueux qui sort du sein des femmes après leur délivrance.	
castañeta ... bruit qu'on fait en //frottant fortement le pouce contre le doigt du milieu.	CASTAÑETA. Claquement avec les doigts, comme ſi c'étoit avec des caſtagnettes. [...]	CASTAÑETA, *s. f.* Bruit qu'on fait en frottant fortement le pouce contre le doigt du milieu. [...]	CASTAÑETA f. *castagnéta.* Castagnette. ‖ Bruit qu'on fait en frottant fortement le pouce contre le doigt du milieu.
empapelar ... envelopper avec, dans du papier.	EMPAPELAR, *v. a.* Envelopper quelque choſe dans du papier. [...]	EMPAPELAR, *v. a.* Envelopper dans un papier. [...]	EMPAPELAR a. *èmpapélár.* Envelopper dans du papier.
enjundia ... graisse de volaille,	ENXUNDIA, *ſ. f.* Graiſſe qui ſort du croupion d'une poule graſſe.	ENJUNDIA, *s. f.* Graisse de volaille. [...]	ENJUNDIA f. *énjoúndia.* Graisse d'un croupion [...]
malograrse ... mourir à la fleur de son âge.	MALOGRARSE. Signiffie auſſi Se perdre, mourir à la fleur de ſon âge par quelque accident. [...]	MALOGRARSE, *v. r.* Échouer, étre prévenu, arrêté par la mort dans ses projets.	MALOGRAR a. *malográr.* Déconcerter. ‖ **SE**. r. [Manquer].
malparado ... en mauvais état.	MALPARADO, da, *part. paſſ.* Perdu, ue, bleſſé, ée. [...]	MALPARADO, *p. p.* V. *Malparar.* ‖ *adj.* En mauvais état.	MALPARADO adj. *malparádo.* En mauvais état.
sofreír ... frire légèrement	SOFREÍR, *v. a.* Frire une choſe légèrement, la paſſer par la friture.	SOFREÍR, *v. a.* Frire légèrement.	

On the contrary, the influence of contemporary Spanish monolingual dictionaries seems to be less important, according to the following table:[18]

Table 2.

Cherezli 1898–99	DRAE 1852 & 1869 & 1884	Gaspar y Roig 1853–1855	Domínguez 1853
calostro (: primera leche de la mujer después de parida) …	CALOSTRO. m. La flor de la leche, ó la primera leche que se ordeña de la hembra después de parida.	CALOSTRO: s. m.: la flor de la leche o la primera leche de la hembra después de parida.	**Calostro**, s. m. Hig. Primera leche que secretan las glándulas mamarias de la hembra después de haber parido.
castañeta (: sonido que se haće ″con el dedo pulgar y el de enmedio) …	CASTAÑETA. f. El sonido que resulta de juntar la yema del dedo de en medio con la del pulgar, y después separarla con fuerza. […]	CASTAÑETA: s. f.: Castañuela, en su primera acepción.– El sonido que resulta de juntar la yema del dedo de en medio con la del pulgar, apretarlas y resbalar la una sobre la otra con fuerza. […]	**Castañeta**, s. f. V. Castañuela, en su primera acepción. ‖ El sonido hecho con los dedos ó con la boca imitando el de una casta-ñuela. […]
empapelar (: emburujar con papel) …	EMPAPELAR. a. Envolver en papel alguna cosa […]	EMPAPELAR: v. a.: […] Envolver en papel. […]	**Empapelar**, v. a. Envolver en papel alguna cosa. […]
enjundia (: la godrura de las aves) …	ENJUNDIA. f. La gordura que las aves tienen en la overa; […]	ENJUNDIA. s. f.: grasa o gordura que las aves tienen en la overa. […]	**Enjundia**, s. f. La grasa ó gordura que las aves tienen en el ovario. […]
malograrse (: morir a la flor de su edad) …	MALOGRAR. […] r. Frustrase lo que se pretendía. Comunmente se dice que se malogran los jóvenes, cuando la muerte frustra las buenas esperanzas que daban de sus adelanta-mientos.	MALOGRAR: […] r.: frustrase lo que se pretendía. Comunmente se dice que se *malogran* los jóvenes, cuando la muerte frustra las buenas esperanzas que daban de sus adelantamientos.	**Malograrse**, v. pron. Frustrarse lo que se pretendía. ‖ Desgraciarse las personas. Comunmente se dice que se *malogran* los jóvenes, cuando la muerte frustra las buenas esperanzas que daban de sus adelantamientos.

(Continued)

Table 2. (Continued)

CHEREZLI 1898–99	DRAE 1852 &1869 & 1884	GASPAR Y ROIG 1853–1855	DOMÍNGUEZ 1853
malparado (: en negro estado) …	MALPARADO, da. adj. El que ó la que ha sufrido notable menoscabo en cualquier línea.	MALPARADO: adj.: el que padece notable menoscabo en cualquier línea, como la salud, la hacienda, etc. Se aplica también a las cosas.	**Malparado, da.** adj. Dícese del que sufre notable menoscabo en cualquiera línea, como la salud, la hacienda, etc. Se aplica también a las cosas.
sofreír (: freír livianamente) …	SOFREIR. a. Freir un poco o ligeramente alguna cosa.	SOFREIR: v. a.: freir un poco o lijeramente alguna cosa.	**Sofreir,** v. a. Freir algo, poco ó ligeramente alguna cosa.

All these facts lead us to think that, at least in the commented samples, the Judeo-Spanish definitions could be determined by French explanations (and not conversely).

4.4. Functions

In general terms, not only paraphrases and definitions but also variants and synonyms appearing together with the lemmas (and sub-lemmas) seek to clarify their understanding.

In several cases, definitions (and variants and synonyms too), serve to specify in which conditions the equivalence with the French expression is valid. That is what we find in the following pairs:

    abaǰar   descendre.[p. 3]
      abaǰar (: haćer más baǰo)   (a)baisser.[p. 3]

    oǰal (: vidro que haće ver las cośas chicas en grandes)   lentille *f.*[p. 10]
      oǰal (ilic [Tk. *ilik*])   boutonnière *f.*[p. 10]

    gastar (: haćer gastes)   dèpenser.[p. 76]
      gastar (boźear [Tk. *bozmak*])   gâter.[p. 76]

    gota (damlá [Tk. *damla*])   goutte *f.*[p. 80]
      gota (: modo de ḥaćinura)   apoplexie *f.*, goutte *f.*[p. 80]

    ĝirar (: dar vueltas en rodeando)   circuler.[p. 85]
      ĝirar (: haćer ĝiro una cambiala [It. *cambiale*])   endosser.[p. 85]

labrar broder. [p. 124]
   labrar (: laborar la tierra)   labourer. [p. 124]

lunar   clair de lune *m.* [p. 127]
   lunar (: manchica preta en la cara)   grain de beauté. [p. 127]

loza (: masa de haćer chinís [*cf.* Tk. sing. *çini*])   porcelaine *f.*, faïence *f.* [p. 127]
   loza (: platos, vaśos... de meśa)   vaisselle *f.* [p. 127]

pepita   pépin *m.* [p. 184]
pepita (: ḥaćinura de_la gallina en la lengua)   pépie *f.* [p. 184]

ponte (cuprí [Tk. *köprü*])   pont *m.* [p. 176]
ponte (: cubierta de vapor)   pont *m.* [p. 176]

quebrado, da   qui a une hernie. [p. 217]
quebrado (: el que hiźo québrita)   failli *m.* [p. 217]

rayo (del sol)   rayon *m.* [p. 223]
rayo (: lo que cae de las nubes)   foudre *f.* [p. 223]

This kind of oppositions is not always explicit in the text. In some cases we have to assume another implicit possible interpretation of the Judeo-Spanish lemma, to better understand why it is followed by a paraphrase/definition in order to justify the equivalence with the proposed French translation.

Thus, in the sample "**agüica (: cura para los ojos)** collyre *m.*" (p. 6), we must suppose some kind of opposition with an hypothetical *agüica* understood as 'a bit of water'.[19]

In "**araña (: guśano que haće la telaraña)** araignée *f.*" (p. 52), Cherezli seems to be pointing out the meaning of 'insect', excluding the reference to the 'spider's web', also called *araña* in some Judeo-Spanish varieties.[20]

In "**carísimo, ma (: muy querido, da)** très cher, ère." (p. 203), Cherezli bets on the meaning of *carísimo, ma* as 'beloved', and not as 'very expensive', even when the French equivalent *très cher, ère* has also both uses. On the contrary, in "**caro (: de mucho precio)** cher" (p. 203) it happens just the opposite and the meaning 'expensive' is chosen for the definition.[21]

In "**duelo (: combate entre dos personas)** duel *m.*" (p. 88), the interpretation of *duelo* as 'mourning' is avoided.[22]

In "**escala** [MGk. σκάρα] **(: reja de fierro para asar)** gril *m.* [gri][23]" (p. 36), other meanings like that of 'stopover'[24] must be considered to understand the presence of the definition.

In the case of "**apetite (: gana de comer)** appétit *m.*" (p. 49), the author seems to establish a difference with the traditional meaning of Judeo-Spanish *apetite* as 'sexual desire', but—according to the already mentioned problems of delimitation—it is not clear whether *gana de comer* is a real definition or just a compound noun acting as a synonym.[25]

Last, in pairs like "**carbonera (: onde guardan carbón)** charbonnier *m.*" vs. "**carbonero** charbonnier *m.*" (p. 202), the definition accompanying the feminine derivative seeks to avoid a possible interpretation as 'woman who produces/sells/works with coal', especially when the French equivalent is the same for both concepts. While, between "**colona (pilar)** colonne *f.*" and "**colono (: morador de una colonia)** colon *m.*" (p. 209), both the synonym and the definition make clear that these are not, respectively, the feminine and masculine of the same word.

Together with the specification of meanings that we have just shown—and always bearing in mind that synonyms or variants play the same role as definitions—, we can presume that definitions in parentheses are added in most cases to explain new or little used words. Unfortunately, the lack of an ample and representative corpus of Judeo-Spanish texts from all places and times prevents us from determining exactly in which cases those lemmas correspond to neologisms or to Judeo-Spanish words which have become obsolete. Let's see some examples to conclude.

More than probably due to their modern incorporation into Judeo-Spanish, we find definitions accompanying several words taken from Modern Romance Languages whose phonetics show to some extent their French or Italian origin, like the following:

> **adío** [It. *addío*] **(: saludo de esparticjón)**   adieu *m.* [p. 8]
> **aĝio** [It. *aggio*] **(: ganancia que toman para trocar un cambio)**   agio *m.* [p. 7]
> **anvelop** [Fr.] **(: capa de carta)**   enveloppe *f.* [p. 45]
> **duch** [Fr., *cf.* Tk. *duş*] **(: baño para ḥacinos)**   douche *f.* [p. 90]

But there are others too, in which phonetic and/or morphological adaptation into Judeo-Spanish does not permit us to affirm clearly whether they are taken from those languages or from Modern Spanish itself, like the following:

> **accento (: tono; varica encima la letra)**   accent *m.* [p. 51]
> **aritmética (: la cencia o el estudio de los números, ḥešbón** [hb. חשבון])   arithmétique *f.* [p. 53]
> **autor (: el que haće un libro)**   auteur. [p. 1]
> **abonamiento (: acheto a un precio convenido por tener parte a alguna cośa)**   abonnement. [p. 4]
> **abreviación (: escritura de un yierbo con mancas letras de las que tiene)**   abréviation. [p. 5]
> **ĝeografía (: la cencia o el estudio de_la tierra)**   géographie *f.* [p. 83]
> **humano, na (: que peten[e]ce a el hombre)**   humain, ne. [p. 12]

Actually, there is some amount of lemmas more than probably incorporated from Modern Spanish like, for instance:[26]

> **abaratar (: abajar, amenguar el precio)**   baisser le prix, rabaisser. [p. 3]
> **agricultor (: el//que labora la tierra)**   agriculteur. [pp. 7–8]
> **ahondar (: haćer más hondo)**   approfondir. [p. 2]

avejentar (: parecer viejo sin serlo)   paraître vieux. [p. 4]
dintel (: la parte de encima afuera de una puerta)   linteau *m.* [p. 97]
grana (: color muy colorada)   écarlate *f.* [p. 86]
mástil (: madero de la nave)   mât *m.* [p. 135]
otoño (: uno de los cuatro tiempos del año)   automne *m.* [p. 10]
topo (: ratón de tierra)   taupe *f.* [p. 110]

There are also others, of Spanish origin too, but scarcely used in Modern Judeo-Spanish, like these examples:

arrabal[27] (: partida de una civdad afuera de las murallas, calés [Tk. sing. *kale*])   faubourg *m.* [p. 51]
umbral[28] (: la parte de abajo afuera de una puerta)   seuil *m.* [p. 12]

Lastly, much more difficult to understand for us is why certain lemmas of Turkish or Greek origin are also defined in the text,[29] as they were supposed to be known by Sephardic readers. That is what happens with words like the following:

[aḥir [Tk. *ahır*]]: **lugar onde guadran los caballos**   écurie *f.* [p. 17]
[cuyí [Tk. *koyu*]]: **color escura**   foncé, ée. [p. 208]
[gul [Tk. *gülle*]]: **piedrećica redonda para ĵugar**   bille *f.* [p. 80]
[dilinŷear [*cf*. Tk. *dilenci*]]: **demandar la limośna**   mendier. [p. 96]
papú [MGk. παππούς] (: **padre del padre**)   grand-père *m.* [p. 171]
sultuca [MGk. σουλτούκο] (: **sorte de sayo**)   pourpoint *m.*, veste *f.* [p. 158]
[tabut [Tk. *tabut*]]: **caĵa onde meten al muerto**   cercueil *m.* bière *f.* [p. 106]

Actually, only two of the words just mentioned (*gul*, and *tabut*[30]) might be considered neologisms or words not commonly used, as they are not included, for instance, in Nehama's dictionary nor in Michael Molho's unpublished "Glosario de voces turcas". In the case of *aḥir* we cannot discard the possibility that Cherezli wanted to specify the meaning as 'stable' as opposed to 'extremely dirty or messy place', according to Nehama's dictionary, s.v. *ajir*.

5. CONCLUDING REMARKS

As shown, Cherezli's use of Judeo-Spanish to explain many of the lemmas included in his dictionary must not be considered as a mere symptom of lack of planning, considering his main purpose of elaborating a bilingual Judeo-Spanish–French dictionary.

Sometimes, monolingual definitions serve to identify meanings and ensure the reciprocation with the French equivalents given. Other times, in the same way that sub-lemmas frequently allude to concepts that can be expressed in French by means of a word but there is not equivalent in Judeo-Spanish, monolingual definitions come to clarify the meaning of certain Judeo-Spanish words not that commonly used in all varieties of Judeo-Spanish, newly incorporated to it, or – who knows – just being promoted by Cherezli himself.

The wording of those definitions seems to be the responsibility of the author in most of the cases, but we cannot ignore the possibility that Cherezli was somehow inspired by former bilingual Spanish-French dictionaries or –although not commented here– monolingual French dictionaries. And, despite the low systematization of the dictionary, the author tries to strictly follow some concrete patterns when defining diverse groups of words formally or semantically related.

NOTES

This chapter has been carried out within the Research Project *Sefarad, siglo xxi (2013–2014): Edición y estudio filológico de textos sefardíes*, funded by the Spanish MINECO (ref. nr. FFI2012–31390).

1. The journal was directed successively by Eli Francés, Yosef Anĝel, Barouh Shibi, Daniel Allalouf and Alberto Molho. In September 1935, *Acción* joined *La Prensa Libre*, changing its name into *Acción-Prensa* (Gaon 1965: nr. 33). *La pita de noche de šabat* texts started appear in 1932 and continued until the newspaper shutdown in 1940; see García Moreno (2011) for further information about them and their contents.
2. This text belongs to the beginning of the issue of *La pita de noche de šabat* entitled "Desfaćedores del añir" of 25th June 1937. For the presentation of samples we follow the transcription system of the *Corpus Histórico Judeoespañol (CORHIJE)*, whose features are exposed at <http://recursos.esefardic.es/corhije/>.
3. Also unpublished materials like Ovadia Camhi's (Kohring 2011: 338–340), Michael Molho's (Kohring 2011: 341–344) and Nissim de Yehuda Pardo's (Kohring 2011: 330–331; Bunis 2011: 394–414) dictionaries—the latter thanks to the kind help of Prof. David M. Bunis—were consulted. Search in Mefanov's work was possible thanks to my colleague Dr. Dora Mancheva.
4. See mainly Bunis (2011) and—to a lesser extent—Kohring (2011) for further information on authors, titles, contents and ideology of these lexicographic works.
5. These are: From Constantinople's *El Ĵuguetón* (Gaon 1965: 42, nr. 86), those entitled *Para haćer franco postiźo* and *Diccionario a la franca*—edited together in García Moreno (2012: 238–247)—, and *Nuevo diccionario* and *Diccionario modern*—edited separately in García Moreno (2013a: 55–57)—; from Izmir's *El Soitarí* (Gaon 1965: 95, nr. 206), the *Diccionario para emveźar a hablar franqueado* and the *Diccionario en otro bichim*, and from Thessaloniki's *Čharló* (Gaon 1965: 119, nr. 279) that one titled *Mi diccionario*.
6. *Apud* Díaz-Mas and Madrid Álvarez-Piñer (2014: 134), in another transcription system.
7. *Apud* García Moreno (2013b: 381).
8. We do not include in this amount all those cases in which a word (or a pair of words) is added as a synonym or a variant of the lemma. Anyway, as we will see below, it is not always easy to make a difference between "real" definitions and certain analytic structures used in Judeo-Spanish just presented as equivalents of the lemmas.
9. When Turkish or Arabic words are included in sub-lemmas, they appear as lexical glosses in parentheses.
10. In Sejournant (1759, s.v. *consuegro, gra*) we read: "Les deux beaux-peres ou belles-meres qui ont marié leurs enfants ensemble", while in Salvá (1862, s.v. *consuegro, gra*): "Les deux beaux-pères qui ont marié leurs enfants ensemble".

11. *NehamaDict.*, s.v. *ñéve*.
12. Written in the original או, it corresponds to the phonetic transcription of French *août*. Brackets are ours.
13. Only *enćina* (p. 25) is defined in another way as shown below in 4.2.7.
14. Related to them, the same happens with the two names of languages present in the text: "**bulgaresco (: la lengua búlgara**) le bulgare" (p. 62) and "**turqüesco (: la lengua turca**) le turc" (p. 112).
15. Thus, *ollero* (p. 12), *aćeitero* (p. 16), *especiero* (p. 36), *bogachero, ra* (p. 61), *chapeyero* (p. 76), *chorapero* (p. 83), *lechero, ra* (p. 128), *panadero* (p. 169), *fierrero* (p. 181), *frutero, ra* (p. 190), *carbonero* (p. 202), *carnicero* (p. 203), *cobrero* (p. 206), *confitero* (p. 215), *queśero* (p. 218) and *jabonero* (p. 231), which could have been easily defined as *vendedor de* ('seller of') *ollas* ('pots'), *aćeite* ('oil'), *especias* (here 'drugs'), *bogachas* ('cakes'), *chapeyos* ('hats'), *chorapes* ('socks'), *leche* ('milk'), *pan* ('bread'), *fierro* ('iron stuff'), *fruta* ('fruit'), *carbón* ('coal'), *carne* ('meat'), *cobre* ('cupper stuff'), *confites* ('candies'), *queśo* ('cheese') and *jabón* ('soap'), respectively, are not defined. Others like *barbero* (p. 59), *cunduriero* (p. 212), *horero* (p. 15), *joyero, ra* (p. 80), *platero* (p. 187), *zapatero* (p. 155), are not defined in the text but appear together with a synonym: *berber, zapatero, saatchí, ŷevayerŷí, cuyumŷí* and *cunduriero*, respectively. Other personal derivatives meaning professions, but not corresponding to 'sellers' like *aśnero, ra* (p. 16), *banquiero* (p. 58), *bañero* (p. 58), *barquero* (p. 60), *cajero* (p. 204), *carrocero* (p. 203), *comerchero* (p. 211), *gaćetero* (p. 74), *gamellero* (p. 75), *hechićero, ra* (p. 18), *hornero* (p. 15), *marinero* (p. 136), *molinero* (p. 139), *pregonero* (p. 191) or *tabernero* (p. 107), are not considered.
16. It is to note that some other *des-* verbs are also defined in the text, but their definitions do not follow the same pattern: *deśdevanar: deśhaćer jovillos* (p. 93), *deśmigajar: haćer migajas* (p. 95); *deśmigar: haćer migas* (p. 95), *despedazar: haćer pedazos* (p. 100). Also, there are many others as *desalar* (p. 98), *desbarazar* (p. 98), *desfajar* (p. 99), *destapar* (p. 98), *destetar* (p. 98), *desteñir* (p. 98), *desterrar* (p. 98), *destrenzar* (p. 98), etc., whose possible definition might have followed a similar pattern with *quitar ...*, that are not defined. Verbs like *deśbarcar* (p. 93), *deśhaćer* (p. 92), *desheredar* (p. 97), *desolar* (p. 98), *desparecer* (p. 99), *despojar* (p. 99), *destruir* (p. 98), etc. are not considered.
17. Although not included in this table, we have consulted other bilingual Spanish-French dictionaries like Berbrugger (1859), Cormon (1803), Gattel (1803), Gildo (1858), Grimaud de Velaunde (1825), Sobrino (1705), Terreros y Pando (1786), Tolhausen (1884) and Trapani (1826). For the complete list of titles produced between sixteenth and nineteenth century, see Bruña Cuevas (2008).
18. This table elaborated thanks to the *Nuevo Tesoro Lexicográfico de la Lengua Española*, available on-line at <http://www.rae.es/recursos/diccionarios/diccionarios-anteriores-1726–1992/nuevo-tesoro-lexicografico>, consulted on July the 31st, 2014. Although consulted, most of the dictionaries are not included.
19. In *NehamaDict*, we find *agwíta* as a kind of 'light drug' (« un médicament très léger »).
20. Both meanings are included in *NehamaDict*, s.v. *aráña*. See Quintana (2006: 180–183) for a complete analysis of forms and meanings.
21. In both cases, both meanings are included in *NehamaDict*, s.v. *karísimo* and *káro*, respectively.
22. Both meanings are included in *NehamaDict*, s.v. *duélo*.
23. Written <גריל> it corresponds to the phonetic transcription of the French form *gril*. Brackets are ours.
24. Also included in *NehamaDict*, s.v. *eskála*.

25. Actually, in *NehamaDict*, s.v. *apetíte*, the expression *gana de comer* is mentioned as a synonym. It is also to note, that the meaning of *apetite* as 'sexual desire' is not included there. The same thing happens to the patrimonial word "**engullos** (: **gana de gomitar**) nausée *f.*" (p. 23); see *NehamaDict*, s.v. *enguyos*.
26. We include in the following list only words not present in Nehama's dictionary but, probably, many other included there might correspond to neologisms at the time of publication of Cherezli's work.
27. Not included in *NehamaDict*, it appears in Ladino Bibles like *Ferrara's* in *Lev.* 25: 34.
28. Included in *NehamaDict*, s.v. *umbrál*, it is marked as *Vieux* 'old' at the end of the article.
29. Definitions (as well as synonyms) accompanying Turkish-origin lemmas never appear in parentheses as the lemmas themselves already appear between brackets.
30. In is to note that *tabut* was probably considered an Arabic-word by Cherezli.

REFERENCES

Berbrugger, A. *Nouveau dictionaire de poche espagnol-français, et français-espagnol*, 5th ed. Paris: Thieriot, 1859.

Bruña Cuevas, Manuel. "La producción lexicográfica con el español y el francés durante los siglos xvi a xix." *Philologia Hispalensis* 22 (2008): 37–111.

Bunis, David M. "Rabbi Yehuda Alkalay and his Linguistic Concerns." In *Zion and Zionism among Sephardic and Eastern Jews*. Edited by Z. Harvey et al., 155–212. Jerusalem: Misgav Yerushalayim, 2002. In Hebrew.

———. "Judezmo Glossaries and Dictionaries by Native Speakers and the Language Ideologies behind Them." In *Lexicología y lexicografía judeoespañolas*. Edited by Winfried Busse and Michael Studemund-Halévy, 339–431. Bern et alii: Peter Lang, 2011.

Cormon, J.-L.-B. *Diccionario portátil y de pronunciación, español-francés y francés-español*, Lyon: B. Cormon and Blanc, 1803.

Díaz-Mas, Paloma and Teresa Madrid Álvarez-Piñer. *Cartas sefardíes de Salónica. La Korespondensya (1906)*. Barcelona: Tirocinio, 2014.

Gaon, Moshe D. *A Bibliography of the Judeo-Spanish (Ladino) Press*. Jerusalem: Ben-Zvi Institute, 1965. In Hebrew.

García Moreno, Aitor. "La serie *La pita de noche de šabat* en el fichero manuscrito sobre léxico judeoespañol de Cynthia Crews." In *Judeo-Espaniol: Textos satíricos judeoespañoles de salonicenses o sobre salonicenses*. Edited by Rena Molho, Hilary Pomeroy and Elena Romero, 26–43. Thessaloniki: Ets Ahaim Foundation, 2011.

———."*Juguetonarios*: diccionarios humorísticos de *El Ĵuguetón*." In *Lengua—llengua—llingua—lingua—langue. Encuentros filológicos (ibero)románicos. Homenaje a la profesora Beatrice Schmid*. Edited by Yvette Bürki, Manuela Cimeli and Rosa Sánchez, 237–254. München: Peniope, 2012.

———. "Juegos de palabras: palabras de *El Ĵuguetón*." In *Judeo-Spanish in the Time of Clamoring Nationalisms*. Edited by Mahir Şaul, 37–59. Istanbul: Libra, 2013.

———. "¿Ante el primer diccionario monolingüe judeoespañol?." *Sefarad* 73: 2 (Dec. 2013): 371–408.

Gattel, C. M. *Diccionario español-francés y francés-español, con la interpretación Latina de todas las voces*. Leon: Bruyset, 1803.

Gildo, D. *Dictionnaire espagnol-francais et français-espagnol*, 2nd ed. Paris: Rosa and Bouret, 1858.

Grimaud de Velaunde, F. *Nuevo diccionario portátil español-frances ó Compendio del diccionario grande de Nuñez de Taboada, mucho mas aumentado que la edicion impresa en Paris en 1823*. Madrid: F. Benné, 1825.

Kohring, Heinrich. "Lexicographica judaeohispanica. Florilegium." In *Lexicología y lexicografía judeoespañolas*. Edited by Winfried Busse and Michael Studemund-Halévy, 287–337. Bern et alii: Peter Lang, 2011.

NehamaDict = Nehama, Joseph. *Dictionnaire du Judéo-Espagnol*. Madrid: CSIC, 1977.

Núñez de Taboada, M. *Dictionnaire espagnol-français et français-espagnol, plus complet que tous ceux publiés jusqu'a ce jour sans excepter celuy de Capmany*, 7th ed. Paris: Rey et Gravier, 1833.

Quintana, Aldina. *Geografía linguistica del judeoespañol. Estudio sincrónico y diacrónico*. Bern et alii: Peter Lang, 2006.

———. "Israel bar Hayim de Belogrado, the 'Write as you speak' principle and the nomenclature in the *Sefer Otsar Hahayim* (1823)." *ParDes—Zeitschrift der Vereinigung für Jüdische Studien e. V.* 19 (2013): 35–55.

Salvá, Vicente. *Nuevo diccionario francés-español y español-francés, con la pronunciación figurada de las dos lenguas*, 4th ed. París: Garnier Hermanos, 1862.

Sejournant, Paul de. *Nouveau Dictionnaire Espagnol-François et Latin, composé sur les dictionnaires des Académies Royales de Madrid et de Paris*. Paris: Ch.-A. Jombert, 1759.

Sobrino, Francisco. *Dicionario nuevo de las lenguas española y francesa*. Bruselas: F. Foppens, 1705.

Terreros y Pando, Esteban de. *Diccionario castellano con las voces de ciencias y artes y sus correspondientes en las tres lenguas, francesa, latina e italiana*. Madrid: Viuda de Ibarra, B. Cano, 1786–1793.

Tolhausen, Louis. *Nuevo diccionario de faltriquera español-francés y francésespañol*. Leipzig: Tauchnitz, 1884.

Trapani, D. G., A. de Rosily. *Nuevo diccionario español-francés y francés-español, con la nueva ortografía establecida por la Academia Española, recopilado de los de Gattel, Capmany, Nunez-de-Taboada, Boiste, Laveaux, etc.* Paris: A. Thoisnier-Desplaces, 1826.

CHAPTER ELEVEN

The Creation OF THE State OF Israel AND Its Impact ON THE Self-Image OF THE Sephardim, AS Reflected IN Judeo-Spanish Parodic War Haggadahs

ELIEZER PAPO
Ben Gurion University of the Negev, Israel

ABSTRACT

Both sub-genres of the parodies of the Ladino translation of the Passover Haggadah, the Polemic and the War Haggadahs, make a neglected genre of the Sephardic humoristic literature. The main aim of the present article is to check the impact of the creation of the State of Israel on the self-image of the Sephardic Jews, as it is reflected in the lesser subgenre: in the War Haggadahs. Out of twelve known War Haggadahs, eleven were written before the creation of the State of Israel and only one in its immediate aftermath, in 1949. Interestingly, in that last known Judeo-Spanish War Haggadah, there are no more traces of the self-humor, so typical of the previous War Haggadoth. The ethos of the group seem to have changed, and with it—it's self-image.

1. INTRODUCTION

Parodies of the Ladino translation of the Passover Haggadah make a neglected genre of the Sephardic humoristic literature.[1] The attitude of the Sephardim toward the creation of literary parodies changed throughout centuries. Very stimulating indulgence ruled on the matter of humor in general and on parodies in particular amongst the Jews of Christian realms in Spain, but following the 1492 expulsion the old rabbinic principle stating "all drollery is forbidden, except for drollery against idolatry, which is permitted," came vigorously into force. The Purim festival offered the only exception to this enforced seriousness, at least as far as written literary expression was concerned, and a variegated humorous literature came into existence relating to it (especially the *koplas* or *komplas*; see Hassán, 1976 for a panoramic introduction). The Purim festival served pre-modern Jewish communities as an escape from tensions and social pressures. Other instances of parody had to be brought into some kind of relationship with Purim in order to be made acceptable or publishable.

Another characteristic that appeared in the post-expulsion period was the gradual introduction of Judeo-Spanish as an alternative language for the humoristic genre. In the beginning Sephardic parodies were created exclusively in Hebrew, following the original sacred text from which they took off. Interestingly, even when the hypotext (the original text) was Aramaic rather than Hebrew, Iberian hypertexts were always in plain Hebrew.[2] After the expulsion, some parodies started incorporating burlesque interjections in Judeo-Spanish thrown in the middle of the Hebrew text. In the third phase, some parodies, such as the *Ketubah of Haman*, also knowns as *Ketubah of the Daughter of Haman* or *Ketuba of Orina bat Zeresh* appeared in two independent versions, one in Hebrew-Aramaic and the other in Judo-Spanish.[3] Finally, parodies were written in their totality and solely in the vernacular.

For a long time, a link with the Purim festival was considered necessary for all parody creations. Generally this was achieved by a nominal attachment to the person of Haman, who is the antagonist of the story of Purim, and thus becomes the legitimate target of derision and symbolic aggression. For example, a humorous take on the marriage contract, the *ketubah*, was presented as already mentioned as the Ketubah of the Daughter of Haman. Other examples include a parody of the Hashkava (in the Sephardic tradition a memorial prayer for a deceased man requested by his descendent, but pronounced by the cantor during the reading of the Scriptures section in the Shabbat service): *Ashkava de Aman o de Zeresh la loka, la mujer de Aman* ["The Hashkava of Haman, or of Crazy Zeresh, Haman's Wife"]; a parody of testamentary disposition: *Ṣavaat Aman* ["Haman's Will"]; and the parody of the lyrics chanted while dancing around the Torah scrolls during the *hakafot* circuits at the synagogue in the Simhat Torah festival: *Akafot de Aman* (which were instead performed around a puppet of Haman). Other parodies were based on the liturgical chants of the High Holidays (Rosh Hashana and the Day of Atonement), the Pirke Avot (moralistic-religious aphorisms by the sages of the Mishna, which in Sephardic synagogues are read in Ladino translation during Shabbat services in the weeks between Passover and Pentecost), or the Passover Haggadah.

In the note introducing the parody of two central chants of the Rosh Hashana holiday ("Et sha'are raṣon" and "Aḥot ketana"), which appeared in the issue of 29 Elul 5697 (1936), the Salonikan newspaper *El Mesajero* justified the practice the following way:

El azer la adaptasion de piyutim i pizmonim ['kantes liturjikos'] de kada fiesta es una eredad por akeyos ke se okuparon por la prima vez de dar a la puvlikasion semanales umoristikos. Este uzo, ke kedo dezde un kuarto de sieklo aki, uzo a una partida de lektores a este plazer, por el kual muchos savorean los versos ke se azen a este propozito, i kon razon.	Making adaptations of the *piyutim* and *pizmonim* ("liturgical chants") of every holiday was a heritage for those who first took charge of preparing satirical weekly editions. This custom, which in our location dates back a quarter of a century, habituated some readers to this pleasure, as many enjoy the verses that are written for this purpose, and for good reason.

The earliest Haggadah parody that I came upon is entitled *Orden de la Agada ke se puede dezir todos los anyos en la Noche de Purim, a la Ora de Seuda* ["Order of the Haggadah which can be said every year on the eve of Purim at the hour of the meal"]. It was written in Curaçao and carries the date of 1778. The text is signed, but its author, Ḥam Ribbi Samuel Mendes de Sola, who was the rabbi of the Curaçao community, chose not to publish it. It survived as a single manuscript penned by its author.

In the modern period, with growing secularization the Sephardic authors ceased to comply strictly with halachic scruples. The tie that had formerly existed between the genre of parody and the Purim festival was severed. Nevertheless in the early modern period the general public stood fast to the traditional worldview. The only literary corpus that the new intellectual elite, which was mostly Europeanized and secular in outlook, shared with the common people was the religious literature, especially the sacred texts that had been translated into Judeo-Spanish, and those remained the basis for the parodies. The reason was simple. At that time most men among the Sephardim knew some Hebrew to read the liturgical texts and to have a basic understanding of their meaning, but did not master the language well enough to discern and enjoy the subtle shifts of meaning that generate humor and is the animating force behind any parody. Furthermore, most authors of the parodies did not themselves know enough Hebrew to be able to create elaborate and sophisticated texts in that language.

Between 1875 and 1949 the Sephardic world witnessed the publication of at least forty parodies of the Passover Haggadah (without counting the pre-modern period Curaçao Purim Haggadah already mentioned). Some newspapers such as New York's *La Vara*, published a new Haggadah parody almost every year. All these parodies followed the Ladino translation of the traditional liturgical text that was read at the Passover Seder.

2. POLEMICAL HAGGADAHS

The first modern Haggadah parodies appeared in the second half of the nineteenth century. The publication of a large number of satirical Judeo-Spanish periodicals during the nineteenth century was a factor favoring the creation of numerous Haggadah parodies in this period. These periodicals composed special issues for religious holidays and they grew the habit of printing in them parodies based on the liturgical texts for these holidays. Originally, they directed the humor that stemmed from emulating the sacred text to whatever internal concerns existed in their community, offering opinions and taking sides in the debates of their day on ideological, economic, or gender issues.

As these Haggadah parodies tried to have an impact on the community public opinion and furthered the political or social agendas of their authors, I decided to call them Polemical Haggadah Parodies. To illustrate the subgenre, I'll bring the example of an ideological debate within Sephardic Judaism that found expression in the Passover Haggadah parodies. The *Agada eskaldada* ["Boiled and Cleansed Haggadah"] published on 14 Nisan 5671 (1911) in the Istanbul newspaper *El Korreo*, which was associated with the Chief Rabbinate of the city, reveals local Ottoman patriotism and takes an anti-Zionist stance, whereas a short time later, the *Agada kompozada i kontada para Pesaḥ de tinyozos de Raban Aman de la Prasa* ["Haggadah Composed and Told by Master Haman of the Leek for the Passover of the Mangy"], which was published anonymously in Sophia as a separate pamphlet in 1914, was the product of Zionist circles and ridiculed the Chief Rabbi of Bulgaria at the time, Rav Mordehay Marcus Ehrenpreis, who was their opponent.[4]

3. WAR HAGGADAHS[5]

During the Balkan Wars (1912–1913), a new type of Haggadah parody, which can be considered a subgenre of the parodic Hagaddah, made its appearance. The words "war Haggadah" were part of the title of many of them, and one can subsume all of them under that label.

Eliya Algazi was the first author who wrote a War Haggadah and invented the subgenre. Algazi hailed from Silivri, a town not far from Istanbul, in Thrace, which is northwestern Turkey. In 1912, during the First Balkan War, when the Bulgarian army occupied Silivri, Algazi went as a refugee to Istanbul. In the month of Nisan (March–April) 1913, Algazi started publishing in installments *La Agada de los Muadjires*, dedicating it to a sick and debilitated fellow refugee ["The Haggadah of the Refugees"—*muhacir*: Turkish for "refugee"]. In this text, with great humor and a good dose of self-derision, he described the trials and tribulations of the Jews of Silivri during the war, their fears, and their "deliverance" at the end. The parody also reveals strong identification with and attachment to the Ottoman cause in the face of its war enemies.

Two other parodic Haggadahs from the Balkan Wars have come down to us. One of them is the adaptation of the first section of the Haggadah ("This is the Bread of Affliction") that journalist David Elnekave published in his magazine *El Judio* (issue no. 109, p. 1). The other is the *Agada echa i approriada por el anyo de la gera* ["Haggadah produced and suitable for the year of the war"], which well-known author and publisher Eliya Karmona produced as a separate booklet in Istanbul in 1913.

After a short hiatus of peace the Balkan provinces found themselves immersed in World War I, and I have found four parodic Haggadahs from that catastrophic period: Yaakov Avraam Yona's *Moadim lesimha: Un remorso por la Agada de Pesaḥ* ["Happy Holidays: A Regret for the Passover Haggadah"] (Salonika, 1915); Eliya Karmona's *Agada de la Gera jenerala* ["Haggadah of World War I"] (Istanbul, 1918), which is the first title to include the words "war Haggadah"; Alexander Ben Giat's *La Agada de Ben-Giat*; and Nisim Shem Tov 'Eli's *Agada de la gera por el dia de Pesaḥ* [Haggadah of the War for the day of Passover], published in Istanbul probably in 1920 (the title page of the only surviving copy is missing).[6] I will offer comments on these in the section on group self-perception further below.

Four more War Haggadahs were written World War II. The most important of them is *La Agada de los Partizanes* ["Haggadah of the Partisans"], which was written for Passover of 1944 (published for the first time in Papo 2009). It was written in the free Yugoslav territory, that is, in the Serb provinces of Croatia, which had been liberated by the Partisan Army early in the war. Its author was Shalom Shani Altarak, an education officer in the Partisan Army. It is preserved in two variants: an audiocassette recorded by the author, and a typescript document of loose pages, which was also produced by the author.

The War Haggadahs differed significantly from the Polemical Haggadahs. Unlike the latter, the War Haggadahs did not take a stance in an internal dispute of the community. Their aim was to build collective memory for the community and strengthen the collective identity, in order to mend the damages that the traumatic experiences of the major wars of the Balkan Peninsula inflicted on community members.

The most recent text to be commented upon in this chapter, "La Nueva Agada de Pesaḥ" (The New Passover Haggadah) can be considered the very last War Haggadah, but at the same time it features characteristics that set it apart from all the rest.[7] It appeared in the Istanbul Sephardic weekly *Atikva*, on Passover eve, 13 Nisan 5709 (13 April 1949). Its author was a well-known Turkish Zionist leader, Sabetay Leon, at that time the owner, manager, and chief editor of the paper. The parody was signed Punchon, as Leon signed his serious pieces in *Atikva* with his full name, his less serious ones with the nickname Sabi, and his humorous writings like the "New Haggadah" with the nickname Punchon, which in Judeo-Spanish means "sting" or "thorn".

As it consists simply of twelve passages and one guiding comment, the "New Haggadah" is the shortest War Haggadah in our corpus.[8] The style of the text is also uninspired, compared to earlier examples. Despite these deficiencies, it remains significant. As far as I know, after that date no other parody appeared anywhere based on the traditional translation of the Haggadah into Ladino. In my opinion, a direct link exists between the brevity of this Haggadah and the fact that it is the work that concluded this genre. The terse language and meager style of the last work to be included in the genre are symptoms of the latter's decline. Also, the "New Haggadah" has as subject matter Israel's War of Independence and it was published only days after the end of the final battles and the signing of the armistices with the Arab countries, except with Syria.[9] It can be considered the first attempt at building the new Israeli mythos by making use of the founding myth of the Jews, that is, to tell the story of the establishment of the State of Israel as a sovereign nation in the language and style of the Passover Haggadah (or, more precisely, in the language and style of the traditional translation of the Haggadah into Ladino), which provides the sacred version of the story of the Exodus from Egypt. It is ironic that this construct was created not in Israel but in Turkey, and not in Hebrew but in Judeo-Spanish. The true uniqueness of the "New Haggadah" lies in its being the illustration of the turning point in the Sephardic ethos and cultural memory that occurred upon the establishment of the state of Israel.

Sabetay Leon was born in 1915 in the Hasköy quarter of Istanbul, on the northern side of the Golden Horn, which was the quarter harboring the largest number of Jews in the city and the setting for a vibrant Jewish life. He had been active in the different Jewish communities of the city, first in Balat and then in Ortaköy. He was a member of the committee managing the various Jewish charitable institutions, such as the Or Ahayyim Hospital, the Jewish orphanage, and the Sedaqa u-Marpe and Bikkur Holim organizations. Leon was a fervent Zionist, propagating his views by various means, including his newspaper *Atikva*. In 1949 Sabetay Leon immigrated to Israel together with his wife Roza, née Chiprut. He served as a social worker in the Lod employment office and then as the secretary of the bureau. In time, Leon was elected a member of the city's Workers Council.[10] In 1963, the Leon family moved to Bat Yam where Sabetay managed "Hameshakem," a society for the employment of the elderly and people with limited working ability. In 1964 he was also the secretary of the Mapai party branch of Bat Yam. Leon continued to be involved in the Judeo-Spanish press. His articles appeared mainly in Israeli Judeo-Spanish newspapers published by Mapai:

El Tiempo (The Time) and *Derecho al buto* (Right to the Point).[11] In 1954 he founded, with Eli Shaul and Moshe Azar, the weekly *La Union—Jurnal sionista, sosialista, politiko i literario* (Unity—A Zionist, Socialist Political and Literary Journal). This was the only independent Judeo-Spanish paper in Israel, but owing to financial difficulties it was short-lived. Moreover, in that period Leon wrote for the Judeo-Spanish broadcasts of Kol Yisrael. His features dealt mainly with *aliyah* issues. In 1968, the Leon family went on a two-month mission to Turkey on behalf of the Jewish Agency in an attempt to convince the remaining Jews in Turkey to immigrate to Israel. Apparently, they had some success in their task, although the testimony of Mrs. Rosa Leon, as written up by Eli Shaul, seems exaggerated.[12]

The newspaper *Atikva*, in whose pages the "New Haggadah" appeared, was published weekly in Istanbul in 1947–1949 in Judeo-Spanish, printed in Latin alphabet, employing the orthography adopted in 1928 to write modern Turkish, which made use of some Latin letters modified by diacritical marks. Leon's Haggadah was written in the same orthography.[13]

4. GROUP'S SELF-IMAGE IN THE WAR HAGGADAH PARODIES WHICH PRECEDED THE CREATION OF THE STATE OF ISRAEL AND IN LEON'S "NEW HAGGADAH"

I need to start this section with a few words on the traditional text of the Passover Haggadah itself.

4.1. The People of Israel in the Passover Haggadah

The tenth chapter of the tractate Pesaḥim in the Mishnah deals with the precepts of the Passover Seder. It included few directions concerning the Haggadah. One of them—stated at the end of *mishnah 4*—is the following: "He begins with shame and concludes with praise, and he expounds from 'An Aramean sought to destroy my father' (Deuteronomy 26: 5), until he finishes the entire section." In other words, even before the Passover Haggadah text used today was set down, at a time when the only framework for the obligation to convey the story was an instruction on what verses of the scriptures to read for the exposition, the rule was already laid down that this explanation must begin with shame and end with praise.

In the Talmud, Rav and Samuel differed on the reasons for the shame and praise noted in the Mishnah. The Babylonian Talmud presents their statements.

> He begins with shame and concludes with praise. What is "with shame"? Rav said: "In the beginning, our fathers were idol worshippers" (*'ovde 'avodah zarah*[14]); (and Samuel) said: "We were slaves." (Pesaḥim 116a)

Therefore, according to Rav, the word "shame" is reference to a stain in the spiritual past of the Jewish people, the fact that its fathers were idol worshippers. That being the case, the exposition should begin with "In the beginning our fathers were idol worshippers."[15] Samuel, however, thought that the shame is due to the political past of the Jewish people, the fact that Israel's fathers were slaves in Egypt. Accordingly, for Samuel the exposition during the Passover Seder should begin with the words, "We were slaves."[16]

In contrast, the Talmud says nothing on the reason for the praise, but from the way the sentences of the two sages end I infer something about it. When Rav says "but God has now brought us close to his service," it is unclear whether the praise is upon Israel or upon God. Yet, even if one thinks the praise is directed toward the people of Israel, it still turns out that all the praise of Israel is due to their closeness to their God. The explanation proposed by Samuel is clearer. The reason stated there, "The Lord our God took us out of there with a mighty hand and an outstretched arm," is patently directed toward God.

Likewise, the text in midrash *Sekhel Tov* (Buber ed.) on Exodus (chapter 12) confirms that the intention of the word "praise" is praise of the Holy One, blessed be He, as stated there: "It starts with shame, that is, beginning by saying 'We were slaves to Pharaoh in Egypt' and ends with praise, that is, ended in praise of the Holy One, blessed be He, "Blessed are You, the Lord, our God, King of the universe, who redeemed us and redeemed our fathers from Egypt," and concludes "Blessed are You who redeemed Israel."

In conclusion, the Passover Haggadah sets forth praise not for Israel but for God. The shame of Israel, irrespective of whether due to a stain in the people's spiritual past or its political past, only further underscores the mercy of the Lord for his people Israel, which is worthy on its own.

This is the approach of the Passover Haggadah, as befits a religious text. I shall now examine to what extent this attitude changed or continued in the Judeo-Spanish War Haggadahs in general and in Leon's "New Haggadah" in particular.

4.2. Group Self-Image in the War Haggadahs which Preceded the Creation of the State of Israel

The Passover Haggadah, as noted, is the story of God, who redeemed the children of Israel from slavery in Egypt in Biblical times. A large part of its plot is devoted to a description of the suffering of the children of Israel from this enslavement, prior to the divine redemption. These passages were used in the Judeo-Spanish War Haggadahs to tell of the suffering of various Jewish communities in the present or the recent past. In contrast to the Passover Haggadah, however, which is a serious ritual text, the Judeo-Spanish War Haggadahs are parodic-humorous texts. That being the case, even when a serious subject such as the Jews' suffering in a war is related by means of the sober, canonical translation of the Passover Haggadah into

Ladino, the authors always intersperse comical elements in their texts. At times, they are humorous segments mocking the group's enemies and ridiculing them, while at others what transpires is self-humor, self-sarcasm, or self-irony.

For example, Algazi begins the "Mah Nishtana" passage (§ 2) of his "Haggadah of the Refugees" with two heartrending "questions", which describe the difficult situation of the refugees from the town of Silivri during the war year in comparison to the conditions in previous years of calm and peace:

How is this year different from all other years? For in all other years, we used to eat by the sweat of our brows while this year with what the community provided as a loan. For in all the evenings, we used to eat one or two dishes, and in these evenings only one dish, sometimes hot, sometimes cold …	Kuanto fue demudado el anyo el este mas ke todos los anyos? Ke en todos los anyos nozotros komiamos de nuestro sudado i el anyo el este de la komunita emprezentado. Ke en todas las noches komiamos a una i a dos komidas i las noches las estas, todo es a una, kuando kaente i kuando yelado.

Notwithstanding the humor injected by speaking of current events in calque sentences modeled after the Hebrew original of the Haggadah (*el anyo el este*, instead of simple Judeo-Spanish *este anyo*), this passage might strike the reader as a passage that deals with a serious subject presented in a solemn manner, by means of a somber text. But Algazi hastens to correct this impression created with the first two question, by switching to jocular language right away, in the third question:

For in all other years, we sat in serenity, and this year we all have scratch sores.	Ke en todos los anyos nozotros estavamos en nuestro repozo asentados, i el anyo el este todos nos areskunyados.

In spoken Judeo-Spanish the adjective *areskunyados* ("with scratch sores") suggests mainly unsightly skin injury due to compulsive itching caused by lice or flea infestation. These passages also reverse the Passover Haggadah's chronology of hardship and redemption to comical effect. The liturgical text proposes: We were suffering before, but we are redeemed now; whereas the general meaning here is: We were doing fine before, and look how wretched we are in this year.

Sometimes just the slightest deviation of this type from the liturgical text is enough to raise a smile, to stir in the reader a sense of closeness and affinity to the group. Likewise, the humorous tone (despite the real pain in the things mentioned) hints that this is "familial" remembering of the suffering and not a formal commemoration. What is this similar to? In mourning rites or establishment commemoration rites, there is no room for levity. In contrast, in traditional culture a controlled, moderate joke is an instrument accepted by the community for coping with mourning. In the Judeo-Spanish tradition, the comforters (in addition to other words of consolation) usually tell anecdotes about the deceased. Frequently, even the mourners respond with humorous memories of their own. This phenomenon is cross-cultural: commemorating the memory of relatives is not formal, and it most often includes humorous elements.

Self-sarcasm, as well, is a common occurrence in the War Haggadahs. For example, Ben-Giat lists in passage 19 of his Haggadah the plagues that the Jewish soldiers endured while serving in the labor brigade of the Ottoman army during WWI:

"*I kon maravias*", sin ver ainda maravias, vamos somportando i penando, kayados, atabafados, amudesidos, yevando befras i korando feridas, feridos komo las ke vos vamos a kontar i ke son dies i negras—i estas eyas:

1. vender la kaza—kedar sin braza,
2. pagar el bedel—i ir yene al askier,
3. partir piedras en kampos de Karides,
4. kaminar deskalsos i tambien desbragados,
5. durmir en tierra—la piedra por kavesera,
6. lavorar istihkiames kon luvias i chayes,
7. komer chevirme a una yirme,
8. aferar mal de pecho i kontinuar en el echo,
9. eskuper sangre—aferar la landre,
10. murir enfin de tifo un buen dia sin aver visto ni a la famiya

"And with wonders", without seeing wonders as yet, we go on bearing and drudging, silenced, our mouths shot, struck dumb, suffering contempt and tending our wounds, wounds like the ten dark plagues, which are:

1. To sell the house and be left without a hearth,
2. To pay the *bedel* (special tax for exemption from army service available as an option to non-Muslims) and still be called up anyhow,
3. To break stones in the wastes of Karides,
4. To go barefoot and also naked,
5. To sleep on the ground, with a stone as a pillow,
6. To work in the trenches under rain and flood,
7. To eat street food and still spend a fortune on it,
8. To get pneumonia and to keep on working,
9. To spit blood, to catch the plague,
10. Finally, one day, to die of typhus, without ever seeing the family again.

This passage is based on that of "And with wonders—this is the [plague] of blood" in the Passover Haggadah. At this point the sacred text lists the wonders that God performed at the time when he redeemed the children of Israel from slavery in Egypt. The parody opens with same bombastic declaration: "And with wonders," but immediately cancels it with a sarcastic comment: "without seeing wonders as yet." Similarly, the usage of the descriptor *dezbragados* ("naked"), a colloquial expression suggesting disdain, in the list of plagues is also undoubtedly a sudden departure from what is expected in a formal commemoration of suffering. Adopting lowbrow, casual, or crude language turns the story, despite all the real suffering in it, into a personal "our own" group story, in contrast to a distant, alienated state-establishment story.

Ben-Giat's is not the only passage where one finds sarcastic remarks. Algazi, too, adds a similar sarcastic comment to passage 34 in his Haggadah (based on the benediction "Blessed are You, the Lord, our God, King of the universe, who redeemed us and redeemed our fathers from Egypt," which appears at the end of the first half of the Hallel and before the blessing over washing the hands):

Blessed are You, Lord, our God, King of the universe, who inspired us to flee from the grip of enemy, and guarded us on the way, and even though we travelled a one day distance in ten days, you gave us the strength to bear hunger, thirst, the sword, and fatigue, and you enabled us to reach Istanbul alive, and you sent us all these good people so that they should help us in this captivity.	Bendicho Tu, Adonay, nuestro Dio, Rey de el mundo, ke mos metites en el korason de fuyir de mano del enemigo, i mos guadrates por el kamino, si anke venimos kamino de un dia en dies, mos dates fuersa para somportar: de la ambre, de la sekera, de la espada, i de la kanseriya, i mos izites ayegar kon vidas a Estambol, i mos mandates a toda esta djente buena—para ke nos aremedien en este kativerio.
So thus, Lord our God, day and night we pray, that the situation will improve, and we will have rest, and all the Jews will strive together, and we will establish associations for the advancement of education, because any evil that comes is due to backwardness, and we will be good citizens, and we will have goodwill for all our brothers, and we will go to Palestine and offer sacrifices at that ruined wall, and we shall sing there a new song, on the salvation of our souls, Blessed are You, our God, redeemer of Israel.	Ansi a Adonay, nuestro Dio, rogamos de dia i de noche a ke esta situasyon se amejoreye i tengamos repozo, i penaremos todos los Djudyos en una, i krearemos sosiedades para adelantamientos, porke todo el mal ke viene es del atrazamiento, i mos aremos unos buenos nasionales, i veremos bien en todos nuestros ermanos, i mos iremos a la Palestina, i ayegaremos korbanot en akea pared derokada, i kantaremos ai kantar nuevo, sovre la salvasyon de nuestras almas. Bendicho Tu Adonay, rehmidor de Yisrael.

This passage is one of thanksgiving to God in the name of the Jews of Silivri for having delivered them from the Bulgarian enemy; in this respect it matches the spirit of the hypotext, since the original passage in the Passover Haggadah as well is entirely one of thanksgiving for the redemption of the Jews from Egypt. And yet the language carried a critical note and is not the religious language of thanksgiving. One doesn't usually find in prayer texts sentences such as "and even though we travelled a one day distance in ten days—you gave us the strength to bear hunger, thirst, the sword, and fatigue, and you enabled us to reach Istanbul alive." But, this is stated in a restrained sarcastic tone, which falls short of full-blown defiance toward the heavens.

The prosodic structure of the passage "How many favors has God given us," which content-wise deals with the incessant acts of loving-kindness that God has bestowed upon the children of Israel, opens it to self-sarcasm. Each line opens with "if" and closes with the refrain *dayyenu* (it would be enough for us). The logic of the structure is clear: if the Lord had granted us only the first favor and had not added the second, it would have been enough for us; if he had granted the second one and not added the third, it still would have sufficed. In contrast, in the first two lines in passage 24 of the "Haggadah of the Refugees", one finds a series of disasters that come without respite, one on the heels of the other. The first disaster would have been enough, but the second one did not relent and came as well:

If a plague had broken out, and the war had not begun—it would have been enough for us.	Si nos venia la kolera—i no venia la gerra—dayenu.
If the war had begun and we did not have to flee the enemy—it would have been enough for us	Si venia la gerra—i no fuiamos del enemigo—dayenu.

Ben-Giat's version of this passage is written in the same spirit, with a similar humorous twist. Passage 22 in his Haggadah lists the misdeeds of Enver Pasha (the minister of war, who was one of the triumvirate of the Union and Progress party leadership and the chief architect of Ottoman participation in World War I), which follow one after the other.

How many great disasters did this worthless Enver bring upon us?	Kuantos males grandes izo este kanyo de Enver sovre nos:
If he had made us sell our houses and collected the *bedel* exemption tax—it would have been enough for us.	Si mos azia vender la kaza—i mos tomava el bedel—mos abastava.
If he had collected the *bedel* exemption tax, and did not call us up for army service anyhow—it would have been enough for us.	Si mos tomava el bedel—i no mos tomava al askier—mos abastava.
If he had called us up for army service, but he had not made us break stone—it would have been enough for us.	Si mos mandava al askier—i no mos metia a partir piedra—mos abastava.
If they had made us break stone, but not make us walk naked—it would have been enough for us.	Si mos metian a partir piedra—i no mos deshavan kaminar dezbragados—mos abastava

If he had make us walk naked, but also fed us—it would have been enough for us.	Si mos deshavan kaminar dezbragados—i mos davan a komer—mos abastava
If they fed us and we did not have to bring purchased food—it would have been enough for us.	Si no mos davan a komer i no avia yevar chevirme—mos abastava
If we had brought purchased food and did not have to sleep on the naked earth and on rocks—it would have been enough for us.	Si yevavamos chevirme—i no era durmir en la piedra i la tierra—mos abastava
If we had to sleep on naked earth and rocks, and not been infested with lice—it would have been enough for us.	Si avia durmir en la tierra i en la piedra—i no aferavamos mal del piojo—mos abastava
If we had been infested with lice, and did not have to die without seeing our families—it would have been enough for us.	Si aferavamos mal de piojo—i no mos muriamaos sin ver nuestras famiyas—mos abastava.

Moreover, in the three Ottoman War Haggadahs even the plagues, which in the liturgical text are brought by God on the Egyptians, land instead on the Jews themselves, either as the refugees ("Haggadah of the Refugees"), or as the Jewish soldiers serving in the Ottoman labor battalions ("Ben-Giat's Haggadah"), or on the entire Ottoman civilian entity, including, of course, the Jews. See the following excerpt from "The War Haggadah for the Day of Passover".

These are the ten plagues the Holy One, blessed be He, brought upon the Jews of Silivri, and they are: cholera, poultry disease, death of the children, boycotting, hail, locusts, earthquake, the war, destruction, and the cursed refugee life	Estas dyes degrasyas ke trusho el Santo Bendicho El sovre los Djudyos de Silivria—i estas eyas: holera, hazinura de aves, muerte de kriaturas, boykotaj, pedresko, langosta, teritemblo, la gerra, espojo i muadjirlik dezgrasyado.

Redirecting the plagues toward the Jews cannot be seen as defiance of the Heavens. On the whole, in Judeo-Spanish parodies of the Passover Haggadah (and the War Haggadahs can be included in this generalization), half the humor has no connection with God, religion, or the Passover Haggadah itself. Faith and resignation remain untouched behind it. For example, already in the passage following the one reproduced above, Algazi hurries to tell us that these plagues were intended to lead the Jews to repent, and once they do so, the Lord will have mercy on them, and he quotes the Sages saying: *mode we—'ozev—yeruḥam*, "whoever confesses and leaves [his sins] will obtain mercy", (one must understand that Algazi was not a highly learned Jew and that he wrote Hebrew as he heard it, so that in *'ozev* the *ayin* was replaced by an *alef* and the *bet* at the end was omitted):

Ribbi Gershon of Silivri used to say: "The plagues that the Holy One, blessed be He, brought upon the inhabitants of Silivri, were invoked, more than everything, so that they should recognize that there is a strong power in the world—and so that they should repent, as it said: "whoever confesses and leaves [his sins] will obtain mercy".	Ribbi Gershon el Silivrili dizyen: Estas dezgrasyas ke trusho el Santro Bendicho El sovre los Silivrilis mas de todos es porke konoskan ke ay un poder mas fuerte en el mundo—I agan teshuva, ke ansi diye el pasuk: umode veoze yeruḥam.

Passage 19 from *The Ben-Giat Haggadah* has already been cited above in its entirety and need not be repeated here. The important point is that also for Ben-Giat the plagues of Egypt are no longer reserved for the enemies of the Jews. At the focal point of his haggadah are the Jewish soldiers who served in the labor brigade of the Ottoman army in WWI—so the plagues are also shifted onto them. With Eli, in variation, the ten plagues descend not only on the Jews, but on all Ottoman nationals, including the Jews. Here is passage 38 from *The War Haggadah for the Day of Passover*:

These are the ten plagues that the war brought upon the inhabitants of Turkey, namely: blood, anger, lice infestation, mixing of people, death of the young men, boils, the hail of bombs, dread, darkness for lack of gas, killing of distinguished people.	Estas dyes eridas ke trusho el kavzo de la gerra sovre los moradores de Turkia, i estas eyas: sangre, ravya, hazindad de piojo, mesklatia de djente, muertaldad de mansevos, hazindad de sarna, pedresko de bombas, la angustya, eskuridad por no aver gaz, matansa de ombres grandes.

This reversal of the "ten plagues" setting is actually the highest point of self-irony in the three Ottoman War Haggadahs (*The Partisan Haggadah* contains no direct reference to the "Ten Plagues" passage). The plagues that God brought upon the Egyptians in Egypt, is made a vehicle to describe the sufferings of the Jews in the present, as if it were not enough, for conveying the current torments of the Jews, to adapt only the passages dealing with the suffering of Biblical Jews in the Passover Haggadah. This invention furnishes one other matter of contrast between Leon's "New Haggadah" and the earlier War Haggadahs. Whereas Leon skips the passages of suffering in the traditional Haggadah altogether, or turns them in his parody into passages of redemption (such as the opening, where he applies the suffering to the Jews' enemies rather than to the Jews), the three Ottoman parodists transform even the passages of divine revenge upon the enemy into a opportunity to tell, half mocking and joking, of the Jews' suffering. Understandably, Leon's passage on the Ten Plagues is also applied to the enemies of Zionism.

4.3. The Perception of Israel in Leon's "New Haggadah"

No self-humor at all is found in Leon's "New Haggadah." First of all, Leon does not deal with the suffering of the Jews, but rather with their victory over their enemies. For example, in his Haggadah the Jews "manage" not to eat the bread of affliction. The enemies try to feed it to them, but the Jews inflict retribution on them:

> This is the bread of affliction that the Arabs wanted to feed us anew, and in the end they ate [it] themselves with even more hardship. Whoever is hungry, should come and stuff himself like a turkey; whoever is in need should come and pamper himself this year here, we are fine, next year in the Land of Israel extra, extra.

> Este el Pan de la afrision ke kijeron los Arabos darmolo de nuevo, i lo komieron eyos kon mas dureza. Todo el ke tiene ambre, venga i se repipileye; todo el ke tiene demenester, venga i se envisye. Este anio aki buenos, a el anio el vinien en tierra de Israel ekstra ekstra.

The Passover Haggadah, as noted, devotes much attention to the suffering of the children of Israel on the eve of redemption. The great revival, too, of the War of Independence was preceded by terrible suffering. But Leon does not speak extensively of the Holocaust. He refers to it in only one passage (§ 2, which is based on the "We were slaves" passage in the Passover Haggadah), and even this passage concludes with language of redemption, by marking the rejuvenation of Israel versus the devastation of Germany.

> We were servants unto Hitler in the past and we survived, we the Jews, from that cursed one, and we saw his downfall and his suffering, for as the Punchon (the sting) says: "The Germans were destroyed and the Jews came back to life."

> Siervos fuimos a Hitler en pasadas i salvimos los judios de este maldiço i vimos a su eskaimiento i sufriensas, ke ansi dize el Punchon: *Los Almanes se destruyeron i los Yisraelim se rebivieron.*

It is also true that in the Passover Haggadah, the section "We were slaves," too, ends in language of redemption, "We were slaves unto Pharaoh in Egypt and the Lord our God took us out from there with a mighty hand and an outstretched arm …," but in the Passover Haggadah there are also passages devoted saliently to a description of the suffering of the children of Israel in Egypt before the divine redemption, and had Leon so desired he could have easily converted one of the passages, such as "The Egyptians treated us badly," "And they afflicted us," "And they put hard work upon us," or "And we cried out to the Lord God of our fathers," to reflect the Holocaust of the European Jews. But there is no hint of these passages in the "New Haggadah." Sabetay Leon's Haggadah is simply as its title states—this is a new Haggadah telling of the new beginning of the Jewish people. With the establishment of the State of Israel a new era began, which was entirely redemption. Not only would the Jews no longer suffer in the new era, but there is no place in it even for a remembrance of the former suffering. This is a new world in which Isaiah's prophecy is already fulfilled: "He will swallow up death for ever; and the Lord God will wipe away tears from off all faces; and the reproach of His people will He take away from off all the earth; for the Lord has spoken it" (25: 8).

Leon's Haggadah reflects the spirit of the times. It cites the statement by Yosef Sprinzak, speaker of the Knesset, made toward the approach of the first Independence Day: "The new Hebrew holiday traverses our history, on one side the lengthy period of the mourning for Zion, and on the other—the period we have entered, with great effort, of consolation of Zion."[17]

The only difference between Sprinzak's statement and the spirit of the "New Haggadah" is Sprinzak's awareness of the tremendous challenges awaiting the young country, its builders and its citizens. This is the element of sacrifice characteristic of the Israeli Zionist ethos. The "New Haggadah," by contrast, does not recognize the challenges or suffering involved in redemption. Its spirit is that of Isaiah: death has been swallowed forever, the tears were wiped away, and the reproach of His people has been removed.

NOTES

1. For an extensive research (in Hebrew) of the phenomena see Papo 2012.
2. Compare, for example, the Hebrew parodies on ketubboth in Benveniste 2003 and Ibn Shabbetai 1991, with the standard Aramaic text of the ketubah.
3. Twenty-nine variants of this parody on ketubah are known; six are preserved in manuscript form, whereas another twenty-three were published in the span of 140 years (1792–1932), usually in different *Komplas de Purim* booklets. For more information about the text see Caracedo 1982 and 1986.
4. *Prasa* ("leek") was the humble vegetable of the poor, thus in funny contrast to the aristocratic pretension of the "de la" part of the imaginary name, but also sounds similar to Ehrenpreis, name of the person who is the target of the satire.
5. For more information about this sub-genre see Papo 2010.
6. For extensive research on 'Eli's parody see Papo 2007.
7. Abbreviated as the "New Haggadah" in the text below. The haggadah's full text, with Hebrew translation and comprehensive commentary that clarifies difficult words and offers basic information about events or persons mentioned in the work, appears as Text 5 in vol. 2 of my dissertation, Papo 2012.
8. Except for the series of adaptations of the "Ha Laḥma Anya" passage by David Elnekaveh, which cannot be considered a stand-alone parody of the Haggadah.

9. On 10 March 1949, IDF forces reached Eilat, and at about the same time they took charge of the Ein Gedi region. These two events, which did not actually involve fighting, concluded the War of Independence. Israel signed its first armistice with Egypt, on 24 Feb. 1949. The agreements with Lebanon and Jordan followed soon afterwards, on 29 March and 3 April. Syria was the last Arab country to sign an armistice with Israel, on 20 July, a few months after the other agreements.
10. See the article on Leon on the occasion of his election as secretary of the Mapai branch in Bat Yam in *El Tiempo* of 5 May 1964.
11. This paper was distributed free of charge to new Judeo-Spanish–speaking immigrants.
12. For additional information on this man and his endeavor, see E. Shaul, *Folklor de los Judios de Turkiya* (Istanbul 1994), pp. 132–36.
13. There are minor differences between this orthography and the one that is currently used in Israel or elsewhere to print Judeo-Spanish (including at present in *El Amaneser* and Şalom periodicals in Istanbul). I will only mention two points relevant to the reading and comprehension of the "New Haggadah": the ג׳ (which is ج in contemporary Arabic) and the traditional Judeo-Spanish ש׳ are written in the Turkish version of the Latin script—and in the Judeo-Spanish orthography of Turkey until very recently—as <ç> and <ş> respectively (represented instead in the orthography of *Aki Yerushalayim* as <ch> and <sh> respectively). As is known, Ottoman Turkish was written in the Arabic script. One of the major projects of Kemal Atatürk's revolution was substituting the Latin script used by the European nations for this older script. The Jewish citizens of the republic too, partly as a result of constant decline in traditional education and partly under pressure from the Turkish government, which did not look kindly upon the use of the non-European Hebrew script for the publication of current periodicals and popular books, began gradually, during the 1930s, to abandon the traditional Judeo-Spanish script and adopted the Latin letters, alongside the diacritical marks and orthographical rules of modern Turkish.
14. Most manuscripts read this way. In the Vilna edition, at the direction of the censor *'avodah zarah* (idol worship) was replaced by *gilulim* (idols).
15. Rav's opinion is expressed in the Passover Haggadah used today, in the passage "In the beginning our fathers were idol worshippers, but now God has brought us close to his service …"
16. Samuel's opinion is given expression in the Passover Haggadah common today in the passage which reads: "We were slaves unto Pharaoh in Egypt and the Lord our God took us out of there with a mighty hand and an outstretched arm. And had the Holy One, blessed be He, not take our fathers out of Egypt, then we and our children and our children's children would be still be enslaved to Pharaoh in Egypt. And even if we were all wise, all discerning, all knowledgeable in Torah, we would still be obliged to discuss the exodus from Egypt, and everyone who discusses the exodus from Egypt at length is praiseworthy."
17. *Divrei haKnesset*, I, minutes of the 28th session of the First Knesset, 3 March 1949, p. 477 [Hebrew].

SOURCES

Anonymous. "La Agada eskaldada, el seder eskaldado", *El Korreo,* 58 (year I, 14 Nissan 5771 = 1911): 2–6.

Algazi, Eliya. *Agada de los muadjires*, Istanbul: Arditi i Kasuto 1913.

Altarac, Šalom "Šani", Parodija—kako su Jevreji neborci, koji su oslobodivši se koncentracionog logora na otoku Rabu, prešli VII neprijateljsku ofanzivu po Lici, Korduni i Baniji, 1944. godine, ms.
Ben Giat, Alexander. *La Agada de Ben-Giat*, Izmir, ~1919.
'Eli, Nisim Shem Tov. *Agada de la gera por el dia de Pesaḥ*. Istanbul, ~1920.
Elnekave, David. "A laḥma anya", *El Judio*, 109 (11 Nissan 5673/18 April 1913): 1.
Karmona, R. Eliya. *Agada echa i approriada por el anyo de la gera*, Istanbul, 1913.
Karmona, R. Eliya. *Agada de la Gera jenerala*, Istanbul, 1918.
Mendes de Sola, Samuel. Orden de la Agada que se puede dezir todos los años en la Noche de Purim, a la hora de la sehuda, Curaçao 5548 [=1778], ms.
Yona, Yaakov Avraam *Mo'adim lesimḥa: Un remorso por la Agada de Pesaḥ* Salonika, 1915.

REFERENCES

Benveniste, Don Vidal. *Melitsat Efer Ve-Dinah,* Studies and Critical Edition by Matti Huss. Jerusalem: Magnes Press, The Hebrew University, 2003.
Hassán, Iacob M. *Las coplas de Purim*. Doctoral thesis, Madrid, Universidad Complutense, 1976.
Ibn Shabbetai, Judah ben Isaac. *"Minhat Yehudah," "'Ezrat ha-nashim" ve-"'En mishpat."* Edited by Matti Huss. Vol. 1. 2 vols. Jerusalem: Hebrew University, 1991.
Caracedo, Leonor. "Un texto burlesco de Purim en judeoespañol: 'La Ketuba de Haman'." *World Congress of Jewish Studies* 8.4 (1982): 7–12.
Caracedo, Leonor. "La copla de El Ajugar de Hamán." *Miscelánea de Estudios Arabes y Hebraicos* 35.2 (1986): 159–186.
Papo, Eliezer. "Reescribir un texto para redefinir una identidad: La Agada de la guerra para el día de Pesah de Nissim Siman-Tov 'Eli y la autopercepción de los sefardíes de Turquía después de la Primera Guerra Mundial." In *Ayer y hoy de la prensa en judeoespañol: Actas del simposio organizado por el Instituto Cervantes de Estambul en colaboracíon con el Sentro de Investigasiones Sovre la Kultura Sefardi Otomana Turka, los días 29 y 30 de abril 2006.* Edited by Pablo Martín Asuero y Karen Gerson Sharhon, 113–128. Istanbul: Isis, 2007.
Papo, Eliezer. "'The Hagaddah of the Partisans': Carnival Laughter as a Way of Facing the Trauma Caused by Persecution and Combat or a Means of Constructing Collective Memory" [Hebrew]. In David M. Bunis (ed.), *Languages of the Sephardic Jews and Their Literatures*, pp. 142–216. Jerusalem: Misgav Yerushalayim and The Bialik Institute, 2009.
Papo, Eliezer. "Konstruksion de la memoria i rekonstruksion de la identidad: Agadot de gerra, un jenero neglejado de la literatura sefaradi." In *Los Sefardíes ante los retos del mundo contemporáneo: identidad y mentalidades* Edited by Paloma Díaz-Mas y María Sánchez Pérez, 205–224. Madrid: *Consejo Superior de Investigaciones Científicas,* 2010.
Papo, Eliezer. *And Thou Shall Jest with Your Son: Judeo-Spanish Parodies on the Passover Haggadah* [Hebrew], II volumes, Jerusalem: Ben-Zvi Institute, 2012.
Shaul, Elie. *Folklor de los Judios de Turkiya*. Istanbul: Isis, 1994.

CHAPTER TWELVE

The Hispanic Legacy AND Sephardic Culture

Sephardim and Hispanists in the First Half of the 20th Century

PALOMA DÍAZ-MAS
Instituto de Lengua, Literatura y Antropología, CSIC, Madrid

ABSTRACT

This article discusses the contribution of the Sephardim to Hispanic studies in the first half of 20th century, and how their participation influenced the appreciation of Sephardic culture both in Hispanists academic circles as among the Sephardim themselves. Attention is paid to the Sephardic studies in the framework of Romance Philology, the role of illustrated Sephardic Jews in the late 19th and early 20th century, the attitude of Hispanophiles correspondents of Angel Pulido, collaboration of Sephardim with Ramon Menéndez Pidal under the Centro de Estudios Históricos and the relations of Sephardim and Hispanists scholars in the United States.

1. INTRODUCTION

When one speaks of the Spanish legacy and the Sephardim, usually what comes to mind is the preservation of elements and features of Spanish origin in the culture of the Sepharadim throughout the centuries, from their expulsion from Spain in 1492 until the present.

A fundamental part of that Hispanic legacy in Sephardic culture is the language itself (known as Judeo-Spanish, Ladino or Judezmo), since it is a linguistic variety derived from medieval Castilian, incorporating elements from other

Ibero-Romance languages, even though throughout its history it has received numerous influences from other non-Iberian Romance languages (such as Italian and French), as well as from Hebrew, Aramaic, Turkish, the Balkan languages and Arabic.

Regarding literature, several aspects of the survival of Hispanic culture among the Sephardim have also been the object of research. To mention only a few, we have the versions of the Bible in the vernacular, which continue a Spanish medieval tradition of Biblical translation; the survival of medieval Spanish themes and motifs in Sephardic oral poetry (in songs and, especially, in *romances* or ballads); and the Spanish antecedents (in several Castilian poems of the 14th century) of one of the most typical genres in Judeo-Spanish poetry: the type of learned poems called *coplas* by the Sephardim, which were developed in the Jewish communities of the diaspora between the 18th century and the beginning of the 20th century.[1]

In this article, however, I will not be concerned with the contribution of Hispanic culture to the culture of the Sephardim, but, rather, with the contribution that the Sephardim have made to the knowledge and appreciation of Hispanic culture.

In an enlightening article, Julia Phillips Cohen and Sarah Abrevaya Stein (Cohen and Stein 2010) have analyzed the contribution by Sephardic scholars from Turkey and the Balkans to the study of Sephardic culture and history from the middle of the 19th century to the end of the 20th. They distinguish four generations: those born between 1820 and 1850; those born between 1850 and 1870; those between 1870 and 1895 and finally those born in the years 1895–1910, most of whom were born or grew up after the migration outside of the traditional Sephardic communities.

Nevertheless, I do not know of any overview article devoted to highlighting the contribution of the Sephardim to Hispanic Studies. This is precisely what I propose to do here. I intend to present a panoramic view of the contribution of the Sephardim to academic Hispanism, pointing out both what we have learned about Hispanic cultures thanks to the Sephardim and how the work of Sephardic scholars have sometimes changed the direction of Hispanic Studies.[2]

My starting point is that the Sephardim have contributed, from the end of the 19th century on, to improve and complete the knowledge of Hispanic culture that Hispanists themselves had. The contact between Hispanists and Sephardim (a) has enriched Hispanic Studies, opening new perspectives and (b) has contributed to the appreciation of Sephardic culture, both in academic Hispanic circles and among the Sephardim.

On the one hand, as a result of this contact, both with Sephardic scholars and with less learned individuals, whose culture was essentially of oral transmission, Hispanists started paying attention to certain aspects of Hispanic culture that until then had been neglected. On other hand, a certain Sephardic intellectual élite made relevant contributions to Hispanic Studies from their double perspective of having direct knowledge of the Judeo-Spanish cultural tradition and of being trained in scholarship.

Here I will focus on specific examples of how that intellectual collaboration developed in the first part of the 20th century, both in Spanish institutions such as the Junta de Ampliación de Estudios and the Centro de Estudios Históricos, and in universities in other European countries, most especially the University of Vienna; as well as in American universities.

2. SEPHARDIC STUDIES WITHIN ROMANCE PHILOLOGY

The first scholars outside of the Jewish cultural world to become interested in Sephardic culture were Romance philologists.

The tremendous growth that philological research experienced at the end of the 19th century and the beginning of the 20th century led some Central-European Romanists to focus their inquiry towards the study of Judeo-Spanish, which had for them a huge philological interest: it was a Romance variety, of Hispanic origin, that crystalized and developed in an environment where non-Romance languages were spoken. It preserved some archaic features of Old Spanish, but it had also evolved through the centuries in a way that was independent from the evolution experienced by Peninsular and Latin American Spanish.

Even though at that time Judeo-Spanish was already starting to be relegated by its own speakers to the domestic and familial environment and was losing ground as a language of culture to other languages, especially French, it was still a living language in relations among neighbors, in commercial transactions and within the community. In the Sephardic communities of the Eastern Mediterranean, numerous newspapers and books were published in Judeo-Spanish in Hebrew characters. There were still schools where the language of instruction was Judeo-Spanish. The language played a role even in religious life, both in the liturgy of the synagogue, which was mostly in Hebrew but on occasion included songs in the vernacular, and, especially, in the home paraliturgy of the holidays. That is, Judeo-Spanish was a minority language that had already started its period of decadence; but it was still alive in the social, commercial, educational and religious spheres and as a language of literature and the media. It was not, by any means, in the situation in which it is nowadays found, where UNESCO lists it as a language in serious risk of extinction.[3]

In this way, there appeared the first fieldwork studies with the goal of collecting samples of the spoken language of the Sephardim. To a smaller extent, some written documents also received philological attention, especially biblical translations and liturgical texts. Among this work, we have the pioneering philological studies of Leo Wiener (1896, 1903–1904), Julius Subak (1905, 1906,

1910; who was also the first to make phonographic recordings of Judeo-Spanish, in 1908, see Liebl 2009), Max Leopold Wagner (1909, 1914, 1923, 1930; whose Judeo-Spanish studies were compiled in 1990) and, later, Cynthia Crews (1932, 1935, 1960).

The University of Vienna became a key location for the promotion of the academic study of Sephardic culture. In Vienna there was an important and active Sephardic community, whose origins go back to the 18th century.[4] In the transition from the 19th to the 20th century, the Sephardic community of Vienna was primarily composed of merchants, businessmen, and students, since the university of the capital of the Austro-Hungarian Empire was, just like Paris' Sorbonne, a center of attraction for the children of the Sephardic bourgeoisie of the Balkans, who went there in order to receive a European university education, especially in specialties such as Medicine and Law.

One of these students of Sephardic origin was Adolfo Mussafia (1835–1905), born in Split, Croatia, in a family of rabbis. Like many other children of the Sephardic bourgeoisie, Mussafia went to Vienna with the intention of studying Medicine. However, in 1860 he was hired by the University to teach Italian, which made him reorient his interest toward the study of the Romance languages. As is well known, Mussafia became one of the great names in Romance Philology, having made essential contributions to the study of medieval Italian, Galician-Portuguese poetry and Catalan literature, among other topics.

As far as we know, Mussafia did not do research on Judeo-Spanish. In order to find the first Sephardic Sephardists of the University of Vienna we must wait until the first decades of the 20th century, when we find names such as Moritz Levi, Kalmi Baruch and Isaac Altarac, three Sephardic intellectuals from Sarajevo, who were educated in Vienna, where they read their doctoral dissertations.

Moritz Levi was an activist of Judeo-Spanish, who vigorously participated in Viennese Sephardic academic life, as co-founder, secretary and later president of the student association *Esperansa*.[5] In the beginning, *Esperansa* was a Sephardist society, promoting the use of Judeo-Spanish, although later it became a Zionist association.

In Vienna, Moritz Levi wrote his doctoral dissertation about the Sephardim of Bosnia (Levi 1911), which was the source of two publications in Judeo-Spanish, an article entitled "Los sefaradim en la Bosnia", published in 1923 in a Viennese journal, *El mundo sefaradí*; and the pamphlet *Los sefardim de Bosnia* (Salonika, 1932).

Another one of the first Sephardic Sephardists was Kalmi Baruch (Sarajevo 1896–Bergen-Belsen 1945), who studied at the universities of Zagreb and Vienna. In the latter university, Baruch was a member of the society *Esperansa* and wrote a doctoral dissertation about the Sephardic language of Bosnia (Baruch 1925). Back in his native Sarajevo, he became one of the founders of the newspaper

Jevrejski Zivot ("Jewish Life"), in 1928, and a frequent contributor to *Jevrejski Glas* ("The Jewish Voice"), between 1939 and 1941. In addition, he became interested in orally transmitted Sephardic poetry, publishing a collection of ballads from Bosnia in the yearly publication *Godisnjak* (Baruch 1933).[6]

Finally, Isaac Altarac was also a contributor to *Jevrejski Glas* and in 1932 he read his doctoral dissertation on the topic of the translations of the Bible into Judeo-Spanish (Altarac 1932).[7]

Both Moritz Levi and Kalmi Baruch had some contact with Spanish intellectuals. Levi was one of the correspondents of Senator Ángel Pulido (see below), with whom he exchanged letters and to whom, in 1904, he sent detailed information regarding the association *Esperansa*, of which he was then its secretary. For his part, Baruch exchanged correspondence with Ernesto Giménez Caballero, who, in 1928, published an interview with him in *La Gaceta Literaria*, a journal that had great prestige and influence in Spanish cultural life at the time.

3. THE SEPHARDIC *MASKILIM* AND HISPANISM

Before the writing of the abovementioned doctoral dissertations, some learned Sephardic intellectuals, known as *maskilim*, had already made contributions to the knowledge of Sephardic culture in academic circles. This is the case of Abraham Danan and Abraham Galante.

There are several remarkable aspects in Abraham Galante's life (Bodrum 1873-Istanbul 1961).[8] He was a teacher of Turkish and French in several schools and in the Ottoman Lycée, inspector in the Turkish Ministry of Education, and Professor of History at the University of Istanbul. Like most Sephardic intellectuals of his time, he carried out an intense journalistic activity, founding the journal *La Vara*, which was published in Cairo between 1905 and 1908, and he collaborated in other Sephardic and Turkish periodical publications. In the academic realm, he distinguished himself as a historian of the Sephardic communities of Turkey and the Dodecanese islands. He also made interesting contributions to Spanish philology, including a small but very interesting collection of Sephardic ballads, which he published in a prestigious academic venue, the *Revue Hispanique* (Galante 1903).

Abraham Danon (Edirne 1857–Paris 1925)[9] was a rabbi who founded the Rabbinical Seminary of Turkey in Istanbul. Like Galante, he was also very active in the newspapers. In addition to contributing to periodicals published in Istanbul, Izmir, Sophia and Belgrade, he founded the newspaper *Yosif Da'at/El Progreso* in Edirne, in 1888. But of special interest for us are his writings in academic venues on popular Sephardic culture, where he presented materials deriving from his direct knowledge of the oral tradition.

In one of the international congresses of orientalists that took place in Paris, Danon read a paper on a topic of ethnographic interest, the superstitions of the Jews of Turkey (Danon 1896). A work of greater importance for Hispanic Studies was an important collection of ballads from Turkey, which he published in *Revue des Études Juives* (Danon 1896). This collection was included by Marcelino Menéndez Pelayo in the section "Romances castellanos tradicionales entre los judíos de Levante" of his *Antología de poetas líricos castellanos* (Menéndez Pelayo 1890–1916: vol. X, 293–357). This compilation was considered the canon of lyrical poetry in Spanish for many years.

When, at the beginning of the 20th century, Ramón Menéndez Pidal started his research on the Hispanic ballads, there were very few academic publications that included texts of oral Sephardic poetry: the articles by Abraham Danon and Abraham Galante, the abovementioned anthology by Menéndez Pelayo (which, in addition to Danon's texts, includes several others from Salonika's oral tradition), and the twenty-eight Sephardic songs from the Balkans published by the Romanist, Leo Wiener (1903–1904).

4. ÁNGEL PULIDO'S HISPANOPHILE CORRESPONDENTS

Both Danon and Galante were correspondents of the Spanish Senator, Ángel Pulido, who, from the beginning of the 20th century started a famous political campaign advocating the rapprochement between the Sephardim and Spain.[10]

In his activity in favor of establishing a closer relationship between Spain and the people he called *españoles sin patria*, Pulido strived to maintain epistolary contact with members of the Sephardic élites around the world, especially in the traditional communities of Turkey, the Balkans and North Africa, but also with Sephardim living in Vienna, Trieste and various countries in Latin America. Pulido was the one who sought that relationship, but, through it, some Sephardic intellectuals acquired visibility in Spanish society, especially in political and intellectual circles.

Pulido's campaign caused a number of very different reactions from the Sephardim that he contacted, ranging from sympathy and admiration to disdain, skepticism and overt rejection (Díaz-Mas 2000, Romero 2010b). Naturally, those who showed the greatest sympathy towards his ideas were some Hispanophile Sephardim, who, precisely because of their Hispanophilia, already had contact with contemporary Spanish culture.

For some time already, an intense debate was raging in the Sephardic press regarding the language that the Sephardim should adopt in the modern world. There were very different positions: from the preservation of Judeo-Spanish to its abandonment in favor of the national languages, Hebrew or western modern languages such as French and German (Bunis 1996, Romero 2010 a and b). One of these positions, which had passionate defenders and detractors (Bunis 2012), was to maintain the Judeo-Spanish language, but purified from Turkisms, Balkanisms and Hebraisms, in order to make it as similar as possible to Standard Spanish.

Several of Pulido's correspondents were in favor of this latter option, and for this reason were interested in establishing a closer relationship with Spain, just like the Senator was proposing. This applies to Pulido's first contact in the Sephardic world, Haim (or Enrique) Bejarano (1846–1931), rabbi, teacher, director of a Jewish school in Bucharest, and strong proponent of the re-Hispanization of Judeo-Spanish in order to bring it closer to modern Standard Spanish (Varol-Bornes 2010 and 2013, Bunis 2013).

This is also the case of Abraham Cappon (1853–1930), founder of the newspaper *La Alborada* (which was initially published in Ploesti, Romania, and later in Sarajevo), dramatist and poet, and also a proponent of preserving Judeo-Spanish through its assimilation to standard Spanish (Schmid 2010); Cappon is also the author of an ode "A España", where he expresses his ambivalence with respect to the country of origin of the Sephardim.[11]

Consistent with his political ideology (i.e. "regenerationist liberalism", a type of moderate left-of-center movement, born in the 1870's), Pulido also proposed a "regeneration" of Judeo-Spanish, purifying it from Turkish and Balkan elements and from the influence of French, to bring it closer to contemporary Spanish. Consequently, he promoted contact between Spanish writers and philologists and Sephardic intellectuals.

In his books, Pulido insisted on the importance of the common language as a factor that favored the relationship between Spain and the Sephardim. Guided by his patriotic ideals, the Senator idealized Judeo-Spanish as a fundamental link between the descendents of the Jews who were expelled and the country that expelled them. He explained the fact that the Sephardim had preserved a Hispanic linguistic variety as a consequence of the Sephardim's alleged love for Spain (a *topos* that was born at that time and since then has had much success in Spanish political and journalistic circles).

It is within this intellectual and political project that we must understand Pulido's proposal to name several Sephardic academics and intellectuals as corresponding members of the Royal Spanish Academy. The list includes the already mentioned Haim Bejarano, Abraham Cappon, Abraham Danon and Abraham Galante.

5. THE SEPHARDIM AND MENÉNDEZ PIDAL'S STUDIES ON THE SPANISH BALLADS

At the time when Pulido was promoting the nomination of several Sephardic intellectuals as corresponding members, Ramón Menéndez Pidal had just become a full member of the Royal Spanish Academy (He read his entrance speech in 1902 and was later director of the institution for two different periods, 1926–1939 and 1947–1968).

This contact with Sephardic intellectuals, in the wake of Ángel Pulido's campaign, was fundamental for the future orientation that Ramón Menéndez Pidal's research on the Spanish ballads would have, since it allowed him to know those ballads that were still in use in the Sephardic communities of Morocco and the Eastern Mediterranean.

His initial research on Spanish medieval epic poetry (and, specifically, on the legend of the Infantes de Lara, published in 1896), had led Menéndez Pidal to the study of folk ballads as a manifestation of the Hispanic epic genre. Since 1900, together with his wife, María Goyri, he had started an investigation of folk ballads that were still alive in the Spanish oral tradition.[12] That same year, volume X of Menéndez Pelayo's *Antología de poetas líricos castellanos* also came out. As already noted, this volume includes a selection of Sephardic ballads.

The first step for the study of the Judeo-Spanish ballads had to be the gathering of more versions of individual ballads, which Menéndez Pidal and María Goyri accomplished with the help of correspondents from several Sephardic communities.

In 1896—exactly the same year when Abraham Danon published his collection of ballads—Salomon Levy, from Oran, sent Menéndez Pidal three versions of ballads. A few years later, Levy would become Pulido's correspondent and would write him letters full of admiration.[13]

In turn, from 1904, when Pulido's first book was published, several of his correspondents started to exchange letters with Menéndez Pidal and to send him ballads that they themselves recorded in their places of origin. This is the case of M. Gany, from Romania and Moises Abravanel, from Salonika.

Abraham Cappon also wrote to Menéndez Pidal to explore the possibility of publishing in Spain his poems in a re-Hispanized Judeo-Spanish. Later, he would serve as contact in Sarajevo for the fieldwork that Manuel Manrique de Lara carried out, which is discussed below. These relationships no doubt contributed to stimulating the interest of the Spanish school of Philology in the Sephardic tradition.[14]

Menéndez Pidal was the founder of a school of Hispanic Studies that has lasted until our days. This school, from the very beginning was enriched by the contribution of several Sephardic intellectuals. A main axis in the formation of the school was the Centro de Estudios Históricos (CEH), a Spanish public institution that was founded and directed by Ramón Menéndez Pidal from 1910 until 1939. It was from the CEH that Menéndez Pidal developed an extensive research program, edited the *Revista de Filología Española* and contributed to the training of researchers, some of whom became the Spanish intellectual élite that was exiled from Spain after the Spanish Civil War.[15]

It was also at the CEH where Menéndez Pidal carried out a good part of his work on the Hispanic ballads, in which the Sephardic tradition played an important role. But here I want to highlight two specific aspects of the relationship between Sephardim and Spanish Hispanists around the CEH: the collaboration between Menéndez Pidal and José Benoliel, and Américo Castro's trip to Morocco.

5.1 The Collaboration Between Ramón Menéndez Pidal and José Benoliel

José Benoliel (1858–1937) was a Sephardi from Tangier, and was president of this city's Jewish community.[16] Between 1881 and 1921 he lived in Lisbon, where he started to correspond by letter with Menéndez Pidal already in 1904 (Catalán 2001: 33–37). As Samuel G. Armistead has pointed out

> El cultísimo Benoliel, buen conocedor de las lenguas española, portuguesa, francesa, árabe y hebrea, había de ser una persona enormemente creativa y dinámica. Poseedor de fina sensibilidad y amplia cultura literaria, así como de gran curiosidad intelectual y entusiasmo por la cultura sefardí, Benoliel resultó ser un colaborador ideal en la empresa pidaliana de documentar el romancero judeo-marroquí. Desde 1904 a 1913 Benoliel mantiene con Menéndez Pidal un intensivo intercambio de cartas y textos [...] Entre otras muchas empresas suyas, enseña en varias escuelas de Lisboa, está redactando un diccionario francés-portugués, escribe poesías propias y además quiere traducir a Camões y a otros poetas portugueses... al español, al francés, al hebreo; ha inventado una máquina para escribir el sistema Braille de los ciegos e idea y construye otro singular aparato capaz de imprimir cinco alfabetos distintos. (Armistead 1978: 15–16)[17]

Armistead himself reproduced part of a letter that Benoliel wrote to Menéndez Pidal, where he shows his enthusiasm for the study of the folk ballads, the need to explore the oral tradition of the Sephardim of Morocco and the necessary conditions for this work:

> Es convicción mía que algunas ciudades de Marruecos, Tetuán, Tánger, Xexuán, Alcázar, Arcila, Larache, Casablanca y quizá algunas más del litoral representan para el estudio de la poesía medioeval española, y particularmente para el romance, una mina inestimable, que hay que explorar cuanto antes y con el mayor cuidado si no se quiere perder sin remedio aquel tesoro tan milagrosamente conservado hasta hoy pero fatalmente destinado a sumirse dentro de poco tiempo.
>
> Las hodiernas generaciones menosprecian y sacrifican a las canciones de moda aquéllos que denominan cantares de viejas, y que éstas mismas ya no se atreven a cantar con recelo de atraerse las mofas y motejos de sus hijas. Es preciso, pues, y lo más pronto posible visitar aquellas ciudades y recoger todo lo que aún subsiste de lo que llamaré la verdadera epopeya española. Pero esta empresa no es fácil ni está al alcance de quien quiera. Son indispensables ciertas condiciones: ser del país, conocer las costumbres e idiomas que le son peculiares, ser judío y más o menos acreditado y conocido entre sus correligionarios;

estar al corriente del asunto y tener la habilidad necesaria para sacar a las recitadoras cuanto saben y encaminarlas en lo que no se les ocurre o han olvidado. Sin vanagloria ni modestia inoportuna [...] creo reunir todas aquellas condiciones [...]. (apud Armistead 1978: 16)[18]

As far as we know, Benoliel never undertook the sytematic task of visiting the Sephardic communities that he mentioned searching for folk ballads; he just gathered the ballads he could find among the Moroccan Sephardim living in Lisbon and in his occasional visits to Tangier. But even so, he sent Ramón Menéndez Pidal more than 150 versions of ballads from Tangier and an additional nine from Tetouan, thus contributing in a decisive fashion to Menéndez Pidal's and the CEH's research on the ballads. In addition, he published, in collaboration with Menéndez Pidal, the first known version of an *endecha* from Morocco (Menéndez Pidal and Benoliel 1905).

The epistolary exchange between Menéndez Pidal and Benoliel shows how the Spanish Hispanist contributed to the training of his correspondent, initiating him on the foundations of the methodology of philological fieldwork. In his first letters, Benoliel explains how he has worked to improve, complete and "restore" (and even recreate) the texts of the ballads that he had gathered from the oral tradition, so they would be more complete and aesthetically valuable. In his response letters, Menéndez Pidal thanks him for his texts, but asks him to apply what nowadays we consider basic criteria of academic fieldwork: not to reform the texts, but to transcribe them as faithfully as possible, respecting even what may look like errors; to document diverse versions and to abstain from elaborating factitious versions by combining several oral versions; to try to gather basic data about the informants (place of origin, age); etc.

In turn, the relationship with Benoliel enriched Menéndez Pidal, forcing him to a constant reflection on the process and methodology of philological fieldwork, and the instructions that should be given to fieldworkers. In addition, Benoliel gave Menéndez Pidal an idea that would prove to be very fertile. In a letter of June 1904, he writes:

> Habrá Ud. pensado en publicar al mismo tiempo las melodías correspondientes a algunos de los romances recogidos? De muchos se podrían obtener en Tánger y Tetuán y me parece que habría verdadero interés en hacer un estudio sobre composiciones musicales de 4 ó 5 siglos a esta parte. (apud Catalán 2001: 37)[19]

As if this wasn't enough, Benoliel is also the author of a fundamental study describing the Judeo-Spanish variety of Morocco, known as Haketia. This is a pioneering piece of work that, nevertheless, has not been superseded by later work. If we consider the date and the venue where it was published, it must have been instigated by Menéndez Pidal's influence.

I am referring to the paper entitled "Dialecto judeo-hispano-marroquí o Hakitía", of more than 250 pages, which was published in four installments in the

Boletín de la Real Academia Española, starting in 1926 (Benoliel 1926–1952),[20] precisely in the year when Menéndez Pidal became director of the Spanish Royal Academy. It is a fundamental contribution by a Sephardic scholar to the philological study of one of the varieties of Judeo-Spanish, the Moroccan one. The study was published in a Spanish academic venue; more precisely, in the official journal of the Royal Spanish Academy. In this manner Haketia, the poor relative of the Sephardic language, was officially introduced as part of the canon of Spanish Philology.

5.2. The *Junta para Ampliación de Estudios* and Manuel Manrique de Lara's Fieldwork

The Centro de Estudios Históricos was one of the research centers created by the Junta de Ampliación de Estudios e Investigaciones Científicas (JAE).[21] The JAE was founded in 1907, by a decree of the Spanish government. Its goal was to promote research in Spain, stimulating the creation of research centers, the training of researchers, and relations between Spanish researchers and foreign institutions.

This formed part of a project that was envisioned within the Institución Libre de Enseñanza (1876–1936), the most progressive pedagogical institution in Spain at the end of the 19th and the beginning of the 20th century. One of the main activities of the JAE was a scholarship program to allow students and researchers to spend time doing research at Spanish and, especially, foreign institutions.

At the moment of its founding, the president of the Junta para Ampliación de Estudios was one of the most prestigious Spanish scientists, Santiago Ramón y Cajal, who had been awarded the Nobel Prize in Medicine the year before. Among the members of it first board of directors was Ramón Menéndez Pidal, together with other scientists, writers and artists.

The Junta para Ampliación de Estudios played an essential role in the study of Sephardic culture. In 1911, at the behest of Menéndez Pidal, the JAE funded Manuel Manrique de Lara to travel to the Sephardic communities of the Eastern Mediterranean with the goal of doing fieldwork in order to collect samples of folk ballads that were still alive in the Sephardic oral tradition.[22]

Manrique de Lara was a military man by profession, as well as a musician—he was the author of several symphonies and a *zarzuela*—and had started to become interested in the oral tradition of the folk ballads a few years before, when he accompanied Menéndez Pidal on a trip to collect ballads in Castile. His musical knowledge made him an ideal collaborator to fulfill the objectives that José Benoliel had suggested to Menéndez Pidal in the abovementioned letter of 1904: to record not only the lyrics of the ballads, but also their melodies, since, as is well known, the *romancero* is the Hispanic manifestation of the ballad, and, consequently, a genre of sung narrative poetry.

In 1911, Manrique de Lara visited the Sephardic communities of Sarajevo, Belgrade, Sophia, Salonika, Izmir, Istanbul, Rhodes, Beirut, Jerusalem and Cairo, searching for Sephardic ballads and folk songs. His fieldwork took place under very difficult conditions, not only because of the difficulties in transportation at the time, but also because the area was suffering the effects of the Italo-Turkish war—the Italian troops took Rhodes just a few days after Manrique's visit—and by a cholera epidemic.

Without a doubt, Manrique de Lara made use of the epitolary contacts that Ángel Pulido had already established in the Sephardic communities. He got in touch with some of Pulido's correspondents (Abraham Cappon, Zeki Efendi, etc.) as a way of being introduced to the Jewish communities of Turkey and the Balkans. But, notably, Ángel Pulido's correspondents gave Manrique de Lara extremely few ballads. This is not surprising, since most of them belonged to the Sephardic bourgeoisie, which was already very westernized. The oral tradition was especially alive among the common folk, and in particular among women. For this reason, his most productive informants were women who belonged to the less affluent classes and lived in the traditional neighborhoods of the Jewish communities of the Eastern Mediterranean (Díaz-Mas 2001).

Later, in 1915–16, the JAE funded Manrique de Lara again to collect ballads in the Sephardic communities of Northern Morocco: Tangier, Tetouan, El-ksar-el-kebir, and Larache.

Putting together his fieldwork in the Eastern Mediterranean and in Morocco, Manrique de Lara interviewed almost 150 informants, most of them women, since women had kept the tradition better. It is surprising to observe the skill and ease with which Manrique, a man and non-Jewish, was able to interview them, in a social and cultural context in which the life of Jewish women took place mostly inside the home. Manrique de Lara gathered almost 2000 versions of balads and orally-transmitted songs, together with over 350 musical transcriptions. In addition, he consulted and copied several manuscripts that contained examples of folk poetry and songs and purchased some pamphlets with Judeo-Spanish ballads printed in Hebrew letters that were still being published in cities of the Eastern Mediterranean such as Salonika.

The materials that Manrique de Lara gathered (and are nowadays preserved at the Archivo Menéndez Pidal in Madrid)[23] gave a new orientation to Hispanic Studies, causing the Sephardic tradition to be considered from then on a key element in the study of the *romancero* and, consequently, of Spanish epic poetry. From that moment on, it became impossible to study folk poetry or the Spanish *romancero* without taking the Sephardic versions into account. This massive gathering of materials also opened the door to the research on the Sephardic ballads that has been undertaken, starting in the second half of the 20th century, by leading

U.S. Hispanists such as Samuel G. Armistead and Joseph H. Silverman, as well as by Diego Catalán and his students.

But, without a doubt, these activities also had an impact on the attitude of the Sephardim towards their own traditional culture. We can see an example of this in one of the few Sephardic women writers of the first half of the 20th century.

Among the papers from Manrique de Lara's fieldwork, we find fourteen ballads recorded in Sarajavo from a 19 year old informant identified as "Miss Laura Levi". Laura Levi is the maiden name of Laura Papo (1891–1942), who wrote short stories, journalistic articles and plays in Judeo-Spanish under the pseudonym of Bohoreta.[24] In her work we find descriptions of traditional Sephardic life, recounting the habits and customs that were found among the women of her mother's generation. In many of her texts, her fictional characters appear singing ballads and traditional songs. According to Laura Papo's own words, her meeting Manrique de Lara in her youth was essential in awakening her interest in traditional culture, the old *romansas* and *canticas*, to the point that they became a very important element in her literary creation.

5.3. Américo Castro and His Contact with the Sephardim of Morocco

Another important event in the history of the influence of the Sephardim on Hispanic Studies was Américo Castro's trip to Morocco in 1922, in order to do linguistic fieldwork on Judeo-Spanish, within the research projects of the Centro de Estudios Históricos.

Américo Castro (1885–1972) highlighted the importance that the *convivencia* of the three civilizations—Christian, Muslim and Jewish—had in the history and formation of Spanish culture. That drift in his thinking towards philosophy of history took place during his exile after the Spanish Civil War, when he was a professor at Princeton University. His initial training, however, was philological and his research and teaching activities were always primarily focused on the study of Spanish language and literature.

In 1910, Américo Castro helped Menéndez Pidal in establishing the Centro de Estudios Históricos, where he directed the Department of Lexicography. He was also one of the founding editors of the *Revista de Filología Española* and continued collaborating with the CEH until the Spanish Civil War. He was a Professor of History of the Spanish Language at the University of Madrid. After his exile in 1938, he became a Professor of Spanish language and literature in several US universities: Wisconsin (1937–39), Texas (1939–40) and, in particular, Princeton (1940–1953).[25]

In 1922, Américo Castro traveled to Morocco, funded by the Junta para Ampliación de Estudios, for several months of fieldwork. In that time, he compiled an important collection of Sephardic ballads and folk songs and took notes about the Judeo-Spanish of Morocco.[26] After this trip, he published, in the *Revista Hispano-Africana*, an article describing some of the features of the Judeo-Spanish of Morocco, and making interesting observations regarding its use and attitudes towards this language (Castro 1922).

Professor Armistead (1988) has commented on the importance that first contact of Américo Castro with the Moroccan Jews may have had in his later research on the three cultures and in the construction of his theories about the history of Spain.

5.4. The Sephardim in the Project *Archivo de la Palabra y de las Canciones Populares*

The next step in the relation between Hispanists and Sephardim is also related to the Centro de Estudios Históricos.

Between 1931 and 1933, the musicologist Eduardo Martínez Torner (1888–1955) and the philologist Tomás Navarro Tomás (1884–1979) undertook the project "Archivo de la Palabra" whose goal was

> recoger y conservar en discos de gramófono aquellos testimonios relativos a la cultura hispánica que puedan ser comprendidos bajo los siguientes aspectos: a) La lengua española, literaria o correcta, en su uso corriente y en sus manifestaciones artísticas. b) Idiomas y dialectos hablados en la Península y en los demás países hispánicos, documentando con los ejemplos necesarios las distintas variedades que constituyen cada unidad lingüística. c) Testimonios autofónicos de personalidades ilustres. d) Canciones, melodías y ritmos populares y tradicionales. (Navarro Tomás 1932)[27]

Within this project, a large collection of commercial recordings was acquired and, most importantly, new recordings were made: 175 gramophone records of folk songs of Castile and Extremadura from the fieldwork of the musicologist, Kurt Schindler and 29 records with speech samples. In the latter, the voices of intellectuals, artists and politicians were recorded; but also some Sephardic voices, including songs and ballads sung by the Grand Rabbi of Sarajevo, Mauricio Levy (who had been Manrique de Lara's informant in 1911) and by two young women from Tetouan, Estella Sananes and Yohébed Chocrón, who were pursuing their studies in Madrid and were lodged at the Residencia de Señoritas, which had been founded in 1915, by the pedagogue, María de Maeztu.

In this way, the Sephardic tradition became part of a documentation project that made use of the new technologies of the 1930s, leading to the academic canonization of the Sephardic tradition.[28]

The Spanish Civil War brought about the closing of the Junta para Ampliación de Estudios e Investigaciones Científicas and of the Centro de Estudios Históricos. The materials and documents that had been collected there were dispersed. Most of them ended up at the Consejo Superior de Investigaciones Científicas-CSIC, which was founded in 1939.[29]

Nevertheless, the relations between Sephardim and Spanish Hispanists continued in the exile. Among the different routes those relations took, a particularly important center was the Hispanic Institute at Columbia University.

6. SEPHARDIM AND HISPANISTS IN THE UNITED STATES

In 1916, New York's Columbia University hired Federico de Onís as a professor. Formerly, Federico de Onís had been professor of Spanish Literature at the University of Oviedo and the University of Salamanca, had collaborated in the *Revista de Filología Española* and, with Américo Castro, had published an edition of the *Fueros leoneses* (1916). At Columbia, Onís was involved in the founding of the Instituto de las Españas (later Hispanic Institute) in 1920. Within this Institute, he promoted the development of a *Sección sefardí*.[30]

It appears that Onís never taught courses on Judeo-Spanish or Sephardic culture at Columbia, but, between 1930 and 1938, he did fieldwork gathering *romances* from Sephardic immigrants from the Eastern Mediterranean and Morocco in New York (Armistead and Silverman 1980: 156 and notes 16–17, Martín Durán 2004). In addition, his influence was essential in inspiring several of his students to become interested in Sephardic language and literature and write their doctoral dissertations in this area.

For instance, under his guidance, Max Aaron Luria, an Ashkenazi Jew, began his own studies on the Judeo-Spanish of Monastir (now Bitola), in Macedonia, initially based on fieldwork with Sephardim from Monastir living in New York, and later traveling to Monastir (Luria 1930a, 1930b, 1930c; see also Liebl 2009), a few years before this community was massacred by the Nazis.

A number of Sephardic students wrote MA theses and doctoral dissertations at Columbia University on topics related to Judeo-Spanish culture. In almost every case, these students were children of immigrants, either born in the US or having moved there with their parents at an early age. For these young Sephardim, studying their parents' culture within the academic field of Hispanic Studies must have had great value in the construction of their own identity, for recovering the memory of their families, and for the preservation of a treasure of immaterial culture that was about to disappear, not only in the context of immigration to the New World, but also in their communities of origin. This was a culture that they had known only indirectly, or was part of their childhood memories.

This development also brought about a change in the direction of the study of the oral ballads. Until then, the fieldwork had taken place in the traditional communities of Turkey, the Balkans and Morocco. The work done in the US started to pay attention also to the second Sephardic diaspora, exploring the oral tradition of the Sephardim who had migrated to the US from those traditional communities.

In this way, the Sephardim in the United States contributed to the knowledge of the Hispanic *romancero* from a double perspective: as informants who had received this oral tradition and as researchers of their own culture in academic circles.

Some of those studies remained unpublished for many years, including Zarita Nahón's doctoral dissertation on the ballads from Tangier and Mair José Benardete's MA thesis, which was based on an excellent collection of *romances* gathered in New York from immigrants who had arrived from the Sephardic communities of the Eastern Mediterranean and Morocco. Both theses were published several decades later by Samuel G. Armistead and Joseph H. Silverman (Armistead and Silverman 1976, 1977, 1981).

It was Mair José Bernadete who Onís asked to direct the Sephardic Section of the Hispanic Institute. Bernadete developed Sephardic Studies at Columbia's Hispanic Institute and, later, in the 1930s, in Hunter College and Brooklyn College, becoming an essential figure in Hispanic and Sephardic Studies.

His doctoral dissertation, *Hispanic Culture and Character of the Sephardic Jews* (Benardete 1952), which was translated into Spanish as *Hispanismo de los sefardíes levantinos* (Benardete 1963), highlights the Hispanic elements of Sephardic culture from the perspective of a Sephardic Hispanist who in his childhood had known the traditional culture of the Sephardim of the Ottoman Empire. Benardete was born in the Dardanelles and emigrated with this parents to New York in 1910, when he was 15 years old.[31]

Another Sephardic scholar associated with the Hispanic Institute was Henry Besso (1905–1933), who was born in Salonika and emigrated with his family to the United States. Besso wrote several papers on Sephardic language and culture, where he comments on the decline in the use of Judeo-Spanish (Besso 1961b, 1962, 1967, 1968, 1970). He also compiled an important bibliography of Ladino publications in the Library of Congress (Besso 1963), and, significantly, is the author of an article where he reviews Menéndez Pidal's work on the Sephardic *romancero* (Besso 1961a), underlining Menéndez Pidal's influence on Sephardic Studies.

The scholarly production by students of Sephardic origin at Columbia University includes Susan Bassan's MA thesis (Bassan 1947; see Armistead and Silverman 1980: 156–157 and fn. 21), and Denah Levy's (Denah Lida, after her marrying Raimundo Lida) MA thesis on Judeo-Spanish as spoken in her native city, New York (Levy [Lida] 1944). This work would have a continuation in her doctoral thesis from the Universidad Autónoma de México (Lida 1953). Denah

Lida would become a distinguished Hispanist who authored very important studies on Spanish literature of the Golden Age and the 19th century.[32]

Columbia University was not, however, the only North American institution of higher learning where students of Sephardic origin became scholars of their own culture. Between 1931 and 1935, Emma Adatto recorded ballads, folk tales and proverbs working in Seattle with informants from Turkey and Rhodes. Some of this work was included in her Washington University MA thesis (Adatto 1935, apud Armistead and Silverman 1980: 156 and note 19).

In the 1950s, Isaac Jack Levy recorded folk ballads in Atlanta and Brooklyn for his University of Iowa MA thesis (Levy 1959, apud Armistead and Silverman 1980: 157 and note 25). Isaac Jack Levy is nowadays a well-known specialist on Sephardic culture.

These Sephardic Sephardists blazed a trail that would be continued in work by distinguished North American Hispanists such as Samuel G. Armistead and Joseph H. Silverman. Notably, one of Armistead's and Silverman's projects was the recovery and publication of the collections of Sephardic ballads and songs that had been gathered in fieldwork by Sephardic scholars such as Mair José Benardete and Zarita Nahón. Armistead and Silverman also gave continuity to the research started by Onís and his students in the 1930s by engaging in additional fieldwork on the ballads among the Sephardim in the USA.

7. CONCLUSION

From the beginning of the 20th century, the interaction between Hispanists and Sephardim has enriched the field of Hispanic Studies, opening for Hispanists new areas of research. A very positive development was that some Sephardim took up the study of their own language and culture from an academic perspective, thus becoming Sephardic Sephardists who contributed to the recovery of the Sephardic cultural endowment and created a link between Sephardic Studies and the wider academic field of Hispanic Studies.

The result was a certain academic canonization of Sephardic Studies, but only in very specific areas such as the *romancero*, folk songs, and linguistic research on the varieties of the Judeo-Spanish language. Other aspects of Sephardic culture, most notably the very rich Judeo-Spanish printed literature in Hebrew characters, which includes from religious literature to secular literature to journalistic writing, had to wait until the second half of the 20th century and the beginning of the 21st century to take their place within academic Hispanic Studies.

To go back to the beginning of the paper, it is common to insist on the Spanish heritage of Sephardic culture, but there is less acknowledgment of how much Hispanic Studies owe to Sephardic Hispanists and Sephardists. The Sephardim have contributed to the knowledge of some aspects of Hispanic culture (traditional poetry, ballads, etc.) as informants, as correspondants and collaborators, but also—and in a very important way—as students and scholars of their own culture.

NOTES

1. There is an extensive bibliography on this topic, including studies and editions of texts of this poetic genre. A good summary, with bibliographical references, can be found in Romero (2011).
2. This paper is part of research project FFI2012–31625 "Los sefardíes ante sí mismos y sus relaciones con España III: hacia la recuperación de un patrimonio cultural en peligro", funded by Spain's Ministerio de Economía y Competitividad.
3. For the concept of *endangered language* and a world atlas see http://www.unesco.org/new/en/culture/themes/endangered-languages/[consulted July 9, 2015].
4. For the Sephardic community of Vienna, its founding, evolution and importance, see the articles compiled in Studemund-Halévy, Liebl and Vucina 2013. Regarding the influence of the Viennese cultural environment for the promotion of academic research on Judeo-Spanish, see Studemund-Halévy 2010.
5. On this association, see Ayala and von Schmädel 2010, 2014, and Vucina 2013.
6. On these periodical publications there is information in Vidakovic-Petrov 2013.
7. Biographical sketches of Moritz Levi, Kalmi Baruch and Isaac Altarac, with bibliographical references, are found at Sefardiweb http://sefardiweb.com/node/734, http://sefardiweb.com/node/48 and http://sefardiweb.com/node/37, respectively [consulted on June 8, 2015].
8. There is a biography of Galante in Kalderon 1983. See also Sefardiweb http://sefardiweb.com/node/399 [consulted June 9, 2015].
9. His bio-bibliography can be found in Sefardiweb http://sefardiweb.com/node/169 [consulted June 9, 2015].
10. See his books, Pulido 1904 and 1905. About this campaign and its outcome, see Alpert 2005. There is detailed information about Pulido's correspondents (Sephardim, Jews of other origins and Spaniards), in Sefardiweb http:///sefardiweb.com/corresponsales-angel-pulido [consulted June 8, 2015]
11. Biographical notes on Cappón and Bejarano can be found in Sefardiweb http://sefardiweb.com/node/115, http://sefardiweb.com/node/49, respectively [consulted June 8, 2015].
12. For Menéndez Pidal's biography, see Pérez Pascual 1998 and http://www.fundacionramonmenendezpidal.org/ramon-menendez-pidal. For the creation of the archive of the romancero, see Catalán 2001.
13. Catalán 2001: 13 and note 30; Armistead 1978: vol. III, p. 78, *encuesta* 1; Pulido 1905: 252, 293, 468–470, 474, 508–509, 619.
14. Catalán 2001: 31–33 and 69; Pulido 1904: 43–44, 111, 161–162, and Pulido 1905: 71, 73–74, 92, 94, 292, 293, 330–336, 396–399, 438–443.
15. A good synthesis of the development and activities of the Centro de Estudios Históricos can be found in http://web.archive.org/web/20111127223629/http://www.ucm.es/info//hcontemp/leoc/taller/centro.htm#La%20investigaci%C3%B3n%20en%20el%20Centro%20de%20Estudios%20Hist%C3%B3ricos. For the CEH's philological work, see Abad 1988.

16. On Benoliel's biography, see http://www.aki-yerushalayim.co.il/ay/084/084_10_donjose.htm. and http://lad.wikipedia.org/wiki/Jose_Benoliel.
17. "The very learned Benoliel, who had a good command of the Spanish, Portuguese, French, Arabic and Hebrew languages, must have been an enormously creative and dynamic person. Having a refined sensibility and a broad literary culture, as well as a great intellectual curiousity and enthusiasm for Sephardic culture, Beloniel became an ideal collaborator in Menéndez Pidal's project to document the Judeo-Moroccan folk ballads. Between 1904 and 1913, Benoliel kept an intensive exchange of letters and texts with Menéndez Pidal [...] Among many other activities, he taught in several schools in Lisbon, worked on a French-Portuguese dictionary, wrote his own poetry, and wanted to translate Camões and other Portuguese poets ... to Spanish, French and Hebrew. He also invented a machine to write in Braille and invented and built another device that was able to print in five different alphabets" (Armistead 1978: 15–16).
18. "It is my conviction that some Moroccan towns, Tetouan, Tangier, Chefchaouen, El-ksar-el-kebir, Arcilla, Larache, Casablanca and perhaps a few more on the coast, represent an invaluable mine for the study of Medieval Spanish poetry, and especially the ballads. This mine should be explored as soon as possible and with great care if we do not want to lose forever a treasure that has been miraculously preserved until now but is destined to disappear soon. The present-day generation sacrifices in favor of fashionable songs and despises those that they call old wives' songs; which old women themselves do not dare to sing to avoid the mockery of their daughters. It is thus necessary to visit those towns as soon as possible and to gather everything that still survives there of what I would call the true Spanish epic poetry. But this task is not easy, nor can it be accomplished by just anyone. Certain conditions are necessary: to be from the land, to know its habits and languages, to be Jewish and more-or-less known among those of this religion; to know the topic and to have the necessary skills to elicit from the singers everything they know, leading them when they do not remember or have forgotten. Without boasting or false modesty, [...] I think I meet these conditions [...]" (apud Armistead 1978: 16).
19. "Have you thought of publishing, at the same time, the melodies that correspond to some of the ballads? Many of them could be obtained in Tangier and Tetouan and it seems to me that there would be a lot of interest in conducting research on musical compositions of the last four or five centuries" (apud Catalán 2001: 37).
20. In Benoliel's life, the first three installments were published, in 1926, 1927 and 1928. The original of the last part of the article was misplaced and was recovered and published in the same journal only after the end of the Spanish Civil War, in 1952.
21. On the JAE, see the articles in Sánchez Ron 1988 and Puig-Samper Mulero 2007: 23–255. See also http://www.csic.es/web/guest/16.
22. Information on Manrique de Lara's fieldwork can be found in Armistead 1978: 18–21 and Catalán 2001: 66–72 y 88–96. On Manrique de Lara as a musician, see Iberni 1997; on his work as a folklorist, see Díaz González 2012.
23. For information of this archive, see the webpage of the Fundación Ramón Menéndez Pidal, in Madrid http://www.fundacionramonmenendezpidal.org/. Some of Manrique de Lara's musical transcriptions can be found in the Tomás Navarro Tomás library of the CSIC: http://biblioteca.cchs.csic.es/podcast/archivos5.php [consulted June 7, 2015].
24. A biography of Laura Papo, with many bibliographical references about her life and work, can be found in Sefardiweb http://sefardiweb.com/node/73 [consulted May 30, 2015].
25. See http://www.fundacionramonmenendezpidal.org/ramon-menendez-pidal/escuela-pidalina/americo-castro [consulted July 31, 2014].

26. See Armistead and Silverman 1971 and Armistead 2001.
27. "To collect and preserve in gramophone records those testimonies related to Hispanic culture that may fall under the following categories: a) the correct or literary Spanish language in its everyday use and in its artistic manifestations, b) languages and dialects spoken in the Peninsula and in the rest of the Hispanic countries, documenting the different varieties that constitute each linguistic unit, with the necessary examples, b) audio records of distinguished personalities, d) Traditional and folk songs, melodies and rhythms" (Navarro Tomás 1932).
28. On the project Archivo de la Palabra, see Navarro Tomás 1932, Gallego Morell and Pinto Molina 1986 and Residencia de Estudiantes 1998. On the Residencia de Señoritas, see Moreno 1993.
29. See http://www.csic.es/web/guest/historia and Puig-Samper Mulero 2008: 251–356.
30. http://www.fundacionramonmenendezpidal.org/ramon-menendez-pidal/escuela-pidalina/federico-de-oni. About his activities at Columbia University regarding Sephardic culture, see Ben-Ur 2009: 161–173.
31. Benardete's biography and his bibliography until 1965 can be found in his Festschrift, edited by Langnas and Sholod 1965: 11–30 and 459–476.
32. Bio-bibliographical data about Denah Lida can be found in her Festschrift, edited by Berg and Gyurko 2005: 5–26.

REFERENCES

Abad, Francisco. "La obra filológica del Centro de Estudios Históricos". In *1907–1987. La Junta para Ampliación de Estudios e Investigaciones Científicas 80 años después. Simposio internacional, 15–17 de diciembre de 1987*. Ed. José M. Sánchez Ron, 503–517. Madrid: CSIC, 1988.

Adatto, Emma. "A Study of the Linguistic Characteristics of the Seattle Sefardi Folklore". M.A. thesis, University of Washington, 1935.

Alpert, Michael. "Dr. Angel Pulido and philo-Sephardism in Spain". *Jewish Historical Studies* 40 (2005): 105–119.

Altarac, Isaac. "Die Spracheigentümlichkeiten der Judenspanischen Bibelübersetzung". Doctoral dissertation, University of Vienna, 1932.

Armistead, Samuel G. *El Romancero judeo-español en el Archivo Menéndez Pidal (Catálogo-índice de romances y canciones)*. Madrid: Cátedra Seminario Menéndez Pidal, 1978, 3 vols.

Armistead, Samuel G. "Américo Castro in Morocco: The Origins of a Theory". In *Américo Castro: The Impact of His Thought*. Eds. Ronald E. Surtz, et al., 73–82. Madison, Wisconsin: Hispanic Seminary of Medieval Studies, 1988.

Armistead, Samuel G. "Seis cantos de boda judeo-españoles (mss. de Américo Castro)". In *La eterna agonía del Romancero: Homenaje a Paul Bénichou*. Eds. Piñero Ramírez, Pedro M. et al., 179–193. Sevilla: Fundación Machado, 2001: 179–193.

Armistead, Samuel G. and Joseph H. Silverman. "Un aspecto desatendido de la obra de Américo Castro". In *Estudios sobre la obra de Américo Castro*. Madrid: Taurus, 1971: 181–190.

Armistead, Samuel G. and Joseph H. Silverman. "La colección Nahón de romances judeo-españoles de Tánger". *La Corónica* 5 (1976): 7–16.

Armistead, Samuel G. and Joseph H. Silverman. *Romances Judeo-españoles de Tánger (recogidos por Zarita Nahón)*. Madrid: Cátedra Seminario Menéndez Pidal, 1977.

Armistead, Samuel G. and Joseph H. Silverman. "Judeo-Spanish Ballad Collecting in the United States". *La Coronica* 8.2 (Spring 1980): 156–163.

Armistead, Samuel G. and Joseph H. Silverman. *Judeo-Spanish Ballads from New York. Collected by Maír José Benardete*. Berkeley-Los Ángeles-London: University of California Press, 1981.

Ayala, Amor y Stephanie von Schmädel. "Identitätdiskurse und Politisierung der Sepharden in Wien am Beispiel des Studentenvereins Esperanza (1896–1924)". *Transversal. Zeitschrift für Jüdische Studien* 11.2 (2010): 83–102.

Ayala, Amor and Stephanie von Schmädel. "Viena y sus estudiantes sefardíes: la Sociedad Académica 'Esperanza' (siglos XIX y XX)". *Ladinar* 7–8 (2014): 21–36.

Baruch, Kalmi. "Der Lautstand des Judenspanischen in Bosnien". Doctoral dissertation, University of Vienna, 1925.

Baruch, Kalmi. "Spanske romanse bosanskih Jevreja". *Godisnjak* (1933): 272–288.

Bassan, Susan. "Judeo-Spanish Folk Poetry". M.A. thesis, Columbia University, New York, 1947.

Ben-Ur, Aviva. *Sephardic Jews in America. A Diasporic History*. New York and London: New York University Press, 2009.

Benardete, Maír José. *Hispanic Culture and Character of the Sephardic Jews*. New York: Hispanic Institute, 1952 (reed. by Marc Angel, New York: Sepher-Hermon Press, 1982).

Benardete, Maír José. *Hispanismo de los sefardíes levantinos*. Madrid: Aguilar, 1963.

Benoliel, José. "Dialecto judeo-hispano-marroquí o Hakitía". *Boletín de la Real Academia Española* 13 (1926): 209–233, 342–363, 507–538; 14 (1927): 137–168, 196–234, 357–373, 566–580; 15 (1928): 47–61, 188–223; 32 (1952): 255–289.

Berg, Mary G. and Lanin A. Gyurko, eds. *Studies in Honor of Denah Lida*. Potomac, Maryland: Scripta Humanistica, 2005.

Besso, Henri V. "Don Ramón Menéndez Pidal and the Romancero sefardí". *Sefarad* 21 (1961): 343–374.

Besso, Henri V. "Judeo-Spanish Literature". *Le Judaïsme Sephardi* 23 (1961): 1016–1022.

Besso, Henri V. "Literatura judeo-española".*Thesaurus. Boletín del Instituto Caro y Cuervo* 17 (1962): 625–651.

Besso, Henri V. *Ladino Books in the Library of Congress. A Bibliography*. Washington: Library of Congress, 1963.

Besso, Henri V. "Causas de la decadencia del judeo-español". In *Actas del Segundo Congreso Internacional de Hispanistas*. Nimega, 1967: 207–215.

Besso, Henri V. "Los sefardíes y el idioma castellano". *Revista Hispánica Moderna* XXXIV (1968): 176–193.

Besso, Henry V. "Decadencia del judeo-español.Perspectivas para el futuro". In *Actas del Primer Simposio de Estudios Sefardíes*. Ed. Iacob M. Hassán, 249–261. Madrid: CSIC, 1970.

Bunis, David M. "Modernization and the Language Question among Judezmo-Speaking Sephardim of the Ottoman Empire". In *Sephardi and Middle Eastern Jewries: History and Culture in the Modern Era*. Ed. Harvey E. Goldberg, 226–239. Bloomington, Indianapolis: Indiana Univ. Press, 1996.

Bunis, David M. "The Anti-Castilianist Credo of Judezmo Journalist Hizkia M. Franco (1875–1953)". *eHumanista: Journal of Iberian Studies* 20 (2012): 63–97.

Bunis, David M. "The Judezmo Press as a Forum for Modern Linguistic Discourse". In *La presse judéo espagnole, support et vecteur de la modernité*. Eds. Rosa Sánchez and Marie-Christine Bornes Varol, 143–180. Istanbul: Libra, 2013.

Castro, Américo. "Entre los hebreos marroquíes. La lengua española de Marruecos". *Revista Hispano-Africana* I.5 (May 1922): 145–146.

Catalán, Diego. *El Archivo del Romancero, patrimonio de la Humanidad. Historia documentada de un siglo de Historia*. Madrid: Fundación Menéndez Pidal-Seminario Menéndez Pidal de la Universidad Complutense, 2001, 2 vols.

Cohen, Julia Phillips and Sarah Abrevaya Stein. "Sephardic Scholarly Worlds: Towards a Novel Geography of Modern Jewish History". *Jewish Quarterly Review* 100.3 (2010): 349–384.

Crews, Cynthia M."Judaeo-Spanish Folktales in Macedonia". *Folk-lore* 43 (1932): 193–225.

Crews, Cynthia M. *Recherches sur le Judéo-Espagnol dans les Pays Balkaniques.* Paris: Droz, 1935.

Crews, Cynthia M."Extracts from the Meam Loez (Genesis) with a Translation and a Glossary". *Proceedings of the Leeds Philosophical and Literary Society* 9, parte II (1960): 13–106.

Danon, Abraham. "Recueil de romances judéo-espagnoles chantées en Turquie". *Revue des Études Juives* XXXII (1896): 102–123, 263–275; XXXIII (1896): 122–139, 255–268.

Danon, Abraham. "Les superstitions des juifs ottomans". In *Actes de l'Onzième Congrès International des Orientalistes*, 259–270. Paris, 1899: 259–270.

Díaz González, Diana. "La labor de folclorista de Manuel Manrique de Lara en el contexto de su vida y obra". *Cuadernos de Música Iberoamericana* 23 (2012): 45–66.

Díaz-Mas, Paloma. "Repercusión de la campaña prosefardí del senador Ángel Pulido en la opinión pública de su época". In *España y la Cultura Hispánica en el Sudeste Europeo*. Atenas: Embajada de España-Instituto Cervantes, 2000: 326–341.

Díaz-Mas, Paloma. "Corresponsales de Ángel Pulido e informantes de Menéndez Pidal: dos mundos sefardíes". *Los trigos ya van en flores. Studia in Honorem Michelle Débax*. Eds. Jean Alsina and Vicent Ozanam, 103–116. Toulouse: Université de Toulouse-Le Mirail, 2001.

Galante, Abraham. "Quatorze romances judéo-espagnols", *Revue Hispanique* X (1903): 544–606.

Gallego Morell, Antonio and María Pinto Molina. *El archivo de la palabra (Catalogación de su fondo discográfico)*. Granada: Universidad de Granada, 1986.

Iberni, Luis G. "Un acercamiento a Manuel Manrique de Lara". *Anuario musical. Revista de musicología del CSIC*, 52 (1997): 155–172.

Kalderon, Albert. *Abraham Galante. A Biography*. New York: Sepher-Hermon Press-Sephardic House at Congragation Shearith Israel, 1983.

Langnas, Izaak and Barton Sholod, eds. *Studies in Honor of M. J. Benardete (essays in Hispanic and Sephardic Culture)*. New York: Las Americas, 1965.

Levi, Moritz. "Die Sephardim in Bosniem". Doctoral dissertation, University of Vienna, 1911.

Levy, Isaac Jack. "Sephardic Ballads and Songs in the United States: New Variants and Additions". M.A. thesis, University of Iowa, 1959.

Levy [Lida], Denah. "El sefardí de Nueva York. Observaciones sobre el judeo-español de Esmirna". M.A. thesis, Columbia University, 1944.

Levy [Lida], Denah. "El sefardí esmirniano de Nueva York". Doctoral dissertation, Universidad Nacional Autónoma de México, 1953.

Liebl, Christian (ed.). *Judeo–Spanish from the Balkans: The Recordings by Julius Subak (1908) and Max A. Luria (1927)*. Vienna: Verlag der Österreichischen Akademie der Wissenschaften, 2009 (= Sound Documents from the Phonogrammarchiv of the Austrian Academy of Sciences: The Complete Historical Collections 1899–1950, Series 12/OEAW PHA CD 28).

Luria, Max A. "A Study of the Monastir Dialect of Judeo-Spanish Based on Oral Material Collected in Monastir, Yugo-Slavia". *Revue Hispanique* LXXIX (1930): 323–583.

Luria, Max A."Judeo-Spanish Dialects in New York City". In *Todd Memorial Volumes: Philological Studies*. Eds. John D. Fitz-Gerald and Pauline Taylor: vol II, 7–16. New York: Columbia University Press, 1930.

Luria, Max A. *A Study of the Monastir Dialect of Judeo-Spanish Based on Oral Material Collected in Monastir, Yugo-Slavia*. New York and Paris, 1930.

Martín Durán, Andrés M. "Noticias de romances y canciones de la tradición oral sefardí grabados por Federico de Onís en Nueva York que se hallan en la Universidad de Puerto Rico". *Revista de Estudios Hispánicos* (Puerto Rico) XXXI.1 (2004): 269–272.

Menéndez Pelayo, Marcelino. *Antología de poetas líricos castellanos. Desde la formación del idioma hasta nuestros días*. Madrid: Perlado y Páez, 1890–1916, 14 vols.

Menéndez Pidal, Ramón and José Benoliel. "Endecha de los judíos españoles de Tánger". *Revista de Archivos, Bibliotecas y Museos* IX.12 (1905): 128–133.

Moreno, Alicia, ed. *Ni convento ni college. La Residencia de Señoritas*. Madrid: Publicaciones de la Residencia de Estudiantes, 1993.

Navarro Tomás, Tomás. *Archivo de la palabra: trabajos realizados en 1931*. Madrid: Centro de Estudios Históricos, 1932.

Pérez Pascual, José Ignacio. *Ramón Menéndez Pidal: ciencia y pasión*. Valladolid: Junta de Castilla y León, 1998.

Puig-Samper Mulero, Miguel Ángel, ed. *Tiempo de investigación. JAE-CSIC, cien años de ciencia en España*. Madrid: CSIC, 2007.

Pulido Fernández, Ángel. *Los israelitas españoles y el idioma castellano*. Madrid: Sucesores de Rivadeneyra, 1904 (reed. facsímil Barcelona: Riopiedras, 1992).

Pulido Fernández, Ángel. *Españoles sin patria y la raza sefardí*. Madrid: E. Teodoro, 1905 (reed. facsimile, Granada: Universidad de Granada, 1993).

Residencia de Estudiantes. *Voces de la edad de Plata. Grabaciones originales realizadas por el Centro de Estudios Históricos (1931–1933)*. Madrid: Residencia de Estudiantes, 1998.

Romero, Elena. "La polémica sobre el judeoespañol en la prensa sefardí del imperio otomano: materiales para su estudio". In *Los sefardíes ante los retos del mundo contemporáneo: identidad y mentalidades*. Eds. Paloma Díaz-Mas & María Sánchez Pérez, 55–64. Madrid: CSIC, 2010.

Romero, Elena. "La polémica sobre el judeoespañol en la prensa sefardí del Imperio otomano: más materiales para su estudio". *Sefarad* 70 (2010): 435–473.

Romero, Elena. "Sephardi Coplas: Characteristics and Bibliography". *European Judaism* 44.1 (Spring, 2011): 72–83.

Sánchez Ron, J. M.,ed. *1907–1987. La Junta para Ampliación de Estudios e Investigaciones Científicas 80 años después. Simposio internacional, 15–17 de diciembre de 1987*. Madrid: CSIC, 1988.

Schmid, Beatrice. "'Por el adelantamiento de la nación'. Las ideas lingüísticas de Abraham A. Cappon". In *Los sefardíes ante los retos del mundo contemporáneo: identidad y mentalidades*. Eds. Paloma Díaz-Mas & María Sánchez Pérez, 99–112. Madrid: CSIC, 2010.

Studemund-Halevy, Michael. "Shem Tov Semo, Sefardi Vienna and the Cradle of Judezmo Philology". In *Los sefardíes ante los retos del mundo contemporáneo: identidad y mentalidades*. Ed. Paloma Díaz-Mas & María Sánchez Pérez, 317–332. Madrid: CSIC, 2010.

Studemund-Halévy, Michael, Christian Liebl and Ivana Vucina Simóvic, eds. *Sefarad an der Donau. La lengua y literatura de los sefardíes en tierras de los Habsburgo*. Barcelona: Tirocinio, 2013.

Subak, Julius, 1905. "Das Verbum im Judenspanischen". In *Bausteine zur Romanische Philologie. Festgabe für Adolfo Mussafia*. Halle: Max Niemeyer, 1905: 321–331.

Subak, Julius, "Zum Judenspanischen". *Zeitschrift für Romanische Philologie* XXX (1906): 129–185.

Subak, Julius. "Vorläufiger Bericht über eine im Auftrage der Balkan-Kommission der kais. Akademie der Wissenschaften in Wien unternommene Forschungsreise nach der Balkanhalbinsel zur schriftlichen und phonographischen Aufnahme des Judenspanischen". *Anzeiger der kaiserlichen Akademie der Wissenschaften: Philosophisch-historische Klasse* 47 (1910): 33–38.

Varol Bornes, Marie-Cristine. "Un erudito entre dos lenguas: el 'castellano' de Hayim Bejarano en el prólogo a su refranero glosado". In *Los sefardíes ante los retos del mundo contemporáneo: identidad y mentalidades*. Eds. Paloma Díaz-Mas and María Sánchez Pérez, 113–127. Madrid: CSIC, 2010.

Varol Bornes, Marie-Cristine. "Hayim ben Moshe Bejarano, maskil, lecteur et collaborateur de presse". In *La presse judéo espagnole, support et vecteur de la modernité*. Eds. Rosa Sánchez and Marie-Christine Bornes Varol, 282–294. Istanbul: Libra, 2013.

Vidakovic-Petrov, Krinka. "La presse séfarade de Belgrade et Sarajevo de 1888 à 1941". En *Recensement, analyse et traitement numérique des sources écrites pour les études séfarades*. Eds. Soufiane Roussi and Ana Stulic-Etchevers, 69–96. Bordeaux: Presses universitaires de Bordeaux, 2013.

Vucina Simovic, Ivana. "Los sefardíes ante su lengua: los esperancistas de Sarajevo". In *Sefarad an der Donau. La lengua y literatura de los sefardíes en tierras de los Habsburgo*. Eds. Michael Studemund-Halévy, Christian Liebl and Ivana Vucina Simóvic, 341–360. Barcelona: Tirocinio, 2013.

Wagner, Max Leopold. "Die Sprache der spanischen Juden". *Revista de Dialectología Románica*, I (1909): 487–502.

Wagner, Max Leopold. *Beiträge zur kenntnis des Judenspanischen von Konstantinopel*. Viena: Alfred Hölder, 1914.

Wagner, Max Leopold. "Algunas observaciones generales sobre el judeo-español de Oriente". *Revista de Filología Española*, 10 (1923): 225–244.

Wagner, Max Leopold. *Caracteres generales del judeoespañol de Oriente*. Madrid, Centro de Estudios Históricos, 1930 (=Anejos de la Revista de Filología Española).

Wagner, Max Leopold. *Judenspanisch*. Stutgart: Franz Steiner, 1990, 2 vols. (= Sondersprachen der Romania III–IV).

Wiener, Leo. "The Ferrara Bible". *Modern Language Notes*, X (1895): 81–85; XI (1896): 24–42 and 84–105.

Wiener, Leo. "Songs of the Spanish Jews in the Balkan Peninsula". *Modern Philology*, I (1903–1904): 205–216, 259–274.

PART THREE

Judeo-Spanish Language
AND Culture Today

CHAPTER THIRTEEN

Contemporary Judeo-Spanish Poetry IN Its Rediscovery OF THE Past

AGNIESZKA AUGUST-ZARĘBSKA
University of Wrocław

ABSTRACT[1]

This chapter focuses on the contemporary Judeo-Spanish poetry and aims at analyzing different manifestations of its rediscovering of the past. The subject of the discussion are poems written by Margalit Matitiahu, Avner Perez, Rita Gabbaï-Simantov, Gracia Albuhayre and Denise León, where their relation to the past—construed either as an individual history or the history of the community which the authors identify with—seems to be one of the crucial themes. It is accentuated that their approach to the past concentrates on three main motifs: recalling places, recalling people and recalling the mere sound of Ladino language. It is also claimed that the poetic expression in Ladino enables the authors to stay in closer contact with their roots and to include this experience in their self-understanding. The Judeo-Spanish contemporary poetry also turns out to be a means of the authors' individual memory as well as contributes to constructing the collective memory of Sephardic Jews.

1. INTRODUCTION

My contribution concerns contemporary Judeo-Spanish poetry produced in Ladino[2] since the 1980s, particularly by several authors chosen as representative. Since at the time they wrote their poems Ladino had already become an endangered language, these authors' decision to write poetry in it must have been, and actually was, a conscious and meaningful act, whose significance needs to be taken into account in our interpretation of their work. For, then, they fully recognized the fact that the Judeo-Spanish literature would certainly lack a natural, wide range of readers, all the more given the fact that even for them Ladino had ceased to be the first language of daily communication. They mostly used to speak it as children at home, or just remembered their grandparents and parents speaking it. Whatever the individual motivations of these authors might be, by writing poems in the Sephardic language they, generally, wanted to pay homage to the culture of their ancestors and to prolong as if it were its life. Accordingly, they took Ladino as a proper device to recall, in poetic images, the memory of the reality of bygone Sephardic communities. They also considered it a means of rediscovering, or understanding better, their own identity.

My analysis will include poems by five authors: Margalit Matitiahu, Avner Perez, Rita Gabbaï-Simantov, Gracia Albuhayre and Denise León. I will make the claim that one of the crucial themes of their work is its rediscovery of the past and I will try to show its various manifestations. The past can be understood both as an individual story (one's own past or one's family's past) and as the history of the community the authors themselves identify with. It is worth stressing that I will take into account only those poems in which the authors endeavor to approach the past—seen as a part of their Sephardic identity. Their recall of it in the poems gives rise to the rediscovery of their identity, and to its reinforcement, in the situation and times in which the question of cultural identity is far from being obvious. All of the above-mentioned authors have their roots in the former Turkish-Balkan Diaspora, but not all of them were born there. Nowadays, they live in different countries and societies with which they also identify. Thus, Sephardity constitutes only a part of their own identity. In addition, as we well know, as a result of the Holocaust, but also as a consequence of the modernization processes, former Sephardic centers that used to be the sanctuaries of Judeo-Spanish culture and of traditional Sephardic modes of life ceased to exist. In effect, there are now no places (such as cities, towns, villages) to go to and experience traditional Sephardic culture and live language. Furthermore, visits to the former Jewish centers in the Balkans always involve facing the terrifying truth about the Shoah and the annihilation of the rich, centuries-old culture that formerly flourished there.

For the poets in question, it is just poetic expression that becomes a means of experiencing the roots of their own cultural community. At the same time, it enables them to include such an experience—to resort to the well-known hermeneutic concept—into their own "Horizons of Understanding", or into their self-understanding, the comprehension of their "being-in-the-world". Perhaps the main factor that invests it with such a significance is the fact that this poetry is written in Judeo-Spanish, so the use of this language is a manifestation of the Sephardic culture and, at the same time, makes it audible again, gives it a new lease of life. It helps the authors to bring back their scraps of memories, which allow them to attain a closer contact with this culture. It is also a record of experiences connected with their strenuous attempts to salvage the memory of the past, and seeking for its traces, which are fading away as time passes. Still, it is just in the poems that they are preserved and thus they have a chance to be saved from oblivion. Accordingly, it may be said that poetry becomes a means of individual memory, and, due to the mere fact of being read, it also contributes to forming the collective memory of the Sephardim.

Although, of course, each of the above-mentioned poets approaches the past in a specific way, some common motifs can be found. Generally speaking, one can say that the poetic images of old Sephardic life focus on three issues: recalling places, people, and the sound of the Ladino language. Often the three motifs coexist in one work, whereas together they all form a family, or communal, "mythology", so important for constituting one's own identity.

2. POETIC RECOLLECTIONS OF PLACES

Poetic reminiscences, and also imaginary representations, of the places important for the Sephardic diaspora are usually outcomes of the author's travels to those places, sometimes taking the form of a travel report. The authors come back to the cities and towns where they were born, or where their ancestors used to live. They want not so much to get to know the places in their present form, but rather, they treat them as a palimpsest; they wish to search out, under their contemporary layer, some traces of their former shape and ambience, and through that to touch "the pre-history of their own biography."[3] This is the case of Gracia Albuhayre, a Bulgarian Jewish poet from Karnobat, who, in the poem *La sivda miya* ("My town") (Jak Albuhayre 2007: 18), described her visit, after years, to her home town. She walked the streets that she had known in her childhood, yet here the family home no longer existed, her familiar yard with the well and with the garden abounding with flowers and fruit trees had disappeared.[4] She remembers her youth, but at the same time faces the impossibility of bringing back the sense of security and carefreeness of those days. With great nostalgia she reflects on the flow of time, and confesses that encountering again this place filled her, first of all, with sorrow:

> La sivda kara miya.
> La sivda ke tanto kiria.
> La sivda ke en mi shunyo vinia
> A mi alma no trusho aligria. (*ibid.*: 18)

> [My dear town/The town that I loved so much/The town that came to me in my dreams/Did not bring happiness to my soul]

In this stanza, what draws our attention is the thrice call to the city. In the first line the city is patently real, while in the next ones we deal with a turn from reality to imagined representations of it. The beloved city of her childhood days appears to be losing its reality and moving completely into the sphere of memories, dreams and emotions. Although in Albuhayre the theme of individual, personal experiences is dominant, in this poem the communal aspect is detectable as well—when she mentions that the name of the Jewish street has been changed, because there are no longer Jews there.

A kind of poetic travel journal may be found in Margalit Matitiahu, whose first bilingual volume of verse *Kurtijo kemado* ("A Burned Yard") is designed as a diary of impressions from her visit to Greece, the homeland of her parents and also, in a broader sense, of the cultural and ethnic community which she identifies with. The author visits first of all Salonika—the home city of her mother—as well as some other towns and places connected with the persecution of Greek Jews during World War II. In the streets of Salonika, she reconstructs a topography remembered from family stories, searching for the places and buildings which her parents recollected, but which were in some way transformed by her imagination in her childhood, when she would listen to those tales:

> En los tertuares de Saloniki
> Kaminava kon prisa,
> Un echiso me travava verso las kayes
> Konosidas por la imajinasion de mi chikes. (Matitiahu 1988: 19)

[In the sidewalks of Salonika/I walked hurriedly/A spell impelled me towards the streets/That I knew from the imagination of my childhood]

In the changed Greek city, she can hardly find them, yet she strives to do this in order, as Shmuel Refael has put it, "to reconstruct her mother's cognitive map—city routes, squares, street names and even inner courtyards do not escape the eyes of the sensitive poet" (Refael 2012: 331). She experiences intense feelings ("La kaye paresia intchirse de mis ondos sintimientos" ["The street seemed to swell with my deep feelings"]) (Matitiahu 1988: 17), when a huge chasm between the old, mostly non-existent reality and the contemporary city, optimistic but rid of its former multicultural past, comes to her mind. Several poems of *Kurtijo kemado* are devoted just to such a confrontation of the imagined city, dear to the poet's heart, with actual, real Salonika, predominantly deprived of the traces of its former Jewish presence. The new Salonika, whose cool indifference remains in contrast with the experiences of her own and of her traveling companions (the second generation members), it appears to be utterly hostile. In her texts, on numerous occasions, we find words and images that evoke associations with violence. They may be understood as echoes of the injustice and harm done to her people during World War II:

Las ventanas seradas paresian metersen/En una gera muda contra el tiempo pasado. (*ibid.*: 17)

[The closed windows seemed to engage/In a silent war against the past]

Las ventanas de las kazas mos miravan kon ojos estranyos/i una negregura enlokesida paresia abashar/De las agilas arrebatadoras vistidas de maldad. (*ibid.*: 15)

[The houses' windows were looking at us with strange eyes/and a crazed wickedness seemed to come down/From the thieving eagles dressed in evil]

En la kaye "Ermu" espunta la madrugada

I los kamiones komo una armia

Atakan las venas de la sivdad.

Una parada de kondanados parecen

La karne i los peshes ke a los bankos del soko

Son yevados. (*ibid.*: 19)

[In Ermu street dawn breaks/and trucks like an army/attack the veins of the town./They resemble a parade of prisoners/The meat and the fish that to the stalls of the marked/are taken.]

The paths of Matitiahu's Greek journey unavoidably bear the mark of the Holocaust, the poems *La plaza de la libertad* ("Liberty Square") and *En el kamino de Athena a Larisa* ("On the way from Athens to Larissa") being explicit examples of that. In both texts, the poetic voice manifests deep grief over the victims of the Shoah and seeks the same sorrow thereabouts. Still, the surrounding neighborhood remains unmoved. For that reason, these works consist of many paradoxes and antitheses that betray acute agitation:

La kayadez korria gritando en muestras venas
En la londjura – la mar kedava blue komo el sielo
Ma nuestros mushos se empretesian.
[…]
Ma de las ventanas ke siempre van kasando la luz
Nunka no podra fuir la eskuridad. (*ibid.*: 15)

[Silence was running around shouting in our veins./In the distance – the sea looked blue like the sky/But our lips were blackening./[…]/But from the windows that always seek the light/Darkness will never be able to escape.]

The scenes of contemporary train travel are superimposed on the imagined pictures of deportations to concentration camps. Traveling between places (the spatial aspect) becomes also traveling in time (the temporal aspect), the former depicting the horizontal movement and the latter—the vertical direction. The poetic voice describes the vision of yawning abyss, experiences the descent into it, which is, simultaneously, the ascent of the highest pain, as groans of the victims are heard and the letters are forming the names of the dead. In the last stanza the duty of remembrance is recited:

> Kon la marka de dolor en el kuerpo,
> Komo mezuza
> Bezar bezar i akodrar. (*ibid.*: 13)
>
> [With the mark of pain in the body/As for a mezuzah/To kiss, to kiss and to remember]

Manifestly, both in Matitiahu and in the other authors whose roots are in the Balkans the duty of remembrance of the Shoah is an inherent element of their Sephardic identity, even if they are not Holocaust survivors themselves, nor are they the children of the survivors.

This is also the case in the poem *Saloniki* by Avner Perez, for whom his visit to this Greek city meant his facing the overwhelming truth that Sephardic Salonika does not exist anymore. When speaking about this inexistence, he uses the metaphor of hide-and-go-seek, which initially seems to be blithe. Yet, the sense of dread grows pervasive when it turns out that what is sought in the game is the old Jewish city and its inhabitants, and that, regretfully, the rules that are usually in effect in a hide-and-go-seek game are not applicable here—the absence of the Jews here is irrevocable. The poetic force of this text relies on equaling the poetic voice's perspective with the point of view of a boy who is gripped with panic fear at the very moment when he is coming to awareness that no one of his family and friends has stayed with him. This figure has a double meaning. Firstly, it articulates the poet's feeling of loss, since he sees himself as a descendant and an heir, when speaking about the culture, of the Sephardic community of Salonika. Secondly, it allows him to experience a sort of empathy with the survivors from the annihilated city, with those who lost both all of their relatives and their own place to live. It was just the survivors that were represented with the help of the picture of a playing boy, his initial carefreeness renders the quietness and confidence of the pre-war life, whereas his despair and fear symbolize their state of mind after they become aware of the fate of all those transported to Auschwitz-Birkenau. It is worth noticing that here, like in Matitiahu, the contemporary inhabitants seem not to share these feelings: some of them are simply indifferent, a few are kind, but there also are those who are utterly hostile. The latter are embodied by a toothless old man, who is telling stories about transportations with a smile on his face, and then tries to chase the child-traveler off by making a gesture as if he wanted to cut his throat. Only a man of the younger generation is ready to offer kindness to him, but simultaneously he betrays complete ignorance of the multicultural, especially the Jewish, past of Salonika.

Perez, like Matitiahu, built his vision of Salonika on the base of both the stories he had heard, or read, and of historical knowledge, irrespective of his personal experience; thus one may say that he belongs to the group of poets who—using the phrase from Shmuel Refael—recreate the Jewish city or create its urban space *ex nihilo* (Refael 2012: 327). He described his attitude to Salonika in the dedication preceding the poem *Siniza i fumo*, published in *Aki Yerushalayim*: "A la memoria de Saloniko—mi esfuenyo i mi amor" ["To the memory of Salonika—my dream and my love"] (Perets 1984: 27) Accordingly, his Salonika belongs to the past, and the image of the city that he keeps in his mind, and that forms his imagination, is a dreamt image fed by his love. In the poem *Saloniki*, his imaginary visions are confronted with the contemporary reality, being so far from them. Perez does not reconstruct any topography of the city,[5] but only says it is quite different today. Salonika before the Holocaust and after it is, in the author's eyes, two different cities, there is no continuity between them. Thus, the final truth is that the Sephardic Salonika no longer exists. It is so vividly uttered in the ending of the poem:

Un djoven atento
Eskuzandose, me dize:
No le des atension.
Me parese ke tienes un yerro en el nombre.
No ay aki ninguna Saloniki,
Nunca no uvo ...
Provate otra vez,
No agora, no aki ...[6]
Saloniki.[7]

[A courteous young man/Begging pardon tells me:/Do not be concerned with it/I think you have made a mistake with the name./There is no Saloniki here./There never was .../Try again/Not now, not here—/Saloniki.]

It sounds very dramatic, "not now, not here"—what is left today is only emptiness. This sense of emptiness, with the feeling of mourning, the poet expressed also earlier in the volume *Siniza i fumo*, where, in the title poem, he depicted an image of the place as if after catastrophe:

Siniza i fumo
Bolando, kayendo
En un esfuenyo malo
Sin salvasion.

En la guerta kemada
Asentada la fija
Pasharos pretos

Apretan su korason.
[…]
Por los sielos, ariva
Pasa la luna
Tapando su kara
Kon una nuve – karvon. (Perez 1986: 6)

[Ashes and smoke/flying around, falling/In a bad dream/Without redemption.//In the burned garden/The girl sitting/Black birds/Oppress her heart./[…]/High up in the sky/The moon goes by/Hiding its face/with a coalblack cloud.]

Hitherto, in the texts discussed above, neither the contemporary city nor its Greek inhabitants care about, or empathize with, the Jews deploring those who died in the Shoah. In *Siniza i fumo*, conversely, the whole cosmos unites with them in grief.

The image of the burnt garden, in Perez, reveals some similarity to the vision of the burnt home and yard from *Kurtijo kemado* by Matitiahu. Both visions become symbols of the annihilation of Sephardic culture in the Balkans during World War II. Matitiahu mentions a sort of force of attraction that makes her keep coming back, both literally and mentally, to the place, where sources of her Sephardic identity are. But such a journey turns out to be also a journey in time, a difficult and exhausting experience—because one of the inevitable stations is the Holocaust:

A mi esprito keria dar
La libertad de fuir,
El kurtijo kemado
Me azia sinios
Sin dizir. (Matitaihu 1988: 25)

[To my spirit I wanted to give/The freedom to flee/The burned courtyard/Was gesturing to me/Without speaking.]

Nevertheless, we will see that Matitiahu will not end her journey by reflecting on this station – for to establish her cultural identity she also needs a variety of scenes from traditional Sephardic life, which she will depict in the volume *Alegrika*, trying to revive old Jewish courtyards. But, besides Matitiahu, the longing for such courtyards could be heard also in the poem *Silencio* (Silence) by Rita Gabbaï-Simantov (1992: 25), who lives in Greece. There, she expresses her empathy with a passer-by that wanders across the Greek streets, perhaps someone seeking for the "pre-history of his own biography". The poetic voice of the poem talks about non-existence of Jewish quarters, courtyards and the Sabbath tales in Salonika. Instead, in the places where they used to be only silence is to be found.

Silent and empty is also Istanbul in the poetic vision of Denise León, an Argentinian poet, whose grandparents were born in Turkey. The words of Elizabeth Bishop "Piensa en el largo viaje a casa" ["Think of the long trip home"] (León 2008: 59), used by the author as an epigraph to the volume of verses *Poemas de Estambul* ("Poems of Istanbul"), suggest that León treats this city as a point of reference in tracing her biography and forming her identity. Still, as Elisa Martín Ortega has remarked, it does not at all resemble the actual Istanbul (Martín Ortega 2011: 355). Its name appears only in the title of the whole book of poems and of one of its parts. One cannot find an aspiration for her reconstructing the topography of the place. Moreover, its image, which we try to figure when reading, turns out not to have any similarity to a typical urban landscape. The city, identified here as "esta sivdad" [this city] (León 2008: 60) appears only in the first poem, where it is left behind—a V-formation of birds is moving away from it, while the city is wavering on the edge of memory and oblivion. The poetic voice verbalizes the fear against oblivion of an unidentified "thou". If we treat the poems as her dialog with herself, we may come to the conclusion that what is sought here is a part of her own self—a part without which she cannot fully understand her "being-in-the-world". But it is also possible that this "thou" refers to another person, probably important for her to form her own identity, for example her mother, who is to be spoken about two poems further. In various poems different elements are dispersed—so that together they give us a fragmentary picture of the city of the title of the book. Its landscape consists of the sea, whose waves are reaching the pillow on the bed, some stones and pebbles that can be touched, salt and ashes, a courtyard described as "kurtijo de ausensias" ["a courtyard of absence"] (*ibid.*: 70), the mother's room seen through the keyhole, and a window. Both open spaces and house interiors merge into each other, although the latter are predominant: silent places, either deprived of people's presence or full of night shadows. One has the feeling that León's poetic journey is the travel into the internal "spaces" of her own memory or consciousness.

3. THE POETIC PORTRAITS OF PERSONS AND THE REMINISCENCES OF THE SOUND OF LADINO

The sphere of memory in the Sephardic poetry involves not only the places that are crucial for the biography and identity of the authors, but also the persons who play an equivalent role, i.e. who are regarded as symbols of old Sephardic culture. Typically, it is the relatives, neighbors or friends from before World War II in the Turkish-Balkan Diaspora, who play this role. They led, or remember from their childhood, the traditional Jewish life with all its customs, feast days and the Ladino language. Their stories sound authentic, for they were either participants of that life, or its witnesses. Frequently, the deceased parents and grandparents are recalled, and the poems devoted to them comprise the authors' own recollections of their childhood and youth, and sometimes evoke the stories about the former Jewish world heard from those people.

The portraits of parents—embodying a feeling of security and parental love – appear in the poem quoted above, *La sivda miya* by Gracia Albuhayre, where the author confesses with nostalgia that in her home town the house of her father does not exist anymore, her mother is not waiting for her to give her a hug. She is disappointed at not meeting any of her old friends, nor any of her neighbors. It is the absence of all these people that makes her feel ill at ease in the town where she spent her childhood and youth. The figure of the mother appears also in the Albuhayre's poem *Komo musika* ("Like music") (Jak Albuhayre 2007: 4), which concerns "djudezmo-espanyol",[8] the language of Sephardic Jews. It was just her mother that taught her to speak this language and its sound will always make the author think of her. Moreover, in the text of *Kantika de mi madre* ("My mother's song") Albuhayre says that her mother was just the person who showed her the continuity of the Sephardic heritage:

> La kaza moestra kedo leshos,
> muy leshos—en Toledo.
> Ayi kedaron la kama y la kuna.
> […]
> Pasimos kaminos largos, largos,
> kaminos no konosidos.
> En la sivda ajena agora bivimos,
> ma la alma en Toledo deshimos. (Albuhayre 2011: 1)
>
> [We left our house far away/very far—in Toledo./The bed and cradle were left there./[…]/ We walked long, long roads/unknown roads./We now live in a foreign town,/but we left our soul in Toledo.]

Similarly, in the poetry of Matitiahu, the mother is presented as a person who played the role of the main link binding her with the sources of Sephardity. The mother is, in her production, the figure that is the most often evoked. The mother and daughter relationship is the subject of the poem *Alegrika* (Matitiahu 1992: 31–39), in which the uniqueness of this relation is captured. In fragment A, the daughter tries to search her memory for the gentle voice of her mother uttering her name, and for the image of her own as a small girl. In the subsequent scenes, the author presents her mother as the one who formed her personality and taught her the life. It is the voice of the women, so to speak, that gives the first shapes the child's personality. The most significant here is scene C, where the daughter, yet again called by her mother, is watching with interest how she is pulling the jewelry from an intricately crafted jewel case. The woman tries the jewelry on, and soon also the daughter, all dressed up, comes out. This situation becomes a symbol of handing down the woman's art of living, but also the tradition[9] and culture. But in fragments E and F we see the converse. Here, it is the daughter—after the death of the mother—that attempts to give shape to the mother's image, now getting more and more blurred in her consciousness.

The next author who brought up the theme of handing down the tradition, in the female line, is Gabbaï-Simantov. In the poem *Shabat* (Gabbaï-Simantov 1992: 30) she captured the scene, where her grandmother is admonishing her daughter-in-law, the author's mother, to observe the Sabbath. The feast day is depicted in its most typical aspects such as festive Sabbath clothes, food, candles. A more detailed portrait of the grandmother may be found, in Gabbaï-Simantov, in the poem *Kuando nona se vistia* ("When grandma was getting dressed") (Gabbaï-Tazartès 2007: 147), where some magical distance between the girl and the mature woman is rendered. The girl is looking at the grandma dressing up elegantly before paying someone a visit, which is for her a sort of strange and mysterious activity, although she, at the same time, feels it is a somewhat important thing to celebrate on occasions.

Coming back to Matitiahu, it is worth noting that *Alegrika* is not her only poem presenting her strong relationship with her mother. One might also claim that her need for poetic expression in Ladino stems from her experience of grief after her mother's death. The image of the mother's figure will always be in her mind in her journey to Greece – her parents' homeland—and Spain, the country of Sephardic origins. When visiting Salonika, Matitiahu is looking for what she remembers from her mother's stories about this former Sephardic city—she is looking at it from the perspective of these remembrances ("Mezo las memorias plantadas en mi por mi madre" ["Through the memories planted in me by my mother"]) (Matitiahu 1988: 17). She has the feeling as if her both deceased parents were there, as if she heard their voices uttering the names of the streets:

Sintia nombres de kayes
Kon la bos de mi padre
I sobre mis ombros konsentia
Los brasos de mi madre. (*ibid.*: 19)

[I was hearing street names/in my father's voice/and on my shoulders I felt/my mother's arms.]

In Athens, the murmur of water in the fountain reminds her, in a way, of the sound of the Ladino language, and thus of her family at home in Tel-Aviv. She is observing the people passing by, trying to search out in their faces the features of her parents (Matitiahu 1992: 43), and hears the warm voice of her mother – which is a sign of her presence:

> En mi memoria subió
> la dulce voz de mi madre
> que me acompañaba
> como un mirador … (Matitiahu 2001: 68)
>
> [In my memory arose/the sweet voice of my mother/who came along with me/like a guardian.]

In the poem *Me visto tu cara sobre la mia* ("I put your face on mine") (Matitiahu 1997: 64) the poet feels as if her deceased mother could see again her old, beloved city and touch its stones – just thanks to the author's presence in this city. But also in her poetic reports from the journey to Spain she stresses that her attachment to and love of this land is a deep feeling that she inherited directly from her mother (Matitiahu 2001: 55). It is there that she also attempts to discover the more ancient—to quote once more this phrase—"pre-history of her own biography":

> Yo, como una hoja
> que llegó con el aire de la poesía,
> abají al nido de raíces y ramas
> encontrando lo pasado
> de los abuelos de mis abuelos. (*ibid.*: 52)
>
> [I, like a leaf/that arrived with the wind of poetry/went down to the nest of roots and branches/finding the past/of my grandparents' grandparents.]

Correspondingly, the sound of contemporary Spanish evokes—for her, living in Israel and usually speaking Hebrew—associations with the language heard at home in her childhood and youth.

The special relationship between Iberian or Latin American Spanish and Judeo-Spanish is to be found in Denise León, whose volume *Poemas de Estambul* is divided into two parts: one in Castilian, *La isla de Alicia* ("Alice's Island") and one in Ladino—*Poemas de Estambul*. Striving, in her poetic work, to search out a part of her own self, she resorts to the language of her ancestors, which sounded, in the past, in conversations between her grandparents, or, perhaps, between her parents. Judeo-Spanish is not her native language, but through its affinity to Argentine Spanish, which is, it can also become the language of her poetry, and by this can be treated as a means that gives her an access to the otherwise unattainable part of her own identity. In her poems one will not find any portraits of persons, and the presence of people is sometimes merely suggested. It is revealed only in some shots and fragmentary pictures: "pieses de alguja/oyos maví" ["feet of needle/eyes of the color of fate"] (León 2008: 68), "una boz/ke es la manyana" ["a voice/which is tomorrow"] (*ibid.*: 64), "el kurtijo de ausensias" (*ibid.*: 70). Once she also writes about the shadows kissing her heart. The world is enveloped in unsettling darkness of the night (*cfr.* Martín Ortega 2011: 356)—the world remembered, or, rather, unremembered—since it precedes what she herself is able to embrace with her memory. Her poems seem to penetrate not only the spheres of her memory, but also the spheres of memory of her parents and grandparents, while the only keys to those spheres are recollections of their stories and just the sound of the language they spoke.

In Matitiahu one could also find shadows wanting to be heard and voices screaming from the walls of the room. Like the poetic voice in the poetry of León, who groped around with her hands for the city's stones, she also feels around with her hands for the past, and "the past like a sail is unfolding before her" (*cfr*. Matitiahu 2001: 30). Yet, Matitiahu's visions take much more specific forms. It is clearly visible in the volume *Alegrika*, where the courtyard—previously presented by her as a "burnt courtyard" (the volume *Kurtijo kemado*), and by León as a "courtyard of absence" (in the *Poemas de Estambul*)—here comes alive with people. They come out of their inexistence with the objects they used, the colors, scents and sounds that accompanied them in their own lifetime. In *Los vizajes* ("Characters") (Matitiahu 1992: 14–27) she creates an image of a traditional Sephardic *kurtijo*, with the people who used to spend time in it. She portraits each of them, depicting his or her characteristic features, gestures or behaviors. Among them are such figures as *tia* Dudun—a cat feeder; *tia* Diamante —singing traditional songs in Ladino; *tio* Shabtay—drowning his sorrows in uzzo and retzina; Yudachi Bahar—whispering the words of a prayer; Sunhula—an overworked laundress; *tia* Ester, in a smell of garlic, who tells off the children playing too noisily; and finally, an unnamed heroin of the poem *Las paredes del tiempo* ("The walls of time") (*ibid.*: 25)—the mother of a large family, who knows very well what the fire of desire means. They are representatives of the bygone Sephardic world—of homesteads and courtyards, mainly from Salonika, but also from Izmir—which Matitiahu cherishes with nostalgia in her heart and memory. They are captured in the situations typical of what used to take place in old Sephardic courtyards, still we have no certainty whether they are just there or in some other place; the memory of those courtyards can be read from their faces. The poems devoted to them resemble descriptions of old, fading photographs.[10] Time flows slowly here, the scenes are lit with the gentle afternoon's light, the shapes are modeled with chiaroscuro, the *kurtijos* are full of smells typical of it, silence reigns around, being from time to time interrupted by the children playing, by *tia* Lea's muttering, by a voice singing a *romanca*, or by the melodious intonation of a prayer.

A similar gallery of portraits representing the types of people from Sephardic quarters in the Turkish-Balkan Diaspora is created by Gabbaï-Simantov in the poems which in the last edition of her poetry *Poezias de mi vida* ("Poems of my life") are gathered in a separate section, *Salonik i Estambol*. The poems mentioned above *Shabat* and *Kuando nona se vistia* – coming just from this section – are not only personal recollections of her family members, but they also commemorate traditions and customs that used to be more commonly practiced formerly than they are today. Such a sense is to be seen in *El aynara* (Gabbaï-Tazartès 2007: 154), describing the practices of protecting someone against a cast spell—with a prayer, an amulet or another magic spell. This poem commemorates, in the figure of Madam Ester, also the type of women that dealt with lifting spells. Another work, *El dervish* (*ibid.*: 157), refers to the stories told by the poet's grandmother and deals with a custom, popular among women, of visiting a dervish so that he would tell them whether their husbands love them. In the poems in question, some figures have been depicted with special esteem, and in the strophes that speak about them, one can feel respect for their fate and their job. These are usually simple souls, whose lives are full of ordinary duties, such as the diligent carrier Itzhak—the father of a numerous family; the *shamash* from the Synagogue, calling men in for prayers and caring for the *minyan* to gather; *tia* Mazalto—laundress, overworked but always cheerful; the beggar Zhakucho, who kept sharing what he had got with other needy people. But there are also figures that have been presented jokingly or humorously, and their poetic portraits can be seen as a satire on human vices, behaviors and tragicomic situations. This is, for example, the case of the stingy *tia* Gracia; of the mother-in-law of poor Yako, buttering in over and over again; it is true about the ugly marriageable girls; about Abramiko, who is handsome but very picky about his future wife; and about the dressmaker Lea, equally fussy about her future husband. Some of the poems are pointed with a Sephardic proverb.[11] Like in Matitiahu's *Los vizajes*, also here we have a gallery of figures representative for bygone Sephardic communities, yet in the Israeli poet (Matitiahu) the reflection on human life going by is predominant, and the tone of nostalgia for the old way of life comes to the fore. In Gabbaï-Simantov such nostalgia is less perceptible, due to the humorous tone of some of her poems, despite the fact that she also wants to preserve the old forms of life in her poetry.

Another picture of the former Jewish community of Salonika is embedded also in the work *Eluenga kortada* ("The cut tongue") by Avner Perez. In the first part of this poem, the author creates an image of a quiet pre-war life, where Salonika presents itself as paradise, in which the angels—speaking in Judeo-Spanish, no less—enjoy to stay:

> En el charshi avlavan kon tio Gavriel el peshkador,
> A las bodas, kon Bona la tanyedera,
> En el meldar kon ham Bohor
> Uzavan a oir la perasha kon su ladino;
> I a la tadre venian a dar la beraha
> A los chikos en la kuna. (Perez 1986: 26)
>
> [In the market square they used to speak with *tio* Gavriel, the fisherman
> In the weddings with Bona, the tambourine-player
> In the children's school with Rabbi Bohor

They used to listen to the Bible reading of the week and its translation
And in the evening they used to come to give the blessing
To the babies in the cradle.]

What appears in this vision is both the common people—such as a fisherman or a folk musician—and a learned person reading out the Torah in the religious school. A special place here is taken by the image of infants in cradles—scenes quite frequent in the culture, in which large families were common. Yet, when juxtaposed with the Shoah, which is the topic of the next stanzas, it becomes a symbol of the wrecked hopes for the future. After the Shoah, only one angel, lonely and mutilated, with the tongue cut out, searches for life in post-war Salonika, but in vain. Especially meaningful is the thought that the angel is just looking for babies in cradles, yet they are no longer there. How much in common he has with the stray passer-by from the poem *Silencio* by Gabbaï-Simantov, who, in the place formerly populous and full of Sephardic culture, faces only emptiness and silence.

Another insight into the rich Ladino culture can be also found in Perez's cycle of three poems entitled *Sarina*, from the volume *Verdjel de mansanas* ("Apple tree orchard"). The figure of the title character has much in common with the poet's grandmother as remembered in his memory.[12] The significant fact is that the life-giving place of Sephardic culture is the *kurtijo*, understood, on the one hand, as a private space—a personal and family one—and, on the other hand, as a junction of many neighborly and communal ties. The charm of the courtyard is epitomized by the ubiquitous smell of jasmine (*cfr.* Perez 1996: 2). Water as well as fish, the latter appearing in a surrealistic, oneiric vision, symbolize fertility and, in a broader sense, also life being led on the *kurtijo* and being revived in new generations. Around the figure of Sarina—a young, scantily dressed woman singing in the *kurtijo*—an air of eroticism definitely stretches; and the first two poems may be simply interpreted as love poetry. Still, Sarina is taken not only to give rise to new life in the literal sense of being able to give birth. Equally essential is the fact that she is also the mistress of a *romance* (folk ballad): she performs and hands over the pieces that belong to this genre. Thus, the poems devoted to her turn out to be also the reflection on the current condition of Judeo-Spanish literature.

In the text *Melizelda* (*ibid.*: 4), a woman appears in the courtyard on a sleepless night and is having a vision—in the sky, she sees Melizelda, the emperor's daughter, coming out from her bath. Here again, Perez pays tribute to the genre of *romance*, alluding to the particular piece *Melizelda, Melizelda la ija del enperante* ("Melizelda, Melizelda, the emperor's daughter") (Perez 2006: XIII). By this, he partly refers also to the current of mystical literature, since this *romance* was included in the group of prayers sung by the Dönmeh sect. The Dönmeh believed it to be of special importance for Sabbatai Zevi—a religious leader taken, by them, to be the Messiah. He reportedly used to sing it, when putting the scrolls of to

Torah to *aron ha-kodesh*, or when leaving *mikvah*. Hence, he must have thought of Melizelda as the personification of *Shekhinah,* the Presence of God (*ibid*.: III).

Similar references to the genres of oral literature are made, in Perez, in the poems *Kantiga de kuna para Selanik* ("Lullaby for Salonika") (Perez 1986: 14) and *La romansa de Rika Kuriel, novia de sangre*, ("Romance of Rika Kuriel, bride of blood") (*ibid.*: 18), both coming from the volume of verses *Siniza i Fumo*. However, Perez does not simply imitate the old genres, instead he draws on literary allusions, affording, in this way, his pieces a modern form of expression. This can be understood as a way to preserve, or revive, Ladino literature. It can also be thought of as an element of his strategy of the re-discovery of the past. For our understanding of Perez's diagnosis concerning the current condition of the Judeo-Spanish culture it is important to take into account also the last poem of the cycle *Sarina—Roza agonizando* (Rose in agony) (Perez 1996: 6). It is deprived of the dynamism and ecstatic aura characteristic of the two poems discussed earlier. Here, Sarina, sad and pale, is coming from a wake, where, as she says, she kissed the rose lying on her deathbed. The rose in agony, mentioned in the title, can be interpreted just as the Ladino language culture, and the very poem remains in harmony with two other poems from *Siniza i Fumo*: *El milagro de la lingua* ("The miracle of the language") (Perez 1986: 32–33) and *La galaksia eskuresida* ("The darkended galaxy") (*ibid.*: 36–38). What is common to both *Roza agonizando* and *El milagro de la lingua* is the form of dialogue between a woman and an interlocutor who asks her some similar questions. In *El milagro* ... the woman speaks about her difficult effort to try to keep the language alive, which resembles gathering ashes in a burnt garden, or planting trees in a barren land—in a word, this borders on insanity. The language itself has been compared to the phoenix, slowly rising from the ashes, which in each successive stanza displays some new signs of life, yet we can never see it flying on its own. Perhaps the conclusion of the efforts undertaken by the woman in question, the efforts to save the life of Judeo-Spanish, is just, regrettably, only *Roza agonizando*. Perez himself confesses that when he began writing poetry in Ladino, first he was a moderate optimist, but with the passing of time he painfully realized that less and less people spoke it and needed to read literature in the language of their ancestors.[13] Therefore, the threat is real that Ladino will soon become only, as he says in *La galaksia eskuresida*, the language of the dead, of the ones that inhabit the dark galaxy.

4. CONCLUSION

The reading of contemporary Judeo-Spanish poetry shows that the rediscovery of the past constitutes one of the most important themes in it. The authors, in their poetic representations, endeavor either to reconstruct or to imagine the places that are important for their own past or the past of their families, but also those that are essential for the history of the Sephardim. Apart from the places, they also commemorate persons that link them with the bygone world of Sephardic communities. Moreover, they present in poems the scenes of traditional Jewish life, associated with the heyday of their culture before the Holocaust. The need to return to these motifs and themes is a result of the fact that the authors find them essential for exploring their cultural identity. The fact that these motifs appear in different authors, belonging to different generations, reveals the existence of a common imagery, or common imagined representations, that are components of their understanding of Sephardity. Thus, we can speak of Sepharad as imagined community—such a phenomenon exists. In many cases, the key to the memory—both in individual and communal aspects—as well as its carrier, becomes Ladino, which formerly was the main element of Sephardic identity. The act of giving it the status of the language of poetry is especially meaningful today, in a time when it is regarded as a dying language.

NOTES

1. This chapter has been translated from the Polish by Tomasz Zarębski.
2. In this text I use the term Ladino in the broad, common meaning as equivalent to living Judeo-Spanish (also known as Judezmo), not in its technical and more precise sense—as the name of the language that used to be employed to translate the Hebrew Bible.
3. The phrase is taken from Olschowsky 2007: 454.
4. In the poem *Una kaza* ("A house") the poetic voice confesses that she often returns in dreams to her family home (Albuhayre 2011: 24).
5. One can speak about the author's intention to render a landscape, or to reconstruct a fragmentary topography of a place, in the poem *Lunes 15.3.1943* ("Monday 15.3.1943"), which describes the first day of transportations of the Jews of Salonika to Auschwitz. Here, the city constitutes the background of the poem and, at the same time, is its main character. For, on the one hand, what has been captured in the poetic images are the changing times of the day (a morning with the moon going off, and, in the ending of the poem, the sunset) and the city's main landmarks such as the railway station, the square adjacent to it and *Beyaz Kule* (the White Tower). On the other hand, the city functions as a metonymy and as such stands for its Jewish inhabitants. In the text, it and they form one inseparable, not to say organic, whole. It is its body—representing both the collective body of the crowd and bodies of individual victims—which is the subject of violence: the portentous, sinister panting of the steam engine reaches its ears together with the shouts of the Nazis, its skin and muscles receive blows, it experiences fear in an utterly physiological way, and finely its heart is stabbed with a knife, or shot with a gun, and is bleeding to death.
6. My emphasis.
7. I obtained this version of the text from Avner Perez. A slightly different version of this poem was published in Refael 2008: 282–283.
8. In the analyzed poem she refers to the language with this word.
9. In the previous fragment B, the girl is accompanying her mother in the preparations for Sabbath.

10. It is worth noticing that on the cover of this volume is a collage made of the scraps of author's family photographs (information given by Matitiahu in private talk on February 24, 2011).
11. In this way Gabbaï-Simantov revives proverbs, the smallest genre of oral literature—today rather forgot, but formerly in common use.
12. Information given by Perez in private talk on February 16, 2011.
13. *Cfr.* Sevilla-Sharon 1982: 18–19. Perez also developed this subject in his talk with the author of this paper on February 16, 2011.

REFERENCES

Albuhayre, Gracia. *Poezia en djudeo-espanyol. Livro no. 2*. Sophia: "Erensia", 2011.
Gabbaï-Simantov, Rita. *Quinientos Anios Despues*. Athens: n.p., 1992.
Gabbaï-Tazartès, Rita. *Poezias de mi vida*. Paris: El Mundo Djudeo-Espanyol, 2007.
Jak Albuhayre, Gracia. *Poezia en djudeo (espanyol)*. Sofia: n.p., 2007.
León, Denise. *Poemas de Estambul*. Córdoba (Argentina): Alción, 2008.
Martín Ortega, Elisa. "I una boz ke es la manyana": El judeoespañol como lengua del rescate en la obra poética de Denise León". In *Del verbo al espejo. Reflejos y miradas de la literatura hispánica*. Edited by Pilar Caballero-Alías, Ernesto Félix Chávez, Blanca Ripoll Sintes, 353–361. Barcelona: PPU, 2011.
Matitiahu, Margalit. *Kurtijo kemado*. Tel Aviv: Eked, 1988.
Matitiahu, Margalit. *Alegrika*. Tel Aviv: Eked, 1992.
Matitiahu, Margalit. *Vela de la luz*. León: Ponte Aérea, 1997.
Matitiahu, Margalit. *Vagabundo eterno (Vagabondo eternel)*. León: Colección Aljama, 2001.
Olschowsky, Heinrich. "Arkadia i Hades. Podróże wydziedziczonych po kataklizmie wojny. Tadeusz Różewicz *Et in Arcadia ego* (1961) i Günther Anders *Besuch im Hades* (1966)." In *Dziedzictwo Odyseusza. Podróż, obcość i tożsamość, identyfikacja, przestrzeń*. Edited by Maria Cieśla-Korytowska and Olga Płaszczewska, 449–459. Kraków: Universitas, 2007.
Perets, Avner. "Siniza i fumo". *Aki Yerushalayim*, 21 (Avril 1984): 27.
Perez, Avner. *Siniza i Fumo*. Yerushalayim: Ed. Sefarad, 1986.
Perez, Avner. *Verdjel de Mansanas*. Maale Adumim: Yeriot, 1996.
Perez, Avner, ed. *Agua, Fuego i Amor. Gazeles i Kantes Mistikos de los Sabetaistas*. Maale Adumim: Instituto Maale Adumim, 2006.
Perez, Avner. "Agua fuego I amor. Introduksion". In *Agua, Fuego i Amor. Gazeles i Kantes Mistikos de los Sabetaistas*. Edited by Avner Perez, I-XII. Maale Adumim: Instituto Maale Adumim, 2006.
Refael, Shmuel. *Un grito en el silencio. La poesía sobre el Holocausto en lengua sefardí: estudio y antología*. Barcelona: Tirocinio, 2008.
Refael, Shmuel. "The Geography of the Memory: The Representation of the Pre-Holocaust Salonican Jewish Community in the Post-Holocaust Sephardic Poetry." *eHumanista*, 20 (2012): 321–333. [http://www.ehumanista.ucsb.edu/volumes/volume_20/pdfs/articles/monographic%20issue/16%20Refael.v20.pdf.].
Sevilla-Sharon, Moshe. "Entrevista con: Avner Perets. El avenir del djudeo-espanyol: kreasion literaria i modernizasion." *Aki Yerushalayim*, 13–14 (1982): 18–19.

CHAPTER FOURTEEN

En tierras virtualas

Sociolinguistic Implications for Judeo-Spanish as a Cyber-vernacular

REY ROMERO
University of Houston-Downtown

ABSTRACT

Although Judeo-Spanish is considered an endangered language, characterized by decreasing domains and a reduced speaker population, modern web-based tools have encouraged the creation of cyber-spaces where the language functions as the sole means of communication. These Judeo-Spanish online communities bring together speakers otherwise separated by geography, and promote a space for language use and maintenance. In addition, these online groups may also provide invaluable data for sociolinguistic research.

1. INTRODUCTION

The plight of the Judeo-Spanish language is echoed in the traditional *kantika* chorus *en tierras ajenas yo me vo murir*, I shall die in a foreign land. And, following this fate, modern Judeo-Spanish is not spoken by a cohesive group in a closely-knit and defined geographical space, but has managed to survive in Jewish communities throughout the territories of the former Ottoman Empire and their subsequent diaspora to Europe, the Americas, and Israel. In addition to geographical distances among these communities, Judeo-Spanish lacks robust intergenerational transmission, and it is spoken at several levels of proficiency and in limited domains, mostly by the older generations. However, in spite of this pessimistic linguistic landscape, Judeo-Spanish has found a new space in the virtual world, *tierras virtualas*. Thanks to web-based tools and advances in electronic communication, Judeo-Spanish users have recreated a digital homeland (Held 2010) in which they can once again utilize their heritage language and promote its maintenance and value.

In this chapter, I plan to contribute to the study of Judeo-Spanish as a cyber-vernacular in light of recent research (Held 2010, Brink-Danan 2011) and new online spaces that facilitate building these cyber-communities. I will situate these online spaces within the context of language domains and provide a survey of several Judeo-Spanish online communities. I will then consider methodological issues and implications relevant to conducting linguistic research in these cyberspace communities, and provide sociolinguistic data and results from the Ladinokomunita (LK) group. The continuous diversity and growth of online communities offer a new set of potential and limitations for sociolinguistic research that have only recently been explored in the context of endangered and Jewish languages.

2. LANGUAGE DOMAINS AND CYBER-VERNACULARS

The assessment of current language domains is central to determine the level of language endangerment. In fact, a Graded Intergenerational Disruption Scale (GIDS) has been proposed to determine the current domains in which an endangered language is used, consolidate its social function, and then strategize its subsequent revitalization (Fishman 1991).

Although bilingualism is required to initiate language shift, it does not always result in language death. A bilingual population may exhibit a diglottic situation in which both languages are used in most social contexts. However, a most-typical scenario is one language assigned or allocated to some domains while another language is exclusively used in others (Dorian 1981, 74–5). Language endangerment begins when the language considered the prestige or official variety, progressively takes over the domains of the heritage language (Schmidt 1985, 4). Eventually, the minority language is reserved to very specific and limited domains, usually not vital to the economic survival of the community, and eventually the endangered language dies when intergenerational transmission fails and it is no longer used. Although language endangerment may occur in immigrant communities who experience extraordinary social pressure for linguistic acculturation to the national language and lead to language death within a few generations, it may also occur in stable monolingual or bilingual situations due to sociopolitical changes and laws governing language policy.

All modern Judeo-Spanish communities exhibit reduced language domains. Harris's (1979) research in the United States and Israel identified six domains in which modern Judeo-Spanish was still used: (1) language of the home, (2) language of the older generation, (3) a secret or code language, (4) the language of entertainment, (5) lingua franca for Sephardim, and (6) modified or accommodated to Peninsular or Latin American Spanish for professional use. More than thirty years later, these domains prevail, but not as robust. Judeo-Spanish continues to be the language of the home for some speakers in Istanbul (Romero 2012, 93), the Prince Islands (Romero 2011, 171), Thessaloniki (Christodouleas 2008, 33), and to a lesser degree in Israel (Kushner Bishop 2004, 64–68). However, it seems the language exists in the home domain only when there is an older relative present, that is, domain 2 is intricately related to domain 1. In Istanbul more than two-thirds of Romero's informants were age fifty or older, and in the Prince Islands most were forty or older (Romero 2012, 70; Romero 2011, 163). In Thessaloniki too, more than three-fourths of participants were older than fifty (Christodouleas 2008, 81), and even in earlier studies such as Luria's (1930) research in Monastir (modern Bitola, Macedonia), Sala's (1971) work in Bucharest, and Harris's (1979) results from New York City and Israel revealed that most fluent speakers were fifty or older (Luria 1930, 9; Sala 1971, 15; Harris 1979, 111). This is a critical age group since intergenerational transmission is key for language survival. The third language domain, Judeo-Spanish as a secret or code language, was reported recently in the Prince Islands (Romero 2011, 173) and Istanbul (Romero 2012, 95–97). It also seems that several heritage speakers and semispeakers were exposed to the language mostly whenever the parents or grandparents wanted to share information without the knowledge of the children or younger generation. In Romero (2012), some members of the younger generation also reported using Judeo-Spanish as a code language, or at least a few Judeo-Spanish code words in Turkish discourse, to avoid disclosing information to strangers.

Judeo-Spanish as the language for entertainment is still present in Istanbul (Romero 2012, 97–98), the Prince Islands (Romero 2011, 171–172), Israel (Kushner Bishop 2004, 155–219), and Thessaloniki (Christodouleas 2008, 33). This function is preserved mostly by the older generation in its traditional form. However, because of the cultural and linguistic content of Judeo-Spanish songs and folk narratives, most modern revitalization efforts address the preservation and fomentation of this particular domain. In several Sephardic communities, these performances serve to create linguistic spaces and promote interest in learning Judeo-Spanish among the younger generation.

The fifth domain establishes Judeo-Spanish as the lingua franca of Sephardim living in the post-Ottoman diaspora. After independence, most countries in former Ottoman territories sought to consolidate governance through a series of nationalistic policies, including official language statutes. This, in addition to the subsequent diaspora to Western Europe, the Americas, and Israel, increased the intra-familial linguistic repertoire of individuals having relatives in countries were the official language was Turkish, Romanian, French, English, and Hebrew, etc. In some families, Judeo-Spanish is the only language members have in common, and therefore it functions as such, but only sporadically and without a defined linguistic space. In spite of this limited function, Judeo-Spanish as the lingua franca among relatives has been attested in earlier research in Bucharest Judeo-Spanish, where most Sephardim had already shifted to German or Romanian, but the older members managed to use the language with relatives outside the nuclear family (Sala 1971, 15). Even in some communities that are no longer linguistically cohesive, such as that in New York City, several informants expressed using Judeo-Spanish when talking to relatives, even if it was just for entertainment or to express concepts that would be hard to translate in English (Romero 2016, 391). In some instances, this domain introduced Peninsular and Latin American phonology and lexicon in Judeo-Spanish from relatives who moved to the United States and Latin America and were undergoing dialect accommodation (Romero 2012, 101; Romero 2013, 293). This is also a consequence of the sixth context listed in Harris (1979), since Judeo-Spanish may be used in the business or professional domain when modified to resemble other varieties of Spanish. Recent dialect accommodation studies (Romero 2013, Romero 2015, Romero 2016) suggest that most Judeo-Spanish speakers are aware of both phonological and lexical differences, but that lexical accommodation is the most common strategy.

These six domains are relevant because they represent the usage of Judeo-Spanish in modern Sephardic communities. Therefore, these domains play an important role in online communities, since Judeo-Spanish users are familiar with the vocabulary and concepts encompassed by these contexts. Amado Bortnick (2001) reflects on these domains in the *Ladinokomunita* Yahoo! forum (henceforth LK), as most messages in the beginning dealt with music, folklore, genealogy, and humorous stories (Amado Bortnick 2001, 5). However, as Held (2010) argues, virtual communities are not just mere spaces for communication, but they have the potential to become "a territory where a culture may be revitalized after having faced a state of severe decline" (Held 2010, 84). From this perspective, these "digital home-lands" use the Judeo-Spanish language as a vehicle to reconstitute Sephardic identity (Held 2010, 83). In other words, Judeo-Spanish is not a by-product of cultural and communal interaction, but rather it is the framework in which culture and community are built. The role these virtual communities play in language maintenance and revitalization is best exemplified by the growing number of domains in which Judeo-Spanish is now used as a cyber-vernacular. Taking the model of reversing language shift proposed by Fishman (1991), cyber Judeo-Spanish is now used to discuss politics and current events, science, religion, history, and even technological advances. Interestingly, although some offline Sephardic communities still use Judeo-Spanish in the religion domain, for the most part, in communities such as those in Turkey and Israel, Turkish and Hebrew have replaced the traditional Judeo-Spanish chants (Romero 2011, 173; Romero 2012, 77). Thus, virtual communities help restore recently-lost domains. The use of Judeo-Spanish in cyber communities has even led to literary and poetic creativity, as users who had hitherto not written anything in their heritage language gain confidence in their proficiency (Amado Bortnick 2001, 10–11). In groups such as *Geon Sefarad* and *Shohrei Ladino*, both on Facebook, even the younger members of the community participate and produce content in Judeo-Spanish. One could say that these digital homelands have succeeded in creating a viable space for the survival of Judeo-Spanish. According to Fishman's (1991) GIDS, modern offline Judeo-Spanish fluctuates between level 7 and 8, high in the endangered scale, since the language is used in peripheral domains, mostly by speakers who are 60 and older, fully integrated in society, and there is no active intergenerational transmission (Fishman 1991, 88–89; Romero 2012, 65–66). On the other hand, cyber Judeo-Spanish is used to discuss a wider array of domains, to produce literary works, and it is used by the younger generation. The language in virtual communities is probably closer to stage 1 or 2 in Fishman's scale (Fishman 1991, 105–109).

3. JUDEO-SPANISH ONLINE COMMUNITIES

Similar to the offline world, it is difficult to define clearly what constitutes the online speech community of an endangered language. For instance, there are no monolingual Judeo-Spanish communities, and therefore every community exhibits a wide range of bilingualism. In the healthier varieties of the language, it is the vernacular in one to five or six of the aforementioned domains, but there are also communities in which Judeo-Spanish is mostly a post-vernacular. That is, the usage of Judeo-Spanish has acquired a special meaning, like a performative act on its own, independent of the utterance's actual message (Shandler 2004, 20). This may also involve sporadic use of Judeo-Spanish through codeswitching, to denote cultural concepts and idioms, and to create an effect on the listener or reader.

In online communities or virtual territories, the parallelism is that the language can be considered a cyber-vernacular (CV) or a cyber-postvernacular (CPV), a terminology previously used to describe Yiddish cyber communities (Sadan 2010, 99–101; Shandler 2004, 20). Both Sadan (2010) and Shandler (2006) propose a postvernacular scale that ranges from the symbolic nature (semantic value) of using Yiddish to the "professionalized, aestheticized, academized, and ritualized" version of Yiddish (Shandler 2006, 153; Sadan 2010, 100–101). Since many online Judeo-Spanish users sometimes write using a professionalized and academized vocabulary obtained from dictionaries, but with the practical intention to communicate solely in Judeo-Spanish without codeswitching to Hebrew, English, or Turkish, the languages that would normally be used for that topic or domain. These cases where the language may be the product of CPV language policies but its use is more closely aligned with PV patterns, I have categorized as PV.

Table 1 illustrates the characteristics of the most significant Judeo-Spanish cyber communities, especially those who have expressed a policy of using only Judeo-Spanish as the vernacular. I have also included other groups that occasionally use it as a CV, but most commonly as a CPV. I have not included groups such as *Our Sephardic Family*, *Sephardic Diaspora* and *Klub de Elevos de Ladino Djudeo-Espanyol* (all in Facebook) where Judeo-Spanish is used more as a topic, rather than the method of communication.

Table 1. Significant Judeo-Spanish Communities Online.

Online community	Year founded	Platform	Members (March 2015)	Usage	Script
Ladinokomunita	2000	Yahoo!	1,518	CV	AY
Ladino Culture Forum	2002–2012	Tapuz	350	Mostly CPV	Mostly Hebrew
Shohrei Ladino	2003	Facebook	7,997	Mostly CPV	Mostly Hebrew
Lovers of Ladino Language, Music, and Culture	2006	Facebook	1,682	Mostly CPV	Several
Ohvei Ladino	2011	Facebook	34	CPV	Mostly Hebrew
Geon Sefarad	2012	Facebook	1,203	CV	Several
Bavajadas en Ladino	2013	Facebook	239	CPV	Several

Most of the communities in Table 1 are located within the Facebook platform. *Ladinokomunita* (henceforth LK) is the only significant community on Yahoo! *The Ladino Culture Forum* (*Forum Tarbut ha-Ladino*) hosted by the Israeli website Tapuz is no longer active, but I have included it here since it was part of Held's (2010) data and it lasted for almost ten years. The group slowly stopped using Judeo-Spanish (curiously most of the time in Hebrew script) and the last comments were almost always in Hebrew. Table 1 also illustrates that most communities use Judeo-Spanish as a CPV. Only LK and *Geon Sefarad* (henceforth GS) have established strict rules regarding the usage of Judeo-Spanish as the sole vernacular. LK goes as far as requiring the Aki Yerushalayim (AY) version of the Latin alphabet, since one of its goals is to promote AY as the standard method of spelling Judeo-Spanish (Amado Bortnick 2001, 7–8). In comparison, GS accepts any kind of orthographic representation, as long as the vernacular is Judeo-Spanish. Other

Facebook groups such as *Lovers of Ladino* and *Ohvei Ladino* post many videos or news related to Judeo-Spanish, and although its use is limited to CPV sharing space with languages such as Hebrew, English, Castilian Spanish, and Turkish, sometimes it exists as CV in some messages. Finally, *Bavajadas* provides a space where Judeo-Spanish is used only for the entertainment domain. The Facebook page has jokes translated into Judeo-Spanish, and members post videos too. However, there are no discussions or extensive communications between the members in Judeo-Spanish, and the language is not used as a CV for the most part. The fact that Facebook is the main platform for most of these cyber communities is both encouraging and risky. On one hand, Facebook is very popular with the younger generation, and those who seek these cyber communities are readily accepted and even learn to use Judeo-Spanish as a CV. This is a great way to revitalize the language and promote intergenerational transmission. However, relying solely on one platform can affect all cyber communities if it changes dramatically, imposes controversial regulations, or if it simply ceases to exist.

Besides these digital homelands, Judeo-Spanish users can find their language elsewhere in the Web. Some of these sites are actually extensions of offline services, such as the online version of the Turkish Jewish weekly Şalom (with one section in Judeo-Spanish) and the monthly *El Amaneser* (fully in Judeo-Spanish). More examples are the online Radio recordings of programs from *Radio Sefarad* and *Kol Israel*. More recently, *Orizontes: Una revista de kreasion manseva*, a new literary magazine completely in Judeo-Spanish was created in 2013 and published via the ISSUU platform. Interestingly, it has been the younger generation of Sephardim, organized via the Facebook forums, who decided to spearhead new literary productions in Judeo-Spanish; some stories even use the traditional Rashi script, formerly employed in secular works in the first decades of the twentieth century. There are also about 3,357 Wikipedia articles written in Judeo-Spanish on a wide range of topics. And, finally, there is a wide variety of Judeo-Spanish videos in YouTube, including the interview archives of the *Autoridad Nasionala del Ladino* and a plethora of Sephardic music. Although all these do not constitute cyber communities per se, they do provide linguistic material readily available online for didactic purposes.

4. METHODOLOGICAL CONSIDERATIONS FOR LINGUISTIC RESEARCH IN ONLINE COMMUNITIES

Cyber communities that use CV varieties of endangered languages represent an additional resource for the study of language variation and change. As previously mentioned, these digital homelands use the language in a wider array of topics than in their offline varieties. Several, such as LK and GS, have monolingual language policies where only the endangered language is allowed as the sole vernacular for communication. In addition, digital homelands have an "in-gathering" effect, in that the sole purpose of promoting heritage language use brings together competent speakers who may no longer be part of a cohesive speech community in the offline world. Having said this, the communication in these digital communities is not the same as in the offline world. To begin with, the interfaces require a written variety of the language, hence significant discussions on orthography and standardization have occurred. In addition, this written communication is asynchronous, that is, interactions do not take place at the same time, but participants have the time and opportunity to reflect before contributing to the forum or wall discussion.

The language of online communities can be best approached as a written corpus, albeit an ever-growing one. Schneider (2004) specified the requirements that written corpora must meet for sociolinguistic variationist analysis. First, written texts must be as close to speech as possible. This prerequisite is met in most digital homelands since Judeo-Spanish is mostly a spoken language, and it is rarely used in a formal or professional setting. In addition, the topics in such forums (recipes, jokes, stories, traditions) are generally discussed in an informal and colloquial tone, thereby reflecting offline usage. Academic and professional conversations in these forums do exist, albeit rarely. Finally, some orthographic representations, such as AY used in LK are highly phonetic, and studies on phonological variation may be possible. The second condition is that texts should come from different sources. Authors must come from a variety of social and age groups, different styles, and include both men and women (Schneider 2004, 71). This is true of even the smallest communities, as cyber space has created a new context and territory for the remaining speakers. For instance, LK, the largest PV community, has more than 1,500 members, from more than two dozen countries and growing (Amado Bortnick 2001, 3). LK users also come from a wide variety of ages, levels of bilingualism, second language background, social networks, and both men and women participate. The third requirement is that these texts have to comprise a large corpus with large token frequencies (Schneider 2004, 71). Since most of these digital homelands already contain thousands of messages, including the impressive number of 52,476 in LK, then these are sizable texts that can provide enough token distribution for the grammatical or lexical item in question. Furthermore, these communities continue to grow, they are not limited by space, and therefore their potential as corpora is just as great. Finally, Schneider (2004, 71) also requires that the written corpus must exhibit some level of variability, that is, that the number of tokens varies according to variables. Since both the morphological and lexical variationist analyses show variability according to the social variables in LK, then the fourth requirement is met. Therefore, using LK as an example of online communities as written corpora can provide additional information on sociolinguistic patterns in endangered languages.

However, availability does not equate permissibility. There are certain ethic and methodological issues that must be addressed when using data from digital homelands. Held (2010), Brink-Danan (2011), and Sadan (2011) do not mention any issues regarding consent in data gathering, but their work is more ethnographic than sociolinguistic, that is, the behavior of individuals is not recorded, but rather the patterns of a group as a whole. Amado Bortnick (2001) uses both personal names and initials, but her study is written from the first person perspective and it does not contain a linguistic analysis. Internet-mediated research (henceforth IMR) is still in its early stages, and only recently institutions, such as the British Psychological Society (British Psychological Society 2013) and the University of California at Berkeley (UCBCPHS 2014), have devised specific guidelines regarding privacy and consent. IMR is defined as research that utilizes data obtained from human participants using the internet and its associated technologies (British Psychological Society 2013, 3). Besides the universal ethical principles for the protection of human subjects such as respect for autonomy and dignity, scientific value, social responsibility, and maximizing benefits and minimizing harm, there are several stipulations specific to online communities.

Regarding privacy, the British Psychological Society (2013, 18) suggests that publishing the name or website of a discussion forum can compromise the anonymity of individuals or have a negative effect. Brink-Danan (2011) did try to anonymize LK in her study (Brink-Danan 2011, 107), citing anthropological ethics. However, these online communities are so specific (compare for instance, to an online forum in English on automobile parts), that it would be near to impossible to keep them in anonymity. On the other hand, given that Jewish populations (and several other immigrant groups and even autochthonous populations who speak an endangered language) experience harassment and persecution, the need to avoid compromising the safety of these digital homelands is self-evident. The job therefore must rest on the moderators of these groups, who must make a choice regarding membership and who have the ability to accept or discard posted messages. Moreover, the British Psychological Society (2013, 19) also indicates that pseudonyms and other usernames must be treated just like a person's real name. If such avatars or pseudonyms must be used in a reports or publications, consent from the participating individual must be obtained (UCBCPHS 2014, 3). Another critical point is to decide when to obtain informed consent and when to waive it. According to the UCBCPHS (2014, 4), data that are both already existing and public do not require CPHS review. Even data that may require log in or other steps to access (for example in Facebook and Yahoo! groups) may still qualify as public. For online communities, the researcher must determine if there is an expectation of privacy within the group. For instance, the difference between an online forum for recovering drug addicts versus a forum that promotes cultural events. Privacy is expected by the sensitive nature of the first. The researcher must be aware of what is considered public or private behavior, including information provided in profiles and avatars such as age, gender, geographical location, etc. (UCBCPHS 2014, 3–4). Consent may also be waived in non-reactive approaches to collect data, that is, when participants are not required to engage with any methodological materials, but their cyberspace behavior is observed unobtrusively, for instance through analyzing their produced online texts (British Psychological Society 2013, 3). If the investigator decides that indeed privacy is expected from participants and that their personal information is essential for the intended research, then consent must be sought. The CPHS of the University of California at Berkeley suggests that consent request should not disrupt normal group activity and that utmost sensitivity must be used when obtaining consent from online communities and chatrooms (UCBCPHS 2014, 3). Furthermore, the CPHS advises that researchers would benefit from having an insider's viewpoint to better determine questions on privacy expectations and informed consent. The UCBCPHS further warns that failure to identify such expectations or issues can lead to hostility from the online community, and that prior experience and sensitivity to the group, both online and offline, can increase the chance of being welcomed and conducting research more effectively (UCBCPHS 2014, 4). For the lexical and morphological studies in LK in the next section, the investigator did not identify any privacy issues, as these messages are written in an open forum for all members to read. Furthermore, no personal or private identifiable information was used as a sociolinguistic variable. The only social variable used, gender, was obtained from the usernames and avatars, and this was the only characteristic I understood I could use without dispersing a sociolinguistic questionnaire. Furthermore, I consulted with the moderators of the group, to make sure this kind of research was permissible and non-intrusive.

5. CHANGE AND VARIATION IN DIGITAL HOMELANDS: USING DATA FROM *LADINOKOMUNITA*

Following the methodological considerations detailed in section 3, I conducted two small variationist analyses on the lexicon and morphology of LK. The lexical variation study focuses on the distribution of *ma*, *ama*, and *pero*, synonymous forms for the adversative conjunction 'but.' I chose the distribution of a conjunction because conjunctions do not have inflection, and searching for exact tokens would facilitate the task. These three tokens also reflect several sociolinguistic bilingual patterns previously observed in the offline community. The first lexical item *ma* is the original Judeo-Spanish conjunction (possibly from Italian *ma* < Latin *magis*), and it was probably the only adversative conjunction in monolingual varieties of Judeo-Spanish. The second choice, *ama*, is Turkish, and its borrowing into Judeo-Spanish may be the result of five hundred years of language contact.

The conjunction *ma* is attested in Wagner's (1914) collection of Judeo-Spanish folktales from Istanbul, but not *ama*, and this may suggest the latter's incorporation as a result of intensified Turkish-only campaigns early in the twentieth century (Benbassa and Rodrigue 2000, 102). The use of *ama* does not necessarily suggest codeswitching, but it is important to understand its distribution in the discourse, especially in a forum where Judeo-Spanish is the mandatory vernacular. Finally, the last token *pero* is the conjunction used in all present-day Peninsular and Latin American varieties of Spanish. Following recent dialect accommodation studies (Romero 2013, Romero 2015, Romero 2016), Judeo-Spanish speakers accommodate lexically when they come into contact with Peninsular or Latin American varieties (Western Spanish in Romero 2013). Although the social dynamics that trigger such accommodation are beyond the scope of this paper, Judeo-Spanish users are aware of such differences and their accommodation may be a combination of language attitudes, professional needs, and exposure to Western Spanish. Lexical accommodation is exhibited by most modern Sephardic communities, including those in Istanbul, the Prince Islands, New York City, and Israel (Romero 2013, 284–286; Harris 1994, 173–175). Therefore, the presence of *pero* in Judeo-Spanish discourse may signal the level of dialect accommodation experienced by the community. I ran a search for each token and annotated whether the user was female of male in accordance to privacy requirements mentioned in the previous section. In addition, I wanted to minimize the effect of the moderators, and therefore I only searched for the first five months of LK history. The results are detailed in Table 2.

Table 2. Distribution of *ma*, *ama*, and *pero* in Ladinokomunita.

Token	Men	Women	Total
ma	46 (57.5%)	34 (42.5%)	80
ama	14 (45%)	17 (55%)	31
pero	8 (72%)	3 (28%)	11

I did not count the total number of tokens per speaker, but only if each speaker used it at least once in the forum. As Table 2 illustrates, it appears that men use the Judeo-Spanish form *ma* more than women, and that women are using Turkish *ama* more. Overall, the Judeo-Spanish form *ma* is used by more participants, and the Castilian/Latin American *pero* is used the least. However, a t-test revealed that for the information in Table 2, $t = 0.3$ and $p = 0.77$, that is, $p > 0.05$ and there are no statistical differences in the distribution of these tokens among men and women. This means that the lexical variation of these conjunctions is not based on gender. There may be other social factors, such as age and geographical location, that determine this variation, but I could not explore this without obtaining informed consent from all 1,518 members of LK.

The morphological study analyzes the interaction between obligatory subjunctive production and the context in which it occurs or fails to do so. Research on endangered languages has demonstrated a tendency towards a reduction or morphological categories (Andersen 1982, 97). In Judeo-Spanish, this pattern suggests that the indicative and subjunctive, two verbal morphological categories, would exhibit a convergence towards one category. In Romero (2012), I investigated the loss of the subjunctive in the Judeo-Spanish spoken in Istanbul. In that study, I concluded that the obligatory subjunctive is highly stable in some semantic contexts, whereas in others it has been replaced by the indicative (Romero 2012, 169–175). Although it is not my intention to provide an exhaustive study on the Judeo-Spanish subjunctive, the five semantic contexts that occurred in the corpus are detailed below:

Obligatory subjunctive occurs after exhortative verbs, such as *kerer* 'to want' in (1):

(1) *Kero ke David venga a Israel*
I.want subordinator David come.subj to Israel
'I want David to come to Israel.'

Verbs expressing a future effect, occurring after the preposition of finality *para* 'in order to, so that,' and its variations, for example in (2):

(2) *Lavoro para ke merkemos una kaza mueva*
I.work. so.that subordinator we.buy.subj a house new
'I work so that we buy a new house.'

Desiderative verbs such as *dezear* 'to wish,' *esperar*, 'to hope,' and *azer umit* 'to hope,' illustrated in (3) below:

(3) *Dezeo ke mi ijo tope lavoro*
I.wish subordinator my son find.subj job
'I wish that my son finds a job.'

Verbs or particles expressing probability, for example *puedeser* 'maybe,' as in (4):

(4) *Puedeser ke sea Amerikano*
maybe subordinator he.be.subj. American
'Maybe he is American.'

And finally, verbs that express emotions, such as *alegrar*, 'to make happy,' as in example (5) below:

(5) *Me alegro ke oy aga luvia*
me make.happy subordinator today make.subj rain
'It makes me happy that it's raining today.'

Since the obligatory subjunctive occurs in subordinate sentences, I ran a search in the LK corpus for the subordinating particle *ke*, (underlined in the glosses above), then recorded the type of semantic context and whether or not the obligatory subjunctive was used. Because I wanted to explore semantic context as a linguistic variable rather than gender, I did not record any information on the speaker. I also limited myself to the first five months of LK history (January-May 2000). The results are detailed in Table 3. The category *indicative means that obligatory subjunctive should have occurred, but the indicative was produced instead.

Table 3. Distribution Obligatory Subjunctive in LK.

semantic context	subjunctive	*indicative	presence %
exhortative	44	6	88
future effect	12	3	80
desiderative	19	1	95
probability	0	16	0
emotions	5	15	25

I conducted a chi-square test to determine if the distribution in Table 3 was significant. Since $X^2 = 65.7$, $df = 4$, and $p \leq 0.001$, the distribution was significant. This suggests that the obligatory subjunctive is more stable in desiderative verbs (95%) and exhortative verbs (88%). The obligatory subjunctive in the corpus has disappeared in the context of probability (0%) and it is in the process of disappearing after verbs expressing emotions (25%). These results from the LK corpus correlate with my findings in the Judeo-Spanish community in Istanbul because exhortative verbs present the highest production of obligatory subjunctive in both populations. Also, both LK and Istanbul exhibit no usage of obligatory subjunctive in probability/dubitative constructions. However, these populations contrast in desiderative verbs, with 95% in LK but an average of 50% in Istanbul (Romero 2012, 172). In Romero (2012), I concluded that distribution of obligatory subjunctive was dependent on both context and age/proficiency. Since I did not have access to the ages of the LK users, my data can only reveal part of subjunctive distribution dynamics. However, and in spite of these limitations, the online LK subjunctive data overall reflect offline usage.

6. CONCLUSION: *EN TIERRAS VIRTUALAS YO VO SEGIR*

Approaching online communities as digital homelands, both as a continuation and expansion of offline communities can provide additional insight into the sociolinguistics of endangered languages. Since these languages are characterized by reduced and peripheral linguistic domains, cyber communities can provide an online territorial space where the language can once again be used as a vernacular and even include new domains. Although online communities that use Judeo-Spanish as CV and not just a PCV are few, their increasing membership numbers and continuous advances in electronic communication provide an optimistic view of their future. No longer limited by geography or offline social group, digital homelands have the potential to grow and revitalize the language.

Because of their reflection of offline language usage, the wide variety of member backgrounds, their large and ever-growing number of utterances, plus the variation of forms and usage, online communities can become new grounds for sociolinguistic studies. However, caution must be exercised when conducting linguistic research in cyber communities, and, above all, the researcher must consider issues of privacy and consent before undertaking any investigation. The two shorts studies on lexical and morphological variation illustrate how digital homelands can contribute to the study of patterns in endangered languages, bilingualism, and dialect accommodation. They also represent the research limitations inherent to research in the digital world. In the lexical study, the only social variable (gender) readily available did not fully explain token distribution. In the morphological study, the linguistic variable (semantic context) did explain the distribution, but comparison to offline communities suggest that the inclusion of a social variable (age) would have provided a more accurate depiction.

Perhaps the greatest contribution of digital homelands, in addition to providing a new ground for linguistic research, is the effect they can have as a resource for language revitalization. Cyber communities have replaced physical space. According to *Ethnologue*, there are about 110,000 Judeo-Spanish speakers distributed throughout the globe (Lewis et al., 2004). That means that digital homelands such as LK, with more than 1,500 users can claim roughly 15% of total language population. That is an impressive number, only possible with modern electronic communication. Most encouraging, is that members in online communities are cooperating and producing new literary, didactic, and entertainment materials. The literary magazine *Orizontes* was the result of a joint effort among the younger members of LK and GS. Members of LK developed an online searchable dictionary to help Judeo-Spanish students, and even the *Ladino Culture Forum* has a small dictionary still available on their site. Members of LK have also organized trips, conferences, and other literary and entertainment activities together in the offline world, and then post comments in the online world. These *tierras virtualas* are no longer *tierras ajenas*, and for many users digital homelands constitute another home.

REFERENCES

Amado Bortnick, Rachel. "The Internet and Judeo-Spanish: Impact and implications of a virtual community". In *Proceedings of the Twelfth British Conference on Judeo-Spanish Studies, 24–26 June 2001 (Sephardic Language, Literature and History)* Edited by H. Pomeroy and M. Alpert, 4–11. Leiden: Brill, 2001.

Andersen, Roger W. "Determining the linguistic attributes of language attrition". In *The Loss of Language Skills*. Edited by D. Lambert and B. F. Freed, 83–118. Rowley, MA: Newbury House, 1982.

Benbassa, Esther and Aron Rodrigue. *Sephardi Jewry: A History of the Judeo-Spanish Community, 14th-20th Centuries*. Los Angeles: University of California, 2000.

Brink-Danan, Marcy. The meaning of Ladino: The semiotics of an online speech community. *Language and Communication 31* (2011): 107–118.

British Psychological Society. *Ethics Guidelines for Internet-mediated Research*. Leicester: British Psychological Society, 2013.

Christodouleas, Tina. "Judeo-Spanish and the Jewish Community of 21st Century Thessaloniki: Ethnic language shift in the maintenance of ethno cultural identity". Ph.D. Diss., The Pennsylvania State University, 2008.

Dorian, Nancy C. *Language Death: The Life Cycle of a Scottish Gaelic Dialect*. Philadelphia: University of Pennsylvania Press, 1981.

Fishman, Joshua. *Reversing Language Shift: Theoretical and Empirical Foundations of Assistance to Threatened Languages*. Clevedon: Multilingual Matters, 1991.

Harris, Tracy K. "The Prognosis for Judeo-Spanish: Its Description, Present Status, Survival and Decline, with implications for the study of language death in general". Ph.D. Diss., Washington, DC: Georgetown University, 1979.

Harris, Tracy K. *Death of a Language: The History of Judeo-Spanish*. Newark: University of Delaware Press, 1994.

Held, Michael. "'The people who almost forgot': Judeo-Spanish web-based interactions as a digital home-land". *El Prezente: Studies in Sephardic Culture* 4 (2010): 83–101.

Kushner Bishop, Jill. "More than a Language, a Travel Agency: Ideology and Performance in the Israeli Judeo-Spanish Revitalization Movement". Ph.D. Diss., Los Angeles: University of California, 2004.

Lewis, M. P., G. F. Simons, and C. D. Fennig, eds. *Ethnologue: Languages of the World, Seventeenth edition*. Dallas, Texas: SIL International, 2014. Online version: http://www.ethnologue.com.

Luria, Max A. *A Study of the Monastir Dialect of Judeo-Spanish Based on Oral Material Collected in Monastir, Yugo-Slavia*. New York: Instituto de las Españas. 1930.

Romero, Rey. Issues of Spanish language maintenance in the Prince Islands. In *Lenguaje, arte y revoluciones ayer y hoy: New Approaches to Hispanic Linguistic, Literary, and Cultural Studies*. Edited by Alejandro Cortazar and Rafael Orozco, 162–187. Newcastle upon Tyne: Cambridge Scholars Publishing, 2011.

Romero, Rey. *Spanish in the Bosphorus: A sociolinguistic study on the Judeo-Spanish dialect spoken in Istanbul*. Istanbul: Libra, 2012.

Romero, Rey. "Palatal east meets velar west: Dialect contact and phonological accommodation in Judeo-Spanish". *Studies in Hispanic and Lusophone Linguistics* 6: 2 (2013), 279–299.

Romero, Rey. "Dialect concentration and dissipation: Challenges to Judeo-Spanish revitalization efforts". In *Judeo-Spanish and the Making of a Community*. Edited by Bryan Kirschen, 50–71. Newcastle upon Tyne: Cambridge Scholars Publishing, 2015.

Romero, Rey. "Trabajar es en español, en ladino es lavorar": Lexical accommodation in Judeo-Spanish. In *Spanish Language and Sociolinguistic Analysis*. Edited by S. Sessarego and F. Tejedo, 381–400. Amsterdam/Philadelphia: John Benjamin, 2016.

Sadan, Tsvi. "Yiddish on the Internet". *Language and Communication* 31 (2010): 99–106.

Sala, Marius. *Phonétique et phonologie du judéo-espagnol de Bucarest*. Paris: Mouton, 1971.

Schmidt, Annette. *Young People's Dyirbal: An Example of Language Death from Australia*. Cambridge: Cambridge University Press, 1985.

Schneider, Edgar W. "Investigating variation and change in written documents". In *The Handbook of Language Variation and Change*. Edited by J. K. Chambers, Peter Trudgill, and Natalie Schilling-Estes. Oxford: Blackwell, 2004.

Shandler, Jeffrey. "Postvernacular Yiddish: Language as a performance art". *The Drama Review* 48.1 (2004): 19–43.

Shandler, Jeffrey. *Adventures in Yiddishland: Postvernacular Language and Culture*. Berkeley, University of California Press, 2006.

University of California at Berkeley's Committee for Protection of Human Subjects (UCBCPHS). *Internet-Based Research: Guidance document*. 8 pages. March 2014 version. Berkeley: University of California, 2014.

CHAPTER FIFTEEN

Judeo-Spanish ON THE Web

ANA STULIC AND SOUFIANE ROUISSI
Bordeaux Montaigne University, France

ABSTRACT

This chapter examines the presence of Judeo-Spanish on the World-Wide Web. We consider two main aspects: The technological issues related to the encoding and recognition of Judeo-Spanish as a separate language in digital environments and the sociolinguistic aspect manifested when we analyze the presence of Judeo-Spanish on the Web.

1. INTRODUCTION

For the past several years we have been exploring the possibility of establishing an electronic Judeo-Spanish corpus. In order to reach and incorporate the full diversity and richness of the sources that are available, we thought it was necessary to first identify and describe these sources and then analyze various aspects related to electronic resources in general (Rouissi and Stulic 2013). As an extension of this research, we offer here some data and reflections on the current presence of Judeo-Spanish on the Internet.

That the use of the Internet, and specifically the Web, has become common practice in all sorts of human activities needs no demonstration. Different digital resources based on Web technologies promote various types of communication and conveyance of information, potentially in many languages.

Although the Web started as an English-language medium, it has since allowed users to "speak" in many other languages as well and at a quickening pace. At the first phase, contents and services were extended from English to other widely-spoken languages, because of their economic and political importance. Eventually, and thanks to the increasingly greater availability of more powerful hardware and the ease with which Web 2.0 software can be used, speakers of "fragile" languages (at risk in their transmission, with few or non-existent strategies for their preservation, with a relatively small number of speakers, lacking linguistics resources, etc.), also seized the opportunity offered by the advent of the Internet, making it possible not only for these languages to be present, but also for them to be used in ways that they would not have been possible otherwise.

In this sense, it can be said that we are now witnessing the appearance on the Web of what could be defined as a distinct, contemporary modality of Judeo-Spanish. A question that arises is to what extent Judeo-Spanish in this new environment reflects the traditional use of the language, as we can observe if through the study of texts produced before the digital age. In order to take a critical perspective and to propose an analytical framework for the use of Judeo-Spanish on the Web, in this chapter we discuss the means of identifying Judeo-Spanish web spaces as well as their characteristics. Our investigation, which aims at understanding the present-day conditions of production of contents in Judeo-Spanish in the digital environment, is a necessary stem prior the formulation of measures that could be taken to favor its deployment.

2. THE PROBLEM

Judeo-Spanish, the traditional native language of the Sephardic Jews who trace their origin to Medieval Iberia, has been in decline in Eastern Europe, Anatolia, and elsewhere since the beginning of the 20th century and is currently classified as "severely endangered," in the red list of languages threatened with disappearance published by UNESCO (Moseley, *Atlas of the World's Languages in Danger*, 2010, online). On the scale expressing the vitality of a language (which goes from 5 to 0: safe; [5-] stable but threatened; [4] vulnerable; [3] endangered; [2] severely endangered; [1] critically endangered; [0] extinct), being classified as "severely endangered" means that it is a language "The language is spoken only by grandparents and older generations; while the parent generation may still understand the language, they typically do not speak it to their children" (UNESCO 2003: 8). The spread of the usage of a language to new domains and media, or its failure to do so, have been recognized as factors that allow a re-evaluation of its degree of vitality, thus taking into account changes in technology and, more generally, in our societies:

> New areas for language use may emerge as community living conditions change. While some language communities do succeed in expanding their own language into the new domain, most do not. Schools, new work environments, new media, including broadcast media and the Internet, usually serve only to expand the scope and power of the dominant

language at the expense of endangered languages. Although no existing domains of the endangered language may be lost, the use of the dominant language in the new domain has mesmerizing power, as with television.

If the communities do not meet the challenges of modernity with their language, it becomes increasingly irrelevant and stigmatized. (UNESCO 2003: 11)

Taking into account the changes that we have witnessed in the last few years, after the publication of this UNESCO document, digital technologies of communication can no longer be considered a merely "new" domain to exert an influence on the use of language. In order to assess whether a language is used at the global level we must include the transformation triggered by digital technologies in the totality of human activities that involve communicating.[1] Because of the widespread use of the Internet, at present the importance of the presence of a language on this medium goes well beyond a fascination for novelty. The degree of the presence of a language is directly related to what we can *do* with or in this language in the digital environment. We should thus ask the question of what it means for a language like Judeo-Spanish to be present on the Web, and, especially, how this presence can be identified, measured, and interpreted.

In order to address this issue, we need to start by considering the complex nature of the Web as an information and communication tool, including both its technological and symbolic dimensions. If we were to summarize the main factors that would ensure the survival of language according to the 2003 UNESCO document, the Web could lead to significant improvement on the following points:

a. The digital environment can become a place for actions that could generate and support positive language attitudes towards Judeo-Spanish.
b. It may also facilitate its documentation, by providing greater accessibility to texts, dictionaries and grammars.
c. The Web creates new opportunities for communication in Judeo-Spanish and, consequently, it may promote its transmission beyond the home environment through formal or informal teaching situations.

3. METHODOLOGICAL CONSIDERATIONS

In less than two decades from its birth, the Web has gone from being a system for browsing and posting pages that were essentially, static, even if they might have been hyperlinked to each other, to an environment that is open to contributions by all users, who go from being simple readers or spectators to being authors or actors, who may intervene and interact by making their own contributions any time and anywhere. With its global reach, the Web now allows users to overcome socio-spatio-temporal constraints. It is thus a place for expression with a very strong symbolic dimension. Social media such as Facebook, Youtube and Twitter offer a perfect illustration of these characteristics.

Since content can be written or spoken in different languages, dialects, styles or registers (that is, across a linguistic repertoire), the Web forms a complex sociolinguistic system, with potentially global scope, given the increasing use of the Internet around the world. Given its open character, the Web may be considered an "emerging global society", in Hymes's sense: "Sociolinguistic systems may be treated at the level of national states, and indeed, of an emerging world society." (Hymes 1974: 44).

Even if this sociolinguistic system does not reproduce perfectly the relations among the different languages outside of the digital world, a quick glance clearly shows that in the digital world as well there is lack of equality among languages in terms of their functioning. Although nowadays it is possible to find traces of use on the Web for almost any language, not all languages allow the same possibilities, because not all languages are taken into account in the development of digital applications or in the digital encoding of contents. Since browser interfaces are found in a limited number of languages (sometimes only in one language), the language of the content may be identified erroneously or not even be identified at all. Search engines do not permit the same degree of search precision for all languages, and, as in the "real" world outside of the Web, not all information is available in all languages. In spite of the obvious progress that has been made in the last few years, a great number of actions that can be taken on the Web require knowing the specific language in which the service is available.

4. JUDEO-SPANISH ON THE WEB: RESULTS OF THE RESEARCH

4.1. Formal Identification of Languages

With the rapid increase of Web content, the identification of a language in the digital environment has become a major issue for finding information in or about it. One of the ways to ensure the identification of the language is to refer explicitly to an internationally recognized standard such as an ISO code. The International Organization for Standardization or ISO is the organization in charge of formulating, establishing and publishing norms or rules. ISO rule 639, which defines the codes for identifying languages, consists of several subsections, such as 639–1 and 639–2, which list the languages most frequently used on electronic media, and 639–3, which aims at providing the most complete list possible of all languages, including all living and extinct languages, artificial languages, languages that are only written or only oral, etc. It is in these two complementary sections, ISO-639–2 and ISO-639–3[2] that we can find the three characters code that refers to the language of Sephardic Jews "lad",[3] which is abbreviated from the denomination "Ladino".[4] Most ISO language identifiers are assumed to denote distinct individual languages. In the ISO code table, "lad" is identified as a living individual language[5] and further information about it can be found in the Ethnologue database, which has been developed by SIL International, formerly known as Summer Institute of Linguistics.[6] This organization has played the role of registration authority for the ISO 639–3 rule. SIL International funds different research activities related to languages and, in particular, to establishing a survey or census of languages, which is the one mentioned with respect to ISO 639–3: 2007. The results of this survey, which can be consulted at ethnologue.com, include 7102 languages, classified according to their level of vitality or official status[7] and by continent[8] (Lewis, Simons and Fennig, 2015). Table 1 shows the description available for this language named "Ladino" and identified as *"a language of Israel."*[9]

Table 1. Information about "Ladino" on ethnologue.com.

A language of Israel	
ISO 639	lad
Alternate names	Dzhudezmo, Haquetiya, Judeo Spanish, Judeo-Espagnol, Judezmo, Sefardi, Sephardic, Spanyol
Population	100,000 in Israel (1985). Population total all countries: 112,130.
Location	Jerusalem District; other scattered areas; used in literary and music contexts
Language Status	4 (Educational).
Classification	Indo-European, Italic, Romance, Italo-Western, Western, Gallo-Iberian, Ibero-Romance, West Iberian, Castilian
Dialects	Haquetiya (Haketia, Haketiya, Hakitia), Judezmo (Jidyo, Judyo), Ladino. The Balkan dialect is more influenced by Turkish [tur] and Greek [ell]. The North African dialect is more influenced by Arabic [arb] and French [fra].
Language Use	Not the dominant language for most. Formerly the main language of Sephardic Jewry. Also use Hebrew [heb].
Language Development	New Media. Newspapers. Radio programs. Bible: 1829.
Language Resources	OLAC resources in and about Ladino
Writing	Cyrillic script [Cyrl], used by Sephardic speakers in the Balkans. Hebrew script [Hebr]. Latin script [Latn], used in Turkey.
Other Comments	The name Dzhudezmo is used by Jewish linguists and Turkish Jews, Judeo-Spanish by Romance philologists, Ladino by laymen (especially in Israel), Hakitia by Moroccan Jews, Spanyol by some others. Different from Ladin [lld] in the Rhaeto-Romansch group. Jewish.

The summary tables presented in Ethnologue refer to another resource, The Open Language Archives Community (OLAC).[10] OLAC is a project that aims to describe language resources with the help of standards of metadescription. This project has two goals: on the one hand, the development of a consensus about best practices in the archiving of linguistic resources and, on the other, the elaboration of a network of interoperational repositories of data and services allowing the storage and access of these resources.

For each language, the OLAC database provides information on primary sources, lexical resources and linguistic descriptions. For Judeo-Spanish, it lists 106 primary sources, of which 105 are interviews recorded within the project *Judéo-espagnol en France*, directed by Marie-Christine Varol and included in the *Collections de Corpus Oraux Numériques*. The remaining entry is a link to a 1931 Ladino translation of Genesis, in Rashi Hebrew letters, which is archived within the Rosetta Project.

Under "other resources about the language" we find ten additional resources of widely different kinds, including two books, the reference for the project *Judéo-espagnol en France,* which we have already mentioned, five other sources included in the Rosetta Project and two entries regarding databases, SIL-Ethnologue and LINGUIST List Resources.

One entry links to the page dedicated to Judeo-Spanish in the *Crúbádan Project: Corpus building for under-resourced languages*, which aims at compiling Web corpora for different languages. The application for Judeo-Spanish, which is only sketched on this webpage, still remains to be developed.[11] OLAC also includes alternate names for the language ("Dzhudezmo, Haketia, Haketiya, Hakitia, Haquetiya, Jidyo, Judeo-Spanish, Judezmo, Judyo, Sefardi, Spanyol") and provides terms that may be useful in searches ("dialect, vernacular, discourse, stories, conversation, dialogue, documentation, lexicon, dictionary, vocabulary, wordlist, phrase book, grammar, syntax, morphology, phonology, orthography").

The use of the ISO code allows the identification of the language of Sephardic Jewswithin language databases. Two initiatives deserve to be mentioned here, that of UNESCO and that of the Max Planck Institute for Evolutionary Anthropology at Leipzig.

UNESCO, the United Nations' Organization for Education, Science and Culture, has as its aim humanity's intellectual and moral solidarity. For this reason, it promotes quality education, the preservation of the cultural and intellectual patrimony of humankind and the conservation of valuable historical sites. It gives particular attention to the world's languages and especially to those that are in danger. These languages are the subject of a particular program[12] whose most notable result is a census of languages in danger of becoming extinct. The languages are represented on an atlas, which in 2015 includes 2467 languages (Moseley 2010). We note that within the UNESCO database the preferred denomination of the language of the Sephardic Jews is "Judezmo" and that is included under two different entries, "Judezmo Europe" and "Judezmo Israel". In Table 2 we reproduce the information available on this Atlas:

Table 2. Judezmo Europe (Atlas UNESCO).[13]

Name of the language	Judezmo (Europe) (en), judéo-espagnol (Europe) (fr), sefardí (Europa) (es), сефардский (ru)
Alternate names	Ladino; Judeo-Spanish; Sephardic; Haketía (local name in Morocco)
Related records	Judezmo (Israel)
Vitality	Severely endangered
Number of speakers	Cf. Judezmo (Israel)
Location(s)	traditionally Greece and Turkey, primarily in the historical provinces of Macedonia and Thrace, but also elsewhere in the Balkans, as well as Morocco, Ceuta, Melilla and Algeria in North Africa; now a few locations in Turkey, where largely concentrated in Istanbul (traditionally in the quarters of Balat and Hasköy), by probably less than 10,000 speakers; in Greece or elsewhere in the Balkans there are very few if any Judezmo speakers left after the Holocaust, and in North Africa the language is extinct
Country or area	Albania, Algeria, Bosnia and Herzegovina, Bulgaria, Croatia, Greece, Morocco, Romania, Serbia, The former Yugoslav Republic of Macedonia, Turkey
Corresponding ISO 639–3 code(s)	Lad

Table 3. Judezmo Israel (Atlas UNESCO).[14]

Name of the language	Judezmo (Israel) (en), judéo-espagnol (Israël) (fr), sefardí (Israel) (es), сефардский (ru)
Alternate names	Ladino; Judeo-Spanish; Sephardic
Related records	Judezmo (Europe)
Vitality	Severely endangered
Number of speakers	400000
	Hetzer (2001: 144): "one can say that less than 400,000 people still have a certain command of [Judezmo]"
Location(s)	resettled communities in Israel where the majority of the speakers live, and in the United States and several European countries; cf. Judezmo (Europe)
Country or area	Israel
Corresponding ISO 639–3 code(s)	Lad

Among the activities of the Max Planck Institute for Evolutionary Anthropology, Harald Hammarström, Robert Forkel, Martin Haspelmath and Sebastian Bank have developed Glottolog, which is a database conceived as an archive of information on the languages of the world, especially the lesser known languages.[15] In this database, Judeo-Spanish is included under the generic name *Ladino*,[16] which has subentries for *Haketiya*, *Judezmo* and *Nuclear Ladino*.[17] Putting all subentries together, the database includes 48 references, of which 26 do not appear to have any obvious relation with Judeo-Spanish, a fact that may be an indication that these references are the result of an automatic search that has not been revised.

We may draw several conclusions from the above. The language spoken by the Sephardic Jews is officially recognized by ISO standards, which allows for its formal identification in databases listing languages and language resources. On the other hand, the information that is found in the archives is incomplete and relatively poor, if we take into account the state of the art in the scholarly production. It appears that only resources whose standards of metadescription and archiving provide machine-readable information have been included.

The formal identification of the Judeo-Spanish language presents a challenge, since the database entries that we have mentioned are linked to each other. This circular structure of the information clearly shows how limited it is and, in cases such as that of Glottolog, the lack of oversight by specialists or experts. Even when the information is correct, its presentation may leave much to be desired. Thus, for instance, in the SIL entry the presentation of writing systems used for this language puts Cyrillic in first place, perhaps following an alphabetical order. Even though it is true that the Cyrillic alphabet has been used for writing in Judeo-Spanish, especially in Serbia and Bulgaria, it is far from being the most characteristic or widespread writing system for Judeo-Spanish.

The fact of creating an ISO code for Judeo-Spanish by itself results in the possibility of creating versions in the language of certain tools with a multilingual nature, an example being the collaborative encyclopedia Wikipedia. As a matter of fact, the open source application Wikimedia permits its native installation in Judeo-Spanish.

The Judeo-Spanish ("Ladino") space http://lad.wikipedia.org[18] has existed since 2005 at the same rank as, for instance, the English-language space http://en.wikipedia.org[19] and the Spanish-language space http://es.wikipedia.org.[20] This "official" existence of the language may help in its development by ensuring an online presence through encyclopedia articles that can be written collaboratively by speakers engaged in this process. It should be noted that, according to the available statistics,[21] the number of active users is considerably lower than that of registered users. The number of articles that have been produced since the creation of the space Wikipedia in Judeo-Spanish is still rather low, only 3361. The relative poverty of the Judeo-Spanish version of Wikipedia is related to the conditions under which it was developed. This initiative has resulted from Wikipedia's goal of extending the project to the greatest number of languages possible. The choices of spelling conventions and lexicon, which must be made at the moment of starting the interface and publishing the first articles, are not the product of well-founded reflection, but, rather the haphazard result of random decisions by contributors without proven competence in Judeo-Spanish. One of these contributors confides the following:

> Yo estoy editando esta Wikipedia porque sé un poco de español, y quiero ayudar a las Wikipedias que no tienen mucha información. No realmente sé algo de Ladino. Lo siente [sic] para mi español, inglés es mi lengua nativa. I'm only editing this Wikipedia because I know some Spanish, and I want to help the Wikipedias that don't have a lot of articles. I don't actually know any Ladino.[22]

Even though the Wikipedia project is collaborative in its essence and thus can always be improved—in fact, some aspects have indeed improved, as it has grown—some features, such as the adoption of an ad hoc spelling system and, especially, a noticeable inconsistency in the application of this orthography, are major obstacles for native speakers who might feel inclined to engage in the project in order to improve the contents, as shown by the following quote found in the discussion archives:

> My grandmother is a native speaker of Ladino, I tried showing her this Wikipedia and she thought it was ridiculous. The alphabet you have "invented" is original research and I regret to tell you that NOBODY will ever spell things like this: "kapítulo", except for you. The point of a Wikipedia is to be readable to speakers of a language, and nobody is able to, or wants to, read an encyclopedia written in your made-up alphabet. This is a travesty, you have ruined something that could have been great.[23]

The choice of spelling conventions thus seems a very important element in the perception of the users of the language. It is important to note this problem is not found in the case of languages that benefit from having a school system in charge of transmitting accepted orthographic conventions. This is not the case of Judeo-Spanish, which has had very different writing conventions, depending on the geographical area, and does not possess a set of norms defining the boundaries of the standard language with precision. A quick glance at the Judeo-Spanish Wikipedia articles shows that, in general, their content is not very different from that of the Spanish version, from which they often derive. This may also affect linguistic aspects. For instance, in the entry *"mar"*, even though the noun is introduced with the feminine article, the agreement with the adjectives in the next sentence is in the masculine, *serrados* and *abiertos*. This sentence appears to have been copied from the corresponding Spanish Wikipedia version:

> La mar es una masa de agua pinta que kubre la mayor parte de la superfisie de la Tierra. Egsisten tres kategorias de mares: mares litorales, mares interiores o serrados i los mares abiertos. Kuando la ekspansion es grande se yama oseano.[24]

Another obstacle for increasing the number of articles and for their improvement—which is always possible at all levels—in Judeo-Spanish Wikipedia is the technological know-how necessary to write or revise articles. In spite of efforts towards greater accessibility, in order to contribute to the creation of an article or its modification one needs certain skills and above all requires knowing that this is actually something that one can do. The undeniable success of collaborative online encyclopedias for a great number of languages should not obscure the fact that the best ones are the product of collaboration among many users with very different levels of education and very different motivations, such as promoting the spread of knowledge on specific topics and specific points of view.

People who are active in a given Wikipedia are nevertheless always only a small part of the total number of speakers of the language. Taking into account the relatively small number of speakers of Judeo-Spanish, in order to ensure the success of Wikipedia in Judeo-Spanish it seems necessary to create conditions for speakers who are already active on the Web to be concerned about this project and see it as a tool for the transmission of the language. The existence of the different Judeo-Spanish Web sites shows that there is indeed an interest on the part of Judeo-Spanish speakers in contributing to the transmission of the language.

4.2. Presence of Judeo-Spanish on the Web

At first glance, it would seem that, in order to study the presence of a given language on the Web, one would need to be able to count numbers of words, sentences or other meaningful units that may provide objective and comparable data. In addition to the technical difficulties that would be involved in this endeavor, including the great number of data to be analyzed, as well as the difficulty of identifying pertinent elements and the relative reliability of the available tools (cf. UNESCO 2009), there is another, methodological problem. Such quantification would mean implementing an analytical strategy with the help of technical tools that are not available to the average user.

Taking inspiration from the ethnographic approach to communication, in the sense given to this term by Dell Hymes (1974), we have chosen to focus on the perspective of the average user who may be interested in looking up information about or in Judeo-Spanish. We thus approach the use of the Web as a complex communicative activity based on navigation in this digital environment and, in particular, in the part of it that is readable/visible by human users and according to a tripartite "consultation-interaction-participation" activity. Our choice of the point of view of the user is not arbitrary, because the immediate availability of relevant information promotes its diffusion. The main idea is to see how in this communicative context Judeo-Spanish appears to users with varied expertise in this domain, from "null" to "confirmed", and how things can be improved in order to increase access to relevant content.

In order to examine the presence of Judeo-Spanish on the Web, we have undertaken a survey of websites that deal with Sephardic culture in general. This survey has produced a proposal for a typology (Rouissi and Stulic 2012). We have proposed that it is useful to distinguish several categories on the basis of editorial responsibility and type of content:

- Associations
- Cultural portals
- Journals and magazines
- Universities and research centers
- Courses and conferences
- Encyclopedias
- Internet guides (lists of sites)
- Library catalogs and digital catalogs
- Web 2.0 and mass dissemination of information

It is important to emphasize the evolving character of this classification, which combines different criteria. The sites that have been identified and classified in these categories do not necessarily include language contexts primarily in Judeo-Spanish, but they all deal with different aspects of Sephardic culture and are inevitable gateways for searches based either on the words used to name the language of Sephardic Jews: *djudeo-espanyol, Judeo-Spanish, judéo-espagnol, judeoespañol, Ladino, Judezmo*[25]. It is worth mentioning that the most common term used among the Sephardim to denote their spoken language, *espanyol*, is not discriminating on the Web as related to Sephardic culture, since it corresponds also to the Catalan word for "Spanish".

The contents in Judeo-Spanish on these websites are of variable proportion, from a few words to entire texts, video or audiovisual files. The majority of the sites identified as relevant are in fact multilingual, and only a few are entirely written in Judeo-Spanish. As a first step toward drawing conclusions from this research, here we present a more detailed analysis of the results regarding some specific Judeo-Spanish web spaces.

There is no need to demonstrate the interest in Sephardic culture and language on the part of the academic world and of official cultural institutions (such as libraries and museums) of different countries that are concerned with the preservation of the cultural patrimony of humanity. These different entities may include resources related to Judeo-Spanish and Sephardic culture on their official websites. However, here we have decided to exclude sites arising from the academic world[26] and have focused instead on the analysis of the conditions and dynamics of production in Judeo-Spanish outside of academia, as can be observed on the Web.

At present, this activity relies on individual engagement within interest groups that are built around the topic of the Judeo-Spanish language, including associations and press outlets, discussion groups and groups of collaborative production. Among all websites that derive from or are related to the activities of these groups of variable organization, we have chosen a few significant examples that illustrate how the concern for the preservation of the Sephardic linguistic and cultural heritage is manifested at the same time in the immediate sociolinguistic environment and within the general conditions of content production on the Web.

4.2.1. Ladino. Lengua y cultura

The website "Ladino: Lengua y cultura" of the Israeli association Arkadash[27] is devoted to the Sephardic tradition and is written almost exclusively in Judeo-Spanish. This association, which is a meeting point for Sephardic Jews originating in Turkey and residing in Israel, has, nevertheless, another website[28] in Turkish, English and Hebrew with a different structure, which gives information about the day-to-day activities of the Association. The site devoted to Judeo-Spanish also has a Hebrew version.

The site interface is written in Judeo-Spanish, although some tabs that had been planned in the architecture of the site are still empty of content (for instance "*Klubes de ladino*", "*La Eskola para estudiar el ladino*" and several others). Within this site, one can find a sample of traditional texts, proverbs ("*Reflanes*") and folk tales ("*Kuentos i konsejas*").[29] There are also several poems by Matilda Koén-Sarano and short articles on different aspects of Sephardic culture. A remarkable aspect of this site is that it also contains an online store ("*Butika*") where one can buy books and CD's. But the interface of the online store and the labels allowing different actions, such as "add to cart" and "proceed to checkout" are in standard Spanish of Spain.

4.2.2. Foundation for the Advancement of Sephardic Studies and Culture

Another example is the site of the Foundation for the Advancement of Sephardic Studies and Culture, located in New York.[30] In 2002, this institution, which works for the preservation of Sephardic linguistic and cultural heritage, appointed a committee dedicated to this goal, the Ladino Preservation Council. Among its activities, one may single out the discussion group *Ladinokomunita* and an audio chat group (with access restricted to registered users), through the application Paltalk.

One part of the website of the Foundation, which is written in English, is devoted to Judeo-Spanish. There one can find an introduction to Judeo-Spanish, the presentation of a publication of the Foundation (*Ladino Reveries* by Hank

Halio, 1996), the presentation of the discussion group *Ladinokomunita*, as well as press dossiers concerning two highly symbolic actions, the participation of the Foundation at a conference organized by UNESCO in 2002[31] and the ceremony organized in 2003 at the memorial of the former concentration camp of Auschwitz-Birkenau, where a commemorative plaque in Judeo-Spanish was solemnly unveiled. The page that introduces the discussion group offers access, through a dropdown menu, to a number of texts in Judeo-Spanish, divided into several categories: "Latest Ladino News",[32] "Personal Expressions, Stories and Fictional Accounts in Ladino", "*Textos relijiozos en ladino*" and "*Sefardim en la Shoa*". It is only in this part of the interface that the tab headings are in Judeo-Spanish, as the rest of the site interface is all in English.

4.2.3. Aki estamos—Association des Amis de la Lettre Sépharade

The site of the French association *Aki estamos—Association des Amis de la Lettre Sépharade*,[33] founded in 1998, is another significant example. Located in Paris, the association brings together Sephardic families who have emigrated from Turkey, the Balkans, Western Europe and all around the Mediterranean, as well as their friends. It sponsors a great number of activities, including courses on Judeo-Spanish and Haketiya, theater, choral music, concerts, conferences, cooking lessons, summer school, etc. Its goal is to promote the transmission of everyday Sephardic language and culture.

Some text contents on this site are written in French and others in Judeo-Spanish; only a few are bilingual (for instance, the proverbs page). As for the distribution of text contents in French and in Judeo-Spanish, there is no classification of topics treated in one language or in the other. Although French appears to dominate both in the interface and in the content of the pages, the demarcation of the two languages is not strict and does not reflect an intention to separate the two languages. Certain headings in the menu are given in Judeo-Spanish (e.g. "*Muestra lingua*", "*Livros... para meldar*"), but they may include content in the two languages on the same page or only in one of the two languages. An important part of the site is devoted to documentation. There one can find videos with recorded interviews, links to external resources, pictures, testimonials in French and in Judeo-Spanish, historical documents, such as a newspaper article in French from 1856, and even a scanned copy of an old book in Judeo-Spanish.

Periodical publications in Judeo-Spanish or about Sephardic culture are closely related to the activities of the associations. *Aki estamos* is a good example of this. As reflected in its name, this association sprang from a periodical publication started by Jean Carasseau, *La Lettre Sépharade*, which was published until 2007.[34] Its more recent activities have given rise to another magazine, *Kaminando i avlando* (in French and Judeo-Spanish), which is accessible online.[35]

4.2.4. Institut Sépharade Européen

The *Institut Sépharade Européen* or ISE, located in Brussels advertises that its aim is to record and transmit Sephardic culture (*"témoigner et transmettre la culture Sépharade"*), which it does through numerous cultural and media activities. ISE has been publishing the magazine *Los Muestros* (in French, English and Judeo-Spanish) since 1990. This magazine is available to readers on the website, and a subscription can also be purchased through their online store, which also offers book titles related to Sephardic culture.[36] The website[37] has been active since 1993 and it offers readers texts from many collaborators on political and cultural topics (often in the form of reviews of books about Sephardic culture), as well as many links to external sites. It also publishes news related to cultural events taking place in Europe and private announcements about family life. The language of the interface and most of the contents is French.

Judeo-Spanish content is found particularly under three headings. *"Muestro kanton en judeo espagnol"* includes 16 spaces in Judeo-Spanish by different authors who write about very different topics and with differing regularity. Among the 16 contributors[38] to *"Muestro kanton"* one finds several individuals who are very well known because of their engagement in the preservation of Judeo-Spanish, including Haïm Vidal Sephiha, Matilda Koén Sarano and Klara Perahya. Seven of these authors publish recipes under the heading *"El gizado sefaradi"*. The third section in Judeo-Spanish *"El komentario de la parashot en judeo espagnol"*, by Yehuda Hatsvi, has a religious theme.

4.2.5. Aki Yerushalayim

Aki Yerushalayim is a magazine written entirely in Judeo-Spanish. Founded in 1979 by Radio Israel, it is published at present by the association *Sepharad*, whose goal is to raise awareness of Sephardic Jewish culture and to contribute to the promotion of literary, journalistic and cultural activities in Judeo-Spanish.[39] Since 1998, this magazine has been published in collaboration with the official Israeli institution in charge of the promotion of Judeo-Spanish, the *Autoridad Nasionala del Ladino*. At present, *Aki Yerushalayim* is published twice a year and is freely accessible online.[40] Like the paper version, the online magazine is all in Judeo-Spanish, including all navigation instructions on the website.

4.2.6. Diario Judío

Diario Judío (*Diario de la vida judía en México y en el mundo*) is a general-interest online magazine published in Mexico.[41] It publishes articles dealing with different aspects of the life of the Jewish community in Mexico and elsewhere. A section specifically devoted to Judeo-Spanish, *"el rincón sefaradi"* includes articles in Judeo-Spanish or about topics of Sephardic culture, as well as videos and sound files with Sephardic songs. An entire section, in Spanish, is dedicated to King Phillip VI's royal decree, giving Sephardic Jews the possibility of obtaining Spanish citizenship. The language of the magazine is Spanish, but one can observe a pronounced interest in the diversity of languages that are found in the community. Thus, in the menu, the user can select contents dealing with or written in Spanish, French, Judeo-Spanish, Yiddish and Hebrew. Most of the articles in Judeo-Spanish in *Diario Judío* have been adopted from other sources, such as *esefarad.com*, *Institut Sépharade Européen* and *Aki Yerushalayim*. Nevertheless, it is worth noting the contributions to *Diario Judío* of two Mexican authors: Julio César Pomposo and Fredy Cauich Valerio.

4.2.7. eSefarad

eSefarad (*Noticias del mundo sefaradí*) is a website created in 2008 by Liliana and Marcelo Benveniste, from Buenos Aires, with the goal of disseminating information on history, customs, news and articles related to Sephardic themes.

On this website it is possible to subscribe to a free weekly email newsletter and there are links that allow access to online radio broadcasts from Spain (*Magacín Sefaradí* of Radio Sefarad) and Argentina (Radio Jai). In addition, the website contains information on cultural events (series of talks *Raíces de Sefarad*) and sells products related to Sephardic culture, including books, CD's, DVD's and souvenirs with phrases in Judeo-Spanish. This is a multilingual website with contents in Spanish, Judeo-Spanish, Haketia and English. The navigation interface is in Spanish.

Among the articles in Judeo-Spanish and Haketia on this webpage one finds many items that are also available elsewhere, such as transcripts of the *Muestra lingua* radio broadcasts by Edmond Cohen and texts by Rachel Amado Bortnick arising from the discussion group *Ladinokomunita* and by Sharope Blanco and Sal Amira from *Sefaradimuestro*. Other prolific authors represented here are Medi Cohen-Malki, Matilda Koén Sarano, Yehuda Hatsvi and Gad Nassi, among others, whose texts were originally published in *Aki Yerushalayim* and other venues. It is also interesting to note the presence of a number of texts from the Torah in Judeo-Spanish, trancribed in Latin letters by Yehuda Sidi, from Turkey.

4.2.8. Şalom and El amaneser

Two remarkable periodical publications from Turkey are also available on the Web: the weekly magazine *Şalom*[42] and the monthly publication *El Amaneser*. Şalom is a magazine of general interest, mostly written in Turkish, which regularly publishes articles in Judeo-Spanish, which are available online.[43] The monthly magazine *El Amaneser*, which is written entirely in Judeo-Spanish, has been published by The Ottoman-Turkish Sephardic Cultural Research Center since 2003 and aims at documenting Sephardic cultural production and promoting the transmission of the Sephardic language and traditions. Although it is not an online publication, the magazine has a blog where one can have access to archived issues through the application Scribd.[44] The interface of the blog is in English and there are notes in English, Judeo-Spanish and Turkish.

4.2.9. Discussion Groups

There are two main online discussion groups containing exchanges in Judeo-Spanish: *Ladinokomunita* and *Sefaradimuestro*. They are both hosted by Yahoo, have international scope, and show a regular and uninterrupted activity since their creation, in 2000 for *Ladinokomunita* and in 2008 for *Sefaradimuestro*.

Ladinokomunita, which at present has over 1500 members, was founded and is moderated by Rachel Amado Bortnick. The most salient feature of this group is the requirement that all members write all messages in Judeo-Spanish. An interest in Judeo-Spanish is also the main thing in common among all members. It should be noted, however, that the official language of the group, as it appears in its Yahoo description, is English.[45] The description of the group is presented in both English and Judeo-Spanish.[46] This is the group that people wanting to learn Judeo-Spanish join. Fredy Cauich Valerio, a Professor of Mathematics from Mexico and contributor to Diario Judío writes this in his own introduction:

> So un namorado del djudeo-espanyol i de la kultura sefaradi, desde septembre de 2010 so myembro de Ladinokomunita, un grupo de korrespondensya mezo internet, ande presonas de los kuatro puntos de la tyerra eskriven solo en djudeo-espanyol, ansi es ke i yo me ambezi el djudeo-espanyol. Dediko este lavoro a todos mis amigos de Ladinokomunita, kon muncho karinyo, djente maravyosa de la ke me ambezo muncho kada ves ke meldo lo ke eskriven.[47]

This group is also often used by people wanting to obtain precise information regarding some specific aspect of the language or the culture, or to conduct opinion polls or surveys (cf. Held 2010, López Fernández 2012–2013: 40–45). Many shared files show an interest in the language and in obtaining scholarly information (one can find, for instance, an article by David Bunis on the name *Ladino*, published on the site of the University of Washington[48]). The interest for documenting is also apparent. Thus, among the files that are available to the group there is a whole book scanned as image (*Agada de Pesah*, 1932). Group members also exchange their own original texts (Buly Hazan, "*De Izmir a la Amerika*", 2012) and their translation projects (e.g. a translation of a fragment of *Don Quixote* by Zelda Ovadia).

Since the online chats of this group are public, they can be used to study the present-day use of Judeo-Spanish. The documentary value of these chats has been recognized by the members of the group, as shown by their putting together an online collaborative dictionary, the *Diksionaryo de Ladinokomunita*.[49] The members of the group have a clear awareness of the role that they play in the process of the transmission of the language. Their activities show reflection on this topic. Among the shared files, we find the results of a 2005 survey among the members of the group, in which more than 200 subscribers participated;[50] as well as two academic papers that study *Ladinokomunita* (Brink-Danan 2010, Held 2010).

The discussion group *Sefaradimuestro* was founded and is moderated by Sharope Blanco (a pseudonym), who also directs a very interesting space within the site of the *Institut Sépharadi Européen*. In the official description that Yahoo gives of this group, which has 766 members, English appears as the official language and Spanish is mentioned as a topic. Unlike in *Ladinokomunita*, in *Sefaradimuestro* on finds messages in French and in English. The group's stated goal is to promote literary and cultural production, as well as the transmission of family history in Judeo-Spanish:

EL BUTO DE SEFARADIMUESTRO es de ranimar la kultura de los djudyos sefaradis, avlar, eskrivir, kompozar poemas, istoryas i kontar kuentizikos humoristikos, akodrarmos de los miembros de muestras familyas, de komo biviyan i komo aziyan las kozas, sus kostumbres durante sieglos, lo todo kon muncho karinyo i amistad ![51]

Sefaradimuestro, just like *Ladinokomunita*, is an online site for informal teaching, where people who want to learn Judeo-Spanish may correspond with speakers. In the following quote from a member of both discussion groups, *Sefaradimuestro* is mentioned together with *Ladinokomunita*:

[...] Komo podesh meldar yo esto tratando de ambezarmi la gramatika del ladino i tengo los primeros manuales de Matilda Koen Sarano traduizidos al ingles Por Gloria Ascher de Tufts University. Yo no tengo a DINGUNOS ke me korije mis yerros mas ke aki en Ladinokomunita i Sefardimuestro. No se si agora ya mijori mi ladino o DAINDA tengo yerros. Aspero repuesta de ti Kerida Mimi.
Ysmael.E.Tisnado.II
de Temecula, California, Estados Unidos.

Ysmael, tu lengua esta kaji perfekta, Bravo! solo dos biervos troki (los meti en majiskulas)
Rb[52]

This exchange, taken from the correspondence in *Ladinokomunita*, serves to illustrate very clearly this didactic aspect, which is found in both discussion groups examined here.

4.2.10. Facebook

The social network Facebook allows users to state what languages they speak, with the help of a menu. The user selects the language from a list that was created using ISO codes. This tool also allows the user to select a language and receive information on it. Going to the page devoted to the language in Facebook, one can know how many people have expressed an interest in the language by clicking "Like". It is also possible to know how many people have stated that they speak the language. This number is 84000 in the case of Judeo-Spanish. One can also access the accounts of people or institutions that have declared Judeo-Spanish as one of the languages they speak. We note, however, that the Facebook interface is not available in Judeo-Spanish.

4.2.11. YouTube

Another important resource on Judeo-Spanish is the video-sharing site YouTube. There one can find interviews in Judeo-Spanish, several series of lessons and a large number of songs. The interface, however, is not available in Judeo-Spanish and the search engine does not provide information on the language of videos. Access to information on content is made possible through a search engine that analyzes the descriptors given by the person who posted the video.

5. CONCLUSIONS AND PERSPECTIVES

In examining the presence of a language on the Web, a first question that arises is that of the official recognition of its existence. We have shown that Judeo-Spanish is in fact officially recognized by the International Organization for Standardization or ISO with its own code. This allows its formal identification in databases concerned with languages and language resources. Nevertheless, the information that is found in the databases is often incomplete and relatively poor, given the state of academic research on this subject. The other problem that must be mentioned is the name of the language. Many speakers of Judeo-Spanish around the world disapprove the use of the term "Ladino" that is clearly referred to by the ISO code "lad" for the vernacular language. Many more do not recognize their language under the denomination Judezmo, which appears in all language information data basis and is even the preferred one in UNESCO's Atlas of the World's Languages in Danger. Official recognition by international organisms dealing with language normalization is essential, but it is important not to fall into technical determinism. As we have seen in the case of Wikipedia, the official recognition has permitted the development of a *lad* version of this space, but with all the shortcomings that we have noted. The symbolic nature of naming a language should be taken into account while configuring language standards.

In addition, through the analysis of a number of websites, we have pointed out the potential these sites offer for developing what we have called "contemporary Judeo-Spanish", through its presence and evolution in discussion groups and social media such as Facebook. Audiovisual resources available through YouTube or similar free platform could also be very useful in the transmission of the language.

The websites that we have analyzed demonstrate a great interest in Judeo-Spanish. As is also the case outside of the Web, Judeo-Spanish is often used in multilingual contexts. At this point of our research, we have found only one Web resource that is written entirely in Judeo-Spanish and is regularly updated: *Aki Yerushalayim*, which offers both original texts and an interface in Judeo-Spanish. This is far from being the norm. In most of the sites with Judeo-Spanish content that we have analyzed, the interface is in other languages and only partially in Judeo-Spanish.

Like many other websites, the Judeo-Spanish sites are characterized by frequent "recycling" of contents. Texts are often adopted from one site to another, although there are also spaces where original creation is on display. In this sense, discussion groups show remarkable richness and dynamics of production, thanks undoubtedly to the use of a device that has become a simple tool of universal availability: electronic mail in all its current forms. Nevertheless, it is still necessary to stimulate greater original production in Judeo-Spanish. With the exception of some texts published in the Turkish magazine *Şalom,* there are very few texts in Judeo-Spanish dealing with present-day affairs, even if such topics are often the subject of exchanges within discussion groups.

Through our exploratory research, we have noticed, on Judeo-Spanish sites, a generalized interest in documentation. Sometimes, interesting documents are made available within these sites, but their visibility tends to be very limited.

The first necessary condition for Web contents and services to be devoted to a specific language is for its existence to be noted and documented in the standards used in this environment. In other words, it is necessary for the "Web World" to recognize the possibility that some users may employ this language. However, the mere presence of a language in the standards does not guarantee that online contents in this language will be described as such. The formal recognition of Judeo-Spanish through the ISO code *lad* makes it possible to identify contents as being in this language, but the fact is that none of the websites that we have identified as having Judeo-Spanish contents uses this label! Among the sites entirely in Judeo-Spanish, *Ladino. Lengua y cultura* uses the code *es*, which corresponds to Spanish, and the pages of *Aki Yerushalayim* do not provide information concerning the language in which they are written. Some of the richest resources in Judeo-Spanish materials, such as discussion groups, are described by Yahoo, which hosts them, as being in English. In fact, the only spaces that can be identified as having a relation with Judeo-Spanish thanks to their ISO code are the

Facebook and Wikipedia sites. Thus, as we can see, the creation of an ISO code has not been sufficient for all producers of content, including the technical staff in charge of developing webpages, to become aware of the existence of such a code.

An activity that seems important, both symbolically and practically, is to develop strategies of diffusion of Judeo-Spanish, starting from domains that concern it closely. It would be a matter of pursuing efforts to make authentic documents available and to work on introducing tools that would allow for these contents to find their way to a large Judeo-Spanish speaking or learning audience.

Regarding perspectives, for Judeo-Spanish to go from being mainly a "topic" language to becoming a "tool" language, in the context of its Web deployment, priority should be given to establishing its presence on interfaces, software and widely used applications. The enrichment of a language and its extension to additional domains often requires an effort of translation. Although translation projects of an open-source type create the possibility of collaborating in translating, we should draw some lessons from the difficult start of Wikipedia in Judeo-Spanish. The adaptation of contents cannot depend only on good will and technical know-how. Traditional tools such as dictionaries and grammars are essential, as well as the engagement of native speakers and of researchers specialized in Judeo-Spanish.

It can be argued that in order to make progress in these matters, the mobilization of scholars is indispensable. Research on online sites is necessary for the documentation of contemporary Judeo-Spanish. Judeo-Spanish culture is now present in research programs and has begun to be taught in academic contexts. The availability on line of authentic documents in digital format has meant considerable progress for everyone interested in knowing about Judeo-Spanish and the Sephardic tradition. However, technical devices are not self-sufficient. They require involvement and mediation of the scientific community We believe that the scientific community must take a step forward in the valorization of the use of contemporary Judeo-Spanish on the Web and, taking into account the characteristics of both the language (its history, linguistic forms, texts, sociolinguistic considerations) and the Web as the medium, work on developing strategies that should increase its visibility and improve conditions of its transmission in this digital environment.

NOTES

1. For a grid that provides a structure for a basic comparison of languages in relation to the Internet, see Diki-Kidiri (2011).
2. Rule 639–3, which provides an exhaustive treatment of all languages, was enacted in 2007. http://www.iso.org/iso/fr/language_codes

3. A table for all the codes, each of which consists of three characters, can be found online: http://www-01.sil.org/iso639–3/codes.asp (last accessed September 1st, 2015).
4. It should be noted that even if this name is nowadays used by some speakers, especially in the USA and Israel, it is not the name unanimously preferred by the research community. Traditionally this term referred only to the language of biblical translations, which closely followed the syntax of the original source.
5. A language is listed as living when there are people still living who learned it as a first language.
6. The Summer Institute of Linguistics is an organization founded in 1934. They describe their own history in http://www.sil.org/about/history. For some controversial aspects of the linguistic politics of this organization, see Calvet (1999: 205–217).
7. Institutional: 578, Developing: 1,598, Vigorous: 2,479, In Trouble: 1,531, Dying: 916.
8. Europe: 286, Americas: 1064, Asia: 2301, Oceania: 1313, Africa: 2138.
9. https://www.ethnologue.com/language/lad.
10. http://www.language-archives.org/language/lad.
11. http://crubadan.org/languages/lad.
12. http://www.unesco.org/new/fr/culture/themes/endangered-languages.
13. This information can be found at: http://www.unesco.org/languages-atlas/en/atlasmap/language-id-374.html.
14. http://www.unesco.org/culture/languages-atlas/en/atlasmap/language-id-2165.html.
15. «Comprehensive reference information for the world's languages, especially the lesser known languages», http://glottolog.org/.
16. http://glottolog.org/resource/languoid/id/ladi1251.
17. It is not clear what is understood by "nuclear Ladino".
18. https://lad.wikipedia.org/wiki/La_Primera_Hoja advertises 3361 articles; page accessed November 30, 2015.
19. https://en.wikipedia.org wiki/Main_Page, with 5020815 articles; page accessed Novembre 30, 2015.
20. https://es.wikipedia.org/wiki/Wikipedia:Portada, with 1215895 articles; page accessed Novembre 30, 2015.
21. https://lad.wikipedia.org/wiki/Especial:Estatistika, shows 10371 registered users, but only 28 « active » users, that is users who have participated in the last 30 days.
22. https://lad.wikipedia.org/wiki/Diskusy%C3%B3n:La_Primera_Hoja/Arshiv_1.
23. https://lad.wikipedia.org/wiki/Diskusy%C3%B3n:La_Primera_Hoja/Arshiv_1.
24. https://lad.wikipedia.org/wiki/Mar. Cf.Spanish version: https://es.wikipedia.org/wiki/Mar.
25. We present only the results of searches based on Latin script.
26. For a presentation of existing resources and developing projects, see Stulic and Rouissi (forthcoming).
27. http://www.myladino.com/.
28. http://www.arkadas.org.il/.
29. The tabs "Romansas" and "Gizar" are still empty.
30. http://www.sephardicstudies.org/index.html.
31. "Judaeo-Spanish Language and Culture: Challenges and Prospects", UNESCO, 2002. http://portal.unesco.org/en/ev.php-URL_ID=4311&URL_DO=DO_TOPIC&URL_SECTION=201.html.
32. Three of the texts in this section are in English, the rest are in Judeo-Spanish.
33. http://www.sefaradinfo.org/.
34. This journal can be consulted on the site of the association: https://sites.google.com/site/lalettresepharade/. Contents can be searched by topic, by issue and by author.

35. http://issuu.com/akiestamos-aals.
36. http://sefarad.org/lm/index.html. The supplement *Kore* is also available online: http://sefarad.org/kore/. In addition to subscription fees, the activities of this organization are financed by selling advertisements on the website and by donations.
37. http://sefarad.org/.
38. It is noted that neither the editorial team nor the advertisers are responsible for the content of the contributions.
39. http://www.aki-yerushalayim.co.il/ay/090/defienda.htm.
40. The oldest issue available online is no. 97–98 of December 2015.
41. http://diariojudio.com/lang/djudeo-espanyol/.
42. http://www.salom.com.tr/news.asp?cat=17.
43. At the beginning, this publication, which started in 1947, was entirely written in Judeo-Spanish.
44. The most recent available issue on the blog is n° 84, February 2012. https://sephardiccenter.wordpress.com/el-ameneser/.
45. Yahoo does not allow the possibiliy to choose Judeo-Spanish as language of discussion.
46. The description in Judeo-Spanish is, nevertheless, shorter: "Keridos Amigos, Bienvenidos a la komunidad virtual de Ladino (djudeo-espanyol.) Mos korrespondemos aki en muestra kerida lingua para ke no mos ulvidemos de eya, ni de muestra erensia Sefaradi. Todos los mesajes deven ser en djudeo-espanyol".
47. http://diariojudio.com/autor/fcauich/.
48. David Bunis, "Ladino" or not "Ladino"?, http://jewishstudies.washington.edu/sephardic-studies/david-bunis-ladino-or-not-ladino/. As the exchanges that can be consulted in the archives show, the issue of the name of the language is something on which the founders and moderators of thes two discussion groups disagree.
49. *Diksionario de Judeo-Espanyol de Ladinokomunita*, por Güler Orgun, Antonio Ruiz Tinoco i munchos otros kolaboradores. http://ladinokomunita.tallerdetinoco.org/.
50. The survey included questions related to the use of Judeo-Spanish: place of birth, place of residence, age, language used at home, where have you learned Judeo-Spanish, other languages that you speak, can read in Rashi and read and write in Soletreo.
51. https://groups.yahoo.com/neo/groups/sefaradimuestro/info.
52. https://groups.yahoo.com/neo/groups/Ladinokomunita/search/messages?query=sefardimuestro.

REFERENCES

Calvet, Louis-Jean. "Politique linguistique et impérialisme: l'Institut Linguistique d'Eté". In *La guerre des langues et les politiques linguistiques*, Paris: Hachette Littératures, Pluriel Sociologie, 1999 [1st ed., 1987].

Brink-Danan, M. The meaning of Ladino: The semiotics of an online speech community. *Language Communication* (2010), doi: 10.1016/j.langcom.2010.08.003.

Diki-Kidiri, Marcel (LLACAN -CNRS/INALCO). "Assessing Language Situation and Planning in Relation to the Internet". In "Towards UNESCO guidelines on Language Policies: a Tool for Language Assessment and Planning", 30 June–1 June 2011, Paris: UNESCO. <http://www.unesco.org/new/fileadmin/MULTIMEDIA/HQ/CI/CI/pdf/assessing_language_situation_and_planning_in_relation_to_internet_marcel_diki_kidiri.pdf>

Hammarström, Harald, Forkel, Robert, Haspelmath, Martin and Bank, Sebastian. 2015. Glottolog 2.6. Jena: Max Planck Institute for the Science of Human History. (Available online at http://glottolog.org. Accessed on 2015–10–24.)

Held, Michal. "The People Who Almost Forgot: Judeo-Spanish Online Communities As a Digital Home-Land". *El Prezente*, vol. 4(December 2010), 83–101.

Hymes, Dell, *Foundations in Sociolinguistics. An Ethnographic Approach*. Philadelphia: University of Pennsylvania Press, 1974.

Lewis, M. Paul, Gary F. Simons, and Charles D. Fennig (eds.). 2015. Ethnologue: Languages of the World, Eighteenth edition. Dallas, Texas: SIL International. Online version: <http://www.ethnologue.com>.

López Fernández, Inés, *El judeoespañol en Internet. Usuarios y recursos*. Oviedo: Universidad de Oviedo, Trabajo de fin de Máster dirigido por el Dr. Alfredo Ignacio Alvarez Menéndez, 2012–2013.

Moseley, Christopher (ed.), Atlas of the World's Languages in Danger. Third edition. Paris: UNESCO Publishing, 2010. <http://www.unesco.org/culture/en/endangeredlanguages/atlas>.

Stulic, Ana and Soufiane Rouissi (eds.). *Judeoespañol digital: datos, documentos, corpus*. Bordeaux: Presses Universitaires de Bordeaux, à paraître.

Rouissi, Soufiane and Ana Stulic-Etchevers. « La métadescription des documents au service de la sauvegarde du patrimoine culturel séfarade », *Horizons Maghrébins* n°67—L'héritage de l'Espagne des trois cultures (vol. II). Edited by Isabelle Touton and Yannick Llored. 2012: 88–94.

Rouissi, Soufiane and Ana Stulic-Etchevers (eds). *Recensement, analyse et traitement numérique des sources écrites pour les études séfarades*. Bordeaux: Presses Universitaires de Bordeaux, 2013.

UNESCO, *Mesurer la diversité linguistique sur Internet*, Un ensemble d'articles signés par John Paolillo, Daniel Pimienta, Daniel Prado et autres, Révisé et accompagné d'une introduction de l'Institut de statistique de l'UNESCO Montréal (Canada), 2005.

UNESCO, *Twelve years of measuring linguistic diversity in the Internet: balance and perspectives*, By Daniel Pimienta, Daniel Prado and Álvaro Blanco, UNESCO publications for the World Summit on the Information Society, Communication and Information Sector, 2009.

UNESCO, *Language Vitality and Endangerment, UNESCO Ad Hoc Expert Group on Endangered Languages*, Paris: 2003. <*http://www.unesco.org/culture/ich/doc/src/00120-EN.pdf*>

Index of Personal Names

Abravanel, Moises 238
Adatto, Emma 247
Albuhayre, Gracia 258–260, 266
Algaba, Jacob 16
Algazi, Eliya 216, 221, 223, 225
Alkalay, Yehuda 193
Allatini, Moïse 114, 136, 139, 141–145
Allatini, Carlo 143
Almosnino, Moshe 5, 14, 18, 44–45, 47–50
Altarac, Isaac 235
Altarak, Shalom (Shani) 217
Amado Bortnick, Rachel 278, 305
Anderson, Benedict 3–4, 16, 78 (notes 2 and 3)
Aristotle 45, 49
Armistead, Samuel G. 239, 242, 247
Aveiro, Pantaleão de 14
Ávila Gallego, Daniel de 15
Asá, Abraham 47, 49
Azar, Moshe 219

Bajar Hayim, Yisrael 193
Baruch, Kalmi 234
Bassan, Susan 246
Bejerano, Hayim (chief rabbi) 167–170, 177, 181
Ben Giat, Alexander 217, 222–226

Ben Rubi, Shmuel 141
Benardete, Maír José 113, 246–247
Benoliel, José 239–241
Benveniste, Itzhak 147–157
Benveniste, Liliana and Marcelo 305
Benveniste, Rabbi Meir 15, 49
Besso, Henry 246
Bunis, David M. 193

Camões, Luís de 239
Canetti, Elias 3
Capsali, Moshe 8
Cappon, Abraham 237–238, 242
Carasseau, Jean 303
Carmona (Karmona), Elijah 133–144, 217
Carmona, Leon 143
Carrión, Sem Tob de 4
Castro, Américo 239, 243–245
Cervantes 16
Chaucer 50
Cherezli, Salomon Israel 20, 192, 194–207
Chocrón, Yohébed 244
Chomsky, Noam 108
Çikurel, Rafael 167
Cohen, Edmond 305

INDEX OF PERSONAL NAMES

Cohen-Malki, Medi 305
Covo, (chief rabbi) (Jacob) 140
Crews, Cynthia 234

Danon, Abraham 50, 116, 235–238

Ehrenpreis, Mordehay Marcus (chief rabbi) 216
'Eli, Nisim Shem Tov 217, 226
Elnekave, David 217
Emmanuel, Isaac 50

Foulché-Delbosc, Raimundo 109, 112
Franco, Moïse 50
Frankl, Ludwig August 141
Fresco, David 50, 137, 138

Gabai, Yehezkel 136
Gabaï-Simantov, Rita 258, 264, 267, 269–270
Gabay, Roza 149
Galante, Abraham 235–237
Gelman, Juan 2
Giménez Caballero, Ernesto 235
Goyri, María 238

Hakohén, Reina 147–157
Halevi, Moshe, chief rabbi 136, 140
Halevi, Saadi 49, 133–137, 141–144
Hassán, Iacob 44
Hatsvi, Yehuda 305
Huli, Yaakov 16, 47–50
Humboldt, Wilhelm von 108

Ibn Abi Zimra, David 6
Ibn Haviv, Yaakov 8
Ibn Paquda 45, 48

Karmona (see Carmona)
Koen-Sarano, Matilda 2, 302, 305
Kohen, Roz 2
Krispin, Eliya 169
Kuli (see Huli)

León, Denise 258, 265, 268–269
Leon, Roza (née Chiprut) 218–219
Leon, Sabetay 217–219, 227–228

Levi, Moritz 234
Levy, Isaac Jack 247
Levy, Mauricio chief rabbi 244
Levy, Salamon 238
Lévy, Shmuel (Sam) 135, 165
Lida, Denah (née Levy) 246
Lleal, Coloma 48
Lehmann, Matthias 45
Lunzano, Rabbi Menahem di 16
Luria, Max Aaron 245

Maimon, Moses ben (Maimonides) 30, 49
Manrique de Lara, Manuel 238, 241–244
Martínez Torner, Eduardo 244
Matitiahu, Margalit 2, 258, 260–262, 264, 266–270
Medina, Samuel de 5
Mefaniv, Daniel 192
Mendes de Sola, Samuel 215
Menéndez Pelayo, Marcelino 236, 238
Menéndez Pidal, Ramón 113, 236–241
Mizrahi, Eliyahu 8
Molho, Michael 49–50, 207
Montalvo, Garci Rodríguez de 16
Moses 48
Moshe, Menahem 192
Mussafia, Adolfo 234

Nahum, Haim, chief rabbi 139
Nahón, Zarita 246–247
Nasi, Doña Gracia 14
Nassi, Gad 2, 305
Navarro Thomás, Tomás 244
Nehama, Joseph 50, 193, 197, 207
Nicoïdski, Clarisse 1–2, 22 (notes 2–3)

Oliva, Palmerín de 16
Onís, Federico de 245, 247

Papo, Laura [Bohoreta] (née Levi) 243
Pardo, Nissim de Yehuda 193
Perez, Avner 2, 258, 262–264, 270–272
Pipano, Albert D. 192
Pulido, Fernández Ángel 164, 231, 235–238, 242

Quintana, Aldina 44, 149, 164, 193

Ramón y Cajal, Santiago 241
Rav 219–220, 229 (note 15)
Refael, Shmuel 260
Romero, Elena 44, 149

Samuel (Talmud sage) 219–220, 229 (note 16)
Sananes, Estella 244
Schaufler, William 192
Schindler, Kurt 244
Schwartzwald, Ora 45
Sephiha, Haïm Vidal 1, 15, 19
Shakespear 50
Sharope Blanco (penname) 307
Shaul, Eli 219
Shaul, Moshe 2
Sidi, Yehuda 305
Silverman, Joseph H. 243, 247
Subak, Julius 233

Thomason, Sarah 116
Thompson, Alexander 193

Usque, Abraham 14

Valente, José Ángel 2

Wagner, Max Leopold 234
Wiener, Leo 233, 236

Yona, Yaakov Avraam 217

Zeki Efendi 242
Zemke, John 48
Zevi, Sabbatai 271

Index of Subjects

Accion (newspaper) 192
agreement (grammatical) 57–58, 60, 63–64, 97–100, 299
Akafot de Aman 214
Aki estamos—Association des Amis de le Lettre Sépharade 303
Aki Yerushalayim 2, 280, 282, 304–305, 309
Al-Andalus 9
Allatini family (Salonika) 114, 136, 141–143
Alexandria 14, 114, 138, 143
Alliance Israélite Universelle 140–141, 143, 165, 167, 183
  languages taught in 110, 113, 147, 164
Amadís de Gaula 16
amor cortés (courtly love) 36
Amsterdam 141
Ancona 9, 14
Andalusia (speech) 11
anticlericalism 141
Arabic (language) 10, 112, 116, 195, 232
Aragon 6, 10, 13
Aragon (congregation in Istanbul, Salonika) 6, 7, 11, 57
Aragonese (language) 10–11, 13, 15, 56, 79 (note 11), 183

Aramaic 14, 18, 80, 104 (note 9), 112, 214, 232
Archivo de la Palabra y de las Canciones 244
Argentina 268, 305
Armenians 110, 112, 119, 125, 138
  alphabet 111
Ashkava de Aman 214
Ashkenazi 8
Athens 267
Atikva (Istanbul periodical) 217, 219
autobiography 3, 133–144, 149
Autoridad Nasionala del Ladino 281, 304

Balat (quarter in Istanbul) 218
Balkan Judeo-Spanish 11, 57, 65, 70–71, 78, 234, 236, 295
ballad (*romance*) 236, 239–247, 271
Bat Yam 218
Beirut 242
Belgrade 235, 242
Bible
  translations to Ladino 45, 47, 73, 104 (note 1), 155, 232, 235, 271
  Ferrara 189 (note 13), 210 (note 27)
  Vulgate 97
  commentaries 48, 50

bilingualism 62, 89, 108, 116, 259–260, 268, 276, 279, 282, 288
Bitola (see Monastir)
Boletín de la Real Academia Española 241
Bosnian Judeo-Spanish 2, 234
Bucharest 14, 237, 277
Buenos Aires 305
Bulgarian 192

c-command 92, 98, 100, 104
Cairo 14, 17, 138, 140–141, 242
calque 65, 70, 87–89,
calque language 15, 19, 45, 47, 92, 116, 185, 221
Camondo family 114, 185
Castile 6, 10, 13, 57, 241, 244
Castilianization 18, 56, 177
Catalan (congregation in Salonika) 6, 7
Catalan (language) 10, 13, 234
  in Hebrew characters 31
Centro de Estudios Históricos 233, 238–240, 243–244
Cercles des Intimes (Salonika) 136, 141
chroniclers (Sephardic) 9
class differences 143, 152
cleft 67–70
clitic pronoun 65, 70, 74–76, 81
code switching 88–89, 93, 116, 285
  to Hebrew 5, 15, 279
Collections de Corpus Oraux Numériques 296
collective memories (of Sepharad) 9, 259
Comentario a Daniel 149
Consejo Superior de Investigaciones Científicas-CSIC 245
Constantinople (Istanbul) 6–9, 14, 109–110, 140, 242, 265, 277, 285
  books published in 45
construct state 90, 94, 96–97, 104–106
contact language 16, 19, 46, 53, 57, 71, 79, 81, 87–88, 109, 114, 116, 123, 163, 169
converso 7–8, 15, 30, 47
  ex-converso 45
convivencia 243
coplas (see *komplas*)
Coplas de Yosef 35
copula 101–104
Cordova (congregation in Istanbul) 6

Coreo de Viena (periodical) 142
Croatia 1, 217, 234
Curaçao 215
Cyrillic alphabet 298

Dardanelles (Çanakkale) 246
deictic 66
demonstrative 70, 98–100
deontic modality 57, 61, 63–65, 80
determiner 67, 70–71, 87, 90–91, 95–96, 98–100, 104–105
Derecho al Buto (Israeli periodical) 219
diachrony 183
dialect accommodation 278
dialect leveling 54–55
Diálogo del Colorado, El 15, 45, 47
Diario Judío (online magazine) 304–306
Diaspora 3,
dictionaries (Judeo-Spanish) 192–194
diglossia
  in Ottoman Judeo-Spanish 44–45
  with Hebrew 45
Diksiyonaryo de Ladinokomunita (online) 307
Dinim de shehitah i bedikah (Judeo-Spanish book) 51 (note 1)
diphthongization 164, 176–177, 182–183
Dodecanese islands 235
Don Quixote 16, 150, 306
Dönme sect 271
dynasties, identification with 4–5

Edirne (Andrianople) 116, 235
Egypt 113, 138
endangered language 257–258, 272, 276, 279, 292
El Amaneser (Istanbul periodical) 2, 281, 305–306
El Cantar del Mío Cid 44
El Catecismo menor, o una corta declaración de lo que creen los protestantes cristianos 193
El Jugueton (Istanbul satirical magazine) 134, 137–138
El Korreo (Istanbul periodical) 216
El Mesajero (Salonika periodical) 215
El Nacional (Istanbul periodical) 142
El Progreso (Edirne periodical) 235

INDEX OF SUBJECTS | 321

El Telegrafo (Istanbul periodical) 137
El Tiempo (Istanbul periodical) 137
El Tiempo (Israeli periodical) 219
élites 7, 139, 142
El-ksar-el- kebir (Alcazarquivir) 242
English 192
epistemic modality 58, 60–62, 64
eSepharad.com 305
Espanyol 7, 9, 184, 301
Esperansa association 234–235
evidentiality 57, 59, 65
Expulsion from Spain 4, 6, 9, 231
Extremadura 244

feature checking 92–93, 96, 100, 102
Fernandez family (Istanbul) 143
Ferrara 14
fieldwork on Judeo-Spanish 113, 168, 233–234, 236, 238, 240–243, 245–247, 283
Florence 11
focus construction 100, 104
Foundation for the Advancement of Sephardic Studies and Culture 302
franco 13, 45
Frankos (Jewish congregation) 113, 165
French 1, 19, 107, 120, 192, 232–233, 236, 278, 303
   language 5, 20, 55, 80, 88 (Canadian), 97 (Old), 104 (Prince Edward Island), 110, 112, 135, 138, 144, 165, 183–184, 235, 236, 278, 304–305, 307
   borrowings in Judeo-Spanish 113–114, 116, 124, 154, 164–181
   in Judeo-Spanish novels 153, 155
   bilingual Judeo-Spanish dictionaries 194–207
fricatives 12
Fuente clara 45, 47, 50

Gaceta Literaria (Spanish periodical) 235
Galician 10, 13, 234
Gallicism 177
Garshuni 46
Genoa 114
genres, literary modern 148
Geon Sefarad (Internet community) 279

German 194, 236, 278
Gerush Sepharad (congregation in Istanbul, Salonika) 6
Glottolog 298
Graded Intergenerational Disruption Scale (GIDS) 276–277, 279
grammaticalization 64
Greece 260, 264
Greek (language) 80, 99, 107, 115, 119, 207
   borrowings in Judeo-Spanish 110, 207
   borrowings in Turkish 115, 117
   in Latin script 110

halakha 7, 8, 215
Haggadah 20, 31, 79 (note 10), 90, 95, 103, 213–214, 219, 221–226
Haggadah parodies 17, 89, 90, 95, 213–227
Haketia 240, 303, 305
Haman 214
Hashkava prayer 214
Hasköy (quarter of Istanbul) 218
Hellenization 7
Hebrew 10, 14–16, 19, 45, 89–105, 112, 119, 166, 192, 197, 206, 214, 218, 232, 239, 268, 278, 280, 302, 305
   rabbinic 49, 90, 94
   adoption as mother tongue 165, 236
   knowledge among Sephardim 49, 54, 215, 226
herem (excommunication) 136–137, 140
heterogeneity
   among Jewish Iberian exiles 6, 113
   linguistic 10
   stylistic in Judeo-Spanish 44
High Holidays 214
Hispanic Institute, Columbia University 245
hispanophiles 231, 236–237
Holocaust (Shoah) 184, 258, 261–262, 264, 271
Holy Land 14
Hovot ha-Levavot 45, 49

idiolect 10
impersonal *se* 57–60, 62–65, 83,
Indépendance [Belge] (Newspaper) 136, 145 note 9
infinitve forms 174

inflected infinitive 75, 81
Inquisition tribunal 13
Institut Sépharade Européen 304–305, 307
Internet 21, 275–288, 291–308
interrogative 65–68, 70–71, 81
Israel 20, 218, 268, 295, 304
Israeli authors 3
Istanbul (see Constantinople)
Italian (Language) 5, 14–15, 19, 74, 80, 107, 110, 113–114, 116, 119, 124, 126, 154, 163–166, 172, 183, 206, 232, 234, 284
Italian Jewish communities 8
Izmir (Smyrna) 114, 140–141, 235, 242

Jerusalem 17, 138, 242
Jevrejski Zivot (Sarajevo periodical) 235
Jevrejski Glas (Sarajevo periodical) 235
Judeo-Fragnol 166, 167
Judeo-Spanish
    as academic prose 2
    in humoristic creations 214, 215
    in Jewish liturgy 233
    18th century style 5, 48–50
    literature origins 43–47
    in Atlanta 247
    in New York 245–247, 277, 278, 285
    in Seattle 247
    in the US 277
    in Israel 277, 285
    on the Internet 275–281, 291–310
    how to identify on the Web 294–299
    as post-vernacular performative 3, 279
Junta de Ampliación de Estudios e Investigaciones Científicas 233, 241–243

Kaminando i avlando (French periodical) 303
Karamanli 45, 110
Karnobat 259
kendi gelen 8
Ketubah of Haman 214
Kol Israel 219, 281
koine 46, 54–56, 79, 164, 183
komplas (coplas) 214, 228 (note 3), 232
Konfidensyas de un amigo 150–157

La Alborada (Ploesti and Sarajevo periodical) 160, 237

La Correspondencia: libro de cartas diversas y de comercho (1906) 193
La Epoca (Epoka) (Salonika newspaper) 133, 135–145, 165, 176, 179
La Lettre Sépharade 303
La Union (Israeli periodical) 219
La Vara (Cairo periodical) 235
La Vara (New York Periodical) 215
la'az 13
labialization 75
Ladino 13, 16, 19, 45, 213–214, 216, 218, 221, 265, 295–298
ladinar (translate) 155, 270
Ladino Culture Forum 288
Ladino. Lengua y cultura website 302, 309
LadinoKomunita 2, 108, 118, 276, 278–282, 284–287, 289, 305–307
language contact 18, 71, 77, 88, 111, 116, 123, 183, 232
    Romance 13, 16, 19, 46, 53, 54–57, 114, 163–166, 169, 183, 285
    Hebrew 15, 87
    Turkish 18, 109, 284
Larache 239, 242
Latin (language) 10, 11, 80, 97, 104, 170
Latin script 16, 22, 110, 112, 119, 129, 168, 194, 219, 229, 280, 295
Latin America 2, 236, 303
    Spanish 12, 18, 233, 268, 277–278, 285
Le Journal de Salonique 135
lengua ajena 45
lenition 13
Leon 7–8, 10
Leonese 11, 15
lingua franca 114, 277
Lisbon 13, 239
Livorno 9
loans from Hebrew 47
Los Muestros (Brussels periodical) 304
Low Countries 6
ludic register 30
Luzero de la Pasensia 169

Macedonia 9
Majorca (congregation in Salonika) 6
maskilim 140, 235
matres lectionis (use of) 48

INDEX OF SUBJECTS | 323

Max Planck Institute for Evolutionary Anthropology 296
Me'am Lo'ez 16, 44, 47–50, 149
memoirs 3
merchant networks 7
Messina (congregation in Istanbul) 6
Mesa de el alma 45, 47–49
meter (verse) 33–34
millet 3, 107, 109
minhag 7
minimalist program 88–92, 102–103
Monastir (Bitola) 74, 245, 277
  Judeo-Spanish 57, 66, 68–73, 76, 78
Morocco 238–240, 242–246, 297
multilingualism 107–109, 123–124, 165,
  Romance 10–12, 14, 18

nation 3
nationalism 112, 120, 147
Navarese 10, 11
New Christians 6, 8–9, 13
New York 245, 246, 302
Nicomachean Ethics 45
Nizâmnâme-i Millet-i Ermeniyân [Armenian Constitution] 110
novels (Judeo-Spanish) 136, 138, 148–157
Nuevo chico diccionario judeo-español–francés 192, 194–207

Obligasion de los korazones 45, 48, 49
online Judeo-Spanish communities 280
online Judeo-Spanish dictionaries 288
Orah hayim 49
Orizontes (Web literary magazine) 281, 288
Ortaköy (quarter in Istanbul) 218
Ottoman Empire 4–6, 8, 15, 18, 44, 46, 54–55, 57, 110, 134, 140–144, 147, 222, 226, 246
  censorship 138
  Ottomanism 112
  patriotism among Jews 165, 216–217

parameter setting 88, 91, 104
Paris 21, 112, 234, 236, 303
parody among Sephardim 214
passive construction 61–63, 65
Passover 214
past tense (see preterit)

patronage, rivalry over 144
Pentecost 214
periodicals (Judeo-Spanish) 16–17, 19, 133–144, 233
  publication license for 137
Persian (language) 112, 116
personal infinitive 72–73, 75–76
philologists 20, 231, 243–244
Pirke Avot 214
Pisa 14
poetry
  Judeo-Spanish 1, 20–21, 257–273
  Castilian Spanish in Hebrew characters 29–41
polemical Haggadah parodies 216
Portugal 6, 9, 14
Portuguese (congregation in Istanbul, Salonika) 6–7, 9, 11
Portuguese
  language 10, 13, 15, 18, 55, 57, 61–62, 65, 70, 72, 74, 80–81, 119–120, 183
  poetry 234, 239
  people 11, 14, 54
prayer for the king in Shabbat service 4
pregunta y respuesta genre 32–35, 38–39
preterit 102, 103, 170, 174, 181
Prince's Islands (Istanbul) 277, 285
Pristina 71
progress 139, 141
pronouns 71, 74, 78
prose, modern Judeo-Spanish 2
Proverbios Judeo-Españoles 109–123
proverbs 107, 120–123
pseudo-cleft 67, 68
Purim festival 214–216

rabbis (haham) 8–9, 49, 119, 136–137, 140–142, 144
  as leaders of Hispanization 7, 15
Radio Sefarad 281
Ragusa 9
Rashi characters 48, 125 (note 17), 168–169, 281, 296
  type for printing 136, 138
Regimiento de la vida 45, 47–50
reflexive pronoun 74
register (linguistic) 10, 48–50

relative pronoun 65, 67, 69–71, 81
responsa 15–16, 116
Revista de Filología Española 238, 243, 245
Revista Hispano-Africana 244
Revue des Études Juives 236
Revue Hispanique 235
rhematic information 59, 65
Rhodes 242, 247
romance castellano 45
Romance philology 233–234, 295
Romanian 119, 278
Romaniyot 7–9, 113
Rosh Hashana 215

Şalom (Istanbul periodical) 281, 305, 309
Salonika 6–9, 14, 114, 139, 149, 236, 238, 242, 260, 262, 264, 267, 271, 277
    Jews who arrived in 11
    Judeo-Spanish publications in 45, 149, 242
    inequality in 141
San Miguel de Tucumán 21
Sapir-Whorf Hypothesis 107–108
Sarajevo 80, 234, 237–238, 242–244
Şavaat Aman 214
Seattle 247
Shoah (see Holocaust)
secularism 139–141
    in language 5
Sefaradimuestro (online discussion group) 307
Shohrei Ladino (Internet community) 279
Shulhan Arukh 45, 49
Sicilia (congregation in Istanbul) 6
siddur (prayerbook) 45, 47
Silivri 216
Simhat Torah festival 214
social media 294, 308
sociolect 10
solitreo (script) 112, 168
    to write Turkish 137
Sophia 235, 242
square (*merubba*) font of Hebrew 112 194
sürgün 8
Spain 2–3, 6, 8–9, 12, 18, 44, 113, 184, 214, 238, 241, 267, 268
    relations with Sephardim 166, 236, 237
Spanish (Castilian) 9–12, 14, 16, 44, 119–120, 131, 165, 237, 268, 302, 305

folk literature 18
in Hebrew characters 30–31, 44–45
northern 15
influence (or lack of) on Judeo-Spanish dictionary 203–204, 206–207
Spanish Civil War 238, 243, 244
Spanish Royal Academy 237, 241
syntax 19

Talmud 5, 219–220
Tangier 239–240, 242, 246, 249
Tanzimat period 112
Tetouan 240, 242, 244
theater, as inspiration for novels 138
thematic information 59,
Thessaloniki (see Salonika)
Thrace 9
time, sacral 4–5
translation
    from Hebrew 15–16, 18, 44–45, 47–49, 51, 73, 88–90–104, 213–218, 220, 232–233, 235, 296
    from French 91, 152
    from Spanish 299, 306
    from Judeo-Spanish 1, 205
Tratado de los suenyos 45
Trieste 125, 236
troubadour poetry 36
turkification 7, 112
Turkey 50, 79, 110, 120, 165, 168, 218–219, 232, 236
    Jewish communities of 21, 236, 242, 246, 258, 265, 278, 302–303, 305
    Jewish elites in 165
    Rabbinical Seminary 235
Turkish (Language) 18, 45, 107–124, 138, 140, 192, 277–278, 280, 235, 309
    in Western Armenian characters 110–111
    fish and seafood words 114–115
    as source of Judeo-Spanish words 19, 117–118, 165–166, 170, 174, 183, 195, 197, 207, 232, 284
    Latin alphabet for writing Judeo-Spanish 219, 229 (note 3)
    in Jewish liturgy 278
Turkish Proverbs Translated Into English (1873) 110, 121–123